Freedwomen and the
Freedmen's Bureau

Freedwomen and the Freedmen's Bureau

Race, Gender, and Public Policy in the Age of Emancipation

Mary Farmer-Kaiser

FORDHAM UNIVERSITY PRESS
NEW YORK 2010

Copyright © 2010 Fordham University Press

All rights reserved. No part of this publication may be reproduced, stored in a retrieval system, or transmitted in any form or by any means—electronic, mechanical, photocopy, recording, or any other—except for brief quotations in printed reviews, without the prior permission of the publisher.

Fordham University Press has no responsibility for the persistence or accuracy of URLs for external or third-party Internet websites referred to in this publication and does not guarantee that any content on such websites is, or will remain, accurate or appropriate.

Library of Congress Cataloging-in-Publication Data

Farmer-Kaiser, Mary.
 Freedwomen and the Freedmen's Bureau : race, gender, and public policy in the age of emancipation / Mary Farmer-Kaiser.
   p. cm.— (Reconstructing America)
 Includes bibliographical references and index.
 ISBN 978-0-8232-3211-6 (cloth : alk. paper)
 ISBN 978-0-8232-3212-3 (pbk. : alk. paper)
 ISBN 978-0-8232-3213-0 (ebook : alk. paper)
   1. United States. Bureau of Refugees, Freedmen, and Abandoned Lands. 2. African American women—Southern States—History—19th century. 3. African American women—Southern States—Social conditions—19th century. 4. Reconstruction (U.S. history, 1865–1877)—Social aspects.   I. Title.
E185.2.F277 2010
975'.041—dc22

2009054041

Printed in the United States of America
12 11 10   5 4 3 2 1
First edition

For my sisters

Contents

List of Abbreviations ix
Acknowledgments xi

Introduction: "a long time in want of a bureau" | 1

1 "that the freed-women . . . may rise to the dignity and glory of true womanhood": The Men, Purpose, and Gendered Freedom of the Freedmen's Bureau | 14

2 "a weight of circumstances like millstones about their necks to drag and keep them down": Freedwomen, Federal Relief, and the Freedmen's Bureau | 35

3 "The women are the controlling spirits": Freedwomen, Free Labor, and the Freedmen's Bureau | 64

4 "to put forth almost superhuman efforts to regain their children": Freedwomen, Parental Rights, and the Freedmen's Bureau | 96

5 "strict justice for every man, woman, and child": Gender, Justice, and the Freedmen's Bureau | 141

Conclusion: "the unpardonable sin" | 167

Notes 173
Bibliography 239
Index 269

Abbreviations

BRFAL   Bureau of Refugees, Freedmen, and Abandoned Lands

BRFAL (M742)   Selected Series of Records Issued by the Commissioner of the BRFAL, RG 105, Microfilm Publication M742, NARA

BRFAL (M752)   Registers and Letters Received by the Commissioner of the BRFAL, RG 105, Microfilm Publication M752, NARA

BRFAL (M1875)   Marriage Records of the Office of the Commissioner, Washington Headquarters of the BRFAL, 1861–69, RG 105, Microfilm Publication M1875, NARA

BRFAL-AL   Records of the Assistant Commissioner for the State of Alabama, BRFAL, RG 105, Microfilm Publication M809, NARA

BRFAL-DC   Records of the Assistant Commissioner for the District of Columbia, BRFAL, RG 105, Microfilm Publication M1055, NARA

BRFAL-FO   Records of the Field Offices of the BRFAL, RG 105, NARA

BRFAL-GA   Records of the Assistant Commissioner for the State of Georgia, BRFAL, RG 105, Microfilm Publication M798, NARA

BRFAL-LA   Records of the Assistant Commissioner for the State of Louisiana, BRFAL, RG 105, Microfilm Publication M1027, NARA

BRFAL-MD   Records of the Assistant Commissioner for the State of Maryland, BRFAL, RG 105, NARA

BRFAL-MS   Records of the Assistant Commissioner for the State of Mississippi, BRFAL, RG 105, Microfilm Publication M826, NARA

BRFAL-NC   Records of the Assistant Commissioner for the State of North Carolina, BRFAL, RG 105, Microfilm Publication M843, NARA

BRFAL-TX	Records of the Assistant Commissioner for the State of Texas, BRFAL, RG 105, Microfilm Publication M821, NARA
BRFAL-VA	Records of the Assistant Commissioner for the State of Virginia, BRFAL, RG 105, Microfilm Publication M1048, NARA
NARA	National Archives and Records Administration, Washington, D.C.
RG	Record Group

Acknowledgments

When I began this project, I set out to learn as much as I possibly could about freedwomen's interactions with the Freedmen's Bureau. What I did not know then was just how much more I would learn about the generosity of those around me. Research and writing may be a solitary pursuit, but this book would not have been possible without a great deal of support and guidance from others.

By way of Kansas, South Carolina, Ohio, and finally Louisiana, I have benefited much from the assistance of a number of individuals who encouraged me along in the research and writing that, in the end and with their help, has become this book. Donald Nieman has promoted this project from its very inception. A wise and generous mentor, he introduced me to the bureau, cultivated my intellectual inquisitiveness about it, taught me to ask the right questions from the records, offered judicious counsel when the evidence did not reveal what I had expected, and allowed me to go my own way. Without question, his expertise in and insights into African American history and the Freedmen's Bureau have shaped this work profoundly. In countless ways, Don taught me by example what it means to be a model mentor, a meticulous scholar, an exacting and gifted teacher, and a remarkable person. I am forever grateful for his guidance and presence in my life. While at Bowling Green State University, I also gained much from the intellectual guidance of Lillian Ashcraft-Eason, Rachel Buff, Sandra VanBurkleo, Scott Martin, Edmund Danziger, Gary Hess, and Don Rowney, all of whom I would like to thank. At the University of Louisiana at Lafayette, the encouragement of my colleagues, especially Thomas Aiello, Vaughan Baker, A. David Barry, Carl Brasseaux, Robert Carriker, Rich Frankel, Julia Frederick, Robin Hermann, Jordan Kellman, Michael Martin, Brad Pollock, Carl Richard, Sara Ritchey, Thomas Schoonover, John Troutman, James Wilson, and Mary Ann Wilson, has been both significant and invaluable. Several other historians have read conference papers, chapters, and drafts of this manuscript, and I am beholden to them too for their insight, critique, and kind encouragement at significant moments in the researching and writing of this book. They include Thomas Aiello, Peter Bardaglio, Ronald Butchart, Paul Cimbala, the late Barry Crouch, Laura Edwards, Leslie Rowland, John Rodrigue, the late Carolyn DeLatte, Carol Faulkner, Richard Paul Fuke, Mary Furner, Elna Green, Morgan Kousser, Michelle Krowl, Randall Miller, Kent Redding, Judith Kelleher Schafer, the late Johnie Smith, Sandra VanBurkleo, Warren Billings, Bradley Bond, Jonathan Bryant, Mark Fernandez, Robert Goldman, Lauranett Lee, James Schmidt, Ted Tunnell, Peter Wallenstein, and Lou Faulkner Williams. I also must thank the anonymous readers for the *Virginia Magazine of History and Biography*, the *Georgia Historical Quarterly*, and especially Fordham University Press. This is a far better piece of scholarship because of their careful reading, perceptive critique, and discerning suggestions.

Institutions also deserve special mention here. My research has been funded by a Mellon Research Fellowship from the Virginia Historical Society; grants and fellowships from the Department of History, the Graduate School, and the Center for Government Research and Public Service at Bowling Green State University; and a summer research grant, a semester of sabbatical leave, and travel grants from the Department of History and Geography and the College of Liberal Arts at the University of Louisiana at Lafayette. This institutional support provided not only the funds but also the time and intellectual space necessary to do archival research and to write. I also have accumulated many debts to the archivists and staff at the National Archives and Records Administration in Washington, D.C., the Virginia Historical Society, Bowdoin College, Bowling Green State University, and the University of Louisiana at Lafayette. When I could not travel to the archives, the interlibrary loan librarians at Bowling Green State University and the University of Louisiana at Lafayette worked diligently to bring the many reels of Freedmen's Bureau microfilm to me. I am thankful to them for this crucial assistance.

I am especially thankful to Don Nieman for introducing me to and making me part of an incredibly giving group of Freedmen's Bureau scholars. Paul Cimbala, the late Barry Crouch, Carol Faulkner, Richard Paul Fuke, Randall Miller, James Schmidt, and Ted Tunnell are but a few of the bureau scholars who have encouraged my work and contributed to my understanding of the federal agency and its agents. I cannot remember how many times I went to my mailbox to discover (and to open eagerly) an envelope that contained copies of one or two bureau documents with information about freedwomen from one of these scholars. I would particularly like to thank Richard Paul Fuke and the late Barry Crouch for graciously sending copies of hard-to-find government documents and publications that proved difficult to obtain through interlibrary loan. Carol Faulkner also warrants special thanks for reading the entire manuscript at a critical moment. Her insights helped me tremendously as I worked to sharpen my argument, and her critique has improved this project in significant ways. I have accumulated a great many debts—perhaps more than to any other individual in recent years—to Paul Cimbala. He has read countless drafts of this book, and his expertise in bureau history certainly informs its every page. His suggestions and critique have made it a far better book than it would have been otherwise. But his contribution to this project has been far more than intellectual. Quite simply, this project's transformation into a book would not have been possible without his encouragement and patience. When broken bones and death seemingly brought my intellectual life to a halt, he was always there with an encouraging e-mail or short postcard (and a gentle nudge). Of course, Paul also brought me to the Reconstructing America series at Fordham University Press, and for that I am most appreciative. I must thank everyone at Fordham University Press who has contributed both time and many talents to the production of this book. It has been a gratifying experience from start to finish.

My friends and family have also provided much encouragement during the completion of this project. I am grateful for their willingness to listen, more than they likely wanted, as I learned to articulate my arguments about freedwomen and bureau men and as I worked to just get the book done. My colleagues at Bowling Green State University, especially Phyllis Gernhardt, Kevin Bailey, Rob Smith, Ron Taylor, Charles Morrisey, Bill Allison, and James Beeby, inspired me with their own scholarly pursuits, and their friendship made my time in Bowling Green considerably more enjoyable. Perhaps my deepest thanks go to friends and family away from Bowling Green, however. I am especially grateful for the new friends I discovered in Louisiana. Robert and Dawn Carriker, Jordan Kellman and Maribel Dietz, and Michael and Amy Martin deserve special praise for always being willing to center me when the challenges of being a scholar, spouse, and parent seemed overwhelming. Their steadfast friendship also nourished me through a difficult loss. The Kaiser family too has offered immeasurable quantities of humor, support, and love over the years. This family embraced me from my earliest days in South Carolina and has become an essential part of my life. Amanda and David Kaiser, and later their daughters, Suzannah and Katie, thus brought not only lasting friendship to my life but also an extended family. I am grateful to them all: Janet and Steve Kaiser, Darrin Kaiser, Linda and Tim Jones, and Davin and Tina Kaiser. I would also like to thank Jess Brown and my nephews and niece, Cody Cox, Daniel Brown, and Courtney Brown, for always knowing when to bring a much-needed smile to my life with letters, cards, and phone calls from afar.

Much love and appreciation go to my parents, Paul and Shirley Farmer, for their unceasing support and encouragement. I have always depended upon them, and they have always been there when I needed them most. Perhaps even more, I am thankful that they blessed me with two sisters, Paula Brown and Lisa Garcia. Although we could not have been more different and we at times disagreed fiercely, we three Farmer girls always knew that we could count on each other. Indeed, since the start of this project, it has often been my sisters, more times than they ever knew, who offered the lifeline to the world beyond academia and the much-needed reminder to trust in my own abilities. I have benefited greatly from their unconditional love. Although she did not live to see this book published, I know that my older sister, Paula, would have been proud. This book is dedicated to my sisters.

Yet I am most indebted to my best friend and husband, Douglas Kaiser, and my children, Peter and Irene. This book may have been part of my life before them, but it is at last complete because of their constant encouragement, patience, and love. They have encouraged me, endured me, and celebrated with me every step of the way. Without them I would be incomplete.

Freedwomen and the Freedmen's Bureau

Introduction

"a long time in want of a bureau"

Not long after the Civil War's end, a "poor colored woman," as Freedmen's Bureau commissioner Major General Oliver Otis Howard would later remember the former slave, made her way to the offices of the War Department in Washington, D.C. Once there, she sought every bit of the freedom that her recent emancipation promised. Having heard about a "bureau" being created for freedpeople as the Civil War ended, she requested one for herself. Telling federal officials in the nation's capital that "she had been a long time in want of a bureau" and that "she understood that there was one there waiting for her," the freedwoman attempted to take advantage of the federal government's generosity—or perhaps to carry away what she believed was her just due for years of work as a slave—by claiming this much-desired bequest.[1]

Congress established the Bureau of Refugees, Freedmen, and Abandoned Lands—more commonly known as the Freedmen's Bureau—in March 1865. And while it would not provide former slaves with the dressing table this freedwoman wanted, the new bureau did accomplish a great deal before being officially dismantled in 1872.[2] Upon its creation, the short-lived and unprecedented federal agency assumed the Herculean task of overseeing the transition from slavery to freedom in the immediate postemancipation South. It became the embodiment of the triumphant North in a defeated South, and its agents the very face of federal authority. The job of the men who served its ranks was, as Georgia freedwoman Susan McIntosh put it some years later, "to get things to going smooth after the war."[3] And even as it would fail at this formidable charge, the bureau stood at the center of Reconstruction and played a critical role in shaping how more than four million men, women, and children defined and enjoyed their lives and labors as freedpeople.[4]

Although known to contemporaries and historians alike as the Freedmen's Bureau—and thus an agency interested most in instructing black men, rather than black women, in the transition from slave to citizen—this bureau profoundly affected the lives of African American women in the age of emancipation. In its efforts to transform the South and define freedom, the federal agency established a multitude of policies designed to guide the former Confederacy in its transformation from a society of slaves and masters to one in which free labor reigned. But bureau policy makers were never concerned only with applying the northern economic theory of free labor in a southern context. Those who created, led, and served the bureau also worked to institute a social reconstruction based on northern middle-class notions of domesticity, dependency, and family relations. Thus the policies crafted by this federal agency touched upon every aspect of African Americans' lives and stood poised to transform not only their legal, economic, and political standing but also familial and gender relations in black communities across the South. Moreover, as bureau agents interpreted and implemented these policies, they recognized a gendered difference between former slave women and men that allowed them to confer upon the former certain benefits unavailable to the latter. Of course, this recognition also allowed them to deal freedwomen devastating, gendered blows. But whatever the intentions and actions of bureau officials stationed across the South, freedwomen—much like freedmen—encountered, trusted, and challenged the bureau and used it to their own ends. This interaction between freedwomen and the Freedmen's Bureau exposes the ways in which both former slave women and northern gender ideology shaped the public policies of early Reconstruction.

Charged with exercising "control of all subjects relating to refugees and freedmen from the rebel states," the bureau's activities were myriad: it assisted in uniting former slave families separated during slavery or as a result of war, supervised labor agreements between blacks and their former masters, monitored state and local officials' treatment of freedpeople, established informal tribunals to settle disputes between whites and blacks (and among African Americans themselves), instituted clinics and hospitals for former slaves, aided efforts to provide freedpeople education, and temporarily provided "issues of provisions, clothing and fuel" to refugees, freedmen, and "their wives and children" in the Civil War's immediate aftermath. To southern blacks like the expectant freedwoman who made her way to the offices of the War Department in the days following emancipation, the bureau's promise was breathtakingly vast and its agents soon became "the government."[5]

In the end, it cannot be questioned that the Freedmen's Bureau fell short in accomplishing all that it promised. Its activities were numerous, but so too were they incomplete. The bureau and its role in the failure of Reconstruction to take lasting hold in the South have generated much debate. Historians, as well as the federal agency's contemporaries, have not always been kind. Its contemporaries damned the bureau for doing too little as well as too much. So too have historians. With the notable exception of W. E. B. Du Bois—who declared at the turn of the twentieth century that the agency had "accomplished a great task"—early scholars of the bureau flatly condemned its presence and activities.[6] As historians in the 1960s began to reconsider the bureau without, as the historian Robert Harrison puts it, "the racial blinkers" that had hindered earlier scholars, they too found fault with the bureau. Seeing it as an "agency of economic and social control rather than racial uplift," historians writing between the 1960s and 1980s concluded that it "exemplified many of the failings of northern efforts to reconstruct the South after the Civil War and, equally, many of the failings of federal policy toward African Americans in their own time."[7] The "new" Freedmen's Bureau historiography, as scholars today label bureau histories published since the 1980s, offers a more nuanced assessment. Recognizing the complicated landscape in which the bureau operated, these works go beyond its limitations, weaknesses, and failures to underscore the significant role that the agency played in former slaves' lives, particularly at the local level, and what it did do for freedpeople. Most grant that the bureau "made an important difference to the lives of freedpeople and left its mark on the social and economic institutions of the postbellum South." Indeed, in many diverse ways, the new bureau scholars would agree with Du Bois's interpretation more than a century ago. "That is the large legacy of the Freedmen's Bureau," he wrote in 1901, "the work it did not do because it could not." Today, bureau historians regard the federal agency as a "limited protector," "guardian," even "ally" of the freedpeople in what Du Bois called the "splendid failure" of Reconstruction and conclude, as Barbara Jeanne Fields has, that most of its "agents seem to have had a genuine sympathy for the freedmen, even if they could never fully understand or appreciate the freedmen's viewpoint."[8]

But there were more than just freedmen involved. Despite the voluminous scholarship on the Freedmen's Bureau, remarkably little has been written about the relationship between black women and the bureau; neglected as well in this scholarship has been the role that mid-nineteenth-century understandings of gender and gender difference played in shaping the outcome of bureau policy.[9] For far too long, historians of the bureau have failed to see that "freedpeople" and "freedmen" are not synonymous and that freedwomen deserve attention in discussions of the former slaves' relationship with the bureau and, by extension, the federal government. By ignoring freedwomen, bureau scholars largely depict bureau policy makers and agents as having acted without regard to gender. They did not. They created and, especially agents at the local level responsible for the day-to-day work of Reconstruction (and with whom freedwomen interacted most), applied bureau policies guided by nineteenth-century ideals of domesticity, dependency, family relations, and gender roles. Moreover, and regardless of the motives of bureau officials, black women used the bureau to pursue their own objectives. In neglecting to recognize freedwomen's agency and overlooking the gendered nature of bureau work, bureau scholarship has failed to understand fully the federal government's relationship with freedwomen, freedmen, and black communities in post–Civil War America.

In the last few decades, Reconstruction scholars more generally have reshaped our understanding of the social and political landscape of the era in profound ways and, in many instances, now see African American women as having agency, although perhaps not self-determination, in their passage from slavery to freedom.[10] In 1988, Eric Foner's *Reconstruction: America's Unfinished Revolution, 1863–1877* transformed how historians understood the age of emancipation. By offering a synthesis that placed the African American experience and the transformation of southern society launched by emancipation at the center of the story, Foner provided a new and powerful vision of Reconstruction—one that integrated the social, political, and economic aspects of these tumultuous years into a master narrative. And the bureau, in his estimation, was central to the story of Reconstruction. To the federal agency, "more than any other institution," Foner maintains, "fell the task of assisting at the birth of a free labor society." While scholars continue to examine the many meanings of northern "free labor" ideology to the policy makers of Reconstruction (including those who created, led, and served the bureau), they agree that a commitment "to lay the foundations for a free labor society" united the bureau's diverse activities and officials. In the end, Foner concludes that bureau leaders never really regarded the agency as representing the interests of either former slaves or former masters per se; rather, it supported the cause of northern free labor. The bureau's interests might have coincided at times with those of southern planters and at other times with those of former slaves, but its officials acted in a consistent way to uphold the ideals of free labor and the contract.[11] Women and considerations of gender, however, are difficult to find in either Foner's appraisal of the bureau or his revision of the turbulent era of emancipation.[12] Nevertheless, by underscoring the extent to which Reconstruction was a social process, Foner opened the door to a research agenda that could both include women and pay heed to the many gendered terrains of freedom.

Scholars such as Nancy Bercaw, Laura Edwards, Noralee Frankel, Thavolia Glymph, Susan O'Donovan, Hannah Rosen, Leslie Schwalm, and Amy Dru Stanley, among others, have since advanced significantly the study of gender and the experience of women during and after the Civil War.[13] Perhaps most noteworthy about this historiographical strand of Reconstruction scholarship is the way in which these scholars have forced a reconsideration of the relationship between the social and the political, the private and the public, in the midst of the era's heated debates over emancipation and citizenship. These historians demonstrate a point now agreed upon—that the politics of the so-called private sphere transformed the public sphere and notions of power within it in profound ways. Indeed, their works show that the very act of drawing a line between the private and the public world was, in and of itself, a brave political act in the age of emancipation. It was an era in which, as the historian Mary Ryan recognizes, the "meaning of gender was being rewritten in broad and basic ways, in everything from political representation . . . to such prosaic matters as gathering trash." It was a time of profound transformation—a time in which, as the historian Thavolia Glymph explains, the "the big abstract story [was] composed of equally big personal stories, from a woman's right to choose the dress she will wear to her right to live." To be sure, these Reconstruction scholars remind us that although mid-nineteenth-century gender ideology proclaimed women's activities and families private, they were anything but. There is no longer any question that in the post–Civil War South, the political went well beyond participating in rallies, voting, running for office, passing legislation, and so forth. By considering the reconstruction of women's labor, marriage, the household, and sexuality as part of the significant—and very public and very political—debates that shaped the meaning and outcome of emancipation, these scholars have remade our understanding of the political culture that was Reconstruction.[14]

What is largely missing in this new scholarship is a significant treatment of the role that the Freedmen's Bureau, its policies, and its agents played in freedwomen's efforts to participate in the contentious—private and public, domestic and political, unquestionably gendered—debates over freedom.[15] That is not to say, however, that the scholarship on freedwomen has not considered the bureau or that it has not drawn extensively from the voluminous records generated by the agency. It has and it does. But, with few exceptions, the histories of black women in the age of emancipation do not depict the Freedmen's Bureau as an agency that brought much good to the lives of African American women.[16] Some of the earliest scholarship on freedwomen argues that black women "resisted" turning to the bureau in their efforts to define a meaningful freedom. The historian Catherine Clinton, for instance, insists that freedwomen "generally sought assistance" from the bureau only "when frantic or destitute, without alternatives." Maintaining that the "desperate circumstances of most women [are] revealed by even a brief survey of the records," she contends that freedwomen came to the bureau primarily for material relief. She also asserts that freedwomen especially avoided bringing "domestic matters" to the bureau and that those who did were not interested in forcing "apprehension or punishment" of the accused wrongdoer but rather "merely" did so "to justify their claims for assistance." Recently emancipated women, Clinton concludes, considered bureau agents, with their racist attitudes, as "allied by color with their former masters" and thus neither regarded it as an agency that could help them nor readily turned to it for help.[17] In the last decade, however, the scholarship on African American women during Reconstruction has come to acknowledge the great frequency with which former slave women appealed to the bureau.[18] These most recent works maintain that freedwomen readily brought labor- and wage-related complaints to the bureau yet were reticent about inviting—although they unquestionably did—federal intervention into their familial relations.[19]

Many works on African American women in the postemancipation South also present the bureau as an agency unresponsive to issues of gender, insisting that, much like white southerners, bureau officials saw freedwomen foremost—if not solely—in terms of their race. They were no more than laborers. Some works, for instance, contend that the central question for bureau agents, as Linda Kerber notes in her consideration of vagrancy during Reconstruction, was about "race, not gender." "For black women" in the postwar South, she concludes, "race trumped gender."[20] Indeed, when it comes to former slave women's labor, much of this scholarship maintains that the federal agency made no distinctions between black women and black men. After all, they were both workers to federal officials. Bureau policies and its agents' actions, these histories insist, were consequences of the racist and gendered assumptions of the day and thus supported views of "freedwomen's industry" in terms that "were not all that different from the interests of ex-masters." Considerations of the bureau's use of free labor ideology and contract further conclude that its officials made no exceptions for freedwomen, refused "to discriminate by sex in enforcing the duty of work," and discounted "all but wage work as idleness."[21] More recent works on former slave women in the postemancipation South continue to explore the gendered consequences of the labor and domestic politics of Reconstruction and, in doing so, address what the historian Leslie Schwalm calls the "formidable, if bungling" bureau and its "interference" in black communities.[22] In the end, and despite cursory comments that "there were many agents scattered across the South who were committed to defending freedpeople's interests" or that freedwomen "occasionally drew support from Freedmen's Bureau agents" who pitied their difficult plight, much of the scholarship on freedwomen concludes, first, that former slave women did not trust the bureau as a mediator of Reconstruction—that they recognized "the limited role the Bureau could play in their lives" and turned to it "only under duress" or as a "last resort"—and, second, that the federal agency, its "coercive policies," and its agents failed to recognize freedwomen's particular gendered needs and were limited in ability or willingness to come to the aid of African American women. The bureau, in short, "proved inadequate" to aid freedwomen as they embraced the blessings and contested the deficiencies of emancipation.[23]

Whatever it concludes about freedwomen and the Freedmen's Bureau, this scholarship on former slave women in the postemancipation South confirms the richness of the federal agency's records for the study of African American women's history. Amounting to more than 1,100 cubic feet at the National Archives in Washington, D.C., the bureau records provide historians a way to hear freedwomen's voices and see their agency.[24] Indeed, the most worthwhile studies of the lives of African Americans in the immediate aftermath of the Civil War, including the incredibly valuable documentary publications of the Freedmen and Southern Society Project,[25] draw heavily from this voluminous collection of manuscript records that document Reconstruction from regional, state, and local perspectives. Perhaps most valuable to works on freedwomen—including this study—are the field office records of the bureau. Providing accounts of local agents on the front lines of Reconstruction, with whom freedwomen interacted most, the field office records include correspondence between bureau offices and with local blacks and whites, labor agreements, complaint registers, endorsement books, and daily logs of agents. It is within these records that the actions and agency of former slave women are most visible. Revealing much more than the actions of a highly bureaucratic federal agency, they offer unique insight into the experiences, culture, consciousness, and aspirations of African American women (and men). Freedwomen speak, though not as much as we would like, through detailed descriptions of the complaints they made to bureau agents. Sometimes they speak in their own words in petitions, letters, affidavits, and depositions. The journals, letters, endorsements, relief rolls, reports of "outrages," and other bureau records further uncover the lives of freedwomen by showing what so many others—southern planters, bureau officials, and black men—expected of them. Visible too in these records is the gendered nature of bureau work, as they document the interactions of local bureau agents with black and white communities across the South and the myriad ways in which agents transformed Reconstruction-era public policy with their varied—and gendered—implementation of federal policies. Archaic and incorrect spelling and grammar in quotations from these bureau records have been allowed to stand as originally written.

Although certainly some former slave women did not, for a whole variety of reasons, turn to the bureau, a great many did. Despite claims that former slave women "resisted" coming to the Freedmen's Bureau and turned to it only "when frantic or destitute" or as a "last resort," bureau manuscript records—especially those from the local field offices—make clear that scores of African

American women interacted with the bureau in the immediate postemancipation South. That is, freedwomen encountered (sometimes willingly and other times by force), trusted (sometimes because they wanted to and other times because it was their only hope), challenged (sometimes with the help of others and other times on their own), and used (sometimes successfully and other times not) the federal agency in their transformation from slaves to freedwomen. Moreover, as they turned to the bureau as an ally in freedom, African American women presented complaints that demanded agents' involvement in a variety of "public" and "private" matters. That is, they came to the bureau seeking relief. They initiated complaints that centered on labor—both their own and that of family members—and involved contract disputes or claims for wages. They also instigated a stream of more personal, in many instances "domestic," complaints that involved marriage and divorce, household support, child custody, and violence both inside and outside their own households. By dragging matters that others, including bureau agents, hoped would be relegated to the private sphere across the line into the political arena, as well as by challenging white notions of their proper place as women, as workers, as former slaves, and as African Americans, freedwomen who turned to the bureau demanded that its agents acknowledge their individual, familial, and gendered needs.

While certainly too bureau officials could be unsympathetic to former slave women and allow their race to "trump" their gender, the federal agency's manuscript records also clearly reveal bureau men[26] who very much considered the gender of freedwomen as they implemented the public policy of Reconstruction. Notwithstanding assertions that the agency's principal interest, as the historian Nancy Cott asserts, was in instructing "freed*men*, not freed*women*," in becoming citizens,[27] and the fact that it issued wholesale proclamations without regard to gender to "freedmen" (meaning, in reality, "freedpeople"), bureau agents and officials struggled with how to view African American women in the wake of emancipation. However much they viewed the former slave women as workers—as white southerners wanted—bureau men did not ignore their gender. To be sure, the predominantly white northern Victorian men who served the bureau, especially those in its field offices, had difficulty classifying freedwomen. To these men, the category of "woman" conflicted in so many ways with the categories of "worker" and "citizen." But the confusion did not stop there. As they attempted to do their job, agents of the bureau, like others in the northern army charged with reconstructing the South more generally, encountered what the historian Nancy Bercaw calls "a bizarre web of contradictory gender, racial, and class ideologies" in which northern notions of "manhood and womanhood, black and white, free and dependent became scrambled and confused." Freedwomen were at once former slaves, blacks, workers, and emergent citizens who were also women, daughters, wives, and mothers. To the bureau men stationed across the South, they had to seem an inherent contradiction—freedwomen were "both male and female, worker and dependent, strong and helpless."[28] Complicating matters further, and regardless of what these federal officials thought about them, freedwomen always seemed to be there, at the doorstep of bureau offices, making demands of the federal government. Indeed, one agent in Georgia described the freedwomen as being particularly "outspoken and aggressive" in their readiness to appeal to federal officials—"Freedmen's Bureau officers not excluded." What was more, these women seemed prepared to demand ever more "loudly," as another agent in Florida put it, that the bureau acknowledge their particular gendered needs.[29] It is exactly this kind of daily interaction with the bureau that underscores the interconnectedness of public policy and private lives during the formative era of Reconstruction.

As they interacted with the Freedmen's Bureau, former slave women and men encountered a highly bureaucratic organization overwhelmingly staffed by northern white men who had served in the Union army and who, now in Reconstruction, willingly (or unwillingly in some cases) occupied posts that made them the face of the federal presence in the war-torn South. Those who led and served the federal agency shared certain goals that, in the end, guided these interactions. African Americans thus discovered in the bureau a legion of men dedicated to establishing a free labor society in the South. So too did they find in these men an unconditional support for policies and more informal efforts designed to reconstruct (or, in their words, to "regularize") African American domestic relations. And thus permeated with nineteenth-century gender ideology, these two overarching objectives—and the multitude of official policies and informal actions employed to achieve them—worked together and reinforced one another through the bureau's interpretation of the ideal of contract. Those who led and served the bureau, as the historians Eric Foner and Amy Dru Stanley have pointed out, regarded the contract as the governing model for all social relations, including both labor and domestic relations. In their minds, it was integral to a successful Reconstruction. As a result, agents worked foremost to enforce the relationship between freedom and contract.[30] *Freedwomen and the Freedmen's Bureau* thus begins in Chapter 1 by demonstrating that mid-nineteenth-century northern ideologies of true womanhood, domesticity, and dependency worked alongside free labor ideology and the contract ideal to form the foundation of the bureau's gendered vision of freedom.

But policy did not always translate into practice in the disorder of the postemancipation South. Ideology was not often reality in the rough terrain of Reconstruction. The remaining chapters of *Freedwomen and the Freedmen's Bureau* illustrate how the bureau's gendered assertions of public policy helped to create—as well as soften or harden—what Susan O'Donovan calls the "numerous and differently gendered shapes" of emancipation.[31] In so many ways, black women both desired and encountered a far different freedom than did African American men in the immediate years following the Civil War, and their interactions with the bureau revealed and contributed to these gendered landscapes of Reconstruction. As agents implemented the bureau's many policies, they demonstrated a willingness to see freedwomen's gender. After all, they were Victorian men who had a strong sense of gender roles. They promoted certain cultural and social notions of womanhood—especially a Victorian gender ideology that valued the dutiful wife and, increasingly, the devoted mother—that, notwithstanding significant legal and political limitations, allowed the bureau to bestow certain privileges upon freedwomen while denying others. Thus influenced by their own gendered assumptions about free labor, domesticity, dependency, and familial relationships—as well as confronted by freedwomen with their own ideas about free labor and domesticity who demanded that their particular gendered needs be recognized by these policy makers of Reconstruction—bureau men came to alter, stretch, and at times ignore bureau policy in their dealings with black women. What resulted were bureau policies that, when enforced, applied to freedmen without much exception and to freedwomen in varying degrees according to their marital and parental status, character, and perceived worthiness. When it came to freedwomen, the bureau's rigid policies just never seemed to translate simply into practice.

Freedwomen and the Freedmen's Bureau proceeds from Chapter 1 to consider the gendered realities of Reconstruction-era public policy in action. In doing so, it moves chapter by chapter to examine the gendered nature of bureau work in four distinct areas of Reconstruction-era public policy—bureau efforts to relieve physical suffering with federal material relief; bureau policies designed to implement a southern free labor system and combat vagrancy; bureau defense of black parental rights and its efforts to regulate, combat, and at times employ the practice of apprenticeship; and finally bureau attempts to secure equal justice for former slaves. Each chapter demonstrates that the consequences of bureau policy at work—rather than as stated in the many policies, orders, and dictates issued with little or no regard for gender—could be far different for freedwomen and men. Chapters 2 and 3, for instance, reveal that the bureau's recognition of freedwomen's gender could bring benefits and protections not available to freedmen. Disregarding restrictive relief policies that limited aid to freedpeople physically unable to work, for example, bureau officials expanded definitions of the deserving poor in a way that allowed them to provide relief to able-bodied "worthy" freedwomen. Amending too the agency's harsh labor policies that called for all able-bodied freedpeople to enter contracts or face prosecution as vagrants, bureau officials—all the while encouraging both black men and women to find work—refused to categorically arrest all African American women who did not enter contracts, work regularly outside their own households, or possess some visible (and acceptable) means of employment. However much the bureau regarded them as workers—which it certainly did—its agents recognized both that freedwomen were now part of freedmen's households and that the labor market regarded them as less productive and less valuable. But freedwomen's gender did not always garner the bureau's largess. Chapters 3, 4, and 5 demonstrate that freedwomen also encountered in the bureau an agency that employed the gendered ideologies of the day to restrict efforts to control their labor, their children, their households, and their bodies. It encouraged black men to control and contract the labor of family members, including that of wives and daughters. It enforced harsh apprenticeship practices against black unwed mothers who could not provide adequately for their children. And it refereed freedwomen's demands for justice in ways that promoted female dependency, black manhood and independence, and northern, white, middle-class understandings of free labor, domesticity, and citizenship.

Studying freedwomen and the Freedmen's Bureau across the South poses certain methodological challenges. Given the sheer magnitude of the bureau manuscript records, in particular, choices had to be made as to the parameters of this study. At the heart of *Freedwomen and the Freedmen's Bureau* is the bureau—the policies and ideologies that guided its role in Reconstruction, the men it charged with enforcing freedom, and its interactions with former slave women. It seeks to provide breadth by looking at policy making across the entire region, and depth by examining the bureau at work at the local level. To do so, this book draws upon the insights of bureau scholars to explain the federal agency's role and policies in reconstructing the South, and it builds upon the work of scholars who have looked at freedwomen's Reconstruction experiences to underscore the gendered nature of the era of emancipation. It relies on the commissioner records and the assistant commissioner records for most states to explain the gendered foundations of Reconstruction-era public policy as understood by those who led the bureau. To demonstrate the gendered implementation and consequences of public policy in the daily lives of freedpeople, *Freedwomen and the Freedmen's Bureau* utilizes the bureau field office records of four individual states—Virginia, Georgia, Louisiana, and Texas—to uncover the gendered responses of bureau agents and officials to both bureau policy and freedwomen's assertiveness. Selected foremost for the quality of the bureau manuscript materials available but also for their geographic, demographic, and economic variation, these states also offer a substantial and growing secondary scholarship on the bureau and Reconstruction more generally. To give emphasis to the gendered consequences of bureau policy beyond these four states, this study also employs the incredibly rich studies of freedwomen and gender in Georgia by Susan O'Donovan; in Mississippi by Nancy Bercaw and Noralee Frankel; in North Carolina by Laura Edwards, Rebecca Scott, and Karin Zipf; in South Carolina by Leslie Schwalm and Julie Saville; and in Tennessee and Arkansas (and beyond) by Hannah Rosen. Finally, it must be noted that *Freedwomen and the Freedmen's Bureau* does not examine the bureau's educational work. Without question, the Freedmen's Bureau played a significant role in facilitating educational opportunities for former slaves between 1865 and 1872. But the bureau played a supervisory or administrative role in the establishment of black education in the postwar South. That is, it advocated and coordinated the creation of schools for freedpeople, but its men did not necessarily control or, in most cases, participate in them directly. Thus bureau policy makers encouraged agents to give attention to and promote educational matters, help secure schoolhouses, and provide transportation (and at times pay) to a great number of teachers, but the job of actually running schools and teaching former slaves fell to individuals, communities, and organizations not employed or controlled directly by the bureau. Thus the reconstruction—or, in actuality, the founding—of black education in the South is a story, although certainly a gendered one, that goes beyond the bureau men and bureau work considered here.[32]

In the immediate postemancipation South, bureau men shaped the gendered outcome of emancipation. The agents and officials employed by this federal agency to enforce freedom did not ignore African American women (even if they could) or their womanhood (even as they understood it differently than former slave women). And quite often, these men acted just as we would expect. That is, they functioned as products, indeed agents, of their society. They were Victorian men, with a strong sense of gender roles, who sought to reconstruct southern society based on their own mid-nineteenth-century, northern, white, middle-class understanding of free labor and domestic relations. In the end, freedwomen who positioned themselves as worthy, appropriately dependent women in need of help benefited from the protection of the bureau. But at other times—and especially when they sought rights and safeguards that white women did not yet possess or appeared to agents as less-than-respectable women—freedwomen lost out in their encounters with this momentary and exceptional federal agency.

But the gendered nature of bureau work is only part of the story in *Freedwomen and the Freedmen's Bureau*. African American women too participated in the remaking of their society in the immediate postemancipation South, and quite often they frustrated the public policy of Reconstruction in the process. Thus the assertiveness of freedwomen is an important part of the Reconstruction experience. And from 1865 to 1868 in particular, when the Freedmen's Bureau was most active, freedwomen's participation in what would become a lengthy battle to define and defend freedom, womanhood and manhood, and citizenship for African Americans on their own terms meant interacting with the bureau they regarded as "the government." In communities across the South, freedwomen turned to the agency and demanded that its agents recognize them as women and that the federal government consider their particular gendered needs.

Yes, the policies of the Freedmen's Bureau and the gendered actions of its men were at times coercive. Yes too, freedwomen sometimes paid the price when bureau policies and agents' preconceived mid-nineteenth-century white notions about gender and race converged to deny them unrestricted and complete control over their lives, labors, families, and bodies. But such was not always the case. Freedwomen found both an ally and an enemy in the bureau. That is, this federal agency, its efforts to reconstruct southern labor and African American domestic relations, and its enforcement of mid-nineteenth-century gendered ideologies worked both for and against former slave women. Rather than being blinded by freedwomen's race, bureau officials and agents saw that they, in fact, were women. And, although not recognizing African American women as emergent citizens equal to men or defending their particular gendered needs to the extent and in the way that former slave women wanted, bureau men awarded freedwomen benefits and protections unavailable to freedmen. In the end, the men who led and served the bureau acted both on ideological impulses and, quite often, in response to freedwomen's agency to enforce the public policy of early Reconstruction. And they did so in ways that helped and hurt African American women.

1

"that the freed-women ... may rise to the dignity and glory of true womanhood"

The Men, Purpose, and Gendered Freedom of the Freedmen's Bureau

There is no being on earth for whom I have higher regard than a true woman; and if there is one thing I desire above another, it is, that the freed-women of this country, so long degraded and made merchandise of, may rise to the dignity and glory of true womanhood.

As part of a series of lectures entitled *Plain Counsels for Freedmen*, Brevet Major General Clinton Fisk, a veteran of the Civil War's western theater and the first assistant commissioner of the Freedmen's Bureau to command operations in Kentucky and Tennessee, imparted these words and "a few additional suggestions" to former slave women as they embarked on their journey as freedwomen. Offering both freedmen and women "a hint or two" about race relations, work and free labor, marriage, home life, and religion, Fisk's *Plain Counsels* was part of a broader narrative intent on defining for former slaves the most important rights, responsibilities, and values of freedom. To African American women, this bureau policy maker readily asserted: "You have serious and important work to do, and you should prepare yourselves for it, and devote yourselves to it."[1]

Assistant Commissioner Fisk, an abolitionist from New York and a devout Methodist, wanted freedwomen to discover and hold fast to the ideals of true womanhood. The "cardinal virtues" of true womanhood—piety, purity, submissiveness, and domesticity—were the standards by which mid-nineteenth-century white American society judged women,[2] and thus to this bureau policy maker, they represented what former slave women should aspire to live by. "A true, honest, wise woman is the best work of God," he told young freedwomen. "She is man's strength," he continued, "the charm of the household, the attraction of the social circle, the light of the church, and the brightest jewel in the Savior's crown." "But," he warned equally, "a foolish, vain, cross, idle, slovenly woman is the meanest creature that ever clotted the fair creation of God." "Let it be your first aim," the bureau policy maker pressed, "to make of yourself a true woman."[3]

For Fisk, like most white Americans, the ideals of true womanhood represented "the centerpiece of nineteenth-century female identity." But the bureau policy maker's promotion of the values present in true womanhood went well beyond what he desired for freedwomen. It said a great deal about his gendered notions of freedom. It got at his understanding of the rights and responsibilities of freedom. It spoke to his white, northern, middle-class definitions of womanhood, manhood, and the home—definitions that seemingly rejected the patriarchal households of the slaveholding South, presented freedmen with "full legal title to citizenship," and welcomed freedwomen "under the mantle of Victorian purity." It was tied too to the cause of free labor and the job ahead of Fisk and his bureau colleagues, who served as policy makers and enforcers of Reconstruction. For the "problem" faced by the men charged with realizing freedom, as the historian Thomas Holt reminds us, "was not merely to make ex-slaves work, but to make them into a working class, that is, a class that would submit to the market because it adhered to the *values* of a bourgeois society: regularity, punctuality, sobriety, frugality, and economic rationality." And acceptance of Victorian gender roles and family relations was part of this charge, for in so many divergent ways household relations represented "the ties which connect society" to mid-nineteenth-century Americans. That Fisk believed it possible for freedwomen to "make" themselves into true women reveals a great deal about what bureau men thought possible at the outset of Reconstruction.[4]

Brevet Major General Fisk was perhaps the most outspoken bureau policy maker to instruct former slave women and men in the gendered privileges and duties of freedom. So too was he one of the most racially progressive bureau officials. But regardless of his abolitionist, more liberal leanings, Fisk was not alone in his paternalistic desire to school the freedpeople in northern ideas about free labor, domesticity, dependency, and family relations. Although more vocal—indeed frank—than others in offering expressions of how mid-nineteenth-century gender ideology factored into the public policy of Reconstruction, this federal official worked in step with his bureau colleagues to guide the transition to freedom with gendered instructions that addressed the agency's most pressing concerns about African American labor and domestic relations. In this sense, Fisk and other bureau men employed the gendered ideologies of free labor and domesticity in ways that "performed [the] political and cultural work" of Reconstruction.[5]

The man responsible for making things "smooth," as Georgia freedwoman Susan McIntosh put it, in the immediate postemancipation South was Major General Oliver Otis Howard. Appointed commissioner of the Freedmen's Bureau in May 1865, Howard was just thirty-four years old when he assumed the monumental post. Known to his contemporaries as the "Christian Soldier," the former commander of the Army of the Tennessee from Maine would serve as the agency's only commissioner until Congress formally dismantled it in 1872. Howard had not been an abolitionist. A wartime convert to emancipation and firm believer in the ability of humanitarian assistance to "uplift" the former slaves, he nonetheless gave the agency its character and course. Calling for the United States to become "a Nation that cares for its children," he provided a moral purpose, an ideological framework, and a vision for the bureau. He was the man who would determine the shape and direction of bureau policy. The task before Howard was formidable to be sure. Upon hearing of his friend's appointment, General William Tecumseh Sherman confided to Howard, "I hardly know whether to congratulate you or not." He cautioned Howard about the inevitable difficulties that lay ahead. "So far as man can do, I believe you will," he told the new commissioner, but "though in the kindness of your heart you would alleviate all the ills of humanity it is not in your power, nor is it in your power to fulfill one tenth of the expectations of those who formed the Bureau." "I fear," Sherman confessed, "you have Hercules' task." Perhaps he was correct.[6]

Howard, stationed in Washington, D.C., was not alone as he embarked on the Herculean mission. Assistant commissioners—at the state level—and their appointees—at the district and county levels—assumed the daunting task of implementing (and expanding) federal laws and bureau policies designed to remake the South. And this too was a formidable charge. Even Howard confessed: "It was easy to write and publish" policies and directives, "but hard to carry such orders into execution." Predominantly military men "of tried courage, of high education, of well-known character, and pronounced friends of humanity," according to the commissioner, the assistant commissioners decided how bureau orders, general as they were, would be applied in their states and issued their own policies applicable to "freedmen's affairs" there. As a result, these men played a direct role in establishing the public policy of Reconstruction.[7]

The men appointed as assistant commissioners had much in common. By the end of the summer of 1865, Howard had filled the agency's leadership positions with twelve assistant commissioners, many of whom embraced their positions with an outlook that, in the words of the bureau historian Paul Cimbala, "could prompt them to make [it] into an agency of change." The first assistant commissioners were mostly college-educated military men from the North with Protestant backgrounds. "It would not be inaccurate to describe" the assistant commissioners as, another bureau historian explains, "quintessentially representative of the Northern middle class." By and large committed to the Christian Soldier's vision for the bureau and to "securing the rights of the freedmen," many also came to their posts with wartime experience with black soldiers and "contraband" slaves. Giving the bureau a more racially progressive character, these initial appointees thus shared an allegiance to the Union cause and, at the very least, an expectation that black and white southerners would accept the consequences of Confederate defeat and emancipation.[8]

The first nine assistant commissioner appointments came in May 1865, in the days following Howard's own appointment to command the bureau. Fisk assumed charge of bureau activities in Tennessee and Kentucky. Selected for the post in North Carolina was Colonel Eliphalet Whittlesey, a professor from Howard's alma mater, Bowdoin College in Maine, and a former minister who had served as the now-commissioner's aid and judge advocate. Whittlesey also had commanded African American troops during the war. Heading bureau work in South Carolina, Georgia, and Florida would be General Rufus Saxton, a West Point graduate and career officer from Massachusetts who had dedicated much wartime effort to enlisting and organizing black soldiers for the Union cause. Saxton, "long . . . distinguished as a friend of the negroes," would ultimately lose his job for working so vigorously for the rights of blacks. Colonel Samuel Thomas, who had worked with the contrabands during the war and was regarded by his bureau colleagues as similar to Saxton in his desire to be "true to liberty," took the post in Mississippi. To lead the agency in Arkansas and Missouri, Howard appointed General John Sprague, an Ohio merchant who had served under his command in the Army of the Tennessee. In Alabama, Colonel Thomas Osborn, an army chaplain who had been Howard's chief of artillery, was tapped to command bureau efforts. Colonel John Eaton, a graduate of Dartmouth College and an ordained minister who had worked to organize contraband camps during the war, took charge of activities in Washington, D.C. Though not known personally to him, Howard, on the recommendation of Secretary of War Edwin Stanton, appointed Orlando Brown, a graduate of Yale Medical School and the army's superintendent of Negro affairs in Norfolk, to the post in Virginia. Also praised by Stanton, Thomas Conway, who had been in charge of freedmen's affairs for Alabama and Mississippi in wartime, was appointed to lead bureau work in the "hard field" of Louisiana. Howard chose three additional men to head bureau activities at the state level in late summer 1865. Brigadier General Wager Swayne, a Yale-educated lawyer in Ohio before the war and son of U.S. Supreme Court justice Noah Haynes Swayne, accepted the post in Alabama when injury prevented Osborn from doing so. General Davis Tillson, an antebellum Republican politician from Maine and decorated soldier who had recruited African American troops, assumed responsibility for the agency in Georgia. Finally, "so fearless of opposition or danger," according to Howard, was radical abolitionist General Edgar Gregory that the commissioner sent him to Texas—"the post of greatest peril."[9]

The Freedmen's Bureau would endure significant change in leadership at the state level over its short lifetime. This was especially true as Congress reviewed its existence and powers in 1866 (and again in 1868) and as Andrew Johnson repeatedly showed, as Commissioner Howard remembered it, "a steady, though underhand, opposition" to the agency.[10] The president's politically motivated investigation of the bureau in the spring of 1866, for instance, resulted in findings that declared it "a Radical corporation" and motivated considerable shifts in bureau men at the state level. "In Virginia," the inspectors told Johnson, bureau officers "were all Radicals. In North Carolina, all we met but one . . . were of the same stripe—South Carolina the same as the other two States." And while Assistant Commissioner Swayne "is a good officer and a man of ability," one of the inspectors reported, "he is as fierce a radical as Thad Stevens himself."[11] Thus, with the president "guiding" his hand—and beginning even before Johnson's inspection—Commissioner Howard replaced some of his most trusted leadership with more politically and, in many instances, racially conservative men.[12] And often these changes contained the bureau's revolutionary potential. "A good many of my present officers lack zeal," the commissioner would comment in the fall of 1866.[13] By the end of the bureau's tenure, fifty-five men had served its ranks as assistant commissioners, and the policy actions of these bureau men would vary considerably.[14]

Whatever Howard's plans from Washington and whoever the leadership in state headquarters, the realization of bureau policy rested foremost on its officials at the local level. Bureau field agents—known as superintendents, assistant superintendents, subcommissioners, or assistant subassistant commissioners in the agency's bureaucratic language—attended to the day-to-day business of Reconstruction. Policy makers charged these local men with implementing bureau efforts as well as aiding and advising freedpeople and promoting and protecting their general welfare. More often than not, northerners and southerners alike would measure the achievements of the bureau by the actions of these agents in the field. Indeed, the very "efficiency" of the Freedmen's Bureau, commented one southern white woman some years after Reconstruction, "depended upon the agent's personality. If he were discreet and self-respecting, its influence was wholesome; if he were the reverse, it was a curse. If he were inclined to peculate, the agency gave opportunity; if he were cruel—well, negroes who were hung up by the thumbs, or well annointed with molasses and tied out where flies could find them had opinions."[15] Although they did not create the policies, orders, and directives intended to enforce freedom and reconstruct the nation, these local bureau were pivotal in this era of civic transformation. For "[u]ltimately," as the historians Eileen Boris and Peter Bardaglio have explained, "public policy is forged in the minute decisions made by those directly involved in translating statutes into rules and regulations, and in interpreting them on a daily basis." In the era of emancipation, it would be the local agent of the Freedmen's Bureau who forged federal public policy.[16]

Most often outsiders by blood, creed, and culture, local bureau men faced a daily deluge of complaints and anxieties brought by both freedpeople and—even as they condemned bureau interference—white southerners. The competence and dedication brought to the job varied greatly among local agents. They came to their positions both willingly and at times unwillingly, with varied backgrounds and motives. While most were white northern military men, some assistant commissioners at the state level began to appoint civilian agents, both northern and southern, beginning in late 1865 and into 1866. Seemingly fearless and faithful to the old abolitionist quest, some bureau officials braved the opposition, hostilities, and outright violence of white southerners to protect former slaves from fraud and violence at any cost. Some sacrificed their lives. Others were not so noble. Desiring acceptance from white southerners and possessing similar racist views about former slaves, some agents and officials blatantly chose to become instruments of the old planter class and aided in efforts to restore slavery in all but name. Most often, however, agents and officials of the bureau fell somewhere in between these two extremes. Many operated with a pragmatism that understood that the bureau was but a fleeting agency and thus focused on the most pressing conflicts between former slaves and former slave owners. Most agents simply tried to do their job, a job that presented fierce obstacles and threatened their very lives. At times, as the historian Eric Foner points out, they came to the aid of freedpeople, while at other times they supported the defeated rebels. In the end, as the agency halted most of its activities in 1868, Commissioner Howard would take pride in the bureau and its men, maintaining that nine out of ten bureau officials had been "efficient and true." Declaring that bureau agents "varied all the way from unselfish philanthropists to narrow-minded busybodies and thieves," the historian W. E. B. Du Bois offered perhaps a more balanced judgment when he concluded in 1901 that "the average was far better than the worst."[17]

Bureau men in the field faced staggering obstacles. To say they were overworked would be an understatement. There never seemed to be enough agents. At best count, 2,441 men staffed the bureau as agents in its brief lifetime. By the close of 1865, only 470 bureau men would unevenly scatter the southern landscape. At the height of its strength, the agency employed only 900 men, with some 300 of these serving as clerks rather than agents. Unbelievably, the bureau in Mississippi operated with only a dozen agents in 1866 and, similarly, the bureau in Alabama employed only 20 men at any given moment during its lifetime. By 1869, the bureau's manpower would wither to a mere 158 men across the entire South.[18]

Numbers aside, the local agent's job, as one Yankee reporter attested in September 1865, was "not a sinecure." The job was intimidating. "It would be accurate to say," he told northern readers of the *Nation*, "that no man can perform its duties, and that most men, finding themselves able to do so little where so much calls loudly to be done, could but become disheartened by the difficulties of the position." Bureau leaders agreed. Upon acceptance of a post in the bureau, Commissioner Howard told the *Washington Chronicle*, the local agent became "a magistrate with extraordinary judicial power—overseer of the poor of all classes in his district, agent to take charge of abandoned lands, and required to settle, in a few days, [the] most intricate questions with reference to labor, political economy, &c, that have puzzled the world for ages." In dealing with the day-to-day work of Reconstruction, the local agent was at once "diplomat, marriage counselor, educator, supervisor of labor contracts, sheriff, judge, and jury." And the demands of the job took their toll. "I am *tired out* and *broke down*," one agent in Georgia would come to confess. "Every day for 6 months, day after day I have had from 5 to 20 complaints, *generally trivial* and of no moment, yet requiring consideration & attention," he lamented in summer 1866. "The result is my time is consumed, and I virtually become a 'pack horse' for the whole county." More sanguine was an agent stationed in South Carolina. "I had often felt depressed at the extent of work before us, but never," declared the young New Englander, who was the son of a radical abolitionist preacher and a Union army officer, was "[I] doubtful of final success in restoring not only the Union in its integrity but of infusing correct notions of government and liberty into the minds of the old slave holders . . . and also of the freedmen." These agents were not alone in their discontent for, as Cimbala explains, the treacherous post often demanded "more motivation than what a modest salary could provide."[19]

If lucky, bureau field agents had a horse and a clerk to help with the responsibilities of office. And, if they were truly fortunate, Union troops were nearby, willing to enforce their orders, make arrests, and provide protection to bureau men. More likely, however, local agents found themselves unaided in a hostile environment and responsible for several counties encompassing hundreds of miles and thousands of people. "My satrapy contained two state districts or counties, and eventually three, with a population of about eighty thousand souls and an area at least two thirds as large as the state of Connecticut," another local agent in South Carolina would recall. "Consider the absurdity," he continued, "of expecting one man to patrol three thousand miles and make personal visitations to thirty thousand Negroes." The agent in Prince William County, Virginia, in January 1866 voiced similar complaints of being overworked, but his grievances went well beyond objections to the size of his jurisdiction. Bemoaning his seeming powerlessness in particular, the discouraged agent vowed, "I am entirely helpless and useless for lack of a horse and one or two good mounted men." "I am openly defied," he protested. "I cannot prevent . . . parties from abusing freedmen and holding them in slavery, and if I could arrest offenders, I have no means of confining them or enforcing any penalties whatever."[20]

Commissioner Howard's men assumed their new commissions with other, more fundamental, limitations too. Incredibly, Congress initially restricted the federal agency's existence to one year following the end of hostilities and appropriated no funds for its efforts in the postwar South. Given a home in the War Department, the bureau had been left to survive off army funds and personnel in addition to the resources and compassion of various private relief, missionary, and educational associations of the North. The official statute creating the bureau permitted (but did not require) the secretary of war to provide both military personnel to staff the bureau and surplus food, clothing, and fuel to aid former slaves and white refugees; it also gave the agency control of abandoned and confiscated lands held by the government and authorized it to divide this land into forty-acre plots for sale or rental to former slaves and loyal refugees.[21] But beyond these provisions tentatively empowering the agency to make some freedmen independent farmers and to provide relief to the indigent, the statute went no further. Thus, as Congress bestowed upon Commissioner Howard and his agents "control of all subjects relating to refugees and freedmen in the rebel states," it gave little support, direction, or authority for doing so. And bureau men, like mid-nineteenth-century Americans at large, were not always of the same mind on these subjects.[22]

Those who created, led, and served the bureau had to contend with significant ideological confines that would check their efforts, as well. Despite widespread political support for the establishment of a federal agency to oversee the transition from slavery to freedom, those who created the Freedmen's Bureau—as evidenced in part by their decision to restrict its existence to one year following war's end—regarded its need as temporary and its responsibilities as exceptional. There was no precedent for the bureau. It represented an unparalleled extension of federal power into the economic, legal, political, and social lives of southerners, both black and white. But these were extraordinary times. Reformers and politicians alike rightly feared that white southerners would not readily grant former slaves even the most basic of freedoms unless forced to do so. The nation "had no right to decree freedom" if it would "not guarantee safe guidance and protection," Representative Thomas Eliot had declared in 1863. As Confederate surrender neared in the early months of 1865, northern voters supported congressional action to protect blacks' newfound status in the rebel states. Thus as part of its plans for Reconstruction, in a quite remarkable move, Congress created the Bureau of Refugees, Freedmen, and Abandoned Lands in March and, in doing so, made the federal government the guardian of the recently freed. That said, politicians, reformers, and bureau policy makers alike never intended this guardianship to be permanent. One northern publication made clear this belief, telling its readers: "Let them [both those in Congress and the leaders of any new 'Bureau of Emancipation'] avoid ... too much guardianship, too much taking care, but recognize in the negro a man fully competent to make his own contracts, if protected from injustice and abuse, and for whom the only necessary compulsion is to be paid fair wages for a fair day's work." Union victory, emancipation, and the nation's interests dictated that the freedpeople be placed on the road to self-sufficiency—to become self-reliant wage laborers or, more ideal yet, independent farmers in a "free labor" South—instead of being forever protected and provided for by a benevolent federal government. Once the former slaves had been "taught" to be responsible, self-supporting individuals who could protect and provide for themselves and their families, those who created, led, and served the bureau agreed, the need for this extraordinary agency would no longer exist.[23]

Bureau policy makers, although they would differ about the best means to accomplish it, held firm to a purpose focused on using the northern ideologies of free labor and domesticity to transform the South. Commissioner Howard expected the men who led and served his bureau to embrace policies designed both to "teach" the freedpeople what it meant to be free and to make them into responsible individuals who would work to enjoy the fruits of their labor, provide for their families, and—when the bureau was no longer—protect their own interests with the political and civil rights earned by way of self-sufficiency and (at least for black men) equal citizenship. A bureau official in North Carolina explained the agency's purpose most matter-of-factly. "What we wish to do is plain enough," he declared in 1865. "We desire to instruct the colored people of the South, to lift them up from subservience and helplessness into a dignified independence and citizenship." But was it so simple?[24]

Commissioner Howard knew better. As he took charge of the bureau, the agency's commander stepped into an already heated "terrain of conflict," in Eric Foner's words, over the meaning of freedom. "It is necessary to define that word," Howard would say of freedom in 1865, insisting that it was "most apt to be misunderstood."[25] As his agents assumed their posts in the summer (although more likely the fall) of 1865, it was readily apparent that white and black southerners possessed fundamentally contrary expectations for life in the postemancipation South. African Americans, on the one hand, craved absolute liberation from white control—meaning that, in freedom, they sought authority over their families and labors, freedom of movement, access to land, control of community institutions such as schools and churches, and rights under the changing laws of the land. For black women more specifically, freedom promised "the right to be mothers, workers, friends, and companions" and, they believed, "the right to citizenship and dignity." White southerners, on the other hand, desired something far different. Former masters wanted to maintain control of a cheap, tractable, permanent labor force and, at the very least, insisted that their former bonds persons treat them with the deference of antebellum times. Despite Confederate defeat, and patently in the face of African Americans' hopes for freedom, they prepared to sustain white hegemony in the postwar South, whatever the cost. The outcome of freedom was far from settled in 1865 even if the peculiar institution was, at least in theory, dead.[26]

Howard's bureau—"the conscience and common-sense of the country," as *Harper's Weekly* would come to describe the agency—was charged with stepping "between the hostile parties and [saying] to them, with irresistible authority, 'Peace!'" In assuming this role of "minister of peace," however, those who led and served the bureau planned to do more than end southern hostilities. Triumphant over the Confederacy, northerners had concluded that their free labor system, which went far beyond ideas about work and economics to define social relations and contractual obligations in Yankee society, was, as one bureau man in Tennessee put it in 1865, "the noblest principle on earth."[27] By removing prejudices from the minds of white southerners unwilling to hire blacks, correcting "false impressions" entertained by freedpeople who planned to "live without labor," and overcoming "a singular false pride" in any helpless souls "willing to be supported in idleness," the bureau, Commissioner Howard insisted, sought to introduce a "practical system of compensated labor" in the South.[28] Thus, as Howard accepted the post in late spring 1865, he was operating with what proved to be the mistaken expectation that southern whites would accept the consequences of emancipation and embrace free labor. He also entered office trusting that former slaves, freed from the clutches of slavery, would continue to work and, in doing so, could achieve independence as self-reliant men and appropriately dependent women (man's "help meet," according to Assistant Commissioner Fisk) who welcomed "the opportunity to labor for themselves as the pathway to freedom and prosperity."[29] Charged with enforcing the federal government's vision of freedom and plans for peace, Howard and his exceptional agency thus prepared to pave the way for "actual freedom," in the commissioner's words, by focusing on efforts to "rehabilitate labor" and "regularizing" black family relations in the postemancipation South.[30]

Bureau men like Howard and his assistant commissioners approached their posts intent on deciding for former slave men and women what their new status meant. And work was certainly at the heart of the freedom that the bureau envisioned for freedmen and, though not the case for the white "true women" that Assistant Commissioner Fisk instructed them to emulate, freedwomen. "I know that it is quite natural that you should associate work with slavery, and freedom with idleness," Fisk had conceded to freedmen and women in his *Plain Counsels*. After all, he continued, "you have seen slaves working all their lives, and free people doing little or nothing. And I should not blame you if you should ask, 'What have we gained by freedom, if we are to work, work, work!'" But this bureau policy maker was quick to correct what in his mind were rash notions about the consequence of emancipation. "There is nothing degrading in *free* labor,—nay, it is most honorable," Fisk told former slaves. Premised on the belief that self-ownership was an inviolable right, the cause of free labor—admittedly meaning different things to the many policy makers and enforcers of Reconstruction—presented workers with the liberty to choose when, where, how, and for whom (but not if) they labored, as well as the chance to realize economic independence and upward mobility through a right to wages, if not land, and control of the fruits of their labor. Insisting that God and "[a]ll the holy angels" were workers, Fisk thus offered an explanation for the change in freedpeople's status grounded in these notions of free labor: "A slave works all his life for others. A free man works for himself,—that is, he gets pay for his labor; and if he saves what he earns and manages well, he can get on so well that he may spend the afternoon of his life in his own pleasant home, and never want for anything." And freedwomen too, this bureau policy maker made clear, were expected to work: "A wife must do her very best to help her husband make a living. She can earn as much money sometimes as he can." For bureau men, emancipation and free labor had not ended African American women's obligation to labor. Colonel Orlando Brown, the assistant commissioner of bureau operations in Virginia, similarly schooled the freedpeople in the difference between their former and present conditions and, like all bureau policy makers, warned them not to "act from the mistaken notion that Freedom means liberty to be idle." Appealing to the values inherent to northern free labor ideology, he told them that as free men and women, they must be prepared to help themselves, instructing: "To do this you must be industrious and frugal. You have now every inducement to work, as you are to receive the payment for your labor, and you have every inducement to save your wages, as your rights in what you possess will be protected."[31]

Like other Reconstruction-era policy makers, officials of the Freedmen's Bureau possessed remarkably idealistic assumptions about the mutuality of interests between labor and capital and how southern antebellum labor relations could be revolutionized to fit a reconstructed free society. Former slaves and former masters had only to renounce the lessons learned in slavery about labor relations and labor control. And, in doing so, bureau men like Fisk and Brown contended, both would reap the great rewards of free labor. As employers, white southerners would get laborers who worked faithfully and industriously. And, in turn, freed blacks would secure wages and fair working conditions—and, at least in theory, economic independence—as employees. Operating on what ultimately would prove to be false assumptions, however, those who led and served the bureau would learn a difficult lesson soon enough. Former masters and former slaves were not going to abandon easily long-held convictions about, and lessons learned from, the nature of slave labor. But for now, in 1865, bureau officials reassured former slaves hopefully: "All good men . . . will recognize your new relations to them as free laborers; and as you prove yourselves honest, industrious and frugal, you will receive . . . kindness and consideration." And so, an unprecedented and Herculean mission, grand hopes, and perhaps even inexperience and a bit of naïveté encouraged the bureau along on its path to instilling northern free labor ideology in the postwar South.[32]

For most bureau officials, understandings of the "solemn obligation of contracts" quickly came to guide federal efforts both to transform southern labor and to school ex-slaves and ex-masters in the meaning of freedom. "While the freedmen must and will be protected in their rights," Assistant Commissioner Brown exhorted in Virginia in November 1865, "they must be required to meet these first and most essential conditions of a state of freedom, *a visible means of support, and a fidelity to contracts.*" Commissioner Howard agreed. If the freedpeople "can be induced to enter into contracts," he had explained just a few months earlier, "they are taught that there are duties as well as privileges of freedom." Northern free labor contained some ideological inconsistencies, to be sure. But, as understood by bureau policy makers, free labor "rested on a delicate balance between individual liberty and public order." "Freedom unrestrained by either self-control or law was not liberty at all" to these mid-nineteenth-century Americans, as the editors of the Freedmen and Southern Society Project remind us. Rather, to them, it was simple "license." With freedom and independence—and, in due course, citizenship—thus came not only rights but also duty and responsibility.[33]

The importance of the "Yankee ideals" of self-support and contract was neither new nor unique to bureau men. The contract ideal would become "above all," as the historian Amy Dru Stanley has compellingly shown, "a metaphor of freedom" in the age of emancipation. In antebellum debates over slavery, abolitionists connected contract to notions of personal liberty, self-ownership, and social order. During the war, the Union army likewise, she notes, "designated contract the instrument of freedom" with its use of contract labor in occupied areas. The American Freedmen's Inquiry Commission too had touted its effectiveness as a tool to promote social order while instructing black (and white) southerners in their new roles. African Americans who willingly worked for wages would "soon get an idea of accumulating" and learn to "stand alone," the commission maintained in the wake of emancipation. Insistent that "free compensated labor" and "legal marriage" could teach the black husband and father the "obligation to support his family" and black wives the "instinct of chastity," it also underscored the northern belief that "work and marriage were mutually reinforcing contracts."[34]

Bureau policy makers followed suit. Assistant Commissioner Fisk especially underscored the bonds between free labor, contract, and marriage. Indeed, in explaining the concept of contract to former slaves in his *Plain Counsels*, Fisk began not with the labor contract but rather with marriage. Having explained that a contract "is something which binds two or more parties," he offered the marital contract as the example: "John and Mary agree together to get married. John promises Mary, and Mary accepts John. That is a marriage contract." Thus alongside bureau pronouncements about the contractual obligations of free labor came instructions that promoted efforts to "regularize"—and reject slaves' notions of—black families and celebrated northern ideals of domesticity.[35]

As it got underway in 1865, the bureau promptly addressed the need for lawful marriage in its lectures to former slaves about the "nature and limits" of a free labor society. To the men of the bureau, like other Americans, the right to marry symbolized perhaps one of the most significant differences between slavery and freedom.[36] And, like abolitionists before the war, most believed that slavery had inflicted "the most cruel wrongs" on the black family. "When you were slaves you 'took up' with each other, and were not taught what a bad thing it was to break God's law of marriage," Fisk told former slaves. "But now you can only be sorry for the past, and," he announced with a clear purpose in mind, "begin life anew, and on a pure foundation." Only lawful marriage, bureau policy makers like Fisk counseled, could provide the purity and security that had been lacking in the familial relations created in slavery. But even the most racially conservative bureau men advanced prevailing beliefs that legally sanctioned marriage among the former slaves, beyond rectifying one of slavery's worst sins, also promoted peace and social order.[37] From the start, then, bureau policy makers undertook the effort to promote and enforce the "sacred institution of marriage" as the answer to "an immensely great and an immensely difficult problem" in the immediacy of emancipation. Commissioner Howard offered the first bureau directive on marriage not long after assuming office in May 1865 with Circular No. 5. Instructing bureau officials "in places where the local statutes make no provisions for the marriage of persons of color" to record black marriages "solemnized by any ordained minister of the gospel," the directive offered little "policy" per se but rather acted to continue wartime practices that had originated in Union contraband camps, where military clergy had sanctified and recorded "the rite of marriage" among fugitive slaves.[38] Given the opening, however, some bureau policy makers at the state level seized upon the opportunity to promote marriage as the way "to correct" what Assistant Commissioner Rufus Saxton in South Carolina called "a monster evil which meets us at the very threshold of our work."[39] With little uniformity, the assistant commissioners responded to Howard's circular in 1865 and 1866 with everything from painstakingly thorough "Marriage Rules" to the appointment of officers to serve as "superintendents of marriages"; suspension or reduction of fees for marriage certificates; licenses for black preachers; authorization of agents to certify, license, or officiate marriages themselves; and, of course, terse orders that instructed agents simply to make known and to enforce state laws regulating marriage.[40] Whatever the variation, the purpose of bureau policies enjoining marriage among former slaves was clear. Marriage was a civilizing element—"a crucial source of virtue"—in an ordered, free society, and the bureau was going to demand it and regulate it as freedpeople began "life anew."[41]

Even as they would lament that the "most difficult questions were those arising from the marriage relation," officials stationed across the South understood that "instructing the freedpeople in the sacredness of the marriage contract" was central to bureau efforts to define freedom and, perhaps more important, to instill in freedmen the rights and obligations of free labor and citizenship. Noting the fundamental role that efforts to "regularize" black families played in the bureau's purpose, the historian William McFeely wrote decades ago: "It would not be an overstatement to say that the bureau men in the field saw marriage and the formation of stable family groups as the most important thing they should accomplish for the freedmen in their charge. Belonging themselves to a culture in which families were of enormous importance, the encouragement of that institution among the freedmen was the natural thing to do." But to bureau men, it was far more than just "the natural thing to do." To them and to those who created the agency, the right to marry promoted "the formation of male-headed nuclear families and was inextricably linked to ... the paramount goal of turning former slaves into wage-workers" and emergent citizens.[42] At the very least, marriage was a contract, and contracts, in their minds, were both essential and sacred to a free labor society. Thus just as labor contracts had granted both rights and obligations to slaves-turned-employees, the marriage contract, according to the bureau, presented freedmen and women with "the mutual rights and privileges of husband and wife" alongside commensurate responsibilities.[43]

Bureau men were unwavering in their expectation of marriage, and their gendered instructions regarding the "the duties and relations of the matrimonial state," as an agent in Virginia put it, were directed first at freedmen. Indeed, it should come as no surprise that white northerners in the bureau insisted that freedmen had gained "duties and responsibilities as free men & as husbands and fathers" with emancipation. Foremost among the privileges and duties in their own northern free labor society were the independent man's right to govern his household (and to command its labor) and the obligation to work to provide for dependent members within it. By war's end, abolitionists and Republicans had long turned to the complementary roles of the right to family and the obligation to work to bolster demands for an end to slavery. A congressman from Pennsylvania forcefully made this connection in 1864 when he asserted that slaves would reveal themselves to be the "hard children of toil" as soon as "the freedman [could] feel that he is a man with a home to call his own, and a family around him, a wife to protect, children to nurture and rear, wages to be earned and received, and a right to invest his savings in the land of the country." The bond between free labor and domesticity was paramount. "Labor is the law of all," this same northern policy maker told freedpeople in Charleston more than a year later. "Work industriously," he advised, and they would "need no longer live in slave huts." "I charge you, men," he said, "to make your homes comfortable, and you, women, to make them happy." Freedom had entrusted the "three great fundamental rights of human society" to the former slave man, explained a different congressman at the outset of 1865— the right to his own "personal liberty," the right of a "husband to his wife," and the right of a "father to his child." Casting the promises ahead in an encouraging light (at least for former slave men)—that emancipation secured African American men a right to households in which women and children were commodities no longer—white northerners thus conveyed the rights and responsibilities of free labor and marriage in tandem.[44]

Bureau men did the same. Underscoring the gendered nature of nineteenth-century understandings of free labor, family governance, and dependency, bureau policy and actions would stress time and again the requirement that freedmen assume control of and provide for their families. Extending the modified patriarchy of northern domesticity to black men and acknowledging that they, as free men, had a "sacred right and privilege" to their families (and also to their labor), bureau policies ordered that "the [black] husband has the same right to control his wife and children that a white man has." But these same policies also were quick to clarify that with this right to household came significant obligations. Addressing freedmen in North Carolina in July 1865, Assistant Commissioner Whittlesey stated it plainly: "Some of you have families; it is your duty to support them." In a matter-of-fact, uncompromising way, the assistant commissioner's straightforward pronouncement was typical of such bureau orders. And the ramifications for failing as a father or husband could be severe. The "Marriage Rules" issued by Assistant Commissioner Saxton in South Carolina, for instance, laid out a potentially ruinous punishment for freedmen in its "Rights of wives and children" section, which powerfully declared: "If a wife be released from her husband for a moral cause proven against him, to wit, adultery or fornication, she shall be entitled to receive one-half of his real and personal property, and all the household effects. If the wife have children by him, she shall have the entire control of such as are minors, and all the property, personal and real, shall be forfeited to the wife and children." But beyond property and possessions, men who fell short in their duty to labor and to family surrendered much more, not the least of which was their independence and their respectability. They failed both their family and their society. They were idle vagrants not to be tolerated, and their dependents—children, wives, the elderly—impending wards of charity or the state. Such men, to nineteenth-century Americans, were undeserving of freedom and, certainly, citizenship.[45]

Guided by his own northern, white, middle-class understandings of manhood, Assistant Commissioner Fisk was exacting in the gendered commands that accompanied his vigorous encouragement of marriage and the formation of black households. "Now you have yourself in charge, and," he told freedmen in *Plain Counsels*, "I want you to make a man of yourself." "*Do not be in haste to get married*," Fisk told young freedmen. Going further, he cautioned: "Wait until you are at least twenty-one years of age, and until you have a home for your wife. To marry a girl, and have no home to take her to, is foolish. She will soon regret that she married you, and you will be sorry you married her. You will have a family of ragged children, and will be dogged around the world like a slave. Wait, I say, until you have a home for a wife, and then if you can find a pure, good woman, who will help you on in the world, marry her." But manhood went far beyond economic responsibilities. Contrary to images of the detached Victorian patriarch focused solely on breadwinning, Fisk's teachings about the familial obligations of freedom emphasized the need for a man's presence in the home and, at least in theory, a partnership between man and wife in marriage. After providing for their families with steady employment, freedmen, he insisted, must "*spend all your spare time at home,*" for the very act of "leaving . . . wives and children night after night alone" was "mean, and bad." Men's absence, the bureau policy maker declared, "disheartens a wife, makes children unhappy, and demoralizes husbands." As a matter of official policy too, Fisk offered marriage directives that made clear the obligations of these emergent citizens, instructing: "Let each man turn his heart and his thoughts toward providing a good home for his wife and children, . . . carefully guard and keep sacred the marriage relation; be lawfully wedded; 'taking up with each other' is an abominable practice, and must perish, with the institution which gave it birth." Marriage may not have been "a business with which the Federal Government had properly anything to do," according to most mid-nineteenth-century Americans, "but," as the *New York Times* asserted in its defense of the agency's extraordinary efforts in 1866, it had been "very properly taken up by the Freedmen's Bureau" and, it told readers, to good effect.⁴⁶

With images of "the men in the fields; the women in their own homes; [and] the children at school" guiding their purpose, bureau men also employed the northern ideology of domesticity to guide freedwomen in their transition from slavery to freedom. To the "women assembled here," the northern congressman from Pennsylvania who had spoken to black Charlestonians in 1865 made clear—and rejoiced with them about—the great changes ahead: "[Y]ou are to be mothers and wives in the homes of free men. You must try to make those homes respectable and happy. You are to be the mothers of American citizens." Like many abolitionists before the war, the men who would become the policy makers of Reconstruction saw freedom and lawful marriage as offering privileges and protections to freedwomen. "[S]o long degraded and made merchandise of" by slavery, as Fisk had said, former slave women would at last be protected by "*woman's grand shield,* MATRIMONY."⁴⁷

Emancipation and lawful marriage had promised much to African American women. But the protections of marriage and familial relations, according to bureau men, were dependent upon former slave women devoting themselves with "noblest enthusiasm" to becoming "true women." Products of the greater society ruled by ideas of separate spheres, bureau men like Assistant Commissioner Fisk emphatically relegated freedwomen to the domestic realm with their gendered instructions about the meaning of freedom. Notwithstanding the regular insistence that "wives must do their part" and that "Eve was made for a 'help meet,'" Bureau instructions to the former slave woman about her changed status informed her of responsibilities to be "a pure, good woman" and "to make a happy home." Telling young unmarried freedwomen to focus their energies on making themselves worthy of marriage and true womanhood, Fisk insisted that they should not even think of marriage until they had learned "to knit and bake good bread, to keep a nice clean house and cultivate a garden, and then to read and write." But more important to this bureau man was the great need for freedwomen to protect their chastity. "Allow no man, under any pretense to despoil you of your virtue," he told young freedwomen. Even going so far as to warn them against "those base white men who come to you with smooth words and good promises," Fisk called on former slave women to "stamp a lie upon the common remark, that colored women are all bad." Insistent that they must no longer be "careless of your morals" as in the days of slavery, he demanded that the freedwoman live a life that "becomes a free Christian woman." To be sure, bureau demands on freedwomen became greater with marriage. Once married, freedwomen, according to the bureau, were responsible (in "partnership" with their husbands) for creating independent, comfortable, clean, beautiful, happy homes. "Much of the beauty and happiness of home depends on the good sense, economy, and industry of the wife," he told black couples. Appealing to northern notions of domesticity, he counseled freedwomen to take seriously their efforts to make black husbands "love home better than any other place on earth." Holding firm with his intent, Fisk told them:

> A man can not make a happy home if he has an idle, shiftless, and scolding wife.
> A wife should take good care of her person, be clean, neat, and look as pretty as possible. I do not see how a man can love a slovenly women, who goes about with her heels out of her stockings, her dress un-pinned, her hair uncombed, with dirt under her finger-nails, and snuff or tobacco in her mouth. And no man can long love a brawling wife. . . . An ill-tempered woman will drive her husband to the evil one.

Although these certainly were not the words with which he would have addressed white women whom he regarded as "true women," Fisk nonetheless made clear his desire that freedwomen aspire to be like them and to create modest, clean homes in the likeness of white families.[48]

In the early moments of Reconstruction, freedwomen who appealed to the bureau as virtuous women in adherence to these northern, white, middle-class notions of womanhood and domesticity—much like a "good colored woman" who made her way to Assistant Commissioner Fisk's office to seek help reclaiming her "stolen" daughter—could find a friend in the federal agency. Readily and "politely" offering a "hearing" to the "neatly dressed" freedwoman "as if she had been white and dressed in satin," this assistant commissioner revealed a willingness in this instance to look beyond African American women's race to recognize their gendered needs as women, and as mothers especially, as well as their desire for respectability. Indeed, in hearing this particular woman's case, Fisk had set aside the complaint of another woman—a white "mountain refugee" who, he insisted, would have to "learn a great deal" and conduct herself "in a much better manner" to "become the equal" of this "good colored woman." "Touched" by the "grateful" black mother's appeal, Fisk ordered his agency into action—to do everything possible to find the girl and return her to her devoted mother—after hearing her "sad" story. The values of true womanhood, Fisk wanted to believe, would transcend racial lines in the postemancipation United States.[49]

Of course there was another possibility. What Assistant Commissioner Fisk did not invite, but what could and did result in the immediacy of emancipation, was condemnation of freedwomen for succumbing to the "evil of female loaferism." Free labor's demand that black women continue to work in the fields and white households of the South certainly compromised Fisk's call for former slave women to make themselves into true women. But there would be bureau concessions beyond its forfeiture of northern domesticity's seeming quid pro quo that a man's labor begat a wife at home. Emancipation and lawful marriage may have brought the freedman, liberated from the control of a master, the "rights and privileges" of a wife, but they also produced a new kind of subordination for freedwomen. That is, the marital contract promoted, indeed demanded, by the bureau (and the ideals of northern domesticity that came with it) dictated African American women's obedience to their husbands. After all, to these mid-nineteenth-century white Americans, "submission was perhaps the most feminine virtue expected of women," and bureau policy makers would readily endorse black husbands' authority over wives as a symbol of their independent manhood and evidence of their readiness for citizenship. Thus even as they would offer a welcome forum for redress and answers to questions about, among other things, the complicated nature of black families in the age of emancipation, bureau men could be quick to resolve freedwomen's complaints about negligent or demanding husbands, with notations in the records that "I told her she must go back to him and dismissed her." There were definite limits to Fisk's appeal for domesticity for freedwomen in the postemancipation South.[50]

"A new life was before us now, all the old life left behind," Susie King Taylor, a former slave in Georgia, declared at the end of the Civil War. But less than a year later, as 1865 came to a close, many—black and white, male and female, northern and southern—would have questioned whether "all the old life" had been left behind in the postwar South. The Civil War had ended. The Confederacy had been defeated. The Constitution had been amended to end slavery. So long awaited, so intensely coveted, freedom had promised African Americans the fulfillment of their dreams. But emancipation, freedwomen and men discovered abruptly, was only the first step, for freedom, as Thavolia Glymph has recently reminded us, "had to be built." Frederick Douglass would have agreed. "Verily," he once remarked, "the work does not end with the abolition of slavery, but only begins." And as they undertook the work of Reconstruction in the immediacy of emancipation and war's end, former slave women and officials of the Freedmen's Bureau alike understood that the realities of freedom were far from what either had envisioned.[51]

As 1865 ended, agents stationed in bureau offices across the South found that the nation had gravely miscalculated the enormity of the task ahead. Despite the bureau's many policies, orders, and dictates outlining the federal government's goals for emancipation and plans for Reconstruction, no successful course of action had developed for accomplishing the Herculean task set before Commissioner Howard earlier that spring. But bureau efforts had begun. The hard work of Reconstruction was taking shape. On a daily basis, bureau agents in the field had begun to encounter—and were being expected to fix—some of the most vexing problems in postwar society. And as they did so, what was emerging already in these first days of freedom was a gendered assertion of Reconstruction-era public policy.

Whatever the outcome, it is clear that the purpose of Reconstruction was not exclusively about free labor to the men of the bureau. Rather, using the gospel of free labor as the platform, bureau officials and agents across the South sought to convey to freedpeople not only the great rewards of free labor but also what they understood to be the rights, obligations, and values of freedom. Thus as it struggled to clarify the organization, supply, and control of labor, the bureau simultaneously sought to instill in former slaves the privileges and virtues assumed by mid-nineteenth-century northerners as integral to a free labor society. Beyond applying the economic theory of free labor in a southern context, then, the bureau sought to initiate a social reconstruction that would transform southern slave society based on northern ideas of domesticity. "Time and experience, with much patient labor and great charity," as a local bureau agent in South Carolina explained it, were what would be necessary to "raise" former slaves "to the full dignity of manhood and womanhood."[52] Whether fully aware of it or not, bureau officials' advocacy of free labor conveyed northern gender ideologies and worked to reconstruct gender's "power to mean" in the age of emancipation. In short, bureau men and bureau work reinforced northerners' desire to supplant southern slave society with, in the historian Nina Silber's words, "the new Yankee order," and with that came the promotion of northern notions of independent manhood, dependent womanhood, and the "proper" family structure.[53]

Alas, that was the plan. Relying on the agency's ever-evolving policies, the men of the Freedmen's Bureau endeavored to bring understanding and resolution to what the *New York Times* portrayed as the seemingly "innumerable social intricacies which had to be dealt with and settled" in the immediate aftermath of emancipation. Whether attempting to regulate federal relief, southern labor relations, apprenticeship laws and practices, or the administration of justice, the federal agency endeavored to use the binary northern ideologies of free labor and domesticity to return former slaves to the workforce, to place freedmen at the head of black households, and to "teach" freedwomen to be the virtuous women, dutiful wives, and devoted mothers of true womanhood. But as they did so, and as the chapters that follow make clear, the bureau men charged with enforcing freedom would discover that—especially when it came to African American women—policy and intent did not translate necessarily into practice. All too often in their dealings with former slave women, local agents found themselves repeating words similar to those of an official in Augusta, Georgia, who informed his superiors: "[T]he present is an instance where the rule above alluded to should not be enforced."[54]

Complicating matters, to be sure, were the many freedwomen who seemed to be there at every instance, demanding their own kind of freedom as well as testing the bureau's every action. Having long rejected the southern domesticity of their ex-masters, former slave women were not ready to consent to another domesticity that disregarded their own desires for freedom.[55] Although not always successful in achieving the freedom that they imagined, freedwomen's persistence in trying to "realize their rights in practice," as the historian Laura Edwards brilliantly expresses it, revealed a resilient determination to disrupt the patterns of white power and domination that had long marked their lives as slaves.[56] Entering the offices of the Freedmen's Bureau across the South was part of this rejection of their past. As they did so, and as Chapter 2 illustrates, former slave women sometimes found an ally that could provide gendered protections from the lasting cruelties of slavery, the losses of war, and the many deficiencies of emancipation. Other times, however, freedwomen discovered in bureau men and their agency a seemingly insurmountable adversary that dealt cruel gendered blows and intensified the plentiful failings of freedom. Whatever the result, the interaction of freedwomen with the bureau revealed that gendered understandings of free labor, domesticity, and dependency, as well as the actions of former slave women and bureau men alike, shaped the outcome of public policy in the immediate postemancipation South.

2 "a weight of circumstances like millstones about their necks to drag and keep them down"

Freedwomen, Federal Relief, and the Freedmen's Bureau

Many destitutes . . . have still to be fed, because they are women, helpless with infants in their arms or unborn, with no place to go in their own counties, totally destitute, utterly helpless who would be beggars anywhere. . . . [T]here are no houses for them, they have no money to pay rent for old ones, or build new ones, their labor is not wanted, and rations cannot be issued to them unless additional . . . help shall be furnished.

Reporting to the assistant commissioner in Virginia more than a year after the Civil War's end, General Samuel Chapman Armstrong, superintendent of the Freedmen's Bureau at Fortress Monroe, attempted to convey the seriousness of the condition in which many freedpeople lived in his district. Unsure what to do with hundreds of destitute black women, in particular, he requested assistance. But that assistance did not come. Less than a year later, in January 1867, General Armstrong was still appealing to his superiors with the same concerns. Not satisfied with what had been done thus far for this "large destitute helpless class," he now requested that "Congressional action . . . be solicited in this matter."[1]

"With a weight of circumstances like millstones about their necks to drag and keep them down," destitute freedwomen represented the epitome of the worthy poor to General Armstrong. Included in this group were not only the wives and children of black Union soldiers—"now widows and orphans"—but also "demoralized, worthless . . . thriftless" freedwomen. It was these "very many" women "struggling to make lives," he told bureau policy makers, who "deserve relief in some form." The situation had to be exasperating to the young field agent. Described by Commissioner Howard as a man with "quick motions and nervous energy" who "wanted matters decided if possible on the spot," Armstrong was one of the many military men who would become the backbone of the agency. He was the son of missionaries and, like many of the first assistant commissioners, had served as an officer of black Union soldiers during the war. He believed passionately in the power of education to uplift former slaves and, in Reconstruction, committed himself to the plight of the freedpeople not only as an officer in the bureau but also as the founder of Hampton Institute and later a mentor to Booker T. Washington. To Agent Armstrong, there was "no duty more imperative and important than to provide for" poor former slave women so that they might rise to their "highest physical and moral well being." Indeed, this bureau field agent was certain that what the federal government did or did not do would be told "in the future . . . interests and destinies of the Anglo African race."[2]

While General Armstrong's answer to the weighty circumstances confronting freedwomen in his district included both congressional action and "a suitable apportionment of lands for which they might pay a reasonable price in a reasonable time," the federal government disagreed.[3] In the immediate postemancipation South, the bureau limited its federal relief activities to temporarily aiding former slaves and loyal white refugees with rations of food, clothing, fuel, and medical care. In doing so, it operated in the short term and worked to avert an immediate need rather than what some reformers recognized already as a long-term crisis of extraordinary times. Bureau policy makers pledged to get the agency out of the "ration business" from the outset. Official relief policy thus charged bureau men in the field with instructing freedmen and women in the importance of free labor, self-reliance, and independence and distributing material relief only to "prevent starvation or extreme want." Agents could provide short-term relief to the deserving poor, but for all others—able-bodied freedmen and women especially—they were to enforce the obligation to work. Promoting free labor came first to those who led the bureau. Providing material relief was secondary.[4]

As was the case at Fortress Monroe and given the policy directives, the appeals of freedwomen for federal relief often represented some of the most troubling cases for bureau men at the ground level of Reconstruction. Indeed, many, if not most, of the requests for bureau aid came from women who, as Armstrong explained, faced "a weight of circumstances." They were elderly or sick women. They were unmarried—single, widowed, abandoned, and separated—women. They were the wives of black Union soldiers who had not yet returned for their families. And they were the "unproductives"—the black mothers who bore sole responsibility for young children and thus faced the toughest of all labor markets—as both bureau men and southern white employers came to label them. Certainly, agents worked to find homes and, better yet, work for these women. After all, the goal of bureau policy was to turn former slaves into free laborers who provided for themselves and had no need for charity. But like Agent Armstrong in Virginia, countless field agents found this preferred course of action futile. Employers did not want them.

Work was not readily available. Yet bureau policy ordered agents to terminate relief to them all the same. What was an agent to do? A constant source of frustration to them to be sure, these destitute, indeed desperate, freedwomen repeatedly returned to bureau offices for aid and, in doing so, underscored some of the many deficiencies of emancipation. Insistent and persistent in their pleas, these poor freedwomen called on agents to disregard policy and to acknowledge their gender, their distinct needs as women and as mothers in particular, by providing assistance. As a result of this assertiveness as well as the willingness of bureau agents in the field to acknowledge a gendered difference between freedmen and freedwomen in the allocation of federal material relief, freedwomen managed to remain on the bureau's ever-dwindling relief rolls.[5]

Perhaps nowhere was it more apparent that both agents' gendered assumptions and freedwomen themselves shaped the actions of the Freedmen's Bureau than in its "war on dependency." All the while working to eliminate freedwomen's need for relief as official policy demanded—by enforcing black men's responsibilities as husbands and fathers to them as wives and mothers, by advocating their employment and relocation as free laborers, and by encouraging the apprenticeship of young children—local agents recognized them as women and acknowledged an appropriate dependency for them based on their gender. Dependency, as they understood it within the confines of northern domesticity, was an expected and normal state of relations begot by marriage, motherhood, infirmity, and old age. Agents, as long as they could obtain material relief, resolved the contradiction between policy and practice by accepting a definition of the deserving poor that could include freedwomen who were elderly or ailing as well as those who were able-bodied widows, wives of Union soldiers, and mothers of young children. Thus in coming to the bureau as deserving women, these freedwomen secured benefits, as scanty as they may have been as the days progressed, granted to them because of their gender and unavailable to freedmen.[6]

Emancipation had granted freedom to more than four million former slaves. But with this freedom came nothing more: no food, no money, no land, no homes. African Americans thus faced the first years of freedom lacking the most basic necessities of life. "Us had no education, no land, no mule, no cow, not a pig, nor a chicken, to set up house keeping," Violet Guntharpe, a former slave woman from South Carolina, later remembered. "De birds had nests in de air, de foxes had hoes in de ground, and de fishes had beds under de great falls, but us colored folks was left without any place to lay our heads." Federal officials could not ignore this harsh reality. Basic humanity, as well as the devastation, dislocation, and destitution raging across the South, dictated that the federal government feed the hungry and care for the weak. And at times, these rations (a military provision that referred to the issuance of some combination of meat, corn meal, flour, and other available supplies) were what kept starvation at bay for many southerners, both black and white. But given the paltry amount of assistance available—as well as the grudging willingness with which it could be distributed—it is not surprising that former slaves remembered the postwar relief activities of the federal government with resentment. "Dem Yankees was mean folks," recalled Sarah Debro. "I was never hungry till we was free and de Yankees fed us," she bemoaned. Some seventy years later, this former slave had not forgotten—or forgiven—the federal government's answer to hunger in the wake of emancipation.[7]

While the records of the Freedmen's Bureau concerning relief are incomplete, inconsistent in the type of data reported and the way it was reported, and generally frustrating for researchers, they nonetheless reveal that the distribution of food, clothing, fuel, and medicine remained a central task through most of the agency's short lifetime. Certainly, there were calls for federal action more far reaching than the bureau would ever attempt. Beyond confiscation and redistribution of Confederate land to assist former slaves, the most radical of freedmen's aid reformers advocated an activist federal government committed to helping former slaves become independent, self-supporting citizens through education, employment, redistribution of land, and sustained direct material relief. They, including white female reformers like Josephine Griffing and Julia Wilbur, both at times employed by the Freedmen's Bureau, insisted that poverty-stricken former slaves, exploited by racism and slavery for far too long, deserved a federal government that would assume responsibility for the "national sin of slavery." But in a time when Americans were wary of expanding federal authority and public charity of most kinds, these answers proved far too radical for bureau leadership, especially Freedmen's Bureau commissioner Oliver Otis Howard.[8]

As he entered office, Commissioner Howard understood that conditions across the South were grave. "In every State many thousands were found without employment, without homes, without means of subsistence, crowding into towns and about military posts, where they hoped to find protection and supplies," he later remembered. But the real "wonder," according to Howard, was "not that so many, but that so few," actually required assistance. Providing material aid may have been part of the bureau's duties, but to those who created, led, and served the bureau, it was an immediate and momentary necessity. "From the start," the commissioner maintained, "I felt sure that the relief offered by the Bureau to refugees and freedmen through the different channels, being abnormal to our system of government, would be but temporary." Public charity was not the answer to southern ills. Rather, like other mid-nineteenth-century northerners, Howard insisted that getting freedpeople back to work so that they would not be dependent on the government for support was the solution to the South's myriad troubles. But, so as to "avoid anarchy and starvation," his bureau undertook the "no ordinary task" of providing material aid. And certainly these relief efforts were critical despite the many obstacles the bureau encountered in meeting the needs of the poor. There was no past wisdom to guide its officials in the distribution of aid on such a grand scale, in such a momentous time, or under such challenging conditions. Moreover, the financial resources of the bureau were never enough to end suffering among former slaves. Congress had approved the use of War Department supplies of food, clothing, and fuel to aid destitute freedpeople and refugees, but—incredibly—it gave no appropriation to facilitate bureau relief efforts. Yet whether viewed as heroic in its compassion and humanity, a movement ahead of its time, or a failure for what it did not or could not accomplish, bureau relief nevertheless stood poised to assist former slaves as they struggled to embrace many of the promises of freedom.[9]

The number of relief recipients aided by the bureau was staggering by contemporary standards. At its inception, the federal agency aided more than 144,000 southerners—black and white—with, as Commissioner Howard put it, "daily rations, medical supplies, and other help." In August 1865 alone, the bureau sustained some 148,120 people every day.[10] To be sure, this figure represented only a small percentage of the southern population, but the distribution of federal relief to even this few was unprecedented. Over its first year of operations, between June 1865 and August 1866, the bureau distributed more than thirteen million rations of food to southerners, almost nine million of which went directly to freedpeople.[11] During this time, however, the bureau continually sought to remove itself from what Howard called the "ration business" by returning responsibility for the poor to charities, poorhouses, and overseers of the poor. But given responses like that of the president of the overseers of the poor for Stafford County, Virginia—who, when asked whether his county would feed poor freedpeople should the bureau cease issuing rations there, replied, "[N]ot a *dam bite* will I give them, I would chose *hell* first"—it is not surprising that bureau relief efforts continued beyond what Howard wanted.[12] Local governments across the South would continue to contest federal demands that they assume responsibility for poor blacks throughout the bureau's brief existence.[13] Yet even in the face of local inaction, by October 1866, following Howard's order to restrict aid to those in hospitals and orphaned children in group homes, the distribution of federal material aid began to decrease drastically (see Figure 1). Over the next year, the bureau would issue just over four million rations, down dramatically from the year before. Even so, more than three-and-a-half million of these rations continued to aid former slaves. The bureau pulled back its relief activities further in 1867. Officially, it provided relief only to those in hospitals or other institutionalized care facilities and offered material aid to others only intermittently. Between September 1867 and September 1868 the bureau would supply only 2,802,478 rations to southerners. Of those, freedpeople received 91.5 percent. By the fall of 1868, according to Commissioner Howard's annual reports to Congress, the bureau had furnished more than twenty million rations of food—almost fifteen million of which directly aided former slaves—in its efforts to reconstruct the South. Perhaps more revealing is that, when the bureau ended all but its educational activities in 1869, Howard would take great pride in estimating that of the four million "thrown suddenly on their own resources" only one in two hundred had received some form of "public charity."[14]

Even as bureau relief activities diminished and the national commitment to relieving former slaves with material aid waned, thousands of black women appeared—and remained—on federal relief rolls. Despite the many deficiencies in the federal agency's records concerning relief, bureau manuscript records clearly reveal that agents viewed freedwomen and children as different from similarly situated freedmen and provided relief to the neediest and most deserving of them. This was particularly true during 1865 and 1866, the years when the bureau was most active in distributing relief (see Figure 1). Between November 1865 and September 1866 in Alabama, for example, bureau assistance increased drastically as drought and crop failure resulted in widespread misery. There, more than 72,000 freedpeople—84 percent of them women and children—received assistance from the bureau (see Figure 2).[15] During the same period in Virginia, already the recipient of the bulk of federal assistance, the bureau aided over 80,000 freedpeople—85 percent of whom also were freedwomen and children (see Figure 3).[16] Even in states where the bureau issued few rations to the destitute, the same held true. In 1865, the bureau in Texas, for instance, issued relief to only sixty-four freedpeople. Yet roughly half of the recipients were freedwomen. By 1868, the number of rations issued in Texas may have decreased, but not the percentage of women receiving them. In June, July, and August of that year, as the bureau prepared to end its operations in the state, the agency issued rations to only sixteen freedpeople—six freedwomen and ten freedgirls. Thus although the number of freedpeople aided by the bureau decreased significantly after October 1866, the agency continued to support southern blacks with well over three million rations, and, as it had been from the start of bureau relief activities in 1865, a disproportionate number of women and children benefited from this assistance.[17]

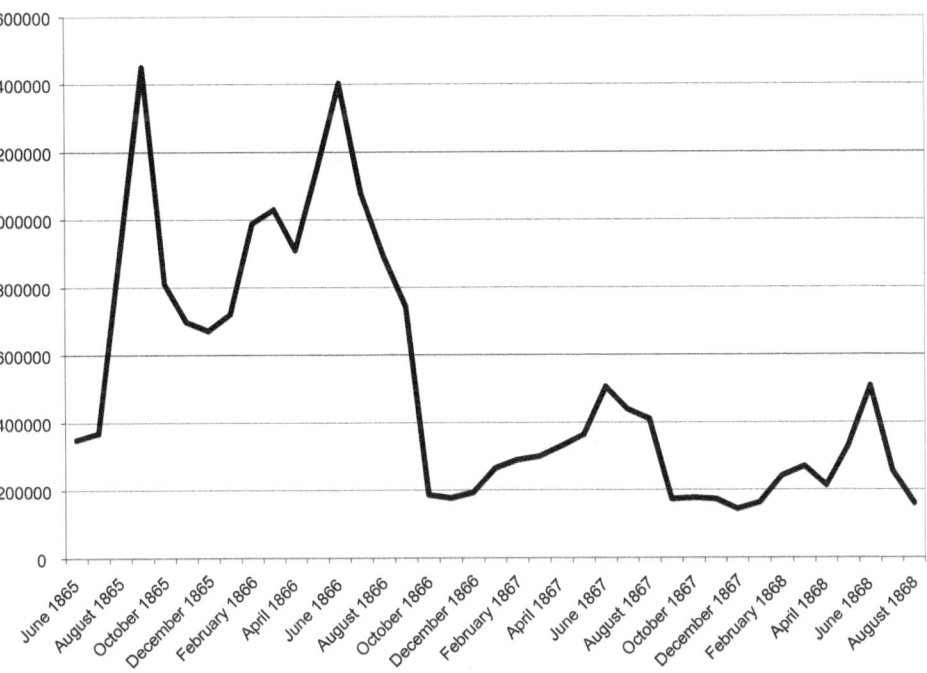

Figure 1. Relief issued by the Bureau of Refugees, Freedmen, and Abandoned Lands, June 1865–August 1868.
Source: U.S. House of Representatives, "Report of the Commissioner of the Bureau of Refugees, Freedmen, and Abandoned Lands [1 Nov. 1866]," 39th Cong., 2nd sess., House Executive Document 1 (Serial 1285); U.S. House of Representatives, "Report of the Commissioner of the Bureau of Refugees, Freedmen, and Abandoned Lands [1 Nov. 1867]," 40th Cong., 2nd sess., House Executive Document 1 (Serial 1323); U.S. House of Representatives, "Report of the Commissioner of the Bureau of Refugees, Freedmen, and Abandoned Lands [24 Oct. 1868]," 40th Cong., 3rd sess., House Executive Document 1 (Serial 1367).

Numbers aside, the words of local agents better illustrate the role that their own assumptions about gender and gender difference played in the distribution of bureau relief. While this was by no means the case for freedwomen receiving aid, agents took extraordinary care to justify any support provided to freedmen. An agent in York County, Virginia, for instance, reported in September 1866 that of the 248 freedpeople who received relief from his office, only 2 were adult freedmen and neither was able bodied—one, he noted, had no hands and the other was blind. He recorded the remaining 246 people receiving rations simply as "women and children." Similarly, of the 195 destitute former slaves on the relief rolls in Mecklenburg County, Virginia, only 16 were adult males—half of whom the agent justified supporting with notations that they were sixty-five

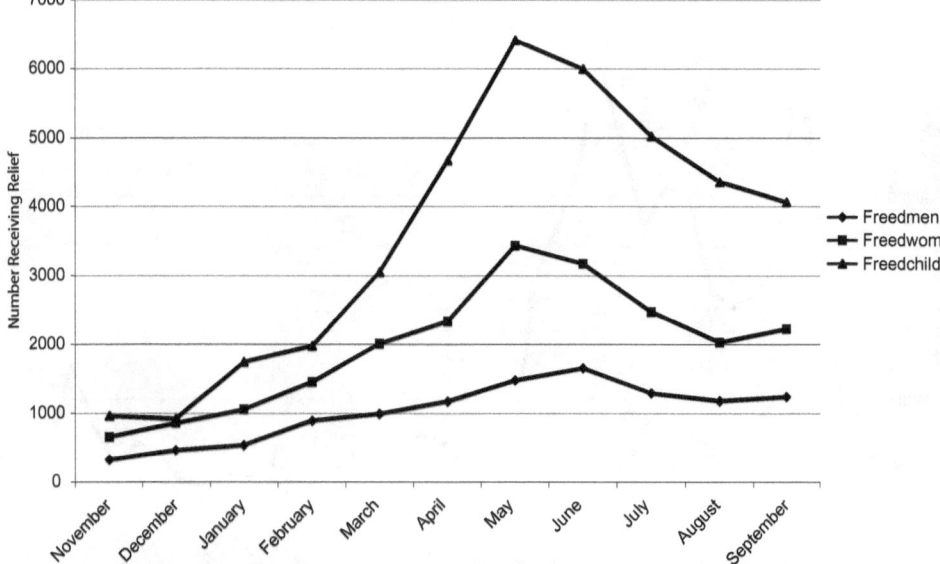

Figure 2. Freedpeople receiving relief from the Alabama Freedmen's Bureau, November 1865–September 1866.
Source: U.S. Senate, "Reports of the Assistant Commissioners of the Bureau of Refugees, Freedmen, and Abandoned Lands and Laws in Relation to the Freedmen [1866]," 39th Cong., 2nd sess., Senate Executive Document 6 (Serial 1276), 9.

years or older. The remaining 179 recipients were destitute women and children. Agents across the South likewise recorded few freedmen receiving relief from the bureau. More telling, however, were the words "old age," "sick," "crippled," "infirm," "helpless," "lame," "blind," and "disabled" that accompanied the names of freedmen on bureau relief reports.[18]

Every day agents across the South made tough choices and real decisions that affected the lives of many—both black and white, male and female, adult and child. Every day they encountered new people, new requests, new needs, and new demands. Every day agents undertook myriad tasks: "Reading and approving contracts[,] visiting the various plantations—allaying strife between husband and wife—deciding the ownership of a hog and last but not least—answering questions in reference to *the Rations*." Without doubt, the administration and disbursement of relief was central to every local agent's job, especially in 1865. For in the end, the local agent translated policy into practice and in doing so determined the very meaning of bureau relief policies. While in some urban areas the bureau issued "soup and bread instead of regular

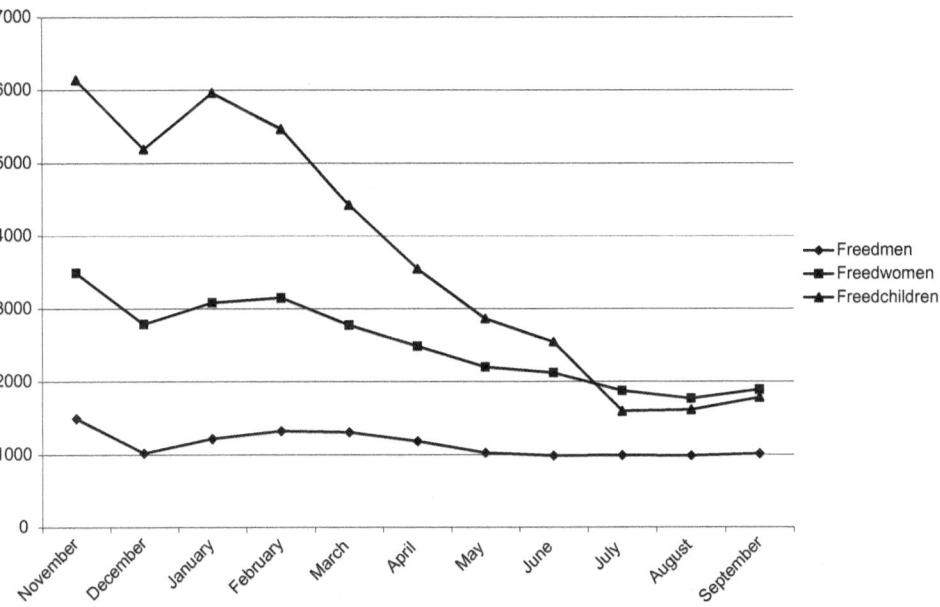

Figure 3. Freedpeople receiving relief from the Virginia Freedmen's Bureau, November 1865–September 1866.
Source: U.S. Senate, "Reports of the Assistant Commissioners of the Bureau of Refugees, Freedmen, and Abandoned Lands and Laws in Relation to the Freedmen [1866]," 39th Cong., 2nd sess., Senate Executive Document 6 (Serial 1276), 161.

rations" in what today would be called a soup kitchen of sorts, in most instances agents doled out relief from their offices to the deserving individually and as supplies arrived intermittently. Thus, in this kind of system of distribution, those who made their way to bureau offices in person and who could present themselves as deserving had the best chance of obtaining relief. Met with petitions of every kind, however, the bureau found distinguishing between the worthy and unworthy poor was no simple task. Indeed, as one agent bemoaned as late as 1868, "[I]t has been impossible to discriminate between the ... deserving poor and the vicious poor."[19]

In answering the question of who was a worthy recipient of federal relief, Freedmen's Bureau policy makers forcefully delineated who was *not* deserving from the outset of the agency's existence. "A man who can work has no right to support by government or by charity," one assistant commissioner exhorted in 1865. Another demanded, "[W]ork or starve." Others readily agreed. Insisting that "[n]o really respectable person wishes to be supported by others," these assistant commissioners' stance reflected contemporary beliefs that poor relief undermined manly independence. Such ideas were not unique to those commissioned by the bureau. Nor were they completely unknown to white southerners. Assertions that men should be independent, show initiative, and provide for the well-being of their families reflected mid-nineteenth-century thinking about both the gendered nature of dependency and the distinction between the deserving and undeserving poor. Federal policies were remaking many things during Reconstruction, but not these concepts; northerners and southerners held similar views about who was worthy of aid. By accepting relief, one became not only dependent on others for support but also independent of the responsibilities of family and employment. Accordingly, the bureau insisted that providing able-bodied black men government assistance encouraged idleness and sapped the very sense of manly independence and responsibility that it hoped to foster among the freedmen. Thus, like Josephine Griffing, at one time the assistant to the assistant commissioner in the District of Columbia and agent for the National Freedmen's Relief Association, bureau officials carefully noted the absence of able-bodied men in relief reports: "It will be observed that no able-bodied man is included and in fact none are connected with the above & within enclosed named families." Agents clearly did not consider able-bodied black men among the deserving poor.[20]

If freedmen were undeserving recipients of government relief, whom then did the bureau support with its relief policies? With few exceptions, agents counted orphaned children of former slaves as well as elderly, infirm, and disabled freedpeople among those deserving of relief. But beyond black orphaned children—who had no means of support—and elderly, infirm, and disabled freedpeople—who lacked the ability to support themselves—agents also counted the families of black Union soldiers as well as single women with children among the worthy poor. Like other mid-nineteenth-century Americans, bureau officials viewed women and children in a state of dependency that, while considered proper for women, was degrading for men. As members of a household, wives and children were politically, economically, and legally dependent on, and thus subordinate to, husbands and fathers. But for poor freedwomen this state of dependency was complicated by both their race and their poverty. Like white women, they fell under the control of male heads of household. Unlike white women, however, black women were regarded by white society—both northern and southern—as dependent too by nature of their race. Attributing black inferiority to racial differences or to the experience of slavery, whites, including those employed by the bureau, accepted prevailing stereotypes that characterized African Americans as mentally, physically, and spiritually inferior to whites and, in the words of one bureau official, predisposed to "idleness, vagrancy, pauperism and crime."

Blacks, contemporary anxieties stressed, were naturally dependent, and emancipation only intensified such fears. Poverty too muddied the waters for black women. Contemporary attitudes toward pauperism, indeed toward the poor of both races, led bureau officials to conclude that recipients of public charity, whatever their race, would eventually defraud the government in an effort to "claim any good that is gratuitous." Thus disability, age, gender, race, and economic standing all factored into mid-nineteenth-century understandings of dependency, which, as the historian Nancy Bercaw notes, "disqualified a person from being able to control his or her own actions" and influenced the decisions of local agents of the bureau. No longer slaves dependent on masters, poor freedwomen and their children would ideally become dependents of black husbands and fathers. But with black families separated or destroyed as a result of slavery and the war, this ideal was not easily achieved. Moreover, given the widespread destitution in the South, even freedwomen fortunate enough to be reunited with family were not assured a future free of economic hardship. Thus until black households could be reunited—as well as reshaped to more closely resemble the federal government's ideal of family life—bureau officials found themselves willing to provide government relief to the neediest and worthiest freedwomen.[21]

In judging black women's petitions for relief, local bureau agents quickly discovered they could not base their decisions solely on whether these women were physically able to work. Underscoring the gendered nature of dependency in nineteenth-century America, agents came to consider factors distinctive to women as they dispensed material aid: Were the freedwomen who petitioned the bureau for assistance married? Were they married to soldiers in the Union army? Were they married to able-bodied freedmen? Had their husbands abandoned them? Were they widows? Did they have children? Were their children infants? Finally, were they deserving or worthy of assistance? In short, were these freedwomen respectable, hardworking members of the community who—because of a weight of circumstances often beyond their control—could not provide for themselves and their children? Poverty alone was not enough to ensure that one would be counted among the worthy poor—even for dependent black women. As Assistant Adjutant General Selden Clark in Washington, D.C., informed agents there, great care had to be taken in relief work. Fostering "idleness and a spirit of dependence" among former slaves, even women, had to be guarded against. Agents, he warned, must differentiate "between poverty and actual suffering," with material assistance going only to the deserving poor who faced the latter.[22]

Freedwomen's pleas for federal assistance and protection were both heartfelt and heart wrenching, and those who were successful—thus making it into bureau records and obtaining actual relief—tended to be those whose requests appealed to bureau agents' middle-class notions of dependency, domesticity, and family relationships. "I rite to in form you that I am suffering for every thing that support[s] life," Feby Leach, an elderly freedwoman in Waynesboro, Virginia, wrote to the nearby agent in Staunton in 1867. Possessing no food, she pleaded with the agent: "I have bin beging for too years and the citizens are geting tyard of my beging and I am verry old and infirm and unless I receive help from you or some other source I can not possible get a long." Too old to work, no longer possessing a master to provide for her, and in a community where blacks could not care for their own and civil authorities were unwilling to provide for the poor without regard to race, Leach, like other elderly freedpeople, turned to the bureau as her only hope. Nancy Flournoy, an elderly freedwoman suffering from "rheumatism & other ailments," had been fortunate in that her former master had allowed her to remain on his place in northern Louisiana, but by 1867 that kindness had worn thin. Viewing this support as something owed to her for years of work, the "poor old woman" now refused, her former master reported, "to leave my house & will not consent to go to any hospital or asylum provided for by the government." Rejecting any sense of obligation to the woman, he demanded that the bureau intervene and provide for her support. The elderly, infirm, and disabled thus found refuge in this agency that worked to provide assistance and to place them in the few hospitals and asylums that cared for freedpeople. Relief to them would be the last withdrawn by the Freedmen's Bureau.[23]

Other poor women too turned to the bureau as an ally in their struggle to make ends meet in the unforgiving conditions of the postwar South. Asserting ideals of domesticity, womanhood, and motherhood more broadly than the "true women" of their time, these African American women understood all too well that the many deficiencies of emancipation did not permit them to entertain "aspirations to be like white ladies" by passing the day "dawdling over their trivial housework, or gossiping among their neighbors," despite such claims by whites. Elite and middle-class white women with husbands to provide for the financial needs of their families enjoyed the luxuries of having servants to carry out household duties and time to devote to child rearing. Poor women did not. Rather, they tended to their households, cooking, cleaning, gardening, and caring for children, as well as worked the fields as the seasons demanded, took in laundry, and did whatever else was needed for their families' survival. Motherhood for poor southern women, black or white, in the words of the historian Laura Edwards, foremost entailed "feeding their children, putting clothes on their backs, and keeping a roof over their heads." Now free to place their own homes, children, and families above all else, freedwomen knew that if economic survival meant at times turning to public charity, to the Freedmen's Bureau especially, and waiting for hours in line for a ration of food or a blanket, clothes, or pair of shoes, that was what they did.[24]

In coming to the bureau for aid, poor black women most often garnered agents' sympathy when they could position themselves as women with distinct needs and weighty circumstances because they were wives—though often separated, widowed, or abandoned—and mothers. Separated from their husbands, the wives of black Union soldiers, for instance, often found respite at the bureau office. Mrs. William Cauldfield, a poor Louisiana freedwoman whose neighbors were "not disposed to help her as her husband is in the U.S. Army" but who was a "very good woman" and mother of three, gained the support of the local agent in Clinton as she sought rations. Mrs. Martin Randale, the wife of a black soldier stationed in Texas, fared equally well in her appeal to an official in West Virginia in 1865. Writing that "if there can be Eny thing don for me I should be very hapy to receve it," the mother of three small children informed the agent that she had not received word—or support—from her husband since he had gone west a year earlier. A "respectful colored woman," the agent reported, with "no means of support . . . except what she earns by taking in washing," Randale gained his sympathy as a soldier's wife and as a mother who was doing what little she could to support her family. But more important than his sympathy, this worthy soldier's wife also obtained the agent's recommendation for rations. Also separated from her husband and "unable to earn a support for . . . [her] family," Mrs. Mary Carbin, a freedwoman from Orleans Parish, Louisiana, obtained ten days' worth of rations for herself and her three children to tide them over while the bureau worked to "take measures to cause Mr. Carbin to support his family." Widows too found sympathy from the bureau. Harriet, a freedwoman from near Savannah, Georgia, faced dire straights. Now pregnant with her fourth child, the freedwoman had traveled to Athens to appeal to the bureau agent for both material aid and transportation, telling him that she had "lost her husband tis now a widow." Reporting that the widow and her children lived in "an open state in the rear of an old Livery Stable," and fearful that they would "necessarily perish" if not aided, the agent recommended that the poor widow's appeal be granted immediately. His superior officers consented and provided transportation to Atlanta, where she could be "confined." Similarly, the "over a dozen" applications for aid from widowed women with families gained support from the agent in the Virginia counties of Washington, Russell, and Buchanan, who recommended aid for "this class" so as to alleviate "a good deal of suffering." But not all were so fortunate. By late 1864 and 1865, former slaves at the freedmen's colony at

Roanoke Island in North Carolina had already begun to face ever more restrictive relief policies, first by the army and then the bureau. Insistent that the freedpeople there could not become self-sufficient without leaving the camp, army and bureau officials adopted policies sharply curtailing rations in an effort to force the destitute to move elsewhere. Even black soldiers' wives did not fare well there, encountering officials like the Reverend Horace James, the army's general superintendent of Negro affairs in North Carolina–turned–local bureau agent, who insisted that to provide even them with "rations without regard to their circumstances is teaching them to be indolent, saucy, and unchaste." As the bureau instituted more restrictive policies and relief became harder and harder to come by, officials looked more and more to freedwomen's individual circumstances, reputation, and respectability when doling out what little aid was available.[25]

Facing the most difficult of labor markets, single mothers of small children turned to the bureau often as their only source of relief. And bureau officials understood, indeed lamented, the dreadful fate that emancipation forced these women to confront. Planters had "turned their backs" on these women, and, as the historian Susan O'Donovan has forcefully demonstrated, shown themselves to be "out of patience with the pregnant, the recently pregnant, the potentially pregnant, and the very young—people who had been reckoned 'a heavy Expense' in bondage but tolerated for the value they had added to a slaveholder's purse." No longer valued for their ability to provide "life-time supplies of perpetually bound labor," freedwomen were, as a bureau official in Alabama reported frankly, "every where regarded and treated as an incubus."[26] Bureau officials did not deny this harsh fate and, paying "special attention" to the "piercing cry" of their children and appealing to shared notions of motherhood and domesticity, came to the aid of black mothers. Maranda, a former slave woman living in Rutledge, Georgia, after the war ended, was but one woman who encountered the weighty circumstances of postemancipation life. A "young and healthy" mother of four children "about to increase her family in a few days," Maranda had embraced the promises of freedom a year earlier by leaving her former owner to "set up for herself." But the young freedwoman had no husband and, it was suspected by the man on whose land she now lived, "her children is by different men who care no more for their offspring than the crockodile." Sympathetic to the young mother's plea for support, the local agent secured relief for the mother and her children as well as transportation and admittance for them to the freedmen's hospital in Augusta. A group of freedwomen and children who had been "driven off" from their former owners' place gained similar compassion in Coffee County, Georgia. Concerned that the women had no husbands to provide for them or their young families, the agent there requested aid for members of "this class," some of whom he was supporting already out of his own pocket. Agent William Tidball in Charlottesville, Virginia, feared the consequences of not coming to the aid of abandoned mothers who possessed "the inability to obtain work" because of young children. While some were widows, he disgustedly reported that "a large majority . . . [were] wives, abandoned by their husbands, who have run away to avoid their support." These women, he believed, the bureau should aid. Even as bureau relief policies in Virginia denied relief to the able bodied, Petersburg officials offered only one exemption, declaring that "the only exception will be in the cases of women, who have no husbands, living or present, to provide for them, who have large families of children, in which cases rations, for part, may be issued." Thus women, particularly mothers, "left without any visible means of Support" obtained aid from agents willing to rely upon common ideals of motherhood and domesticity, in the words of an agent in Richmond in the fall of 1866, to "afford . . . relief . . . to prevent actual starvation." But like black soldiers' wives, even able-bodied mothers of small children increasingly found that motherhood alone was not enough to guarantee bureau support. Both widowed freedwomen with several young children who had been drawing rations for some time from the bureau at Fortress Monroe, Virginia, Georgiana Smith and Margaret Hawkins faced the loss of this assistance in July 1866. Observing that "these rations are issued to the mother as a convenience only," General Samuel Armstrong and the assistant commissioner's office in Richmond instructed agents to exercise "discretion" in such cases and reminded them that these kinds of "exceptional cases . . . should not be too frequent." Eliminating their need for public charity, not the promise of continued federal relief, was the answer, according to even the bureau's most sympathetic agents.[27]

In the end, former slaves who positioned themselves as worthy women and appealed to the northern ideals of dependency, domesticity, and motherhood that bureau men promoted proved the most likely to obtain the federal aid—whether material aid or transportation—that they sought. Agents could reconcile aid to these freedwomen, unlike similarly situated freedmen, by seeing them as part of the worthy poor. Moreover, and perhaps more important to the pragmatic among them, bureau officials knew that their federal agency, and the dwindling relief it provided, was but temporary and would not last long. Thus, even freedwomen deemed deserving would find bureau relief increasingly difficult to secure as the agency worked to dispose itself of the burdensome task that Commissioner Howard had once called so "abnormal to our system of government." By 1867, for certain, the bureau was out of the "ration business" and bureau men found themselves making reports like that of the agent in Albany, Georgia. "Everyday," he reported, former slaves would come to "me with starvation" plain "in their faces, and I am obliged to send them away empty handed."[28]

Providing any relief to freedpeople, even to the most deserving black women, made bureau men uneasy. Historians of Reconstruction have long noted the ambivalence of bureau officials—like that of Commissioner Howard and his assistant commissioners—toward federal relief efforts. Yet even as it issued broad statements condemning public assistance to the poor, bureau men in the field expressed apprehension, and great frustration, over the many able-bodied but unemployed and destitute freedwomen seemingly destined for, if not already on, the agency's relief rolls. Despite a seeming awareness of an appropriate dependency for women and children, bureau officials feared the danger of an inappropriate dependency developing among black female recipients of public charity. They worried that bureau actions, as one official explained it, were "confirming one dependent population in their worst of habits or rather of crimes—confirmed pauperism," a "condition that destroys self respect, demoralizes and ruins any people." Moreover, emancipation, at least according to bureau men and white southerners alike, had not ended the black woman's obligation to labor. Idleness was not acceptable. Given such misgivings, bureau policy makers and agents in the field advanced a variety of steps to end the need for material relief among freedwomen.[29]

Reflecting its desire for freedmen to assert their newfound independence properly, the Freedmen's Bureau first attempted to reduce material aid to freedwomen by holding black men accountable as heads of their own households. Freedom and citizenship, according to bureau men, required freedmen to embrace free labor, enter contracts, and provide for their families. Promoting male independence, industriousness, and responsibility, bureau pronouncements, regardless of time or place, thus directed local agents to impress "upon the freedmen's minds their duties and responsibilities as free men and as husbands and fathers." Telling black husbands to provide for their families, Clinton Fisk, assistant commissioner of the bureau in Kentucky and Tennessee, insisted: "By industry and economy you can soon provide a real good home, and plenty of food and clothing for your family; and you should not rest until this is done." Indeed, he instructed, "This is your first duty, and the most religious thing you can do." But the bureau did not stop there. African American men, according to the federal agency, also possessed an obligation to see that wives and children contributed as well. Thus agents encouraged the complete authority of freedmen over their households, including the power to control the labor and earnings of their wives and children. Where employment was abundant, as in Texas, for example, agents embraced the practice of making contracts with the male head of household that bound all members of his family. Reflecting the law passed by the Texas legislature in 1866, for instance, the bureau there ordered that all labor contracts "be made with Heads of families" and "embrace all the members of the family who are able to work." Whether labor was abundant or scarce, however, in the eyes of both agents of the Freedmen's Bureau and white southerners, freedmen did not become more manly by removing wives and children from the postemancipation workforce. Motivated by more than the fear of idleness developing among former slaves and a desire to end federal material relief efforts to be sure, bureau men readily condemned the withdrawal of freedwomen from the workforce as well as the "hen pecked" husbands who allowed it.[30]

Despite such efforts, poor freedwomen continued to besiege bureau offices across the South.[31] Agents found especially alarming the many complaints against freedmen who deserted wives "so soon as there is a prospect of additional mouths to feed" or left "their old wives, the women they have lived with for years, because they are encumbered with children." Aware of the harsh conditions faced by abandoned women with children, especially, bureau officials thus went beyond pronouncements to get freedmen to support their families. As early as May 1865, military authorities in Virginia ordered that able-bodied freedmen who had left their families "without good cause" be sent home. Similarly, in an effort to prevent freedmen from escaping their marital and familial obligations, South Carolina officials denied free transportation to black men who were not accompanied by their families.[32] In addition, the bureau endeavored to help freedwomen locate husbands who had deserted families and return them when possible or, at the very least, compel them to support their wives and families. In most instances, agents reminded freedmen of their marital and familial responsibilities with lectures on "connubial bliss" and used their authority to force delinquent husbands to support their families.[33] The Virginia bureau, for instance, helped Lucinda Molley locate her husband and, in doing so, lectured the parties on their marital duties, ordering the husband and father to provide for his dependents. In granting a petition for divorce, the freedmen's court in Richmond, Virginia, went much further than lectures when it directed Henry Woodson to pay $25 per month to his former wife, Rebecca, for the support of herself and three children. It granted custody of the children to Rebecca and enjoined Henry from "molesting" his now-former wife. And lastly, even as it noted Henry's payment of the first month's support to Rebecca, the court put some additional weight behind its decision by conveying exclusive control of a boat and mule to the freedman "so long as he performs this judgment without default." Chastising the husband for not assuming his duties, the court granted control over the couple's economic resources—the boat and the mule—to him so as to enforce its decision and thus prevent his dependents from having to rely on others for support. In a similar move, an agent in Louisiana ordered one father to pay child support in the amount of $4 a month for his daughter until she reached the age of ten. Bureau officials in Charlotte Courthouse, Virginia, went further when they helped Ann Marie Brown locate her husband, James. As her husband was now "doing well" in Maryland, Brown desired to go live with him but complained that he neglected to support or send for her. The bureau ordered James to send for his wife. In an attempt to offset the need for relief as well as to liberate the federal government from having to provide it, these bureau officials worked to get black men, now free men, heads of household, and emergent citizens, to assume responsibility as protectors and providers for their dependents.[34]

In cases where black men could not be held accountable for the women on its relief rolls, the Freedmen's Bureau adopted a more rudimentary approach to reduce the large number of dependent black women. With varying degrees of encouragement, and outright coercion in some instances, it sought to return them to the workforce. Despite the fact that they considered many women drawing rations "unproductives," officials of both the Union army and the bureau proved intent on ending federal material relief. Bureau officials in Richmond, Virginia, directed agents in August 1865 to investigate thoroughly relief cases by visiting "each and every family now representing themselves as Destitutes." As if that were not enough, the bureau there also provided certificates confirming privation to be "signed by one or more respectable clergymen residing in the County."[35] Officials elsewhere were more forceful. Officers in the Union army occupying Manchester, Virginia, in 1865, for instance, "packed off" "idle" freedwomen to a nearby island to do soldiers' laundry. Another army official in Richmond even went so far as to advocate gathering all the unemployed women in his city to "hire them out." But if that did not work, he recommended trying to find work for them as nurses in hospitals or as seamstresses or washerwomen for prisoners and blacks, or detailing them out as laundresses to the military. Finally, if "every source of labor fails," he thought it wise to "gather these women and children into buildings and open a grand *general* washing establishment for the city, where clothing of any one will be washed gratis."[36]

Like these army officials, bureau agents also employed force to get freedwomen working. After going to much trouble to find work for Anne Virginia Brown, the local agent in Alexandria, Virginia, found himself frustrated with her determination not to accept it. Although this freedwoman had "a house to live free for herself and her Family," she had drawn rations for some time when the agent finally ordered her "to hire herself out to a lady . . . to help attend to a little house work, in a small family." But to this agent's great dismay, Brown refused, telling him "that she was not going to work." In turn, he responded by "coaxing her," but Brown stood firm nonetheless, stating "that she would not go any how." As resolute as Brown, the agent did not concede defeat, however. Promising to step in if she "was illtreated in any way or manner," the agent returned with a guard and instructed her "to work or she would have to be punished." Brown at last yielded to his demands. Freedom may have ended slavery, but to federal officials like this one in Virginia, the free labor system that they promoted in the wake of emancipation would not permit the choice not to work. He worried that by providing Brown material assistance, the bureau was sanctioning an understanding of freedom tantamount to idleness, and that would not happen on his watch—even if it meant using coercion to promote regular employment and self-sufficiency among former slaves. Following policies from above both curtailing relief and promoting regular employment, bureau officials looked for every opportunity to discontinue federal material aid to freedpeople, even freedwomen, able to work.[37]

In areas of the South where jobs were scarce and finding employment for black men, let alone black women, was difficult, agents tried another approach: relocating the unemployed to areas where employment was more plentiful.[38] Given the disruptive impact of the Civil War on labor patterns throughout the South, the relocation of laborers at times seemed the only feasible answer to unemployment and its resultant poverty. Such was the case in the District of Columbia, Virginia, Georgia, and North Carolina, where assistant commissioners reported labor supplies that squarely outstripped labor demands. As early as the summer of 1865, Virginia assistant commissioner Orlando Brown, for instance, insisted that only a large-scale exodus of 50,000 freedpeople would alleviate the labor surplus in his state. By December, he exhorted: "The exhausted condition of the State will not allow the employment, even at 'Starvation rates' of the entire laboring population." With no action taken, according to Brown, the outcome was easy to predict: "The best hands only will find employment, leaving a large class of inferior laborers dependent on the Government or charity."[39] Given such realities, Commissioner Howard argued that it would be far cheaper to transport the former slaves to new jobs than "to feed them in idleness." As a result, the Freedmen's Bureau provided free transportation to tens of thousands of former slaves to places where, it was hoped, "the promise of economic betterment was greatest." For the "hundreds of perfectly helpless yet strong and willing women who must be rationed or starved or resort to those crimes for which destitution is fertile soil," in particular, the bureau hoped to end their dependency by relocating them to former homes where family members or former owners could support them or to areas where employment was available.[40]

Many freedwomen seized bureau transportation as an opportunity to return to former homes. Charity Cox, a freedwoman living in Charlottesville, Virginia, when the war ended, for instance, sought transportation from the bureau as an avenue to return to her home in Tennessee, where she had last seen her children. Similarly, Sarah Sanford appealed directly to Commissioner Howard, hoping to secure transportation from Washington, D.C., to Alabama. "I come to make application to you to see if in the goodness of your heart you will give me a free pass to my people in Alabama," she petitioned in 1869. Noting her desperation, she insisted, "I would not come to you if I could possibly in any way earn enough to take me there."[41] Like Cox and Sanford, many of those who turned to the bureau did so in an effort to reunite families, although, certainly, the bureau saw such cases as a way to ensure support for them other than the federal government. More than fifty Virginia freedwomen and children secured transportation from the bureau to Texas, where their husbands and fathers, who were stationed there with the army, could provide for them. Hoping to be reunited with her husband, Georgia freedwoman Caroline Thomas bolstered her request for free transportation by warning the local agent in Augusta that she would "become a burden on public charity" if the bureau did not help her get to Montgomery, Alabama, where her husband was gainfully employed as a carpenter.[42] Other freedwomen discovered in bureau transportation efforts an opportunity to go north. With the assistance of the Freedmen's Bureau as well as northern benevolent associations, thousands of former slaves relocated to Brooklyn, Boston, Pittsburgh, New York, Portland, and other northern cities where work was more readily available.[43] And success stories seemingly abounded. The American Freedmen's Friend Society, which under the "auspices" of the bureau had relocated more than fifty freedpeople from overcrowded Richmond, reported victory in early 1866. At last, "suffering mothers" were able to "earn their own subsistence." Although "bathed in tears" after "giving up" children to the Colored Orphan Asylum in New York City, the mothers among those transported north—"who but a few days ago had nothing but suffering and utter destitution before them"—were "now earning from eight to twelve dollars per month."[44] By giving freedwomen "a fair chance to find work elsewhere," the bureau hoped to relieve the government of their support and reduce dependence among freedpeople.[45]

Not all were pleased with the bureau's approach to relocation, however, and thus its official transportation policies did not last long. The *New York Herald* charged the bureau with "traffic[king] in negroes," and President Andrew Johnson—long an opponent of the bureau—criticized Howard's agency for endorsing a practice "little better than another form of slavery." At issue was the use of forced transportation, and certainly the appearance of coercion was evident in the bureau's effort to use relocation as a way to curtail federal relief. Although in principle Commissioner Howard approved the use of relocation for "those only . . . who can be induced voluntarily to do so," bureau officials worked to induce freedpeople to relocate with varying degrees of pressure. Officials in Washington, D.C., for instance, threatened to cut off rations to those who refused to accept contracted work or move elsewhere. Indeed, the district's assistant commissioner sternly informed Josephine Griffing, then an employment agent for the bureau who vehemently objected to, though was obligated to uphold, such coercive policies: "It is important . . . to have the women provided for before winter. None who refuse to go (without good reason) will receive any aid from the government here." Similarly, after forcibly relocating hundreds of unemployed blacks in his state to Alabama, Mississippi, and elsewhere, Georgia assistant commissioner Davis Tillson warned lingering jobless freedpeople in December 1865 to find work or bureau officials would "make contracts for them."[46] Charges of coercion aside, other problems arose as local agents became for all intents and purposes labor brokers or, as was the case in Washington, D.C., turned to employment agents and intelligence offices to facilitate the relocation of poor freedpeople and solve the myriad problems of unemployment. Accusations of abduction, kidnapping, and corruption revealed the many imperfections in bureau transportation efforts. For, as the historian Carol Faulkner reveals in her study of female reformers in the freedmen's aid movement, agents working both for and with the bureau "unwittingly separated families, mistreated freedpeople in transit, sent freedpeople to the wrong destination, or lost track of them altogether." General Samuel Armstrong at Fortress Monroe, Virginia, a bureau official who initially had fully embraced the transportation of freedwomen to the North as a way to meet their needs and satisfy bureau directives, for instance, apprehensively reported "the abduction" of some twenty freedgirls he had sent to Boston in the spring of 1866, declaring somewhat helplessly: "The Lord knows where they are!" Bureau officials in Georgia were accused of using relocation to mask their participation in the trafficking of freedgirls for the purpose of prostitution. And black parents especially called into question bureau actions as it relocated freedchildren. By taking custody of and apprenticing or sending north (in a practice akin to apprenticeship) black children assumed to be orphans, the dependents of impoverished parents, or those purportedly sent with parental consent, the bureau interfered with efforts to reconstruct black families. Indeed, writing for a freedwoman who had "lost" her child to bureau relocation efforts, Anna

Earle, a Quaker abolitionist in Worchester, Massachusetts, expressed her displeasure with the situation: "I pity the child's mother very much and I feel sorry that the Bureau should suffer as it does when its agents so wantonly violate the laws of humanity." A year later, with the freedchild still lost to her mother, Earle directed her displeasure with the bureau more directly—at the "agent" responsible, Josephine Griffing—telling officials in Washington, D.C.: "I refrain from expressing my feeling in regard to Mrs. Griffing, who it seems to me [h]as clearly kidnaped little Kitty as if she had been a slave trader." Proceeding in the face of such criticisms and at the command of the president, Commissioner Howard officially ordered bureau transportation to cease on 15 April 1866.[47]

Agents of the Freedmen's Bureau employed other more coercive measures to curtail federal relief. Perhaps the most draconian method used by the bureau to reduce dependency among freedwomen with children was its reliance on the apprenticeship system. While the bureau officially advocated the use of apprenticeship only for orphaned freedchildren or with the consent of black children's parents, agents also seized custody of freedchildren and apprenticed them when parents were unable to support their families. Freedwomen on bureau relief rolls were particularly at risk, for some agents clearly employed harsh apprenticeship practices in an effort to combat both their unemployment and their dependence. Agents reasoned that after apprenticing children to employers who could provide "good homes" where they would "be well fed, well clothed & receive a good education," mothers would be able to find work. Moreover, white employers were certainly more willing to hire freedwomen with children if the latter were legally bound to them. Thus the indenturing of freedchildren served as an indirect method of securing employment for mothers, for all involved understood that mothers were less likely to leave while their children were held to service.[48]

The bureau's policy of apprenticing freedchildren (discussed in Chapter 4) varied widely within states and across the South. Bureau officials at the state level in Virginia, for instance, ordered local agents in Lynchburg "to bind out the child" in "*any case* where the parents receive government support." Similarly, bureau policy makers in South Carolina readily used children as a weapon in its "war on dependency." In addition to endorsing apprenticeship policies designed to "relieve" destitute parents of the financial burden of supporting children, agents there required freedpeople seeking custody of their children to demonstrate first their ability to provide for their household. Though not as severe, the bureau in Texas nonetheless indicated to local agents that women who "have so many children they cannot support them all, should permit" them to be bound to "good" men. In other areas, bureau policy makers proved more reluctant to force poor freedwomen to apprentice children.

Insisting that the "practice of binding out children is dangerous inasmuch as it fosters the old ideas of compulsory labor and dependence," these officials desired apprenticeship with "proper safeguards." Most important, they sought parental consent when indenturing freedchildren. Thus agents counseled, advised, and urged destitute mothers receiving relief to apprentice their children voluntarily.[49]

Certainly not all agents thought the practice of binding out black children was harmful in every case. Operating in a way consistent with national poor-relief practices and in a move seemingly at odds with their own promotion of domesticity and the sanctity of the family, these bureau men failed to see any injustice in turning to apprenticeship in cases of destitution.[50] Seeing apprenticeship as offering a twofold solution for curtailing bureau relief and finding black mothers work, one North Carolina agent expressed great satisfaction with the practice. "[T]his system of Indentures is an excellent one," he commended his superior officer in late 1865. Having issued apprenticeships for several children whose fathers, but not mothers, were absent, this agent saw only success in having "relieved" the poor women of the children "they cannot support." Indeed, he insisted, the practice offered "the children good homes—a trade—& a sum of money to start them in life—& at the same time—let the mothers . . . have the freedom to go & find work for them-selves." Bureau men like this North Carolina agent viewed apprenticeship as an answer to the problem of women deemed "unproductives" and failed to see the harm in asking them to turn over all rights as parents. The experience of Phillis, a Louisiana freedwoman, clearly demonstrated this sentiment among bureau officials. After initially supporting the mother's efforts to reclaim her daughter in 1866, the local agent in Franklin, Louisiana, concluded that although "by the law the mother is the natural guardian of her child," in this case—because "it appears that . . . [the] mother has done nothing for the support of the child for the last five years"—it would be better to reject her appeal. Poor freedwomen in Georgia faced similar actions as the acting assistant commissioner made modifications in bureau apprenticeship policies in late 1865. While the official policy of the Georgia bureau had insisted that only minor children without guardians or those whose parents consented to the indenture could be apprenticed, the acting assistant commissioner informed agents: "If a woman has more children than she can support, they can be bound out with her consent. . . . If she becomes a pauper, then the children can be bound out with the consent of the Agent of the Bureau." Deemed a "vagrant" by the "citizens of the neighborhood" and found living "in a state of starvation" in the woods with her children, Sylvia Darden, a freedwoman living near Fort Gaines, Georgia, experienced the wrath of such policy shifts. The local agent took Darden's children from her and bound them to a nearby white planter. Virginia Berry, another Georgia freedwoman, experienced similar consequences in 1866. The local agent ordered Berry, found "loafering about the county," to apprentice all but two of her children. Adhering foremost to the bureau's commitment to promoting free labor and self-sufficiency among former slaves, these agents welcomed apprenticeship as a way both to end freedwomen's dependence on relief and to help them realize economic independence.[51]

Even in the face of such tactics, black women themselves challenged bureau efforts aimed at ending, or at least reducing, their dependence on government relief. In its war on dependency, the Freedmen's Bureau encountered responses and resistance from black women that its officials neither fully anticipated nor wholly understood. Most notably, freedwomen sought to decide for themselves where and how they—as well as their families—would both live and work, even if it meant losing material aid from the government. And despite the combination of bureau incentives and threats aimed at ending their need for relief, many destitute black women stood firm in the face of bureau policies. To agents' great surprise, freedwomen did not always labor how, when, and where the bureau desired; some rejected transportation offered on terms they deemed unacceptable; and many resisted any effort to take their children. Thus as the bureau attempted to implement its relief policies, the federal agency discovered that its own expectations for freedom and those of freedwomen were, at times, very different and that freedwomen could be formidable adversaries.

Despite the bureau's blandishments, many former slave women resisted the bureau's coercive efforts to transport them to former homes, the countryside, the North, or other areas where employment was more plentiful—all of which tended to mean returning to the fields as field hands or to white households as domestic servants. While some freedwomen, like Charity Cox and those who went north, voluntarily accepted transportation from the bureau, many did not. Georgia freedwoman Mary Burch effectively countered bureau efforts to force her relocation. Considering her a "destitute," the local bureau agent had worked to find employment in Boston for the young woman and now sought to force her to move there. But Burch, the agent reported, "declined" to move north and, in a positive turn of events, in his mind, chose instead to find work as a nurse. Whether she was working in the North or across town mattered little to this agent. Either way, Burch was no longer dependent upon his agency for relief. Insistent that Burch had proved that she would no longer need bureau assistance, he contentedly informed his superiors that the young freedwoman now had "more than $10 saved from her wages" and was working for "$5 per month." Not as fortunate as Burch in finding employment nearby, other poor freedwomen resisted the bureau's manipulative offers of transportation even in the face of agents' threats to cut off rations if they failed to move. Facing the choice of relocating out of the freedmen's camp in Arlington, Virginia, or surrendering bureau rations, freedwoman Lucinda, for instance, chose the latter, telling bureau officials: "I dont want the rations if they will let me alone." Frustrated, agents across the South reported that black women were "reluctant to go North," did "not desire regular work in the country," and were, in fact, "very unwilling to go any distance into the country and cl[u]ng with pertinacity to" cities, towns, and freedmen's camps. Bureau agents were perplexed. Indeed, an agent in Virginia noted in disbelief, freedwomen and their children "are here who could if removed to other places find employment and . . . comfortable homes but seem to live here in almost starvation." Far from passive beneficiaries of the government's benevolence, these women rejected notions that their very real needs, their status as dependents, and their appeals for aid made them subject to the bureau's demands.[52]

Black women's behavior may have befuddled agents, but it rested on a powerful logic well understood by former slaves. They seemed willing to risk starvation rather than move away from the cities and camps now their homes. Fearful of former masters, these freedwomen refused to return to their old residences; suspicious "of any effort to find employment for them elsewhere," they proved more resistant to moving to the North than freedmen; possessing "small lots of land under cultivation" or "having rented a small plot of land," they sought to enjoy the fruit of their labors; and having been gone for so long, they realized that the likelihood of family and friends remaining at their former homes was often slim. In short, freedwomen proved inclined to withstand the hardships they faced—the weight of their circumstances—because they understood that what awaited them elsewhere, by comparison, could easily be much worse. Cities and camps offered a kind of protection, and moving away from them often involved separation of families. Describing the impulse for blacks' migration to Atlanta, one black Georgian explained: "The military is here and nobody interferes with us here." Freedpeople in Virginia put it more bluntly to an agent nearby: "We knows old master bettern'n you."[53]

Freedwomen's opposition to returning to the countryside certainly coincided with their determination to keep families together. Beyond conferring legal recognition on their married status, freedom had finally offered women the opportunity to reclaim children and reconstruct families. Their hopes and expectations for freedom could not be separated from their roles as mothers who understood all too well the toll that slavery had taken on them and their children. Emancipation presented black women with the chance to finally place the welfare of their own families before that of their former masters. Few freedwomen were willing to give this up without a fight. Moving back to the countryside entailed considerable risk to freedwomen themselves, their families, and, more important, their control of their children. Black women understood that accepting employment on farms and plantations would require them to leave more secure communities for areas where they would be subject to close supervision and abuse by whites. Relocating to the countryside and accepting labor in the fields or as domestic servants more often than not also meant accepting wages that would not fully support them and their families. With labor-starved planters and farmers nearby, and at a time when civil authorities—as well as the bureau—did not hesitate to remove children from parents incapable of supporting them, poor freedwomen especially understood the very real threat that moving to the country posed. Going north posed similar risks. Although the bureau policies ordered agents to investigate family connections before sending freedpeople away, this did not always occur and resulted in unfortunate consequences. Families were separated. Freedchildren, older ones in particular, were sent away—even north—without parental consent. And the bureau pressured poor parents, especially poor unwed mothers, to apprentice children or leave young ones in orphan asylums so they could accept work elsewhere.[54]

Former slave women recognized that their ability—or, in reality, inability—to provide for their children made any assertion of parental rights difficult. Whether single, married, widowed, or abandoned, poverty-stricken black mothers were especially vulnerable to the many injustices of apprenticeship. As discussed more fully in Chapter 4, "poor" freedchildren across the South were bound out all too often with little or no regard for parental consent. Indeed, Thomas Tredway, a wealthy planter in Virginia, was but one who looked to apprenticeship to offer answers to the labor "crisis" as well as the impoverished condition of single mothers. He hoped to seize the labor of at least four children born to his former slaves—all single mothers who remained on his plantation after the war. Like other whites, this Virginian believed that southern apprenticeship laws and practices, in some ways like those of the bureau, held the most "promise" for mothers with large families who had been abandoned and were now penniless. They might have been free, but poor black mothers occupied an ambiguous position in society. They were free persons but still dependents unable to sustain their families in legitimate households of their own. Tredway, like many white southerners, simply sought to ignore the issue of black parental rights altogether. But the irony of the situation could not be missed. As Marylander William Taylor told Congress in 1867, "The children who were able to support their families were the very ones they took away."[55]

To be sure, freedwomen vehemently resisted efforts to seize custody of their children. As a result, when the Freedmen's Bureau instituted policies aimed at ending freedwomen's reliance on government relief by apprenticing their children, it encountered opposition. Incredibly, many bureau agents seemed puzzled when freedwomen balked—even to the point of forsaking or rejecting government relief altogether. After advising several poor women to apprentice their children, an agent in Richmond, Virginia, for instance, reported to the state's assistant commissioner, "in each case I was met with the reply that 'they could not part with them.'" Puzzled, he noted, "[I]t seems they would rather see their children starve, than have them provided for" by apprenticeship. An agent in Lauderdale, Mississippi, was similarly taken aback when a group of freedwomen employed at a nearby asylum for freedpeople stepped in as he attempted to apprentice the orphaned freedchildren cared for by the institution. Reporting that these freedwomen refused "to let their children go," the frustrated agent was helpless to handle the situation.[56]

While maybe not to bureau officials, the resistance of freedwomen to federal policies aimed at ending their dependence on public charity made sense to former slaves. These women sought to protect and keep their families together, as well as to create and maintain a safe, secure home and community away from the old threats of slavery. If achieving these goals meant accepting (or even resisting) public charity, turning to haphazard rather than regular employment, or resisting employment and transportation offered by the bureau, that seemed reasonable to them. To agents of the bureau, however, these actions only served to intensify concerns that former slaves would interpret freedom as a license for idleness.[57] Still, since it was freedwomen who refused to yield to their orders, it was possible for bureau men to discount such fears. Keeping watch over and instructing freedmen in the rights and responsibilities of freedom was, after all, the foremost concern of the federal agency. Providing momentary material relief to freedwomen who could reasonably be seen as dependents among the deserving poor in nineteenth-century America did not jeopardize that purpose.

"With a weight of circumstances like millstones about their necks," the freedwomen who became the exception to bureau relief policies were, as General Armstrong once lamented, the ones "struggling to make lives."[58] In the end it was the combination of black women's assertiveness and bureau men's grudging willingness to refrain from fully enforcing official policy that afforded some black women a modicum of protection from the vicissitudes of an already harsh reality of extreme poverty, large families absent of husbands and fathers, and a labor market that labeled them "unproductives." In coming to the bureau as deserving women worthy of assistance, these freedwomen secured benefits, meager and short lived as they were, granted to them because of their gender and unavailable to freedmen. Until black households could be reunited—as well as reshaped to more closely resemble northern ideals of family life in which husbands were independent, self-supporting free laborers who assumed responsibility for their wives and children—the bureau continued to provide government relief to the neediest and worthiest poor freedwomen. Working at once both to meet and to end their need for assistance through a variety of means, bureau men sought homes and work for former slave women. But when that was not possible, and as long as they could secure material aid, local agents expanded their understanding of the deserving poor to include not only the elderly, sick, and disabled but also the wives and children of Union soldiers, widowed women, and unmarried mothers with small children. Still, always viewed as a temporary necessity, federal material aid would come to an abrupt end even for worthy black women. In the interim, though, bureau benevolence had eased the weight of circumstances they faced.

No longer the dependents of a master and not yet dependents of black husbands or fathers, as bureau officials desired, these poverty-stricken yet worthy freedwomen had become dependents of the federal government. Thus black women gained federal material assistance and protection on the basis of their standing as dependent women—as wives, mothers, daughters—rather than as impoverished former slaves who were owed something because of years of exploitation by racism and slavery or as citizens of a nation that protected and cared for them as a matter of public responsibility with sustained material aid. As dependents, they secured benefits from the Freedmen's Bureau, and, in the case of relief, found that this status and the federal agency could work to their advantage. Most black women welcomed this arrangement, accepted a status as dependents in their households, and even argued for federal material assistance from the bureau based on their distinct position as women—and as wives and mothers in particular—and what that meant to them. But even though they embraced the contours of a system that promoted the appearance of an outwardly patriarchal hierarchy in their own communities, families, and households, black women contested contemporary negative understandings of dependency and resisted the notion that they, as women and dependents, possessed no rights, authority, or voice in how they should be treated and what they could or could not do. When the demands became too great—when, for instance, the bureau wanted them to accept employment they did not desire, to relocate to places they did not want to go, or to sacrifice their children to apprenticeship indentures—freedwomen resisted, even if it resulted in the loss of material aid.

Black women's insistence that womanhood and dependency did not necessitate the unconditional surrender of authority, indeed freedom, to others—

whether it be the federal government, white employers, or black men—was readily apparent as they struggled to define for themselves when, where, and how they labored. And the relationship between black womanhood and free labor proved especially troublesome to agents of the Freedmen's Bureau as they worked to establish a new system of labor in the South. Bureau men's understandings of freedwomen as workers, as women, and as dependents would both challenge and influence how agents implemented federal labor policies in the face of black women determined to decide for themselves just what freedom and free labor meant in this new age of emancipation.

3

"The women are the controlling spirits"

Freedwomen, Free Labor, and the Freedmen's Bureau

Perhaps a mere majority of the women are hired at present on farms, but a very large number are doing nothing at all towards supporting themselves and their children. They are found occupying all the vacant houses in the villages and country that they can get into, loitering and lounging about, some of them pretending an occupation, but most of them sponging upon the scanty earnings of their Fathers Husbands and friends. Many of them are mere . . . dead-heads on the plantations—the employer having agreed to furnish provisions for them in order to command the labor of the Husbands and Fathers.

Reporting that the freedwomen in Houston County, Georgia, refused to work as they had in slavery, Freedmen's Bureau agent J. D. Harris appealed for guidance from the state's assistant commissioner during the summer of 1866. "These women seem to feel that they ought not to work," the agent explained. Indeed, he exhorted, "This year has demonstrated the fact that they *will not* work." Clearly annoyed, Agent Harris insisted that not only had the freedwomen "been worthless as labourers . . . but they have given their employers a great deal of trouble." "Nine tenths of the cases brought before me for adjudication," he further alleged, "originated with these women." "They are not only lazy but exceedingly sensitive and ungovernable," the agent concluded about the freedwomen he regarded as incorrigible.[1]

Planters and former slave owners were similarly troubled by black women's conduct—or at least what was perceived to be their conduct—when it came to work. Certainly, the allegation that they had all "retired from the fields" elicited perhaps the most frequent, bitter, and hostile complaints from both planters and federal officials alike when it came to freedwomen.[2] For in the former slaves' demands to determine how, when, and where they would work, as a Georgia planter once remarked, "[t]he women are the controlling spirits." Hoping to regain control of the black labor force, the local planters in Agent Harris's district had initiated steps to retaliate against freedwomen who attempted to direct their own labor. "[O]ur planters," he reported, "universally concur in the resolution not to employ the women next year at all." But the planters' reprisal did not stop there. "They further resolve," he added, "to furnish rations for those only that actually work."³

The situation had become serious. "What . . . is to become of the women and children? How are they to subsist? . . . With no bread, no money, no employer. How are they to be fed?" With every word, Agent Harris's concerns became more momentous. "These are serious questions arising from facts that already stare us in the face," he insisted, continuing:

> The county swarms with vagrants. . . . Next year the plantation women will nearly all be vagrants, I fear, for those who would work will be unable to get employment. I see no other alternative but for thousands of them to perish during the next winter and spring, and it will be the case unless they can by some means be induced to work, and the planters satisfied that it will pay to hire them.

But, at least according to this agent, there was hope. If black women's instincts for self-preservation could be aroused, the "boon of liberty" would not be lost to them. "To my mind," he ultimately concluded, "there seems but one remedy. Induce the women . . . to assist in cultivating the soil . . . and do it by compulsion if necessary."⁴

Like other bureau men stationed across the South, Agent Harris had found himself squarely in the middle of the battle between white southerners, emancipated slaves, and the federal government over defining the meaning of freedom and free labor. And freedwomen who insisted on working "in their own time, as they see fit," were often at the heart of this contest. Emancipation had destroyed the established ways of living and working in the South. Unsure what would replace slavery, former slaves and former slave owners now grappled with their new conditions as employees and employers. This contest between freedwomen and white planters in Agent Harris's district and the role that he played in mediating it were not unique. Neither was the agent's response, nor his suggested remedy. As bureau officials undertook the task of laying a foundation for a free labor society—one where blacks consented freely to work and whites granted them the benefits possessed by laborers in the North—they regarded employment as the cure-all to southern ills. If work could be provided to former slaves, they reasoned, the best interests of blacks themselves, their former owners, the South, and the nation as a whole would be served.⁵

In their efforts to transform the South into a free labor society, officials of the Freedmen's Bureau encountered an employment landscape complicated greatly by issues of gender. Reconstruction-era policy makers believed that both

African American men and women should remain active participants in the southern workforce. Emancipation had ended the obligation to labor for neither black men nor black women. As a result, the bureau's official stance on labor—permeated with both an insistence that freedom required employment and a formal refusal to provide relief to persons physically able to work—called for freedmen and women to continue working in the fields and households of the South. Indeed, the agency's free labor experiment depended on it. A complex labor situation seemed ready to thwart such policies, however. Labor supply and labor demand seemed uneven across the South. Complicating matters further, bureau men encountered a determination among African Americans—much like that of the freedwomen in Houston County, Georgia—to decide for themselves how, when, and where they would work. Frustrated by these factors, bureau labor policies did not easily translate into reality.

As it sowed the seeds of free labor—and despite policies demanding that blacks work regardless of their gender—the bureau came to enforce its labor policies differently against freedmen and freedwomen. In adjudicating employment disputes—particularly those involving the dismissal of contracted workers and the use of corporal punishment—agents showed an especial disgust for the exploitation and abuse of freedwomen. However much they regarded them as workers—which they certainly did—agents recognized both that former slave women were vulnerable in a labor market that saw them as less productive and less valuable and that they were now part of freedmen's households. In enforcing the obligation to work too, bureau men acknowledged a gendered difference. What developed was a labor program that, when implemented, applied to African American men without exception and to African American women in varying degrees according to their marital and parental status and character. In short, unemployed able-bodied black men were vagrants. But the same did not always hold true for similarly situated black women. Bureau men proved unwilling to categorically arrest as vagrants all freedwomen who did not enter contracts, work regularly outside their own households, or possess some visible (and acceptable) means of employment. Thus whether trying to settle their labor disputes or to get black women to work, bureau men in the field sought to uphold the ideals of free labor and contract but recognized a gendered difference between freedwomen and freedmen in doing so. They used complaints involving freedwomen's labor to reach into black households to promote manly independence, female dependence, and nuclear families in which male heads of household enjoyed control over their wives and children.

From the first days of freedom, those who led and served the Freedmen's Bureau preached the gospel of free labor—the "noblest principle on earth," as one agent had described it—to southerners both black and white. Despite such praise for the principles of free labor, it would not take long for federal officials to comprehend the enormity of the task that lay ahead. Some bureau men openly expressed doubt in the ability of free labor to thrive in a society so long dependent upon slavery. "The negro seemed resolved and obstinate, and the white indifferent and careless, and full of evil forebodings," reported one agent as he assumed his bureau duties in postwar Georgia. The fear that slavery had deprived African American men of their "freedom and manhood" especially concerned federal officials. Some worried that, robbed of independence for so long, former slaves would never become the truly self-reliant and industrious individuals required in a free labor society. "Slavery prevented all forecasting of thought, and, in general, every possibility of improvement," maintained one bureau inspector in January 1866. "Time," he insisted, "will be needed for the whole effect. Much patient instruction is called for." Commissioner Howard certainly agreed. Creation of a free labor South was going to require much diligent instruction and effort on the part of his men. But time was not something on the bureau's side. Not more than two weeks after his appointment in May 1865, Howard thus set off his agency's free labor experiment by ordering officials and agents across the South to "introduce practicable systems of compensated labor" that taught "whites that they should pay their laborers and blacks that they could not live without labor."[6]

Regardless of federal officials' and white southerners' efforts to get freedwomen "back" to work and to "teach" African Americans that freedom in fact included work, freedwomen—like freedmen—boldly struggled to define how, when, and where they labored in the postemancipation South. That is, they demonstrated an intense desire to define the meaning of free labor on their own terms and they turned often to the bureau for assistance in doing so. Indeed, the sheer number of complaints brought to the bureau against white employers by black women, and vice versa, demonstrated freedwomen's fortitude in the matter. While myriad and diverse, most of freedwomen's labor complaints sought redress for violation of contract obligations, nonpayment of wages, and physical abuse by particularly spiteful employers. In adjudicating their many claims against exploitive and abusive white employers, agents and officials of the bureau treated freedwomen differently, all the while seeking to uphold the ideal of free labor and the sanctity of the labor contract.

Freedwomen understood that their labor had worth and thus worked to define the meaning of free labor on their own terms. Thus what white southerners and federal officials repeatedly called the "withdrawal" of black women from the workforce would perhaps be better characterized as a redistribution of their participation. Black women did not stop working. Rather, they had stopped working according to the dictates of white southerners. Indeed, what white southerners' complaints most clearly revealed was their abhorrence at any effort beyond their own to control the extent, terms, and rate of freedwomen's participation in the southern workforce. However black women responded to free labor and whatever white southerners' vehement complaints about their absence or poor work habits, one thing that cannot be questioned was freedwomen's knowledge of the value of their labor. Aunt Phillis, an elderly black woman in South Carolina, for example, did not hesitate in answering a question posed to her by a northern reporter during the war. "Where did your master get so much money?" he had asked. With great force, she replied: "Whar he git he money? Whar he git he money? Is dat what you ask—whar he git he money? *I* show you, massa." Pulling up her sleeve, she struck her arm and exhorted, "You see dat, massa? Dar's whar he got he money—out o' dat black skin he got he money."[7]

Perhaps most vehemently freedwomen demanded that labor in freedom differ from that of slavery, and one of the first opportunities encountered by former slave women to assert their new rights as free laborers was in the decision to stay with former masters or to seek out new employers. Some chose to remain with former owners in places and with people long familiar. Elsie Reece, a former slave from Texas, for example, vividly recalled the confusion faced by freedpeople as they considered the consequences of emancipation. She remembered black community members, not knowing what to do or where to go, asking: "Where are we going to live?" "What are we going to do?" Only after their former master "laughed heartily" and "said they could stay for wages or work for halves" did the uncertainty settle. "[T]here were a bunch of happy colored folks," Reece recalled, "after they learned they could stay and work." Freedwoman Julia Francis Daniels described the decision to remain with former masters in terms that gave more agency to former slaves making tough choices with limited resources. "The men talked it over a-twixt themselves and concluded to stay," she recalled years later. "They said we might as well stay there as go somewhere else, and we had no money and no place to go." More resigned, a former Mississippi slave woman flatly recalled, "[D]ere wusn't no difference in freedom cause I went right on working for Miss." Whatever freedwomen's reasoning, the decision to remain and to work certainly satisfied former owners, who longed for stability and hoped to provide no more than quarters, provisions, and perhaps clothing after emancipation.[8]

Black women feared owners-turned-employers and at times turned to collective action to resist returning to the days of old. Determined both to stay in the area that they had long recognized as their home and to resist being forced into a contract with their former master, freedwomen on the Sea Cloud Plantation at Edisto Island, South Carolina, for instance, came together in opposition to him as well as the local bureau agent. Now pardoned by President Andrew Johnson, the former Confederate turned to the bureau for assistance in reclaiming his property in the spring of 1866. "I was beset by the women on this place in a very serious manner, and was obliged to use decisive measures for the preservation of the property as well as for my own head," the bureau agent reported to his superiors. Continuing, he attempted to convey the seriousness of the situation as well as to justify his actions:

> After I had made known my errand, and told them who I was, and what I came for, and being also in uniform, they absolutely refused to give me any information. . . . They then said I wouldn't have durst come there had not part of the men gone to the city. . . . They said they would not make any arrangement whatever, for me or anybody else; that they cared for no United States officer: the Govt brought them to the island & "they would burn down the house before they would move away" or "farm it themselves until put out."

Met by two women who then threatened to set fire to the house, the agent arrested the mother-and-daughter team and attempted to take them away. In doing so, however, he reported: "The people followed me about a half a mile with hoes and sticks, and I got sick of this business." Telling the women, "[T]his is the last time I tell you this," and meeting their continued refusal "to obey," the agent drew his revolver, "faced my horse about and charged them back to camp." Although he believed that the mother and daughter (as well as another woman whom he identified as "the oracle") deserved prosecution, the clearly frustrated agent nonetheless concluded: "I do not think I can unaided arrest them, but if you order it, I will try, begging to be excused from any consequences arising from the attempt."[9] Freedwomen elsewhere turned to strikes, work slowdowns, and stoppages as well as other forms of group resistance to get white employers (and bureau officials) to yield—or, when that was not possible, to listen—to their labor demands. While perhaps exceptional, these kinds of resistance nonetheless demonstrated participants' belief in the potential for change. Routine or rare, such organization proved alarming enough to white employers and bureau men alike. Complaints like that of the white Georgian who insisted that freedwomen "are constantly striking for higher wages" seemed to emerge in bureau offices across the South.[10]

Not all freedpeople were so willing to continue living and working as they had in slavery. Insistent in their determination to claim freedom, freedwomen demonstrated great courage as they rejected employment from former owners. After hearing that she was free, Sarah, a Virginia freedwoman, for instance, ran seven miles to confront her former mistress as well as to assert her worth. Looking at her "real hard," she proclaimed: "I'se free! Yes, I'se free! Ain't got to work fo' you no mo'. You can't put me in yo' pocket now!" Equally defiant and determined was Adeline, a Louisiana freedwoman who went to the local bureau agent in Amite City to voice her objection to being held by her former owner away from her husband. Insistent that she was "free and at liberty to work for who she pleases," Adeline asserted herself in free labor terms and demanded—and got—action from the bureau. The agent who heard her complaint agreed with Adeline and ordered her employer to "let her go immediately" as well as to let her "retain all of her private property." But not all assertions of freedom came so boldly. Others revealed their unhappiness with the status quo by departing quietly without regard or concern for former owners. "Adeline cooked us an elegant Christmas dinner," recorded Susan Bradford Eppes in a diary entry not long after the planter family in Florida had "settled" the wages for slaves-turned-employees in this first year of freedom. Something was amiss, however. "Each man and maid were in place, attending to their various duties, but," she wrote, "the atmosphere of merriment and good-will was lacking." Mocking the appearance of peace and harmony, reality soon revealed the former slaves' discontent. By the time the new year had dawned, Eppes reported that she and her family were "all alone on the hill." Adeline, along with other the former slaves, had departed in pursuit of a greater freedom.[11]

Without question, compensation headed freedwomen's lists of demands in the postemancipation free labor system, and disagreement on wages led many to leave former masters. Harriet, a Texas freedwoman, for instance, attempted to negotiate for wages from her former mistress but soon found herself unwilling to live and work in an environment too much like the days of old. "Harriet," the white woman declared after the sheriff read the Emancipation Proclamation, "you are free, Harriet! From this hour [you are] as free as I am. You can stay here, or go; you can work or sleep; you are your own mistress, now, and forever." Harriet understood. For when her now-former mistress asked, "Will you hire yourself to me, Harriet?" and told her she would pay six dollars a month, the freedwoman responded uncooperatively. "Six dollars [is] too little," Harriet protested. "I 'long to myself now. I want eight dollars now. When a nigger free, they worth more." Harriet's employer yielded and agreed to her terms. But still unsatisfied, after only three days of employment, Harriet left in search of a new employer. Kate, an ex-slave in Georgia who had remained a "faithful" to the daughter of her former owner, similarly asserted herself in 1867 on the question of wages. "I wish to tell you if you give me twelve dollars per month I will stay with you," she explained, "but if not, I have had good offers and I will find another place." The mistress of the household refused and, true to her word, Kate left—"with a very impertinent air," according to her former employer. Freedwoman Mary Lindsay similarly left her employer when her earnings in freedom proved not to be what she had hoped. Unsatisfied with the new dress and promise of food and shelter offered to her, this former slave wanted wages. "After a while I asked her [her former mistress] ain't she got some money for me," Lindsay recalled some years later. But the woman "say no" and asked, "[A]in't she giving me a good home?" Disappointed with the response and without saying "nothing to nobody," Lindsay packed her things (including the new dress) and left for a nearby town.[12]

Beyond wages, freedwomen also demanded a say in defining the terms of their labor. Caroline, a freedwoman in Mississippi, for instance, contracted with her employer "to do the cooking, washing, ironing, and general housework and anything about the yard or garden that may be required of her." Although hired as a cook, Venus William agreed in her contract "to work in the field when necessary." South Carolina freedwoman Emmie Gray likewise contracted to "do the cooking washing and all other necessary work about the house," as well as field labor, in return for "one half of the corn & cotton cultivated by herself." Other former slave women were more exacting in their contracts. In particular, some sought to control what services they would and would *not* provide. Freedwoman Georgia Roberts, for instance, contracted to labor "either as House Servant or field hand, with the exception she was not to plow." Similarly, Hagar, a South Carolina freedwoman, willingly agreed to provide domestic help for her employers but flatly refused to touch the laundry. Claiming she "was not strong enough" to do the washing, complained her employer, Hagar refused to wash "even a towel." The wife of freedman Edward Lynch demonstrated similar resolve to have a say in the terms of her labor and, like many, complained to the local bureau office when her labor negotiations did not go as planned. Having stayed with her former master following the war, the woman finally built up the courage to ask him "on what terms he would employ her." Unfortunately, and like too many others, according to the bureau official in Lynchburg, Virginia, the woman was met with a stern reply from the master-turned-employer that "he would not have any of his slaves about him that considered themselves free."[13]

As they put their freedom to the test and attempted to negotiate the terms of free labor with recalcitrant former owners, freedwomen turned often to the Freedmen's Bureau for assistance. And, without question, the failure of white employers to compensate freedpeople—both women and men—elicited perhaps the greatest number of complaints to the federal agency. Most grievances initiated by black women involved the nonpayment of wages due for services or work performed. The seeming unwillingness, and in some instances inability, of white southerners to pay wages produced one of the greatest sources of conflict between former owners and former slaves. Women complained of being cheated out of the already small wages promised for their labor. Such protests at times came alongside reports that freedwomen kept working even as they remained unpaid. As one passerby explained in the immediacy of emancipation, "Still, here—as elsewhere, people with ready money leave their washing-bills unpaid; and I visit many women stooping over their washtubs, weak in body and hopeless in mind, who say, 'I keeps on washin for em, for if I leave em they'll never pay me what they owe me.'" Other freedwomen were not so fortunate. Many, like North Carolina freedwoman Betsy Powell, complained of employers who had "driven her away without pay for her labor." Thus report after report of local bureau agents repeatedly listed "Complaints for non-payment of wages" and "Discharge of laborers without payment of wages, & without just & sufficient cause" as the most numerous cases coming to them for resolution.[14]

Both freedwomen and their white employers turned regularly to the Freedmen's Bureau with complaints that the other had violated their contractual obligations. Georgia freedwoman Fanny Clinton, for instance, implored the bureau to hold her employer accountable to the terms they had verbally agreed upon. Apparently, Clinton's employer had deducted from her wages the time on Saturdays that she used to do her washing despite having agreed that she was to have "every half Saturday for that purpose." She also alleged that they had an understanding that "she should be permitted to leave . . . whenever she became dissatisfied." The bureau agent sympathized with Clinton. Recognizing that "these *verbal* promises were made to her as *bait*," he informed the employer that he was required to fulfill the verbal contract. At the same time, however, the agent admonished Clinton to return and live up to her obligations as a free laborer. To his great surprise, Clinton refused. Despite the employer's demand that the bureau force her to return, the agent refused and instead worked out "a settlement . . . between the parties in which they come out nearly even." After being struck by her employer, another Georgia freedwoman received similar consideration from the bureau. Although the local agent had authorized—or "forced" in her words—the contract between the woman and her employer (who also happened to be the agent's brother), the agent was nonetheless "ordered to give the woman her liberty [for] there was no reason for considering her a vagrant." Indeed, proof of this statement came the very day the woman received her "liberty"—for later that day she had contracted with another employer.[15]

Bureau officials strived to uphold the terms of labor agreements, especially against employers who turned freedwomen away without payment or just cause. Mary Easton, a freedwoman employed by a planter in Walton County, Georgia, for instance, complained to the bureau that he "treated her cruel" and thus had caused her to leave his employ. Insistent that she had done nothing wrong, Easton demanded everything her contract had promised—wages in the amount of $35 per year, one blanket, two suits of clothes, and one pair of shoes. Agreeing with the freedwoman, the local agent ordered Easton's employer to release her from her contract and pay her $20, one suit of clothes, and one pair of shoes for the seven months of service she had provided. Angaline Robbins filed a similar suit with the bureau through her brother, Robert Campbell, in August 1867. A "widow woman with three little children and no one to help Her," Campbell explained to the bureau, his sister had been "driven off" by her employer because "He had no further use for Her." Robbins, the agent determined, had contracted in January with the white planter "to work for Him during this year, in His corn & cotton field," and had done so "faithfully" until now. Settling the case in her favor, the agent secured $32 for Robbins.[16]

Not just freedwomen paid attention to the terms of a labor agreement, however. So too did their white employers. Black women who protested taking on tasks they considered beyond their work obligations—the ones who, according to white employers' many complaints to the bureau, were "imprudent and saucy," as well as "disrespectful and abusive," and "refused to obey" orders—suffered consequences for such evaluations. Lethy, a freedwoman living in postwar Virginia, for instance, openly challenged white expectations for her employment. Richard Eppes, her employer and former owner, repeatedly complained of her "airs" and poor work habits after the war. Eppes would have just assumed that Lethy would save him the trouble of feeding and employing her by leaving. "[W]ere it not for the obligations I feel . . . to her for the preservation of the property . . . during the war and her most excellent husband," he wrote about the nervy freedwomen, "she would not stay a day on the farm." The planter's family was certainly not opposed to firing freedwomen. Eppes's wife discharged another freedwoman for declining to do anything beyond cooking for the family. After only two days of employment it seems that Anna, hired as a "house servant," refused to take on any extra duties involved with helping with the wash. "[A]s we could not keep a servant to do only the cooking," Eppes explained, "we were compelled to discharge her." Others longed to be released from their contractual obligations. Hoping to move closer to her husband, a Louisiana freedwoman pleaded with her employer to allow her to leave. Ignoring her pleas, the unrelenting planter refused to let her go. "Don't you know that you contracted with me for a year?" he asked the defiant freedwoman. "Don't know nuffin about it," she replied bitterly. "I wants to go 'way." But the planter was not going to yield. "Well, I'm keeping my part of the contract, and you've got to keep yours," he exhorted. "If you don't, I'll send you to jail, that's all." Rosetta Taylor, a laundress in Mississippi, similarly defied her white employer's expectations as she endeavored to do her work in the manner she saw fit. Complaining directly to the assistant commissioner of the Freedmen's Bureau in his state, the infuriated employer insisted that she had "neglected ½ of her house work." But perhaps most upsetting to this employer was that Taylor had blatantly disregarded his instructions and washed his family's clothing with that of "some hireling white laborers" and, more disturbing, that of her own family.[17]

That white employers turned to the bureau with complaints of freedwomen who tested their freedom by seemingly becoming ever more defiant in their demands as free laborers confirmed the forever-changed relationship between former owners and former slaves. "Have you noticed that when you call they will never answer," one former mistress inquired as she bemoaned the attitude of her female house servants to another southern lady. Continuing, she insisted, "[T]hey seem to think it is a sign of their freedom." Freedwomen were determined to perform work differently—and as they desired—in freedom and quite often that determination revealed itself in their refusals to labor the same hours they had in slavery. The demand to regulate their own work schedule, in particular, revealed itself over and over again in the many complaints of white employers that former slave women spent too much time "keeping house" or "playing the lady." In what became a rather typical criticism of African American women, the local bureau agent in Wharton, Texas, reported in summer 1866: "The Principal Complaints are against the women who have a disposition to keep the house too much and generally they do not go out *early* enough or work *late*."[18]

Given the importance placed on the labor contract by bureau policy and bureau men, it should not be surprising that many agents sided often with frustrated planters in contract disputes involving freedwomen who brought suit as independent women. Despite her complaints of having been driven off her employer's land without any kind of payment, freedwoman Mary Magruder, for instance, gained little sympathy from the bureau in Cuthbert, Georgia. Concluding that she was "decidedly loose, both in tongue and morals, swears a great deal, had a quarrel with [her employer] . . . & left on her own accord," the agent ordered Magruder "to go back to work and to be more civil in [the] future." Angeline Sealy, another freedwoman in the area, fared little better when she appeared before the bureau. Having received and sustained the complaints of her employer that she was "lazy" and did not pick enough cotton, the agent gave Sealy "a lecture on her duties" and "told [her] that if she did not average from 75–100 [pounds] . . . of cotton per day . . . a deduction will be made from her wages."[19] In a world in which the bureau upheld the sanctity of free labor and thus viewed the contract as the governing model for labor relations, agents were unwilling to tolerate individual freedwomen (or freedmen, for that matter) who did not live up to their obligations as free laborers.

Bureau men did not uphold labor contracts in every case, however. As they endeavored to enforce the contractual obligations of both freedpeople and white employers in this free labor South, bureau men also worked to protect the rights of African American men as heads of household, free laborers, and emergent citizens. As a result, it was not uncommon for them to discard the labor contract in favor of the marital contract. Operating with an understanding of the contract as the governing model for both labor relations and domestic relations, these men thus acted to uphold the sacredness of the marriage and the right of black husbands to control wives and their labor. And, to be sure, they showed little hesitation to void contracts forced upon black wives without their husbands' approval or consent. Freedwoman Louisa Bealfree Green, for example, gained release from her employer when she married. For, in the words of the agent who adjudicated her case, as Green "ha[d] made a marriage contract[,] any previous contract or indenture is void." Freedwoman Emma Regan enjoyed similar support from the bureau. Writing to her present employer, the agent in Albany, Georgia, explained: "A bona fide contract of marriage annuls a labor contract." As a result, he concluded, she must be allowed to "join her husband." Texas agent Byron Porter reported similar conditions in his state, insisting that "wives are in nearly every case given up, when parties holding them receive orders to do so." Not so fortunate, Texas freedman Pattis Brown had a much harder time trying to obtain the release of his wife from a particularly stubborn employer. The planter in Walnut Run was not at all eager to release the freedwoman. Indeed, in this case it would take not only a bureau order but also military assistance and protection for the freedman to successfully "take away" his wife. Bureau men in Georgia showed similar determination in efforts to secure husbands' rights to remove wives from undesirable contracts. Indeed, in the case of freedwoman Delia, the agent informed her employer that Edward (her husband) "had a perfect right to take his wife away," contract or not. The only remedy open to the employer, he insisted, was "a suit for damages under the civil law." But left to the bureau, in this instance, the marital contract trumped the labor contract.[20]

In an effort to protect the sacred bonds of family and the authority of black husbands in another way, bureau men also often prevented black family members under contract together from being unjustly separated or discharged by white employers. Specifically, they endeavored to prevent planters from discharging one spouse and then compelling the other to remain under the terms of the labor contract. Bureau officials in Georgia, for instance, prohibited freedman Stephan Williams's employer from discharging him without also releasing his wife. Similarly, when freedman James Washington proceeded to the bureau to stop his employer from forcing his wife to leave the plantation on which they both worked, agents stepped in. In this instance the bureau sternly informed their employer: "[T]he dismissal of the wife necessitates the discharge of the husband consequently you will please settle in full with each of them to date of discharge, giving them a written statement of the fact, or show sufficient cause at this office why said settlement should not be made." Likewise, when the wife of freedman Harrison Hugan decided to "quit working" and the couple's employer retaliated by trying to fire her but keep him, the bureau intervened. Although sympathetic to the employer's unwillingness to allow "any one . . . [to] occupy his quarters if they did not work," the bureau agent allowed dismissal but demanded that both be allowed to leave. Thus supportive of Hugan's refusal to remain "if his wife could not stay," the agent informed their employer that he could not oust the couple until they had found other employment and a new home together.[21]

Even in instances in which bureau agents enforced a married freedwoman's obligation to fulfill a contract entered into on her own accord, they still endeavored to protect her husband's rights. As a matter of free labor, these officials were reluctant, in particular, to invalidate labor contracts agreed to in earnest by freedwomen prior to marriage. Not uncommon, then, were bureau endorsements like one from an official in Georgia that declared: "The husband of a freedwoman hired out, contract approved, cannot take his wife away from her employer, when he knew that she was hired for the year before marring her." In a similar directive, the agency further ordered that in such cases "the woman must perform her contact and any person interfering with its fulfillment should be punished." Yet at the same time it upheld the authority of freedwomen to contract in such instances, bureau men still worked to protect black husbands' rights to "reasonable" access to their wives. While the bureau in Texas, for example, readily confirmed freedwoman Jane's right to "make any contract . . . that she sees proper" and held that her husband could not "remove her . . . without her consent," it simultaneously insisted that he could not "be prevented from coming to see her while she is his wife." In fact, an employer's denial of this right to a black husband could result in the cancellation of the wife's labor contract by the bureau. Freedman John Barton, for instance, went to the bureau in Texas for assistance when his wife's employer prohibited him from visiting her. Informing his wife's employer that Barton "will be allowed to visit his wife," the agent went so far to assert that if she was "willing to go with . . . her husband[,] She must not be prevented from doing so by any one." The employer of freedwoman Eliza received similar warnings from the bureau in Texas. Having been informed that her husband, Mingo Charles, had been prevented from visiting Eliza, the local agent in Houston told her employer flatly: "If her husband is not allowed to visit her, she will be under no obligations to stay with you but will be allowed to leave if she chooses, and you will be obliged to pay her for the time she has been with you."[22]

The defiant words and actions of freedwomen determined to define free labor on their own terms did not come without consequence. A black woman's gender certainly did not shield her from physical abuse or violence at the hands of her employer. Nor did it guard her against unwelcome dismissal. Agents stationed across the South filed report after report exposing the cruel misdeeds of white employers. W. B. Stickney, the agent in Shreveport, Louisiana, for instance, filed this report in early July 1865:

> There are now filed away in my office the statement[s] of ten freedmen who complain of having been brutally treated by their former masters. Some of them come to my office with the marks of brutality still plainly visible. One woman had received a long gash upon the top of her head, and a cut under the eye, and her dress was stained with the blood from these wounds. Two old men brought me the hickory sticks with which they had been beaten.[23]

In behavior reminiscent of days of old, white employers did not hesitate to use violence to demonstrate their resolve to retain labor control even after emancipation. And it took little to provoke such violence. Mary Connor, a freedwoman in Mississippi, suffered at the hands of her employer simply because she "did not know how to plough." Bettie Kelson was whipped and beaten by both her employer and his wife "because she had not made the Beds," despite pleas that "she had not had time" to do so. It was not as if she had not worked that day, Kelson told the local agent in Alexandria, Virginia, for she had been expected "to sweep the House and make the beds, and bring the wood from the cellar and make the fires, also to take care of 4 children." Also in Virginia, freedwoman Dilsey and her son were choked and whipped for having stolen "a few ears of corn from the cornfield." In Louisiana, Annie Walker was beaten for complaining that "she did not receive food" from her employer. Across the border in Mississippi, freedwoman Naomi Smith was struck for "not washing the clothes clean." A Georgia freedwoman withstood severe consequences for "carelessly burning up four lbs. of coffee," while another was shot through the hand for continuing to nurse her child after having been told "to lay it down and unload a wagon full of corn." A Virginia freedwoman was badly injured for simply rejecting her employer's allegation that she was a "dirty slut." And freedwoman Sarah Bolton endured the wrath of her Georgia employer for "influencing her husband to vote the Radical Ticket."[24]

Having the audacity to reject work as employers offered it, to ask for wages, or to refuse to show deference was a sure way to provoke a master-turned-employer. Offered a contract in Georgia, freedwoman Amanda Kemp, for instance, was "tied her up by the thumbs to force a compliance with" it. Producing more devastating consequences, the case of a freedwoman in South Carolina who refused to sign a contract "for life" showed the lengths to which some white southerners would go and, indeed, the viciousness to which they would resort. After having driven her and her husband off the plantation without food or wages for the work they had already performed, the employer retaliated with violence and murder. Explaining that the planter had hired men to murder the woman's husband and another man, the assistant commissioner reported that they "stripped the woman naked, gave her fifty (50) lashes on the bare back, and compelled her to walk back to the plantation. She was then put at the plough by day and confined by night for a week without anything to eat." As if this were not enough, not long after enduring this cruelty, she "gave birth to a dead infant." In a similar act of cruelty, the employer of a Mrs. Tyrell, a freedwoman in Mississippi, beat her "with a stick . . . and tied her thumbs & drew her up by them" and then demanded that she "call him master." Knowing her rights and with her contract in hand, Mrs. Tyrell went straight to the bureau and registered a complaint. Freedwomen who demanded payment for their labors similarly placed themselves at risk. An elderly freedwoman in Tennessee was "cruelly beaten" for "demanding of her employer a settlement for labor [she] performed for him." Likewise, when Harriet Murray asked her employer for the amount owed, he responded by taking "her to the woods. . . . [W]ith the help of another man, one sat on her head the other . . . stripped her of all her clothes naked, her hands were tied up at a limb. . . . [T]wo candles were burned out in the time occupied whiping her."[25]

In adjudicating freedwomen's appeals for justice against such recalcitrant white employers, bureau men were not blind to their gender. When faced with cases revealing white employers' continued use of corporal punishment to maintain control over labor, in particular, agents responded with a willingness and desire to protect black women. "Disobedience," Agent William Sims Tidball warned the justice of the peace in Albemarle County, Virginia, "is not such a provocation as will justify an assault and battery upon, and threats against the life of a woman." Agent Samuel S. Sumner in Jackson, Mississippi, agreed. Indeed, he exhorted, "there can be no excuse for beating a *woman*."[26] Surrounded by the vigilante justice and violence all too common in the state of Texas, Agent W. B. Pease made similar demands to a judge in Houston as he reported an assault upon a freedwoman by two white men. "These cases of maltreating freedwomen are becoming all too frequent," he charged. Although Pease readily admitted that heretofore even he had allowed such cases "to pass unpunished," he no longer thought that wise.

> Any man who assaults a woman is worse than a brute, for brutes do not bite or injure females. . . . It may have been well enough in former times for a white man to "wallup" a wench the state of society prehaps demanded it. But those days are passed and men who now presume to indulge their brutish propensities by beating and kicking women must be taught that in the eyes of the law the wench is entitled to the same privileges and immunities and the same protection that is accorded to the wife of their neighbor or the daughter of the Mother.[27]

Officials across the South decreed that such use of violence against black women by employers could not be tolerated. By reporting a "peculiarly aggravated" case to the county court, the agent in Albany, Georgia, warned the community what would happen if such violence did not stop. Appalled by the case of a white employer who had "first beat and bruised" a freedman's wife and then "shot the husband because he resented it," the agent demanded that the offender be punished for attempted murder as well as assault and battery. "If women-whippers and negro shooters go unpunished in this section of the United States," he threatened, "it will be many years before the removal of the curse of military rule as it is termed by the people hereabouts."[28]

Agents everywhere responded with especial repugnance as they considered cases of violence against black women who had accepted their new status as free women and free laborers. As proponents of free labor, they objected to the use of corporal punishment to obtain laborers or to secure labor force discipline. That perhaps is not surprising given that most were white northern men who had long been part of a society that believed in internal discipline and self-control and condemned the outward brutality of slavery. The "days for whipping colored people for amusement & gratification of passion &c," as a bureau official in Georgia explained, "have passed away." "Moral Law, has superceded, lynch law in this country," he demanded. But in the case of women, bureau men also objected to corporal punishment as both Victorian men who had been taught to protect and defend the favored sex and as northern men who had been influenced by abolitionist depictions of naked slave women being brutalized. "[T]here can be no excuse for beating a *woman*," an agent in Mississippi would declare with disgust in 1867. But the fact remained that, to white employers, these workers were not women. Race unmistakably complicated freedwomen's status as women in the postemancipation South.[29]

The bureau expressed disapproval of the use of corporal punishment against women workers in both words and action. Horrified, Georgia agent Frederick Mosebach endeavored to hold one employer accountable for his "cruelty" as he beat a freedwoman "with a heavy stick" and set "the dogs upon her, so that medical treatment became necessary." Annie Walker, the freedwoman who had been abused by her employer for having complained that she was given no food, found similar support from the local bureau office of the bureau in Amite City, Louisiana. Ruling that Walker had not violated her contract but that her employer had, the agent ordered a settlement that would punish the man by allowing Walker "to depart in peace with her children, chattels, and whatever is due her." The agent in Richmond, Texas, was likewise aghast at the abuse of a young freedwoman and her four siblings by the man who held them—allegedly their employer, although he had not paid "a dime for their work." Having suffered the last of her employer's "diabolical outrages"—stripped "to nakedness" and "whipped . . . as in the time of slavery with a large whip"—the young woman, bearing the marks and scars of his wrath, appealed to the bureau for assistance. The agent answered the young woman's plea by doing what was within his power—fining her employer $100 and "taking all this family from him."[30]

The admonitions of bureau officials against the abuse of African American women were not restricted to white southerners. Even as some agents were not inclined to protect freedwomen and, in some instances, used corporal punishment themselves, bureau officials at the district and state levels were quick to condemn such behavior. Upon hearing the complaint of a freedwoman against a local Georgia agent who had tied her "up by the thumbs for two hours and a half upon the representation" of her employer, the superior bureau official at Savannah chastised the agent for carrying his authority "as Ag[en]t of the Bureau" too far. Officials across the South similarly denounced both abuse and threats of violence by employers against female workers, resorting to their own northern understandings of free labor and telling employers: "If you are not satisfied with her labor, you can discharge her [by] paying her for the time she has been with you." But, they warned, "you have no right to use physical force to make her work."[31]

Bureau labor policies that emerged in the postwar South were far from perfect. Despite stipulations that blacks were now free to choose their own employers, the agency's ever-evolving labor program—like that of the military during wartime—sought to return blacks to the plantation fields and households of the South with various degrees of compulsion. What developed seemed an inherent contradiction—a "compulsory" system of "free" labor. "While the freedmen must and will be protected in their rights," the bureau had ordered in November 1865, "they must be required to meet these first and most essential conditions of a state of freedom, *a visible means of support, and a fidelity to contracts.*" In short, former slaves could choose where and for whom they worked, but they were not free to reject labor altogether. Thus, with its many orders, policies, and dictates governing labor, the Freedmen's Bureau proclaimed a twofold message. Now free, former slaves possessed the rights of free men and women, but with those rights came an obligation to labor. Liberty, in other words, would not tolerate laziness, idleness, dependency, or vagrancy.[32]

At the heart of the labor program developed by the bureau in the immediate postemancipation South were provisions guarding against vagrancy. Vagrancy policies served as the enforcement mechanism for the agency's insistence that former slaves return to work and enter contracts. In short, these policies gave force to federal officials' words encouraging immediate employment among former slaves. The bureau "induced" freedpeople to make contracts with white employers, insisting that "a little wholesome constraint" would in the end result in "larger independence" for those recently freed. The message from bureau headquarters was clear. Freedpeople were expected to contract their labor and thus work for wages or a share of the crop. Regardless of gender, they were responsible for providing for themselves and their families—and this required work. Thus bureau labor policies ordered, first, that all freedpeople be urged to find work and make contracts and, second, that those who rejected labor be considered vagrants, fined, imprisoned, and "hired out" to employers until they understood the virtue of honest toil. At a policy level, then, the bureau approved the general rule "to require *all* freed people to enter into contracts, irrespective of their willingness to labor."[33]

The labor landscape in the South quickly impeded bureau policies, however. Confronted with a complex labor situation—that is, white employers who refused to accept emancipation and free labor, black laborers who demanded that they alone would define their role as free laborers, and an employment outlook in which the labor supply and labor demand at times appeared irreconcilable—agents across the South soon found themselves asking how, and even if, bureau labor policies could be uniformly applied. To be sure, the seeming incompatibility of labor supply and demand posed overwhelming difficulties for the bureau. As the historian William Cohen notes, "All over the South, or so it seemed, labor supply and labor demand were out of phase." Planters and bureau officials in the southwestern states of Texas, Arkansas, Mississippi, and Alabama, for instance, complained of profound labor shortages. At the same time, officials in Virginia, the District of Columbia, and parts of Georgia and

North Carolina bemoaned the opposite—too many laborers and not enough work for them. "The labor of the State is, indeed, so inadequate to the demand," insisted Texas assistant commissioner Edgar Gregory, "that from twenty to fifty thousand additional plantation hands could be at once absorbed. All those who are represented in other departments of the south to be unemployed and starving, could at once find work, bread, and wages on the rich bottoms and fair uplands of Texas." But while Assistant Commissioner Gregory recounted such tales of labor-starved planters and premium wages, Virginia assistant commissioner Orlando Brown insisted that only an exodus of some 50,000 blacks could allay the labor surplus in his state.[34]

It would be bureau men in the field, those who came into daily contact with freedpeople, who ultimately discovered that rigid labor policies did not always translate into practice. Agents thus found themselves at times insisting to their superiors that bureau policy should not be, even could not be, enforced. Such assertions especially came to characterize the bureau's labor encounters with freedwomen.[35] As they endeavored to enforce the agency's labor policies, bureau officials were especially conscious of a freedperson's gender as well as their own assumptions about the proper place and role of black women and black men in a free labor society. Thus, the enforcement of labor policies against freedwomen varied depending upon an individual woman's circumstances. Rather than categorically regarding every unemployed but able-bodied freedwoman as a vagrant as they did for jobless freedmen, agents frequently looked to her marital and parental status, the labor market in which she lived, and her character and worthiness as seen by those around her. In the end, black women who could not find work, as well as those who restricted their labor force participation for a variety of reasons, discovered that their gender could shield them from the harsh realities of the postwar labor market.

Eager to inform former slaves how to live as free women and free men, bureau officials instructed black women—like black men—in the meaning of freedom, as well as in their new rights and duties. In particular, agents hastened to inform black women of their continued obligation to labor. "No discrimination will be made between males and females," pronounced a bureau policy maker in Florida in January 1866. Continuing, he insisted, "[A]ll who are able to work on a plantation & their families will be" required to do so. Just as Assistant Commissioner Clinton Fisk had said at the outset of freedom, these officials insisted until the very end that freedwomen "must do their part" and continue to fulfill their obligation to labor. "As far as possible," the assistant commissioner of the bureau in South Carolina, Robert Scott, would decree as late as 1868, "this office endeavors to discourage the notion that freedom and work are incompatible, and that wives should not assist in supporting their families."³⁶

Despite such policy directives from the bureau, white southerners remained steadfast in their complaints that freedwomen refused to work. Indeed, if measured only by the protests of white southerners, such words and policies failed miserably. With African American women's efforts to seize greater control of their labor force participation came the loss of, as one Georgia planter put it, "a very important percent of the entire labor of the South." Bitterly disapproving any effort by freedwomen to forsake labor in their former owners' fields and households, southern whites as well as military officials and bureau agents stationed in the South complained of "idle women whose tongues are busier than their hands," who "put on airs" and long to "play the lady and be supported by their husbands like the white folks," and who "are . . . absolutely clogging the advancement of the colored men" with their "foolish notions" and idleness. Indeed, John William De Forest, a bureau agent in up-country South Carolina, flatly denounced "the evil of female loaferism." "[M]yriads of women who once earned their own living now have aspirations to be like white ladies," the agent complained and, "instead of using the hoe, pass the days in dawdling over their trivial housework, or gossiping with their neighbors."³⁷

Like those in Houston County, Georgia, white employers bemoaned black women's struggles to define—or, in the white planters' words, end—their labor force participation and they wanted action from the bureau. "Allow me to call your attention to the fact that most of the Freedwomen who have husbands are not at work—never having made any contract at all," one planter complained to bureau officials in Georgia in 1866. "Their husbands are at work while they are as nearly idle as it is possible for them to be, pretending to spin—knit or something that really amounts to nothing," he persisted. Continuing, he demanded: "Are they not in some sorts vagrants as they are living without employment—and mainly without any visible means of support—and if so are they not amenable to [the] vagrant act?"³⁸ This Georgia planter's question pinpointed the dilemma. If bureau policy was so intent on returning the former slaves—regardless of gender—to the labor force, why were freedwomen who opted to redirect their labor not held accountable to the agency's policies that demanded otherwise? In short, why were unemployed black women not considered vagrants by the bureau and forced to enter contracts, or hired out, when they refused?

It was in answering this question that agents proved powerfully if not consciously influenced by their own assumptions about gender and gender difference. White northern men commissioned in the bureau feared—just as white southerners had—that the "evil of female loaferism" endangered the effort to transform the southern labor system. Without any hesitation, they exempted black women from the northern middle-class ideal of full-time domesticity. Moreover, making freedwomen work in the fields was reconciled easily by the fact that, like immigrant women who labored in the factories and mills of the North and poor white women in the South, necessity demanded that they labor for the benefit of their families. At the same time, however, bureau men at the local level found that they were not prepared to categorically arrest and punish all freedwomen who did not enter contracts, work regularly outside their own households, or possess some visible—and acceptable—means of employment. Apart from prostitutes, vagrants were male in the minds of these bureau men, whose ideas were shaped by mid-nineteenth-century northern middle-class concepts of gender roles, domesticity, and free labor.[39] In the end, local bureau men looked to factors beyond race when it came to applying the agency's labor policies—vagrancy policies in particular—to jobless black women. Although they clearly preferred former slave women to work, the simple fact that a freedwoman was unemployed did not convince agents she was a vagrant. (Though the same easily convinced them that a freedman should be prosecuted as a vagrant.) Rather, and much as they did when doling out federal material relief, agents considered other factors. Was she married? Did she have an able-bodied husband to support her? Had her husband abandoned her? Did she have children? Did the age of her children prevent her from working? And, finally, was she a woman of good character? The answers to these questions proved critical to agents as they determined the fate of unemployed freedwomen.

First and foremost, bureau officials responded to women's refusal to work as they had in slavery by relying upon freedmen to remedy the poor work habits of female family members. Blaming the "withdrawal" of freedwomen from the workforce on the "hen pecked" husbands who allowed it, agents thus demanded action from black men as heads of households worthy of citizenship. As with all bureau undertakings, these men called on African American men to assume responsibility for and authority over their families as free men. Although the law of domestic relations was changing in the mid-nineteenth century, married women of all races and classes still largely lacked independent legal recognition as well as control over their own person, property, and wages. Thus, in the eyes of these bureau men, freedmen needed only to assert authority over black wives and command their labor. "There is still a complaint that the freedmen exercise no control over their families," reported Agent Edwin Lyon to his bureau superiors in May 1866. More than a year after war's end, freedmen in his Virginia district were "allowing their children to follow their own inclinations" and, even more disappointing to him, some were "encouraging their wives to idleness." Despite such reports, and rather than intervening directly by arresting the women and apprenticing the children, agents chose a more indirect route for "encouraging" black women in productive family units—that is, those in households with able-bodied black men at the head—to return to work and contract with white employers. They appealed to freedmen, urging *them* to compel their wives and daughters to return to work in southern plantation fields and white households. The agent in Cuthbert, Georgia, for example, suggested—perhaps somewhat naively—that the solution to freedwomen's refusal to work was obvious. Countering complaints about a particularly unruly freedwoman who refused to work and "damned the Bureau"—insisting that "all the Bureau out cant make her work"—this agent went to the "impertinent" woman's husband and ordered him to control his wife. Indeed, the agent made the freedman promise "to work faithfully & to keep his wife in subjection." Bureau records provide no indication as to whether the husband was able to do so. Nonetheless, bureau men readily demanded that freedmen assert their newfound rights as husbands and control their wives and grown daughters by putting them back to work. That is, they attempted to hold freedmen accountable for the actions of female family members while also respecting the authority of black men to maintain and control their families.[40]

While it may have been a "matter of pride" for freedmen to assert authority over their families—and, in doing so, the labor of dependents—not all black women agreed. As Chapter 5 makes clear, the battleground over the meaning of freedom extended well into black households. Black women and men disagreed about how their labors, families, households, and familial relationships would be reconstructed after emancipation. Thus, even convincing black men of the need to put their wives and daughters back to work did not necessarily mean women would return to postwar labor. "[M]any negro women," reported Joseph Thorp, an agent in Arkansas, "have failed to perform their part of the contracts . . . claiming the husband has no powers to control her labor. She being free & responsible as himself." Certainly, this agent concluded, the absence of "harmony" between black workers and white employers in his district was to be blamed on "the negro women [who] have failed to perform their part of contracts." Perhaps what frustrated bureau men like Thorp, among others, most was that despite the growing inclination among freedmen "to put their wives and grown daughters to work," freedwomen were "determined on resisting the authority of their liege lords." Another much disappointed agent in Abbeville Parish, Louisiana, similarly reported that although the freedpeople in his district were "Steady" and "Sober," the freedwomen were "not inclined to be industrious . . . and through idlenss refuse to work the fields with their husbands."[41] In the end, it was not uncommon for agents' reports to resemble that of Agent J. Jordan stationed in Virginia, who insisted:

I have made every effort, embraced every opportunity, to impress upon these people that their wives and children must aid them and will not be suffered to live in indolence. And while my advice and explanations were received in the kindest manner & every assurance given that these evils should be abated, the fact still is evident and demonstrated daily that a very large portion of colored women in this country are by their course of living absolutely clogging the advancement of the colored men.[42]

Freedwomen were expected to work, the bureau demanded, and it was the job of their husbands and fathers to make sure that happened.

Beyond lectures encouraging freedmen to compel their wives and daughters to embrace free labor and enter into wage work, bureau officials countered the perceived withdrawal of freedwomen from the workforce with more concrete steps. Most notably, these officials demanded that contracts be made with heads of households and in a way that embraced the labor of entire families. That is, the bureau called for labor agreements that promoted nuclear families and enjoined the labor of not only husbands and fathers but also wives and children able to work. In labor-starved states, in particular, bureau officials (as well as state legislatures) responded to freedwomen's efforts to restrict their labor force participation, actions that clearly aggravated labor shortages, with policies that bound entire families in yearlong agreements. As early as October 1865, Assistant Commissioner Edgar Gregory in Texas, for instance, flatly ordered that all contracts "be made with Heads of families [and] . . . embrace all the members of the family who are able to work." The following year, the policy was sharpened, ordering that every detail of the agreement must "be *specified* in the contract, and not left to be '*understood*' . . .—whether the women are to work or not, if not, at whose expense are they to be fed and clothed." Clearly, black Texan women were not exempt from working and black men had an obligation as free men to make certain that they continued to labor. Further enforcing notions of an independent black manhood and a dependent black womanhood—and thus denying black women an independent identity with rights—Assistant Commissioner Gregory told freedmen that they, as free men with a right to property and household, "could purchase and own any kind of property that a white man could—his wife, his children, a horse, a cow or lands."[43]

While the Freedmen's Bureau demonstrated great interest in the work habits of married freedwomen who had redirected their labors, it also showed concern with the labor of other unemployed African American women. As demonstrated in Chapter 2, bureau men proved particularly troubled by the agency's call for the application of labor and vagrancy policies—and their harsh sanctions—to former slave women who were "idle from necessity" rather than any choice of their own. While not always charitable, understanding, or fully sympathetic to the needs and concerns of black women who encountered a "weight of circumstances" in emancipation, such officials nonetheless expressed consideration for those they considered worthy. By acknowledging the lack of employment opportunities available to many former slave women, both the words and actions of these officials illustrate that, despite the letter of bureau labor policy, the agency did not hold all freedwomen to the same labor standards as freedmen. In particular, it recognized that freedwomen with children were especially vulnerable in the postwar southern labor market. Economic hardship, large families with small children, and a harsh labor market had combined to create a new kind of bondage for these economically vulnerable black women. As a result, many were forced to accept whatever work was available or turn to charity or the federal government for support. In other words, in parts of the South where jobs were scarce for freedmen, let alone freedwomen, the bureau understood that it simply could not enforce vagrancy policies against all unemployed able-bodied freedwomen.[44]

"Woman-hood in these circumstances is not possible," reported bureau agent Samuel Armstrong at Fortress Monroe, Virginia. For destitute black women were, in his words, "what slavery—what the worst form of it—ignorance has made them—and in such homes as they get here there is no hope for their improvement." "Female labor commands very low wages," Armstrong explained, and in consequence, "[t]heir sphere here is one that presents no cheerful phase. No opportunities of improvements." Indeed, he insisted:

> It would however be unjust to many very worthy widowed women who have large families, who, poorly off as they are here, can do no better elsewhere, who have no assurance of getting employment away from here, have not the means . . . of moving and setting up new homes in other parts, and who are, withal, too weak minded and ignorant to discern and act according to their best interests. This class demand[s] sympathy, firm but tender and patient treatment, and, in the distribution of gratuities should be the most favored; although it is not always easy to discriminate.

Elsewhere too agents similarly insisted that freedwomen with large families found it difficult to find employment. "I will also bring to your notice another class of unfortunates," the agent in Richmond wrote his superiors. "[T]hese are freedwomen whose husbands have either died or deserted, leaving behind them several small children." Continuing, he insisted, "[T]hese poor mothers with their helpless and dependent family of little ones are totaly debarred from obtaining employment because of their encumbrances." In this agent's mind, there could be no question that these women were worthy and deserving of the nation's sympathy. They "eke out a miserable existence, notwithstanding their industry and willingness to work there can be no question raised involving the perseverance or self denial of many of these women." Quite simply, this agent concluded, despite their unemployed status, such women could not be considered vagrants.[45]

In the end, the decision to regard unemployed black women as vagrants often came down to a question of their perceived "worthiness"—that is, their condition, reputation, and character combined. And, to be sure, the bureau did regard some freedwomen as unworthy and vagrant. More often than not, however, these women were neither the married freedwomen who limited their labor force participation nor the black mothers of large families who received government assistance or charity. Rather, they were the women who most openly rejected the obligation to labor or, in the words of the historian Linda Kerber, the obligation "not to be *perceived* as idle and vulnerable to punishment for vagrancy." Moreover, black women who appeared to be of bad character or ill repute were especially at risk for prosecution as vagrants by both the bureau and state authorities. Indeed, in the case of the bureau, freedwomen with degraded and troublesome dispositions or those who practiced the "oldest profession" of prostitution proved likeliest to be considered vagrants.[46]

Like civil officials, the bureau regarded freedwomen who stirred up trouble as vagrants. Having been found guilty of "beating a black man . . . and throwing a quantity of drift-wood which he had gathered into the river, and . . . vagrancy in general terms," Louisiana freedwomen Margaret and Harriet Sharpe, for instance, were fined $5. Indeed, after their encounter with the bureau, the two women "promised to do better and try to find employment." Cecilia, a freedwoman in New Orleans, encountered a much harsher fate at the hands of civil officials. When they arrested the woman for quarreling with another freedwoman, civil authorities sentenced her to three months' "hard labor in the city work house for vagrancy." Although the local bureau official recognized her troublesome behavior, he nonetheless thought this was a particularly callous punishment—especially since, in his words, "she could prove that she had a husband working on a steamboat steady." Yet the agent did little beyond making an appeal for a "fair trial" for the woman. Similarly, Georgia freedwoman Virginia suffered the loss of her children for being "a bad tempered & vagrant woman." Found "loafering around the county," she was picked up "as a vagrant" by the local bureau agent, who then recommended to civil authorities in Clay County that her two daughters be bound out.[47]

The bureau also threatened black women who gave their employers trouble or raucously refused to accept employment with prosecution as vagrants. For instance, a local agent warned Leathy, Jane, and Ester—three freedwomen employed by Charles Gordon near Meridian, Mississippi—that, should they abandon their employer "without due cause" again, they would be jailed as vagrants. More devastating, however, was the case of Harriet King. After several months of giving the local agent in Morgan, Georgia, trouble, she faced reprimands, arrest, and ultimately imprisonment. The sharp-tongued freedwoman, it seems, "would not Contract at all"—choosing to "work a few days here and there"—and went around trying to "persuade other freed people not to work with the old poor Rebs." After it had gotten "so that she could scarcely get any work to do," the agent responded, telling her "if she did not go off and get work that I should take her up for a Vagrant." But King was not easily bullied. Several weeks later, she came by the agent again and he—clearly curious if she had found herself a job—asked where she had gone. Thinking it was none of his business, however, King, "in a Vulgar manner . . . kicking up her heels & dancing . . . her tongue going at a terrible rate," simply proceeded to walk past. Within moments, two young men who witnessed the exchange went after the woman. In the process, much "excitement" ensued, during which she experienced "several blows over the head." Ultimately, the woman "of dispirate character" was carried to jail, where the doctor dressed her wounds and she remained. The consequence of such repugnant actions was manifest. If not jailed like Harriet King, unruly freedwomen were arrested and hired out. "A great number of vagrants and people are around the towns . . . living in an idle and immoral way," reported another official in Georgia. Determined to rid his district of "such men and women," he ordered agents to hire them to "good imployers for good pay as the demand for labor . . . is very great." Insistent that such action would serve "as a Double Benefit," the official maintained it would do the community good both by requiring that "this class of people [be] bound over to honorable lives and by compelling other[s] . . . to go voluntarily to work."[48]

Finally, and most frequently, agents and officials of the bureau considered freedwomen of notoriously bad character and morals as vagrants. The agent in Fort Gaines, Georgia, for instance, was troubled by three particularly unruly black women. For more than a year, he had been plagued by the case of freedwoman Eliza and her two daughters, Mary and Martha. Although he had asked them several times to "get home," the imprudent women were still "loafing upon the Streets of . . . town, and engaged in adultery and Fornication, and corrupting the morrals of the young Freed girls, and also the morrals of the youngsters." Regarded by both himself and the "good citizens" of the town as "a public nuisance—and vagrants," the three women had no permanent home and went about town "clad in old mutilated garments of an indecent order" and "not a shoe to their feet." Almost four months after his first encounter with the women, the bureau agent finally took action beyond scolding. Fed up with these "vagrants," he hired the three women—as well as a freedman who "claimed to be the Husband of Eliza"—to a "responsible and reliable gentleman" in a neighboring county.[49]

Somewhat ironically, the only instances in which agents and officials of the Freedmen's Bureau consistently applied its vagrancy provisions to freedwomen were cases in which former slave women were, in fact, employed and receiving wages for their services. That is, bureau men without fail regarded as vagrants black women who worked as prostitutes. And, to be sure, officials showed little compassion for these women, whom they deemed the worst of vagrants. Indeed, the agent in Houston, Texas, urged the civil authorities to bestow "the severest punishment that the law provides" upon young black women who kept "a disreputable house" in his city. Officials in other states were no less harsh when it came to prostitution. Charged with "keeping a House of Prostitution and Disorderly Conduct" in the freedmen's court in Drummondtown, Virginia, freedwomen Maria Handy, Nancy Bundy, Sally Bundy, Leah Colburn, and Kitty Joins faced prosecution as vagrants in May 1865. "[N]ot being able to satisfy the court that they have any visible means of obtaining a livelihood," all but Kitty Joins were found guilty; fined $3.50 each; and, in default of payment, sent to the city jail. Within the week, Agnes Ann Gunter also appeared before the court for "attempting to entice enlisted men from the camp for the purpose of prostitution." And, similarly, when Gunter could not "give account of herself," the court sentenced her to jail for a week.[50]

Although bureau men stationed across the South shared a general abhorrence of prostitution and vagrancy, punishments for freedwomen whom agents regarded as morally debased varied greatly and could include imprisonment, fines, hard labor, and even exile from the community. Indeed, many women were not fortunate enough to receive sentences like those issued by the court in Drummondtown, Virginia. Found guilty of prostitution and vagrancy, Laura Elliot and Caroline Young, for instance, were ordered to leave the county within five days by the court in Elizabeth City County, Virginia. But faced with the same charges and the same court, Phillis Barber did not fare as well. Having appeared before the court twice before—and already having been expelled from the county—she was sentenced to three months' hard labor for being "a notorious prostitute." Perceived to be similarly troublesome, freedwomen in Savannah, Georgia, faced both ejection from the city and hard labor for such undesirable behavior. Appealing to the bureau in August 1866 for assistance, the mayor of Savannah asked for "cooperation in relieving the community of a nuisance, in the shape of a large number of shameless colored prostitutes, who nightly infect our streets, to the annoyance of all well disposed persons." Continuing, he explained, "These prostitutes are arrested . . . arraigned & fined . . . for lewd behavior & often times committed to the Jail for non payment of the penalty inflicted on them." Acknowledging that the civil authorities' efforts to discipline these women had not been successful, the mayor now asked the bureau to send them "down to the islands" and hire them out as agricultural or domestic laborers. "This course," he insisted, "would effectually put a stop to the evil complaints of & bring about a better state of morals in the colored population of the City." Bureau officials in Savannah agreed, endorsing the mayor's proposal with the conclusion that "these colored prostitutes are daily becoming worse, they insult people in the street & laugh at the punishment inflicted for their offence. The jail is full of them & there is no place here to lock them up. They are a perfect nuisance."[51]

More often, however, bureau agents and courts reprimanded freedwomen convicted of prostitution and vagrancy and sentenced them to time in jail or prison for periods ranging from one week to three months. In Norfolk, Virginia, for example, Harriet Hanberry, Lavinia White, May Williams, and Alma White received sentences of thirty days in jail for "walking the streets." Not as fortunate, Mary Edwards was convicted of "being a prostitute, notorious character and old offender and vagrant" by the freedmen's court in Richmond, Virginia, and sentenced to three months' imprisonment at Castle Thunder prison.[52] Similarly, another bureau court in nearby Fortress Monroe condemned Francis White, Timpy Liggins, and Mary Wilson to three months at the military prison for prostitution and vagrancy after being found, ironically enough, "in an out building of the Military Prison, acting with open and gross lewdness, in the company of enlisted men" and refusing to leave when ordered.[53]

Were freedwomen without employment "not in some sorts vagrants," as one Georgia planter bemoaned to the Freedmen's Bureau in 1866? If the federal agency intended to return former slaves to the workforce, regardless of gender, why were freedwomen who chose to redirect their labor force participation not held accountable to its policies that demanded they enter contracts, return to work, or face prosecution as vagrants? In confronting this question, agents of the bureau proved powerfully influenced by their own assumptions about gender and gender difference. For these officials, the decision to treat unemployed able-bodied freedwomen as vagrants hinged upon understandings of worthiness. In the end, officials evaluated a freedwoman's condition, reputation, and character when deciding whether she was a vagrant. And, if the federal agency protected any former slaves from prosecution as vagrants, it shielded only "worthy" freedwomen and looked upon "unworthy" freedwomen—like unemployed freedmen—as vagrants whom it would not tolerate. Thus, at times, black women who could not find work as well as those who restricted their labor force participation used their gender to shield themselves from the harsh postwar labor market.

In the end, a set of complex realties faced bureau officials as they sought both to enforce the federal agency's labor policies and to adjudicate labor disputes between white employers and freedwomen. In doing so, the bureau clearly supported the cause of free labor that viewed the contract as the governing model for all social relations, including both labor and domestic relations. The bureau did not necessarily see itself as representing in these cases the interests of either white planters versus freedwomen or even freedwomen versus freedmen. Rather, and as the historians Eric Foner and Peter Bardaglio have pointed out more generally, bureau officials sought to represent the interests of free labor. These interests might overlap at times with those of southern white planters, and at other times with those of freedwomen and freedmen, but they always remained independent. Thus steps that might look contradictory within a dualistic framework of former masters and former slaves produced fairly consistent outcomes when viewed as a response to a separate set of forces outside a southern Reconstruction-era context.

From this perspective, the agency's refusal to treat "worthy" freedwomen—particularly the wives and daughters of African American men who had embraced emancipation by taking on the responsibilities of employment and family—as vagrants worked to uphold the contractual terms of marital and familial relations. Compelling such freedwomen into the workforce would have interfered with, indeed directly challenged, freedmen's authority over their own families. Doing so also threatened to destroy the very sense of manly independence and responsibility that bureau officials hoped to foster among African American men as free men and emergent citizens. Thus, rather than prosecuting as vagrants married yet "worthy" freedwomen who chose to redirect their labor force participation, bureau officials attempted to combat their actions by circumventing the women altogether. African American men's changing status from slave to independent citizen informed such actions. The federal agency resisted married women's efforts by going straight to African American men. Officials lectured freedmen about getting their wives and daughters to return to the workforce or, in some instances, demanded that contracts be made with heads of households to embrace the labor of entire families. In the end, the bureau acted to uphold the rights of freedmen as well as the ideal of the marital contract.

As for other unemployed freedwomen, agents of the Freedmen's Bureau found themselves perplexed over what to do. Prosecuting other "worthy" freedwomen—including those "idle from necessity" rather than choice—as vagrants simply defied the realities of the labor market in many parts of the postwar South. Bureau policy demanded that agents deny federal relief to unemployed able-bodied freedpeople, for emancipation had not ended anyone's obligation to labor. But when circumstances made it difficult for needy yet "worthy" freedwomen to find work, the bureau was much more likely to consider them dependents than vagrants. Like other women in the nineteenth-century United States, then, African American women in the immediate aftermath of the Civil War had become part of an intimate patriarchy. No longer dependents of a master, they now became dependents of their husbands or fathers. And, in the many instances when no able-bodied male was present in their lives, freedwomen encountered a Freedmen's Bureau prepared, albeit at times reluctantly so, to assume this patriarchal role for the federal government.

Historians have long debated the degree to which black women withdrew from the workforce in the Reconstruction-era South.[54] To a certain extent, however, there can be little doubt that freedwomen remained active participants in the southern workforce. Even Agent De Forest in South Carolina, who complained about the "evil of female loaferism," was careful to qualify his reports about freedwomen, noting that he "did not mean that all women were idle; the larger proportion were still laboring afield, as of old." Postwar realities—or "rigid necessity," as De Forest put it—"held them to it."[55] Quite simply, few African American men had the means to support both themselves and their families without the contribution—whether full time, part time, or seasonal—of wives' and other female family members' labor. Moreover, the many freedwomen who were not part of productive family units headed by male family members could never have considered rejecting work in the fields and white households of the South without severe consequence. Thus, despite the seeming barrage of complaints by whites insisting otherwise, former slave women continued to work in the immediate aftermath of emancipation. Lizzie, a Mississippi freedwoman, readily described this reality: "I used to think if I could be free I should be the happiest of anybody in the world. But when my master come to me, and says—Lizzie, you is free! it seems like I was in a kind of daze. And when I would wake up in the morning I would think to myself, Is I free? Hasn't I got to get up before daylight and go into the field to work?"[56] Freedom had ended neither the obligation nor the need for black women to work. And freedwomen understood this. Wherever they lived and whatever their circumstances, virtually all black women labored in the postemancipation South. Survival, as well as white southerners and federal officials, demanded it.

And so freedwomen seeking support from the bureau as free laborers discovered in it a supportive agency dedicated to the ideals of free labor and contract. Understanding that they now were free "to work and live for themselves," and often having no other choice because their very survival depended on it, African American women undertook the struggle to define and defend freedom in the workplace.[57] Freedwomen challenged the traditional patterns of employment power relations by tenaciously endeavoring to protect their freedom in the fields and households of the South. In doing so, they labored differently and with the guiding principle that free labor should not resemble slavery in any way. When conflict arose, as it inevitably did, freedwomen as well as their white employers turned to the Freedmen's Bureau for assistance. When freedwomen refused to work or acted in defiance of the terms of a labor agreement, the bureau counseled, reprimanded, and warned them to do better as free laborers. Likewise, recalcitrant planters who acted arbitrarily in their relations with black laborers made it necessary for the bureau to step in. Although in each instance the Freedmen's Bureau came down on different sides of the issue, it acted consistently to uphold the interests of free labor and the ideal of the contract.

To the extent that both freedwomen and men remained at work, emancipation failed to bring about radical change in the lives and labors of African Americans. Freedwomen recognized the mockery of free labor that developed in the postwar South. They understood that their obligation to work had not ended. They also understood that their freedom to "choose" free labor was restricted by necessity as well as the reality that if they did not choose it, work could be chosen for them. Most would have agreed with the Mississippi freedwoman who bitterly asked, "Is I free? Hasn't I got to get up before daylight and go into the field to work?" But bureau men acknowledged that achieving a southern society that accepted, supported, and valued free labor would take time—though ultimately more time than this temporary, understaffed, and poorly equipped federal agency had. Whatever the hopes and expectations of bureau men and white southerners for free labor, it was clear that freedwomen and men had their own. The many defiant words and actions of freedwomen—indeed, the very act of making an employment complaint in bureau offices in and of itself—demonstrated their determination to define and defend free labor on their own terms. The wife of freedman Daniel Bell certainly made it clear how she thought emancipation and free labor had changed her status when asserting to the bureau that "[M]y wages were my own" and "My husband had nothing to do with them." With such words and actions, freedwomen sought to claim the rights and privileges they believed were their due as free women and free laborers.[58]

African American women would show extraordinary strength too as they fought to reconstruct families and to assert a right to their children in the days that followed emancipation. Thus just as they insisted that freedom was incomplete if they did not have the ability to control their own lives and labors, in their own time as they saw fit, black mothers demanded the same for the reconstruction of their family lives. Claiming a right to children taken by slavery and war as well as by apprenticeship laws and even black fathers in the immediate days of emancipation would be a formidable task. And again it would be a fight in which the Freedmen's Bureau was both freedwomen's ally and adversary.

4

"to put forth almost superhuman efforts to regain their children"

Freedwomen, Parental Rights, and the Freedmen's Bureau

Families, torn asunder by the various forms of violence which had become an essential part of slavery, came with tears and sighs for reunion. Now and then an old master, still holding to the idea of chattels, resisted. Husbands and wives, fathers and mothers, sons and daughters, brothers and sisters, limited by no shade of color or grade of intelligence, sought each other with an ardor and faithfulness sufficient to vindicate the fidelity and affection of any race—the excited joys of the regathering being equalled only by the previous sorrows and pains of separation.

Mothers, once fully assured that the power of slavery was gone, were known to put forth almost superhuman efforts to regain their children," continued Brevet Brigadier General John Eaton, assistant commissioner for the District of Columbia, in his report to the commissioner of the Freedmen's Bureau in December 1865. Much impressed, he described their efforts in the first days of freedom as truly remarkable. Indeed, he explained, they were "travelling any distance, daring any perils, and even beating the pugnacious specimens of Christian chivalry in hand-to-hand conflict, and bearing off in triumph the long-sought child."[1]

Now free, however, African American mothers in Washington, D.C., found themselves in a troublesome situation, at least according to this bureau official. Having escaped the "tortures and terrors" of slavery, many had gathered in his "city of refuge" in pursuit of "safety from their bitter foes." In doing so, they now found themselves alone. For, as Eaton explained, they often "had no adult male support." Rather, their men, having "been run off by the enemy," still serving in the military, or having been lost to slavery or the war, were nowhere to be found. Moreover, the question of male support aside, Assistant Commissioner Eaton was concerned about these mothers' abilities to assume their parental rights and obligations. "Wisdom" was clearly necessary as the bureau aided freedwomen, he explained. For "sometimes," Eaton cautioned, "the mother was not sufficiently emancipated from the brutal ideas of her bondage to understand the duties of a Christian parent."[2]

With emancipation, former slave women and men demanded that freedom grant, above all else, the opportunity to reclaim families torn asunder by slavery and war. Emancipation and the legal recognition of the African American family that it conferred had granted, at least in theory, black parents the right to claim and control their own progeny. And, as historians have demonstrated, for freedwomen especially, freedom was foremost familial. They focused first on reclaiming children and placed the highest priority on the right to marry, procreate, and nurture their families without white interference. Doing so would not be easy. In some ways, black parents found that maintaining the integrity of their families in emancipation could be as difficult as it had been in slavery. With freedom in hand, African Americans—like the freedwomen in Washington, D.C., about whom Assistant Commissioner Eaton wrote—soon discovered that they may have acquired the obligations of freedom, but the rights commensurate to their new status were harder to come by. Emancipation had readily granted black parents the responsibilities of supporting their children in the postwar South. But the privileges that came with parenthood—that is, the right to custody and control of children—were far more difficult to secure. Perhaps the most serious threat to black families and African American parental authority in the immediate postemancipation era was the apprenticeship system. Yet black mothers also faced custody battles with freedmen who sought to assert their rights as free and independent men by claiming control over the lives and labors of their families.[3]

The battle for custody and control of black children exposed the great lengths to which freedpeople would go to reconstruct their households in the aftermath of slavery. "Our homes are invaded and our little ones seized at the family fireside," black Marylanders proclaimed as they fought the practice of apprenticeship in the first days of freedom. And both black mothers and fathers encountered formidable obstacles—including bureau officials who endorsed the use of apprenticeship for poor freedchildren—as they endeavored to defend family autonomy as free women and men. But the experiences of former slave mothers differed considerably from those of black fathers as they battled a variety of forces—white planters and farmers, southern laws, each other, and even the Freedmen's Bureau—for the freedom to reunite and protect families, as well as the right to control their labor. Perhaps no complaint brought before the Freedmen's Bureau more clearly revealed how Reconstruction had disrupted the old notion of what politics was and who could participate in it than those involving disputes over freedchildren. In resisting male—both white and black—authority over their children, freedwomen who asserted an unrestricted right to their children made clear their intention to participate in the ongoing debate over the meaning of freedom, family, and free labor. How could they be free, they asked, if their children could be ripped from their arms as easily as they had been in slavery? How could their children be seized without their consent? And, in an era when children supplied essential labor to families, how could they maintain their households without the labor of their children? Custody disputes between African American parents over freedchildren, as well as clashes with white southerners and bureau agents over apprenticeship, revealed the many complexities regarding the legal status, guardianship, and control of black children. And, certainly, the struggle for control of freedchildren's labor figured prominently in these disputes.[4]

Clashes over freedchildren also demonstrated the willingness of the Freedmen's Bureau to intervene in African Americans' lives in an effort to defend free labor and, with that, to prevent black parents from being "deprived of the services of their children."[5] Thus agents' adherence to free labor ideology certainly shaped how they responded to apprenticeship. But here too it was not just about free labor to bureau officials overseeing the transition from slavery to freedom for former slave children. Conflicts over custody and labor also revealed bureau policy makers' preconceived notions of black and female dependence, as well as the agency's intent to promote among black families a family structure in which male heads of household enjoyed control over wives and children. These federal officials thus understood that custody disputes involving freedchildren went well beyond issues of dependency, familial support, and labor control. Such confrontations also brought together African Americans' intense desire to exercise control of their families and their labor with their determination to secure social, legal, and economic independence. And freedwomen, as they fought with seemingly superhuman strength, discovered that while the bureau could at times be an ally in the battle for their children, even this friend was unwilling to come to the aid of poor mothers and mothers who laid claim to children as autonomous individuals rather than as dependent women. Thus, in the case of freedwomen's assertions of parental rights, either against labor-hungry white southerners or rights-driven black fathers, the recognition of their gender by the Freedmen's Bureau again worked both for and against them.

In the immediacy of emancipation, the status and custody of black children was a social and legal quandary. Who was responsible for the hundreds of thousands of minor African Americans now free whose parents, because of the disruptions caused by slavery and war, could not provide "acceptable," "stable," "legitimate" households to support them or, worse, were not physically present to do so? What was more, who now controlled the labor of freedchildren? To be sure, custody disputes were commonplace as African American communities reconstructed families, and the extra few dollars earned by a child could make the difference between solvency and deprivation for black families. But the real threat to black parents in the days following emancipation came from labor-starved white planters and farmers who resurrected the apprenticeship system as both a method to secure labor and an instrument of racial control. By way of the courts, and some bureau offices, as pointed out in Chapter 2, white southerners used apprenticeship to become the legal guardians of minor black "children"—many of whom were young men and women well beyond childhood—and, in doing so, procured their labor until they reached adulthood. This system, also known as binding out or indenturing, was not new, but as white southerners reshaped the practice in the immediate postwar South, it brought to the surface their powerful determination to reassert control over African Americans' lives and labors. White southerners exploited apprenticeship to wield extraordinary authority over their former slaves' families and households. Thus freedparents' struggles to achieve family autonomy remained constrained by white southerners decidedly committed to reasserting control over black labor and restoring slavery in all but name.[6]

Looming large over black parents' efforts to claim control of their offspring and defend family autonomy were new apprenticeship statutes that granted local magistrates the power to disrupt the African American family by seizing control of and binding out black children. In the months following the war's end, southern legislatures responded to defeat and the loss of slave labor by enacting the black codes, which included such laws.[7] Antebellum racial anxieties had resulted already in judges having greater discretion to bind out black children and black apprentices benefiting from fewer protections than their white counterparts. So too had antebellum laws long since sanctioned gender-biased provisions that permitted courts to apprentice the children of single mothers, black or white, and even some widowed women. And the apprenticeship laws and practices that emerged during Reconstruction differed little in these two respects. Perhaps the most evident way in which the postwar southern laws differed from antebellum apprenticeship statutes was that most directed employers to teach black children not only a skill of some kind but also to read and write; most also ultimately came to eliminate racial distinctions in their various provisions (this would be especially true after passage of the Civil Rights Act of 1866). In practice, however, provision of a "reasonable" education and the application of these laws without regard to race were highly capricious at best in the Reconstruction South. These new legal codes, according to a bureau inspector in Texas, had given the freedpeople "about the same protection a wolf does a lamb."[8]

The postwar laws and practices governing apprenticeship reflected southern whites' apprehensions about free labor, their worries about the scarcity of labor, and their continued adherence to a belief in the innate dependency and inferiority of African Americans. These laws, answering whites' need for laborers, for instance, authorized the indenture of African American boys—or, more appropriately, young men—until the age of twenty-one, and girls—in fact, young women—until the age of eighteen or marriage. Moreover, most, like the Alabama and Mississippi laws, granted "preference" to former owners in the binding out of African American children. Beyond these provisions, the reshaped laws presented civil authorities ample latitude and significant loopholes that took advantage of the broken nature of former slave families. The laws that emerged in the days following war's end generally called for the binding out of children whose parents could not provide for them adequately—and unsurprisingly the courts, rather than parents, gauged this capacity. They also went well beyond considerations of familial economics. North Carolina judges, for instance, could bind out children whose parents did "not habitually employ their time in some honest, industrious occupation." The South Carolina law similarly sanctioned the apprenticeship of children "whose parents are not teaching them habits of industry and honesty" or "are persons of notoriously bad character, or vagrants." But officials in Maryland enjoyed perhaps the greatest discretion in apprenticing black children. There, the child of "any free negro" could be summoned and bound out whenever the orphans' court, "upon examination," determined that "it would be better for the habits and comfort of such child . . . [for him or her to] be bound as an apprentice to some white person." The postwar laws, although frequently requiring parental consent, thus offered black parents little hope in challenging the binding out of their children. The Georgia statute, for instance, allowed civil authorities to disregard the issue of parental consent altogether when binding out any child who was poor, orphaned, or left by parents who "reside out of the county." More troubling for freedwomen was North Carolina's law. In that state, the law permitted judges to apprentice any children "whose father[s] . . . deserted their families."[9]

White southerners wasted little time putting their renewed apprenticeship statutes to use. Within days of emancipation, planters and farmers across the South legally seized the labor of black children. Georgia planter William Henry Stiles was but one who recognized the rewards of the practice. Black youngsters, he informed his wife in 1865 as he sought out several apprenticeship agreements, "would be exceedingly useful" on their farm because "they would not have the run-away & fortune-making nature of the men." He planned to "try & get the best of the [former slaves'] children bound to me—such I mean as are now or will shortly be able to work." By convincing courts to bind their former slaves' children to them as apprentices, white southerners gained an abundant, ready—or near-ready—and extended supply of involuntary labor. While impossible to quantify accurately, thousands of apprenticeships were reported by southern courts, the United States Army, and the Freedmen's Bureau between 1864 and 1868. Marylanders, for instance, were quick to note the staggering number of freedchildren bound out. Reporting just days after slavery officially ended in his state in late 1864, a lighthouse keeper recounted the "upwards of hundred young Neagroes on the ferry with there old Masters draged away . . . from there parents for the purpose of Haveing them Bound." In the following weeks, whites seized custody of almost one thousand freedchildren in two Maryland counties alone. And apprenticeship in these two counties continued to flourish. By the fall of 1866, the local bureau agent there reported that an additional 1,200 "unjust" indentures had been made. Officials elsewhere in Maryland made similar reports. In the eastern shore counties, they reported the seizure of some 1,600 black children in the first days of freedom. By late 1867, an official in the state's capital continued to report a deluge of apprenticeship complaints. Over a period of twelve months, he had witnessed some 2,000 complaints made by anxious African American parents and relatives. African American children elsewhere in the South experienced a similar fate at the hands of their former masters. Stationed at Forsyth, Georgia, Edwin Belcher, one of only a few northern bureau agents with African blood serving in the federal agency, reported that in Monroe County alone local civil authorities had apprenticed one-third of the freedchildren residing there. By taking advantage of black mothers—who, "being ignorant," according to this bureau official and later Republican politician, were "easily duped"—and driving off black fathers, white planters in Georgia had so successfully abused the state's apprenticeship law that the bureau there concluded that black youngsters had been "already brought back into Slavery" in the spring of 1867.[10]

Former slave women in the immediate postemancipation South found themselves especially vulnerable to the denial of parental rights as a result of reconstructed apprenticeship laws. Although the postwar laws forced both freedmen and freedwomen to endure bewildering losses as parents, they proved particularly detrimental to black mothers, who now as freedwomen faced relentless poverty and poor job prospects and were forced to face head-on the harsh legacies of slavery as they struggled to reclaim children. Not legally married when their children were born, they found themselves the mothers of "illegitimate" children. Having borne children fathered by more than one man or by white men, they found themselves the mothers of "bastard" children. Sold away from, abandoned by, or temporarily separated from the fathers of their children, they found themselves the mothers of "fatherless" children. Now liberated with little more than their freedom and lacking the most basic necessities of life, they found themselves the mothers of destitute and "vagrant" children. And often "encumbered" by several young children and unable to secure employment, they found themselves labeled "unproductives" or women of "notoriously bad character." The cruel effects of slavery and the great deficiencies of emancipation had provided, in many ways, a fertile foundation for postwar apprenticeship laws and practices.[11]

Without doubt, black mothers who attempted to retain custody of their children without the support of husbands or fathers encountered formidable obstacles. The wives of absent black Union soldiers suffered the loss of children to apprenticeship in remarkably significant numbers in the first days of freedom. This proved particularly true in Maryland, where, as the historian Richard Fuke has demonstrated, the absence of black men in the tidewater region of the state "manifested itself starkly in orphans' court records." With close to 3,000 black men enlisting in the Union army between 1863 and 1864 from this area, black women faced supporting and defending their families alone. At the same time, local magistrates seized the opportunity to put the state's apprenticeship laws to work. The consequences were soon readily apparent. In just one week the Talbot County "Negro Docket," for example, recorded 221 children as appearing before the orphans' court. In doing so, however, it listed only 66 of the black children as "orphans" or children whose parents were "absent." The remaining 124 had appeared before the court with their mothers in tow, although most to no avail. The records of the Kent County justices of the peace reveal similar results. Of the 130 children bound by the justices, the "remarks" listed only 21 children who had "no parents." The remaining 110 included 21 children bound "without consent of their parents," 3 whose parents were "present and objected," 9 whose fathers were "present and objected," and 68 whose mothers were "present and objected." The words of freedwoman Charlotte Hall rang true for many black soldiers' wives: "I think it is hard that my companion should be away from me in his country service and I at the same time deprived of my only child, contrary to the free laws and institutions for which he is fighting."[12]

Black mothers of "orphan"—meaning, in reality, "fatherless," "illegitimate," or "bastard"—children also endured the frequent wrath of labor-hungry white southerners in the postwar South. Indeed, the term "orphan" proved particularly injurious to freedwomen's parental rights following emancipation as civil and military officials—including some bureau officials—construed it to mean a fatherless child and used it as a pretext for apprenticeship. Facing the challenge of a black mother to two of the indentures he held, a Virginia planter provided a fairly standard defense for white southerners' custodial rights. The two children bound to him, the planter explained to the bureau agent in Danville, were "both illegitimate children, neither of them having any recognized father." And southern courts readily sustained this planter's understanding of the postwar status of freedchildren. According to a bureau official in Texas in late 1865, the courts in his state had ruled that any "*fatherless* child" was an orphan. Mississippi courts had taken similar steps. By ruling that the word "orphan" signified a fatherless child, southern courts ensured that the wholesale indenturing of black children would continue even as freedmothers objected and sought to demonstrate their own ability to support and care for their children.[13]

White southerners and the courts were not alone in accepting this detrimental understanding of "orphan." Even federal officials turned to it in a way that often denied freedwomen parental rights. Alarmed by one of his agent's reports listing the indentures of nineteen "colored orphan children" in the summer of 1866, a bureau superintendent in North Carolina felt compelled to investigate. Replying to the shocking report, he asked: "How is it that there are so many (Colored) orphan children in Northampton County? Have the parents been swept away by Plague or by the ravages of War?" Clearly doubtful of the legality of the apprenticeship agreements, the superintendent cautioned in his response that great care had to be taken to ensure "that *none* except orphans, or children whose parents give consent, be bound out as apprentices." In response to this superior officer's inquiry, the local agent finally revealed that he had defined "orphan" as a fatherless or motherless child. Defending his actions, the local agent disdainfully noted: "Nearly all these children were bastards and in many instances the father is dead and in the others no person knows whether he is dead or alive." Black mothers who lacked support from male family members, particularly fathers of their children or husbands, faced formidable odds as they worked to reconstruct their families in freedom.[14]

Freedwomen's ability—or perhaps more appropriately, inability—to support children proved most dangerous to their assertion of parental rights. Whether single, married, widowed, or abandoned, poverty-stricken mothers were susceptible to the cruel injustices of apprenticeship. In an act long consistent with national poor-relief practices, courts across the South bound out poor freedchildren with little or no regard to the wishes of their parents. Thomas Tredway, a wealthy planter and former Virginia legislator, was but one who recognized the opportunity offered by the harsh situation faced by impoverished single mothers. Indeed, in the days following war's end, he hoped to seize the labor of at least four children born to his former slaves—all single mothers who had remained on his plantation. This Virginian believed that apprenticeship held the most "promise" for poor mothers with large families of children who lacked male support. And often it seemed there was little that freedwomen could do to stop southern whites like Tredway from taking their children. Georgia freedwoman Rebecca Parsons found out as much. Upon discovering that she was free, the freedmother notified her former master of her intention to take her children and go "to her kindred." But much to her dismay, Parsons was met with his prompt reply that "she might go but her children belonged to Him." Unwilling to leave her children, she, like so many other freedwomen, stayed. However, Parsons was soon "turned off" and had to contend with the legal indenture of her children to her former master. Having been told that she could not have her children back "unless she paid Him four thousand dollars," the freedmother eventually turned to the Freedmen's Bureau for help. They may have been free, but black mothers occupied an ambiguous position in postwar southern society. They were freedpersons, yet they were still regarded as dependents who could not sustain their families in legitimate households of their own. And even as southern whites ignored the issue of black parental rights altogether, the irony of the situation could not be missed. "These youths," criticized a contemporary Baltimore newspaper, "were able and eager to help support their younger brothers and sisters, and aged parents," yet "were ruthlessly taken from them."[15] Marylander William Taylor confirmed the mockery inherent in southern apprenticeship practices when he told Congress in 1867: "The children who were able to support their families were the very ones they took away."[16]

As agents of the Freedmen's Bureau made their way across the South as the federal agency took shape in the summer and fall of 1865, they quickly discovered that white southerners had begun to resolve for themselves the social and legal questions posed by freedchildren in the wake of emancipation. And settling complaints involving the custody and control of black children soon became an everyday chore for agents. "Almost daily applications are made to me by parents or relatives for minor children who are held by some of the planters or by other freedmen," the agent in Baton Rouge, Louisiana, would report as late as 1867. But it was not just former slaves who made complaints to the bureau over freedchildren. Given widespread fears about free labor and the loss of workers among white southerners, agents also fielded queries from whites trying to claim control of black youngsters' labor. "As a necessary result of the scarcity of labor," the local bureau agent in Sampson County, North Carolina, informed the state assistant commissioner in the spring of 1866, "quarrels are arising between whites—the new masters by Indenture and late employers who were paying many of these minors good wages." Making sense of these complaints was no easy task. For even as bureau officials rejected the worst abuses by white southerners who sought to use apprenticeship as a system of racial control, they nonetheless saw the practice as a "temporary expedient" in their own agency's efforts to transform the South.[17]

From the start, agents and officials of the federal agency expressed disgust at abuses of the practice of apprenticeship and offered criticism of its resemblance to slavery, defiance of the principles of free labor that they espoused, and inhumane disregard for black family bonds. Admitting that the practice was widespread in North Carolina, the assistant commissioner there in 1865 and 1866, Eliphalet Whittlesey, for instance, vigorously voiced concerns about apprenticeship from his first days in office. One of the more radical of the bureau officials appointed to leadership positions in 1865, Whittlesey lamented to his friend and superior officer, Commissioner Howard, in early 1866: "The practice of binding out children is dangerous inasmuch as it fosters the old ideas of compulsory labor and dependence." An agent in Florida similarly objected to apprenticeship, noting that it "made no obligations which will benefit the children." Rather, he perceptively observed, it made freedchildren "the same as slaves till they become of age." Expressing his opposition to "this system of slavery," a Mississippi agent likewise declared disdainfully: "I am not aware of any minor[s] apprenticed . . . who are not able to support themselves—and I have yet to see the first one thus apprenticed who had . . . [learned the] ABC[s]."[18]

One of the most common complaints about apprenticeship from these federal officials centered on southern whites' resistance to the bureau's free labor plans. "A good many of these children are old enough to hire for good wages and can get plenty of labor," a provost marshal in Maryland protested in the first days of emancipation. The denial of black children's right to free labor especially troubled bureau officials. Above all else, Assistant Commissioner Whittlesey instructed agents in his state, they should object to indentures of older children "capable of self support." Insistent that older orphaned children were "capable . . . of supporting themselves as hired laborers" or, "if not orphans," these children who were not yet adults could "assist in the support of their parents," these federal officials flatly condemned apprenticeship abuses for infringing upon former slave children's right to their own labor.[19]

Going perhaps the furthest in his critique of apprenticeship was John C. Robinson, one of three consecutive military men appointed to the post of assistant commissioner in North Carolina following Whittlesey, who condemned the practice for the dangers it posed to black domestic relations. Perhaps a bit idealistic as he assumed his post in mid-1866, the confident assistant commissioner committed the agency to destroying the practice in his jurisdiction, declaring: "The worst feature of slavery was the forcible separation of families, and by Gods help I will prevent its reestablishment within the limits of my command." The danger of apprenticeship was manifest. It aimed, in the words of the bureau agent at Liberty, Texas, A. H. Mayer, "to enslave the rising generation" of African Americans and promised a "worse condition of slavery than they have ever seen." If left untouched, bureau policy makers agreed, southern apprenticeship stood poised to restore "an intolerable oppression and revive African slavery under another name and with increased horrors." Such "an instrument of oppression" and "crying evil," they vowed, demanded the utmost scrutiny.[20]

At the same time they offered condemnation, however, bureau men were not unfamiliar with the practice of apprenticeship and, in many instances, ultimately agreed with white southerners' rationale for its use. Assertions that the practice was, as one Maryland newspaper had justified it in 1864, "prompted by feelings of humanity towards these unfortunate young ones" moved some. More likely, however, defenses of the system like that of the Texas judge who argued that it granted "justice to these children" by placing them in "good comfortable homes" where they would "receive some education" appealed to the more pragmatic side of agents trying to restore order to the disordered postwar South. But such excuses for apprenticeship went beyond expressions of compassion to reveal whites' preconceived notions about African American parents, and bureau men were not immune to such beliefs. For just as John Eaton, the bureau assistant commissioner in Washington, D.C., had questioned whether the black mother had been "sufficiently emancipated from the brutal ideas of her bondage to understand the duties of a Christian parent," many nineteenth-century whites—northern as well as southern—expressed grave misgivings about former slaves' parenting abilities.[21] And reports such as that in the *New York Times* in February 1866 reinforced these doubts, informing readers:

> In the matter of rearing their children is where the true issue and true danger lies. . . . They [the freedpeople] have not themselves sufficient weight of character to enforce that *steady* moral discipline so necessary to the growth of good habits and principles of life. Still, if these children get habits of *labor* simply, it is a great point gained, and the rest will come by slow degrees.[22]

Certainly, more racially conservative bureau officials such as Texas assistant commissioner Joseph Kiddoo readily agreed. To this injured brevet major general of the Union army who had been appointed to his post in the spring of 1866 as part of President Andrew Johnson's efforts to reshape the bureau, the freedpeople were "as a class, perfect children, intellectually" and thus needed "to be taught the simplest lessons of practical life."[23]

Even more racially progressive bureau men—indeed, its most voracious critics of apprenticeship abuses like Assistant Commissioner Whittlesey in North Carolina—expressed paternalistic views of their responsibility to freedpeople. They, possessing many of the racial attitudes of their time, believed that slavery had deprived its victims of the ability to step independently into lives as free men and women. Former slaves, these bureau officials thus insisted, required careful guidance to be capable of assuming their newfound rights and responsibilities—including those that came with parenthood. Accordingly, even the most devoted friends of the freedmen among bureau men revealed significant ideological constraints as they defended former slave parents' rights to their children. Whittlesey, for example (like other more progressive bureau men who initially constituted the agency's leadership at the state levels, such as Rufus Saxton in Georgia and Clinton B. Fisk in Kentucky and Tennessee), approached his post with the belief that only through "proper instruction" and hard work could African Americans successfully assume familial responsibilities as free men and women. Assistant Commissioner Fisk offered exactly this sort of paternalistic instruction to freedmen in his jurisdiction when he warned: "Your children will not run to meet you, dance before you, and climb upon your knees, and call you 'papa,' if you make beggars of them."[24]

Surely instructions offering "a few hints" to black parents by telling them that they were now "charged with the care, government, and education of their own children" and that "*Children must be taught to work*" had to seem ludicrous to former slaves who had labored their entire lives and so desperately longed for the opportunity to care for their children without white interference. But there was another side to such benevolent, although clearly intrusive, notions espoused by bureau policy makers. While their instructions can be read easily as paternalistic, the convictions behind them, as the work of the historian Paul Cimbala has made clear, "prompted officers and agents to take seriously their role as guardians" and to work on the behalf of African Americans. This was certainly the case for Assistant Commissioner Saxton. The "guardianship of these defenceless ones," this career officer and former leader of the army's Port Royal free labor experiment in South Carolina would tell agents in his state about freedchildren, was "a sacred trust." It was in the role of guardian and protector that bureau men of all ideological stripes made it a matter of policy to protect freedchildren and black parents who sought to reclaim families torn apart by slavery, by war, and increasingly by apprenticeship.[25]

All the while expressing repulsion at southern apprenticeship's infringement upon their notions of free labor and domesticity, these Reconstruction-era policy makers considered the practice an unavoidable evil in the immediacy of emancipation and adopted guidelines to regulate its use. With these policies, the bureau acknowledged black parents as the natural and, finally, legal guardians of their children and "instructed" them in their obligations as such. "Parents should be advised that they are responsible for their children . . . and must labor for their support," assistant commissioners told agents across the South. But for black children whose parents were absent or incapable of supporting them for whatever reason, bureau policies designated local agents as guardians of freedchildren and approved of efforts to bind them out.[26] With its apprenticeship polices, the bureau clearly specified the children for whom indentures should be considered (minor children without guardians and children whose parents consented), the indenture terms (reasonable services in exchange for "comfortable clothing, board, medical treatment . . . schooling, and permission to attend church on each Sabbath"), and the length of indentures (until age twenty-one for males and age eighteen for females).[27] Bureau policies also warned agents to exercise caution when selecting individuals to whom to bind former slave children and flatly prohibited their indenture to "unkind" and "unfaithful" persons. "Children will not be bound to persons who were unjust and cruel to slaves formerly owned by them" or to those "who have been guilty of such acts to the freedmen since their emancipation," asserted bureau policies in Georgia, for instance.[28] Bureau policies also directed agents to recognize and support state laws governing apprenticeship if they made "no distinction of color." If racial discrimination existed, bureau policy instructed agents to apply state laws regulating the indenture of white children to freedchildren. If colorblind apprenticeship laws existed, however, these federal policies ultimately directed that black parents' complaints be turned over to southern courts and civil authorities for resolution.[29] In the end, bureau policies encouraged agents to respect the African American family and protect black children. Commissioner Howard told agents in May 1865 to "carefully guard" the "unity of families and all the rights of the family relation" and, in doing so, entrusted to them the weighty responsibility of looking out for "the best interests of the child" as they considered complaints over the labor and custody of freedchildren.[30]

While bureau policies established these broad guidelines governing the fate of former slave children, they also left much room for interpretation by those charged with implementing them at the state and local levels. What resulted was a system in which most bureau men came to embrace apprenticeship's use to varying degrees, particularly, as seen in Chapter 2, in cases when parents'—especially single mothers'—abilities to provide for their families were uncertain. The bureau in South Carolina, for instance, readily endorsed policies that used apprenticeship to "relieve" destitute parents, particularly unmarried mothers, of the financial "burden" of supporting children. Officials there even went so far as to require black parents seeking custody of children to demonstrate an ability to provide for them without the assistance of the government before the bureau would consider their appeal.[31] In Lynchburg, Virginia, bureau agents similarly welcomed policies that ordered them "to bind out the child" in "any case where the parents receive government support."[32] Zeroing in on poor mothers specifically, the bureau in Texas informed agents there that women who "have so many children they cannot support them all" should "permit" the bureau to bind them to "good" men who would "bring them up properly."[33] The bureau in Georgia likewise told agents: "If a woman has more children than she can support, they can be bound out with her consent. . . . If she becomes a pauper, then the children can be bound out with the consent of the Agent of the Bureau."[34] Thus while bureau officials expressed concern about the worst abuses of the system of apprenticeship, these same officials welcomed the practice as an appropriate remedy to the many deficiencies of freedom that freedwomen faced. Promoting the binding out of poor freedchildren with "proper safeguards," such as parental consent and the assurance that state apprenticeship laws applied equally to the children of both black and white women, bureau policies in the end instructed agents to advise, counsel, urge, and at times force impoverished black mothers to apprentice their children.[35]

"My object is to get good homes for these children," an agent in Virginia thus explained in a rather typical bureau response to complaints over freedchildren. "The question is," he reasoned, "in the present state of affairs, and considering the conditions of the col[ore]d people, are they . . . ready to undertake these obligations" of parenthood. While this agent may have been more sympathetic than others—for at least he conceded that "[w]ealth, power or influence does not make a good home always"—local bureau agents across the South investigated this fundamental question as they considered custody disputes brought before them. And, at the end of the day, for black parents prepared to assume the rights and obligations of parenthood—which as a general rule meant being gainfully employed, able to support their children, and preferably married—bureau officials defended their right to custody and control of freedchildren against abuses of the apprenticeship system and challenges from former partners. But for freedpeople who bureau officials believed were not yet able to "undertake these obligations"—particularly poor single mothers—these same agents embraced apprenticeship as an answer to some of the most troubling shortcomings of freedom.[36]

In the chaotic transition from slavery to freedom, black mothers demonstrated extraordinary strength in their efforts to regain control of families in the face of apprenticeship. Intimidation, threats, and outright violence were met head-on. Hester Anthony, a freedwoman in postwar Maryland, put up with repeated clashes with her former master over the custody of her two boys only to be forced to concede for fear of her life. Not content simply to let the man have her children, however, the freedmother complained to federal authorities, telling them that her former master said that "if I did not go he was going to shoot me." Indeed, the frightened mother reported, "[H]e says that before I shall have my children he will blow their brains out."[37] Louisa Foster, the wife of an absent Union soldier, suffered similar vile threats as she endeavored to recover her children. Pleading for help, she told federal officials that her former master promised to "chain me down to the floor and whip me, if I asked for my children any more."[38]

But intimidation was not all that black mothers encountered as they sought to assert a right to their children. Countless black mothers experienced physical violence as well as imprisonment as they took matters into their own hands. One Arkansas freedwoman met a horrific fate as she confronted her child's former mistress. Demanding that she "would have her child," the black mother told the woman that she was now "as free as" she. Her defiant words did not go without consequence. The gutsy freedwoman was "horsewhipped" and "clubbed" by an enraged husband incensed that his wife had been "sauced" by a former slave.[39] An Afro-Virginian woman also experienced bewildering viciousness as she repeatedly attempted to claim custody of her granddaughter. In the face of threats to her life by the man who held the child, the desperate woman would not give up hope and ultimately arrived with a policeman in tow to demand her rights. Although the man promised the policeman that he would give up the child, when the grandmother returned to claim the girl, he "knocked her down several times, put a rope around her neck, dragged her to the fence," and, according to bureau reports, "choked her . . . . then took whips and whipped her on her bare back."[40] Just as sobering, black mothers also endured the wrath of arrest and imprisonment as they fought to recover children. Phillis, a freedwoman from Franklin, Louisiana, resisted the indenturing of her fourteen-year-old daughter even to the point of being put in jail herself.[41] Equally defiant, Julia Handy, the mother of five children, similarly chose to resolve the situation herself. Despite the reassurance of a respected community member that three of her children were old enough to care for themselves and that the mother could, herself, find "a comfortable home for the other two," Handy lost all five children as a Maryland judge authorized their indenture to her former master. The desperate mother responded by attempting to recover her children on her own. After multiple attempts, Handy faced arrest and was ordered to court.[42] No less determined but more successful than these black mothers was Jane Kamper—a freedwoman who "kidnapped" her own children. Upon discovering that her former master considered their indenture the cost of her liberty, the black mother recovered her children "by stealth" and moved to Baltimore, Maryland. Recounting the events to military authorities, who she hoped would now help retrieve her personal belongings, Kamper reported that the former slave owner had "locked my Children up so that I could not find them" and then "pursued me to the Boat to get possession of my children but I hid them."[43]

Even in the face of intimidation and violence, black mothers objected to what they considered unjust claims to their children by white southerners and fought back. Both stunned and somewhat perplexed, one Alabama judge remarked of African American mothers' efforts: "Freedwomen I find have a great antipathy to their children being apprentices." Casting aside their protests, this judge discounted African American women's opposition to the practice as the result of an inability to appreciate the importance of free labor. "I think," he informed the assistant commissioner of the bureau in his state, "it is the result of ignorance of the contract and want of confidence in the faithful performance of the guardian." Freedwoman Linday Robbins perhaps better understood why mothers like herself so vehemently resisted apprenticeship. "[A]lthough I have been ill-treated at different times, I put up with it," she explained to federal officials in 1865. But faced with "an old mistress" who had taken her children and had them "bound in slavery," the former slave woman asserted her position as a mother aware of both the illegality of slavery and the availability of forums like the bureau to demand legal redress. "I cannot rest until I know whether it is a lawful proceeding or not," she insisted.[44]

At times successful and at other times not, black mothers like Robbins turned often to the Freedmen's Bureau to answer these kinds of questions and, in doing so, attempted to assert both a familial understanding of freedom and an unequivocal right to their offspring. "Not a day passes," a bureau official in Maryland noted as late as 1867, "but my office is visited by some poor woman who has walked perhaps ten or twenty miles to . . . try to procure the release of her children taken forcibly away from her and held to all intents and purposes in slavery." Like this agent, bureau officials across the South regularly encountered former slave parents, both mothers and fathers, who sought to convince them that a meaningful freedom necessitated the removal of freedchildren from white control. Indeed, at least one historian has suggested that discharge from apprenticeship "might have been the most common legal action undertaken by African Americans" in the postwar South.[45]

Proceeding to the bureau office in Greenville, South Carolina, a "ragged" and "poverty-stricken" freedwoman was one such parent who attempted to convey the intense desire of former slaves to regain control of their families to officials of the bureau. "I wants to know ef I can't have my little gal," the mother appealed to bureau agent John William De Forest. Understanding the realities of apprenticeship, she addressed the issue of consent straightforwardly by telling him: "I ha'n't bound her out . . . an' now I wants her back." The resolute mother went on to assert herself as an independent woman and emergent citizen with rights, demanding: "She's my little gal, an' I has a right to hev her, an' I wants her." Unsympathetic and indifferent to the single mother's assertion of what she believed to be her rights, however, De Forest reported derisively that "by dint of ridicule, coaxing, and arguing, I prevailed upon her to leave her child with Mr. Jack Bascom, in whose care the pickaninny was of course far better off than she could have been with her poverty-stricken parent." Revealing both doubt in this freedmother's ability to care and provide for her child and an unwillingness to acknowledge the rights she claimed as an independent woman, this official's response attested to the preconceived notions of black and female dependence held by bureau agents. His actions also underscored their commitment to the federal agency's mission to promote a Reconstruction based on northern middle-class notions of free labor, domesticity, and family relations.[46]

An adherence to free labor ideology undeniably shaped the response of the bureau to African American parents' complaints about apprenticeship. After all, at the heart of these disputes was the issue of who controlled the labor of freedchildren. And certainly it was the desire to transform former slaves into free laborers able to provide for their families that guided many bureau officials to challenge white southerners' most overt use of the practice to reassert control over blacks. Bureau men had placed their faith in the concept of free labor and in the sanctity of labor contracts, especially, and African American parents often found success in appealing to these notions when unfair apprenticeship laws and practices led to the indenture of their children. When it was revealed that white planters had obtained contracts of indenture fraudulently, without—or with forced—parental consent, or violated them with wanton disregard, these federal officials found themselves compelled to get involved. And, in doing so, the policies that guided them readily dictated that black parents were not to be "deprived of the services of their children." These same policies also demanded that older children "should not be apprenticed," for they were "capable, if orphans, of supporting themselves as hired laborers, [and] if not orphans . . . assist[ing] in the support of their parents." Thus so as to protect the rights of black parents and to ensure that young men and women themselves were not denied the fruits of their labor, the bureau at times intervened in apprenticeship in an effort to defend free labor.[47]

Perhaps what troubled bureau men most about apprenticeship abuses were the many white civil authorities who openly disregarded bureau labor policies by using the practice to "accommodate their friends willingly with cheap labor." Bureau officials in Florida, for instance, complained of local magistrates who made corrupt indentures whenever they could get "a large fee." But friendships and fees aside, officials of the federal agency also proved especially suspicious of the swift indenturing of freedchildren in the early days of emancipation and the binding out of freedchildren who were all but grown. The speed with which planters and farmers proceeded to apprentice freedchildren—and especially older "children" of working age—led countless agents to call into question white pronouncements of humanitarian concern for black youths. "The avaricious Slaveholder of former days," explained a bureau official in Mississippi, saw in apprenticeship "a chance to effectively apply it in case[s] of young bright & active children." Continuing his early 1866 report, this agent underscored white Mississippians' hurry to bind former slave children. They did not wait "for the law to be carried out by proper officers." Rather, he insisted, they "run . . . before snatching all irrespective of orphanage, willingness or ability of parents or relatives to take care of their children. In many cases the aged parent & gradnd parents last dependence for support is taken away from them." White southerners' obvious preference for older "children" of working age patently challenged their assertions of selfless concern in the eyes of bureau officials. And agents in North Carolina complained of conditions much like those in Mississippi. There, Assistant Commissioner Whittlesey informed bureau headquarters in Washington, former masters "in many instances" selected only "the older children" for binding, "leaving the younger children to be supported by their parents." Seeing these kinds of apprenticeship practices as a denial of the principles of free labor, bureau officials often backed African American parents who worked to release children from such unjust bonds of apprenticeship.[48]

White southerners' reliance upon fraud, force, and intimidation to obtain legal guardianship of black children—even under the guise of parental consent—led many bureau agents to object to indentures resulting from trickery or duress. Deception was not an uncommon practice among those eager to apprentice black youths. "Children are almost invariably bound out from two to 12 years younger than they are," reported an agent in Mississippi in January 1866. Upon investigating one complaint in particular, this agent had discovered an eighteen-year-old freedman identified in his indenture as being only six-and-a-half years old. Fraud was not limited to legal documents, however. After having been told that "the law" required her to apprentice her children, one black mother in Georgia finally relented to doing so. But the profound callousness of this deception revealed itself only upon the discovery that the children's new master planned to deny the industrious and "respectable" freedwoman all contact with her children once he had them bound. Appalled, the assistant commissioner in Georgia directed the agent who investigated the case to confront the local magistrate and "demand that the Indentures be revoked and the children restored to their mother." Yet force, and even outright kidnapping, was also not uncommon in white southerners' efforts to reassert control over freedchildren. Grace Jenkins, a freedwoman in North Carolina, appealed to the bureau to challenge the violent removal of her fifteen-year-old son, Henry, by her former master in September 1865. When the young man protested, the devastated mother told bureau officials, the former master informed Henry that "he would have to go 'dead or alive.'" White southerners readily turned to this kind of intimidation to obtain consent from black parents to bind out freedchildren. In a direct appeal written to the commissioner of the Freedmen's Bureau, freedwoman and mother Mary Porter reported that she had only reluctantly—and quite fearfully—stood before the orphans' court to give her consent to the indenturing of her children. If she "did not let her have them," Porter explained to Commissioner Howard, the white plantation mistress to whom they were to be bound promised that she "wold have them bond to some one that wold treat them bad." Dina Williams, a Georgia freedwoman, faced a similarly horrific ultimatum. With her husband in jail, the mother had been warned that he would be "sent to the Chain Gang where she should not see him again" unless she agreed to apprentice her son. Only out of fear for what would happen to her husband, Williams told bureau officials in Albany, did she consent to the child's indenture. Across the South, "I consented for I was afraid for my life if I did not" were words heard often by bureau officials as they endeavored to resolve apprenticeship disputes.[49]

Even African American children whose parents had the courage to refuse their consent to indentures were not safe from the injustice of southern apprenticeship laws and practices. As Basil Croudy and his wife appeared before the orphans' court in Calvert County, Maryland, in 1866, for instance, they watched the court legally seize custody of their children even as they voiced clear objections. Obeying a summons to appear, the black parents went before the court and "steadily refused to consent to the binding" of their children to no avail. The devastated parents protested so much that, "finding the mother obstinate, and deaf to reason," the constable violently struck the woman "in the face with his fist in the presence of the Judges." Another black mother experienced an equally appalling fate as her former owner, who, also in the presence of the judges, warned that "if she did not cease talking *he* would break her d———d head." Freedwoman Maria Nichols met circumstances just as frustrating as she attempted to resist the binding out of her son. "[T]hey sent for me to come to the courthouse and i refused to go," she later told Commissioner Howard about the experience. The mother's defiance had been made in vain, however, for, as she told Howard, the court sent "high sheriffs after me and taken [me] by force." When Nichols finally arrived before the court, the judges proceeded as if she were not present. "[A]fter i got there," the exasperated mother explained, "they did not ask me anything but they taken him and bound him and they would not let me say a word." Over and over again bureau agents and officials worked to annul fraudulent indentures and to cancel, or at least review, indentures that black parents insisted they had not consented to or that they had been forced to accept.[50]

The issue of parental consent was of paramount concern to bureau officials at the highest levels. "Consent must be obtained" to bind out a child, Commissioner Howard declared as early as the summer of 1865, "otherwise the parent will have the right to the child." Upholding the sanctity of the contract and the ability to consent to it, in particular, bureau policy makers demanded that indentures be entered into honestly, without deceit, and with the knowledge and approval of black parents. Knowing this, bureau officials were particularly alarmed to report the actions of civil authorities in Maryland. There, local agents informed Commissioner Howard, "[c]onsent of parents has not been obtained, or they have not been summoned before the court, or there has been no proof that they could not support their children." With yet more disgust, they added that "in many cases, children apprenticed have been able to support both themselves and their parents." Considering indentures made under such circumstances both illegal and clear violations of the free labor principles they sought to instill, these bureau officials concluded for themselves that "the court had no right to . . . bind them out." So enraged by cases of such blatant disregard for the rights of black parents as well as those of black children old enough to support themselves was the bureau chief in Alabama, Assistant Commissioner Wager Swayne, that he put forth similar challenges to unjust apprenticeship practices there. In one instance, the bureau official ordered a Mrs. Thomas Harrell to liberate two former slaves' families from her unwarranted detention or face armed troops and a charge for the expense of sending them.[51]

Consent to contractual terms thus mattered to bureau officials across the South, and freedwomen like Phillis Peebles at times reaped the benefits of their allegiance to such free labor principles. Reporting that she had consented to the indenture of her children only after the man who held them had "cut her throat & hit her in the head with a whip handle . . . & cut her finger off," this anxious freedmother informed the agent at Belton, Texas, that the man now whipped the children and she wanted them released. Appalled, the agent recognized that the mother clearly had not consented, restored custody to her, and relayed his disgust in the matter to the local magistrate. Freedwoman Rosa Seymour gained similar support from the bureau in Georgia. Claiming that the man who held her child had known she was living when he obtained a court-ordered indenture for them, she appealed to the bureau, asserting that the indenture was illegal because he had represented the child as an orphan. Believing the man was a "consumate Scamp" who was "acting in a very rascally manner," the agent in Savannah agreed and declared that he had "no right to hold this child from its Mother." Upholding the ideal of consent, bureau officials thus demanded that the utmost care be taken to protect black parents' rights as indentures were made. And such orders applied to themselves as well. Upon discovery that the mother of four freedchildren whom he had apprenticed under the pretext of being orphans was in fact living, Atlanta bureau agent Frederick Mosebach, for instance, was quick to correct the injustice. Noting the mother's objection to the indentures, the agent ordered the children returned to her custody. By employing the requirement of parental notification and consent in bureau apprenticeship policies, these agents provided some much-needed assistance to black parents in reclaiming family members held under duress and obtained through force or fraud.[52]

Upholding free labor ideology and the sanctity of the contract required agents to do more than insist upon parental notification and consent in apprenticeship agreements. Such noble principles, according to bureau men of every ideological stripe, also demanded that they work diligently to enforce indentures as binding contacts once entered into. For some bureau officials, the enforceability of contracts was of paramount importance even above directives to protect black parental rights. Such was certainly the case for Major Clinton Cilley, a bureau superintendent in North Carolina who once praised the bureau system of apprenticeship as "an excellent" practice that gave children good homes, and mothers "the freedom to go & find work for them-selves." Upon learning in July 1866 that an agent in his jurisdiction had wrongfully authorized the indentures of a number of freedchildren, this bureau official opted to uphold the contracts nonetheless, declaring, "[T]he same reason as here given [in this instance, the desire of black parents to provide for their children] may be brought forward in hundreds of instances in the course of 5 years and the persons taking children wd be justified in charging the Bureau with bad faith if this reason alone was held to be sufficient cause for canceling an indenture." In the end, Cilley concluded, "[I]t would be a bad precedent to cancel these Indentures, as they now stand." Although the local agent had discovered that he granted the agreements because of false statements and insufficient evidence, he had, according to Cilley, authorized them in good faith and thus now must uphold them despite lesser concerns about black parental rights.[53]

For other bureau agents and officials, however, an adherence to free labor and the enforcement of contracts meant annulling apprenticeship agreements when it became clear that one of the parties had violated the terms of contract. And, to be sure, freedwomen readily reported employers' failures to fulfill apprenticeship agreement terms to bureau officials across the South. Eliza Elder, a former slave woman residing in Georgia, for instance, proceeded directly to the local agent in Athens when the man to whom she had apprenticed her three children did not live up to his end of the bargain. Having negotiated the terms of the children's indentures to include the provision of a house for herself to live in on his plantation, Elder reported that the man had reneged and, in fact, had driven her off his land altogether. Upon discovering that the employer of her six-year-old son had taken the child out of town against the terms of his apprenticeship agreement, freedwoman Annie Gibbs similarly demanded that the bureau in Georgia intervene to enforce the contract. So persuasive was Gibbs that she convinced bureau officials to annul the agreement altogether as well as to provide transportation for the boy back to her on the grounds that he had been "abducted." Black mothers also brought employers' neglect or abuse of freedchildren to the attention of the bureau and in doing so similarly alleged contractual violations that could result in the cancellation of an indenture. Louisiana freedwoman Edna Chapman, for example, regained custody of her indentured children after alleging that they had not been properly clothed or fed and, in fact, were abused by the man who held them. The bureau in Clinton rescinded its own apprenticeship agreement in this instance and ordered the man to restore Chapman's children to their "natural protector," their mother. Beyond asserting complaints of neglect and abuse, black mothers further objected to the failure of white employers to pay for the services of freedchildren. After having sent two orders (to no avail) with a black mother to recover the wages of her apprenticed son, bureau agent L. Jolissaint in New Orleans finally informed the employer: "I have no desire to be harsh with you untill all milder measures are exhausted." But, he steadfastly warned: "I send this one for the *last time* if you do not appear I will send a squad of U.S. Soldiers to compel you."[54]

Beyond notions of free labor, bureau officials' own nineteenth-century assumptions about the sanctity of the family and its domestic relations also shaped how the federal agency responded to complaints involving apprenticeship. That is, and to the benefit of black parents (especially married couples), these federal agents at times supported breaking indentures because not doing so would, as the historian James Schmidt has demonstrated about southern courts that decided Reconstruction-era apprenticeship cases, disrupt black families that were no longer enslaved. Following northern free labor ideology, these policy makers insisted that independence—in both labor and familial relationships—served as the source of all rights. In a free labor society, bureau men believed, and as Schmidt points out, "[t]he right to work and the right to undisturbed family relationships laid the foundation from which all other matters of society and politics" flowed. The understanding that freedom entailed independence and, with it, both the obligation to provide for and the right to control others in dependent relationships motivated bureau policy makers to assert that former slaves had a right, although within certain limits, to control their families, their children, and the labor of each.[55]

To say the least, appeals to domesticity went a long way with bureau men, who by and large lived according to middle-class notions of family themselves and desired that former slaves do the same to uphold the "domestic altar." Ever encouraging and enforcing the familial obligations of freedom, bureau policy makers readily told former slaves: "The sacred institution of marriage lies at the very foundation of civil society." Thus it should come as no surprise that freedwomen had the best chance of using the bureau to combat white claims to their children if they presented themselves as married women who, together with husbands, could support, maintain, and care for their families. Whether knowingly or not, black mothers who emphasized their position as dependents—as both wives and mothers—in apprenticeship complaints strengthened their position considerably with these federal officials. Freedwoman Elizabeth Kennard, for example, gained support for her cause as she protested to the bureau that "without my knowledge or consent, or that of my husband," three of their children had "been put to service beyond [our] control." Appealing for the return of two children, Mary Anne Ran similarly asserted: "I am able to provide for them and with the aid of my husband the father of them to protect them." Freedwoman Ann Maria Tripp likewise professed in her plea to recover her son: "I, with the help of my husband, am able to support him." In her petition for the recovery of children bound "without her consent and against her protest," former slave and mother Ellen Cole also endeavored to demonstrate her ability to provide a financially secure male-headed household. Stressing to bureau officials in Georgia that together she and her husband had "considerable means and are amply able" to support the children, Cole ultimately gained the agency's support. The couple, the local bureau agent informed Commissioner Howard as he forwarded the case for review, were "steady and industrious colored people" and "in every way deserving" of assistance in recovering their family. In the end, bureau authorities—as well as southern civil authorities—took notice of these domestic details, for all too often it was freedwomen's status as wives (rather than necessarily as mothers) that validated their assertion of parental rights.[56]

Her position as a wife proved critical in Texas freedwoman Sarah Lacy's efforts to successfully ward off, with the support of her husband, Moses Lacy, threats to her parental rights from both a former mistress, Mary Timmins, and the father of three of her children born in slavery, Harry Pope. A complicated case to be sure, the Lacys' fight to retain the right to control the labor of Sarah's children revealed the multifaceted nature of black familial relationships in the first years of freedom. Although sold away from the Timminses' plantation during slavery (and thus separated from his children), Pope returned after the war and contracted his labor to his former mistress and her son, Robert. He also agreed to contract the services of his three children—two sons, Elkin and Chuff, and a daughter, Leney—to the Timminses in a year-to-year agreement until 1868. Sarah, remarried to Moses Lacy by this time, also remained in the vicinity at war's end and, at least until the end of 1865, worked for the Timmins family. As 1866 opened, however, the Lacys embraced the principles set forth in the labor system promoted by the Freedmen's Bureau and chose to contract with a different employer for the coming year. Sarah also resolved to hire out her children in hopes that she and her husband, Moses, with the support of their children's labor, could "take care of themselves." Yet, perhaps to no one's real surprise, when she tried to hire out Elkin and Chuff, she met opposition from the Timminses. Robert Timmins, with the help of a double-barreled shotgun, forcefully reclaimed the two freedboys from their new employer. As 1866 came to a close, however, Sarah again decided to contract out the labor of her children, this time agreeing to bind each of them to a different employer for annual earnings between $30 and $40 and food, clothing, and medicine. But for a second time, the Timminses contested the freedmother's right to control the labor of her children. Using the law instead of a shotgun this time, the Timminses acquired an order from the local county court to reclaim the two boys in January 1867 until it could hear the case. The Timminses' case for possession of the freedchildren was strong; perhaps that was the reason Robert Timmins did not rely on the shotgun this time around. Just before year's end, on 27 December 1866, Mary Timmins had obtained permission from Pope to apprentice all three children to her until they reached adulthood. The agreement—and certainly a reason that had to have factored into the father's decision to consent to the indentures—entitled each child to one hundred acres of land when they came of age. The legal battle that ensued eventually made it to the state supreme court, and in the process the Lacys, to their great benefit, presented themselves as a couple with a "comfortable home" who desired only to "be let alone" and "permitted to have the management and control of" their children.[57]

Even in the face of the persistent appeals of Mary Timmins and seemingly unsympathetic judges—including Ninth District Court justice Reuben Reeves, a former slaveholder, secessionist, and captain in the Confederate army—Sarah Lacy was able to regain custody and control of her children as their natural guardian. The Texas Supreme Court later agreed with the decision when it considered the case in April 1867. Writing for the court, Chief Justice George F. Moore, also a former Confederate officer, held that Harry Pope's consent to the indenture of his biological children offered insufficient grounds to "rob" Lacy of her children. Born in slavery, the children of Pope and Lacy were bastards according to the law and, Moore pointed out, it was "a universally recognized principle of the common law, that the father of a bastard has no parental power or authority over such illegitimate offspring." Emancipation, he went on to affirm, had legitimatized the Lacys' marriage and, as a result, Moses and Sarah were the legal guardians of the children in question. Thus it was less her position as the children's mother than her position as a dependent wife assured of male guardianship and support that secured Sarah Lacy a right to her children. Reluctant to end on such a narrow, formalist reading of the law, however, the chief justice carried forth the court's opinion by insisting that even if Pope had a legal right to his children, it would be erroneous to interpret the Texas apprenticeship law in a way that permitted freedchildren to "be taken from [their] mother against her consent, and apprenticed solely at [the father's] will and pleasure." Indeed, he insisted:

> Surely it is not to be supposed that merely because the father, when discharging his duties as such, is regarded as the head of the family, [he] may, after years of desertion and abandonment, during which he has left his wife to struggle unaided for their support, rob her, by means of this law, of the society of her children, and thus add to the injury already done her by the severest blow which can be inflicted upon a woman, whatever may be her condition or sphere of life.

By calling on contemporary understandings of vagrancy and domesticity, as well as by disregarding the particular hardships placed on former slave fathers by the complex nature of black family relationships in slavery, war, and emancipation, Moore at once reprimanded "fathers who abandoned homes, wives, children, and domestic responsibility"; suppressed the efforts of former masters to use apprenticeship as a tool to reassert slavery; and offered freedwomen a bit of hope in reconstructing families threatened by myriad forces.[58]

How the Texas Supreme Court ultimately agreed that this former slave mother deserved her children more than either their biological father or their former mistress came back largely to deep-seated nineteenth-century notions of domesticity. So too did the outcome of another prominent apprenticeship case, *In the Matter of Harriet Ambrose and Eliza Ambrose*, that had reached the North Carolina Supreme Court a few months earlier, in January 1867. The *Ambrose* case brought to a head a battle between North Carolina freedpeople, aided by the Freedmen's Bureau, and a prominent white planter over the apprenticeship of a number of black children. All told, in 1866, Daniel Lindsay Russell Sr., a former slaveholder and justice of the peace in the Cape Fear region of the state, near Wilmington, had managed to seize—kidnap, in some instances—and have bound to him some twenty freedchildren. In fact, Russell's actions had become such a concern to the bureau that in October 1866 Assistant Commissioner John Robinson threatened to cancel all the indentures made to him, telling the governor of the state: "Mr. Russell seizes with violent hands children . . . living with their parents who support them, carries them off, the Court binds them, they are thrown into prison for safe keeping, and then carried to his home; he is asked to restore, he refuses and threatens the vengeance of the Court, the Court of which he is a member, and which Court binds to him these kidnapped children." "Is this not a case where discrimination is made, and that too greatly prejudicial to the Colored people and their children?" the bureau official asked. Offering his own answer to the governor, Robinson maintained: "It looks to me like the reestablishment of slavery under the mild name of apprenticeship." Among the freedchildren bound to Russell were the daughters of two freedwomen, Lucy Ross and Hepsey Saunders. And while both mothers turned to the bureau in an effort to reclaim their children, the differences between their individual appeals and domestic situations would result, as the historian Karin Zipf has shrewdly shown, in two very different outcomes. The fate of the complaints of Ross and Saunders confirmed the very important role that middle-class domestic ideals played in helping black parents obtain, and retain, custody and control of freedchildren in the years following emancipation.[59]

In September 1866, Lucy Ross appealed to the bureau for assistance in reclaiming her daughters, Maria and Delia, ages sixteen and twelve respectively, from what she considered an unjust apprenticeship. In making her case, she told the bureau that Russell had kidnapped, thrown into jail, and unfairly bound the girls, who were old enough to "earn good wages for themselves." Ross begged the bureau to intervene on her behalf: "I pray you to assist me to get my children as I have no other hope as Mr. Russell is Chareman of the Court and no justice can be had here." The freedwoman presented a compelling case. The single mother first insisted that she "never gave any consent" to have her daughters apprenticed. She also told the bureau that she "was, and is, fully able and willing to support" her children. In addition, Ross brought forth a number of male witnesses to support her challenge to the indentures. Her two brothers, for instance, told the bureau that their sister "was fully able to support and provide" for her daughters. And a neighbor, freedman Charles Aubriden, also testified on Ross's behalf, informing officials that the self-reliant freedwoman was "freely able to support her children, having made a good crop during the past season." The freedmen recognized Ross as the head of her own family and supported her contention that the indentures of the freedgirls had been unwarranted. The local agent agreed, although for different reasons, and requested permission to cancel the indentures so as to protect the girls' rights to their own labor, telling his superior officers that they "were both earning wages" and that Maria was, in fact, "a grown woman."[60]

Like Ross, Hepsey Saunders appealed to the bureau for its assistance in reclaiming her children from Russell. But unlike Ross, she came to the bureau with the support of her husband, freedman Wiley Ambrose. As a former slave once owned by Russell, Saunders had given birth to three children—Harriet, Eliza, and John Allen—all of whom had different fathers. After the war, she married Ambrose, and he thus took on the responsibilities of both husband and stepfather. Together with Ambrose, Saunders had managed to ward off efforts by her former master to seize the labor of her children from the first days of freedom. That accomplishment ended in December 1865, however, when Russell convinced the Robeson County Court to bind the three children to him. Thus began a prolonged legal battle to claim custody of Saunders's children. Presenting herself and her husband as a "well to do" couple with "good character," the freedmother turned to the Freedmen's Bureau in the summer of 1866 for help in retrieving her children. The bureau obliged the request. Saunders obtained a bureau order to retrieve her children, proceeded directly to Russell's place, and took them away. But the former master possessed similar resolve to keep the freedchildren. In September of that year—the same month he seized custody of the Ross children—Russell again obtained apprenticeships for Saunders's children through the county court. Just as determined, the black mother again proceeded to Russell's place in December 1866 to reclaim her children. This time she and her husband went without an order from the bureau, however, and as a result promptly encountered Russell's threat to have them arrested and jailed for illegally seizing the children.[61]

Bureau officials in North Carolina responded to both of these black mothers' appeals with sympathy and support, for in Russell they saw a "designing and unscrupulous man" intent on restoring slavery in all but name. That is, they cancelled the indentures and ordered the former master to return the children to their mothers. They did so to no avail, however, for Russell accepted neither the authority of the bureau nor the contention that he held the freedchildren illegally. As a result, Assistant Commissioner Robinson, with the full support of Commissioner Howard, committed his agency to making an example of Russell by challenging the indentures (and the state's apprenticeship laws and practices) in the courts as violations of the Civil Rights Act of 1866. The Civil Rights Act had offered the bureau and freedpeople a way to counter blatant racial discrimination in the postemancipation South by declaring that "citizens, of every race and color, without regard to any previous condition of servitude . . . have the same right as is enjoyed by white citizens." In terms of southern apprenticeship practices especially, the federal law offered black parents a great deal of hope. Interpreted to mean that the binding out of black children could occur only under the same circumstances and terms as that of their white counterparts, the law was seen by the bureau as offering black parents a legal avenue to recover their children. Under a writ of habeas corpus, indentures made in violation of the law could be invalidated. Thus to recover children under the act, black parents needed to obtain a writ of habeas corpus, demonstrate that discrimination existed before the courts, and prove they could support their children. Assistant Commissioner Robinson's hope in the bureau's case against Russell was that one court victory would result in the cancellation of all the indentures obtained by this unrepentant former master. Pursuing this goal, however, would force the bureau to make a decision—a decision of great gendered significance—about which complaint against Russell to pursue.[62]

As the bureau in North Carolina prepared to take on Russell and sought the "best legal advice . . . in the country," its lawyers—a Mr. Pearson and Mr. French—developed a strategy that revealed much about the agency's devotion to nineteenth-century middle-class domestic ideals. To be sure, the bureau's attorneys recognized that centering the case on the complaint of Lucy Ross presented fundamental problems. Lucy Ross was an unmarried woman who had responded to freedom in a way that challenged nineteenth-century dictates of womanhood. She lived independently, rejected the status of a woman dependent upon men, and claimed an unrestricted right to her children. Perhaps more troublesome, North Carolina apprenticeship law permitted courts to bind out any child "not living with fathers." That is, it allowed for the apprenticeship of children of single women without their consent and regardless of their race. Thus there was no case of racial discrimination to allege, no violation of the Civil Rights Act. Certainly, then, fastening the bureau's hopes to the claims of an unmarried freedwoman was not the best choice. A case that rested on the efforts of a freedman who sought to assert his newfound parental rights as a free and independent citizen by claiming control over the lives and labors of his family offered significantly more promise. After all, the North Carolina law called on courts to apprentice the legitimate children of free black, but not white, parents who were "not industrious." Thus bureau lawyers chose to center its challenge on the complaint of Hepsey Saunders and, more significant to them, Wiley Ambrose. Indeed, they selected Ambrose as their petitioner. In the end, then, the bureau opted to challenge Russell and the North Carolina apprenticeship law and practice by defending African American men's rights as parents and citizens and, in doing so, allowed gender distinctions that denied full and unconditional parental rights to mothers to remain in place.[63]

As *In the Matter of Harriet Ambrose and Eliza Ambrose* made its way to the North Carolina Supreme Court in January 1867, the case centered on the alleged illegal indentures of, tellingly, Ambrose's stepdaughters, and ultimately its outcome hinged on the domestic sentiments of those who heard it. In a petition for habeas corpus, bureau lawyers offered the court two principal reasons to invalidate the apprenticeships. First, Pearson and French insisted, the thirteen- and fifteen-year-old freedgirls should never have been apprenticed in the first place. They were from an industrious and, indeed, legitimate family headed by Ambrose and thus did "not come within any of the classes which the court is empowered to bind." "Great 'inconvenience' would arise," they maintained, "from holding that the Ordinance of Emancipation" or the law legalizing slave marriages allowed courts to use apprenticeship to disrupt free and independent black households. Second, the bureau lawyers argued, the indentures should be voided because the lower court had violated the U.S. Constitution's habeas corpus privilege by failing to notify Ambrose, as well as the children themselves, of the apprenticeship proceedings. "It is a clear dictate of justice," they asserted, "that no man shall be deprived of his rights of person or property, without the privilege of being heard."[64]

While bureau lawyers put forth these arguments defending Ambrose's rights as an independent head of household and an emergent citizen, Chief Justice Edwin Godwin Reade relied instead on notions of domesticity and the rights of the children to overturn the indentures. Indeed, the court's written opinion largely disregarded the line of reasoning offered by the bureau and stated flatly that it was "not necessary" to consider the claims or status of the parents. Rather, Justice Reade appealed first to middle-class notions of propriety and domesticity to justify the court's decision. He pointed out that Harriet and Eliza were "industrious well-behaved" young women who had been "amply provided for in food and clothing." They also, Reade noted, lived "with their mother and step-father," who possessed "good character" and were "well to do." "What better off could they be, or need they be," he asked and continued: "What interest had society in having their relations broken up, and themselves put under the care of strangers, with no affection for them, nor any other interest, except gain from their services." The chief justice insisted that it was "a high duty" of the courts to turn to apprenticeship only "to protect . . . helpless children, and not only to prevent oppression and fraud, but to act as friends and guardians, and improve their condition." To make his point, Reade reflected upon an antebellum case that considered the apprenticeship of the "neat and clean," though fatherless, children of "an honest, industrious woman." He recalled that the mother, likely a poor white woman, "cried much but did not say a word" as the Granville County Court decided her children's fate. Upon "inquiry," the judge reported, the court found that she was a widow "who had labored hard for her children, and that just when they could begin to help her the rapacity of some bad man sought to take them away." Moved by her circumstances, Reade told the court, "some gentlemen of the bar . . . readily responded" and collected enough funds to enable the poor widowed mother to retain her children. The chief justice used this rumination to underscore his belief in the "propriety" of having the children as well as "their parents or friends who have charge of them" in the courtroom so as to "hear their own simple story." In the end, Justice Reade turned to the issue of notice to cancel the apprenticeship agreements in question. Reade was certain that, had the children been present and had the "humane and intelligent judge" been able to "look behind the order of binding," the court would never have seen a reason to apprentice Ambrose's children. The freedgirls, he concluded, "were entitled to notice before they could be bound out, and, as they had no notice, and were not present, the binding was void." At "an age" when they were "most in need of the oversight of their parents and friends," the freedgirls, he concluded, had been the victims of "a gross outrage."[65]

Whatever the legal line of reasoning offered, Reade's ruling in *Ambrose*, according to bureau policy makers, offered freedpeople a great victory that both recognized and protected their domestic relations. Although the court had technically demanded only prior notice for apprenticeship proceedings, bureau policy makers went a step further to insist that the decision confirmed their belief that by apprenticing freedchildren without the consent—not just the notification or knowledge—of parents, former masters and southern courts discriminated against African Americans in violation of the Civil Rights Act. Howard and his agents stationed across the South thus began using the *Ambrose* ruling to demand parental consent in many of the indentures made for freedchildren.[66] The decision "will operate to annul all cases of apprenticeship in the State, where the children have been bound out, against the will of their parents," insisted the acting assistant commissioner of the bureau in North Carolina in his Circular No. 5, issued in February 1867. The new circular ordered agents to revoke indentures made without proper parental notice, although agents also interpreted it to require consent. So confident were bureau policy makers that the end of unjust apprenticeship practices was in sight that Commissioner Howard told Congress in late 1867 that the Civil Rights Act and the nation's highest court promised "the liberation of hundreds of freed children wrested from parents who were too poor or too humble to battle successfully with unjust tribunals."[67] And, to a certain extent, the commissioner was correct. Armed with the Civil Rights Act, favorable decisions like *Ambrose*, and orders like that of Circular No. 5 in North Carolina, many bureau officials began canceling apprenticeship agreements with the simple notation that they were voided "in accordance with the recent decision of the Supreme Court of North Carolina in the Case of Ambrose v. Russel."[68]

Without question, many black parents benefited from the legal recognition of their domestic relations offered by the bureau and southern courts that considered apprenticeship complaints like those made by the Lacys in Texas or Wiley Ambrose and his wife, Hepsey Saunders, in North Carolina. But not all black mothers were so fortunate. While some married freedwomen had found that bureau agents' desire to promote northern free labor and domesticity could benefit them in their resistance to apprenticeship, that was not the case for a great many others. Certainly, freedwoman Lucy Ross would have disagreed with Commissioner Howard's assessment that the cruelties of apprenticeship had ended. Even after the *Ambrose* ruling, Ross continued to struggle to regain custody of her daughters, Maria and Delia, from Daniel Russell. Beginning in February 1867, the former slave master had returned to the Robeson County Courthouse to obtain apprenticeship agreements for freedchildren including, yet again, Lucy Ross's daughters. And as late as October 1867, the freedmother was still appealing to the bureau for help in recovering her children from Russell.[69]

Other former slaves too would have challenged Commissioner Howard's insistence that freedchildren were being liberated from the unjust bonds of apprenticeship. At the same time that they sought to protect the needs and rights of the black family as a matter of policy, bureau men assigned limits to the rights of African Americans attempting to reconstruct their families. Thus while bureau policy and bureau men defended black parental rights, they were far less certain about appeals made by other relatives to bound freedchildren. Recognizing African Americans' widespread resistance to apprenticeship, obdurate agents complained regularly of grandparents, aunts, uncles, and so forth, who seemingly came out of the woodwork as soon as the bureau tried to indenture a black child. "The binding out of children Seems to the freedmen like putting them back into Slavery," complained one more racially conservative agent in Louisiana. Annoyed and unsympathetic to the plight of freedpeople, he continued sardonically: "In every case where I have bound out children, thus far some Grand Mother or fortieth cousin has come to have them released."[70] Agent De Forest in upstate South Carolina expressed similar sentiments about relatives who "pestered" him about freedchildren. The "problem" with apprenticeship, he explained, was that all too often black relatives "wanted to regain possession of the youngsters." "If the father and mother were not alive to worry in the matter," De Forest protested, "it would be taken up by grandparents, aunts, and cousins."[71] Such was certainly true for one particularly persistent grandmother of an indentured freedgirl in Texas. Indeed, so relentless was this freedwoman that bureau officials in the state alerted incoming agents to the area of the troublesome old woman. "Every time a new officer is appointed to the bureau in your neighborhood the old woman makes a fresh effort," the bureau official in Austin warned the new agent in Goliad. "It has been the opinion of all the agents here (& it is mine) that the girl is much better off where she is than she would be with her grandmother."[72]

Falling back on paternalistic notions that African Americans were a dependent race largely incapable of organizing their domestic relations in freedom without some kind of benevolent guidance, these bureau men granted little appreciation to relatives and "fictive" kin who sought control of freedchildren. Although admitting that such relatives expressed a "natural affection" for freedchildren, these agents were unwilling to abandon their free labor goals by terminating apprenticeship agreements on their behalf. Ignoring the realities of slavery and wartime upheavals that separated black families, some insisted, like one bureau official in Georgia, that relatives who had neglected black children "at a time when most in need of their protection" could not decide now to return and rob "the parties, who cared for [them], in this emergency" of their services. Thus even though some black relatives—especially those with the support of churches, northern benevolent societies, or attorneys—were successful in challenging the indentures of freedchildren, a great many were not. Having the support of their pastor certainly buttressed the claims of five black women from Philadelphia to their nieces and nephews living in Fairfax County, Virginia. Despite assertions by the children's former mistresses that there was "not force enough to take them" and that "blood should be shed before they would give them up," the aunts, "who wished to take and rear them," in the end gained bureau support to secure custody of the children and return home with them. More often, however, bureau men pointed black relatives to civil officials and local courts for a remedy to their complaints. Yet even as they did so, these federal officials understood the unlikelihood of freedpeople being able to bring a case before the courts, for, as Agent De Forest so readily pointed out, "As an application for a writ of habeas corpus costs money, I never knew a mother, grandmother, aunt or cousin to make it."[73]

All too often bureau officials' own preconceived notions about female (and black) dependence combined with white northern assumptions about domesticity to lead them to sanction efforts—both their own and those of other Reconstruction-era policy makers—that used apprenticeship to deny African American women parental rights. When, for example, the North Carolina General Assembly acted shortly after the *Ambrose* decision to reform its apprenticeship law by removing racial distinctions and inserting a new provision that allowed courts to bind out any child, regardless of race, who had been born out of wedlock and whose mother "may not have the means or ability to support" him or her, the bureau did not object. Likewise, bureau officials at the local level regularly employed policies that disregarded freedwomen's parental rights as they advised, counseled, urged, and forced poor unmarried mothers to bind their children as apprentices. Although some freedwomen—like Ailsie Merrit in Texas, a black mother who combated these kinds of policies by supplying "satisfactory evidence of her respectability and [proof] that she is able to take care of her child"—managed to force the surrender of their children, that was a rare occasion given all the obstacles they faced. In the end, like Sylvia Darden and Virginia Berry, the Georgia freedwomen discussed in Chapter 2 who lost their children to apprenticeship after bureau officials found them unable to support their children, many African American women lost their children to the bureau's "war on dependency" and regarded the federal agency as an enemy in the struggle to retain their children.[74]

Like other policy makers of their day, bureau officials failed to see an injustice in turning to apprenticeship in cases of destitution. The case of Phillis, a Louisiana freedwoman, demonstrated this sentiment. Three months after he reported the mother's seemingly unjust arrest and incarceration for resisting her daughter's indenture, the local bureau agent in Franklin finally concluded in the fall of 1866 that although "by the law the mother is the natural guardian of her child," it was necessary to reject the poor mother's appeal for bureau assistance because "it appears that . . . [she] has done nothing for the support of the child for the last five years." Agent De Forest was more forceful. Refusing to come to the aid of poor, unmarried black mothers against white planters and farmers who offered freedchildren "good homes," he protested that these women acted out of a "combination of affection, stupidity, and selfishness" in issuing demands that they "wanted their children." Bureau policy makers may have objected to the use of apprenticeship as a method of racial control, but the same simply could not be said when it came to using the practice as a way to limit the rights of mothers.[75]

A recognition of African American women's rights as mothers or citizens did not motivate bureau officials to support black mothers like Lucy Ross and the "ragged" freedwoman in South Carolina who sought to rescue their children from the bonds of apprenticeship as autonomous individuals. Rather, nineteenth-century notions of domesticity and dependency shaped how agents, and indeed the courts, responded to freedmothers' appeals for their children. And while these notions prompted sympathy for black mothers from some bureau agents, they were unlikely to result in the unconditional support of the federal agency for freedmothers who battled southern apprenticeship laws and practices outside the marriage relation. Most often, agents and officials of the bureau responded with reservation to these mothers and, even as the more sympathetic bureau officials recognized the travesty in taking children old enough to work away from poor freedmothers, support for the use of apprenticeship. Thus all the while acknowledging that binding out freedchildren deprived "a mother of the labor of a child that would be nearly if not quite able to support her," they nonetheless saw promise in the practice. In their eyes, apprenticeship provided homes to freedchildren and released freedwomen from the encumbrances of motherhood to find employment—ideally with their child's employer. The more compassionate agents thus worked to negotiate agreements with terms more beneficial to mothers and their children than those dictated by law; and, even though not necessarily required to do so by law or bureau policy, they also sought the consent of poor mothers to apprenticeship agreements. Such was the case for an agent in Columbia, Texas, for example, who worked to obtain a poor freedmother's consent to an apprenticeship agreement that consigned her son to short-term servitude, in the agent's mind, in exchange for a chance at future independence for her family. Going well beyond the state's requirement of food, clothing, medical attendance, education, and "humane" treatment, the bureau-negotiated indenture required that the young man receive forty acres of land and the seed necessary for him to begin farming upon its conclusion. According to the contract, the boy's former owner also agreed to provide an ox, horse, saddle, and bridle. Desiring the consent of a similarly situated black mother, another agent in Texas attempted to cushion the blow of apprenticeship by negotiating into the terms of indenture that she be allowed to visit her children "whenever she sees fit and no matter where they may be" and that the children "be taught who is and to respect their mother." Thus rather than objecting to the wholesale apprenticeship of poor freedchildren or offering unilateral support for the rights of black mothers to their children, these bureau men promoted the practice as one that, in the long run and in their own minds, would benefit both freedchildren and their mothers by acting as a cure-all to the weighty conditions freedwomen faced in the immediate postemancipation South.[76]

In their struggle to obtain and assert parental rights, black mothers also encountered adversaries beyond white planters and farmers, southern courts, and bureau agents intent on taking possession of their children by way of apprenticeship. Black fathers as well as black children themselves also challenged African American women's parental rights following emancipation. And here too the Freedmen's Bureau played a role in defining black mothers' rights to their children as its agents considered, among other factors, the "character of the parents and the wishes of the children" to resolve custody disputes. One of thousands, the complaint brought by Madison Day and Maria Richardson to bureau offices in Florida was emblematic of some of the complexities of black family relations that former slaves sought to sort out in the first years of freedom. So too was the local bureau agent's uncertain response to it. Following emancipation, the couple, in the words of the agent who received their complaint, refused to be "regularly joined in the bonds of matrimony." Although no longer committed to one another, however, both remained devoted to their three children, and now they turned to the bureau to determine which parent would enjoy custody and control of their offspring. Unsure how to resolve the complaint before him, the local agent relayed his concerns up the bureau chain of command. "I must confess that I am at a loss to decide which of the two is to have the children or what disposition is to be made of the children," he wrote to officials in Lake City. "Neither husband or wife seem to be in a condition to provide for the children in a manner better than is usual with the freedpeople," the agent reported. "[S]till," he concluded with an acknowledgment of the family bonds at hand, "both appear to have an affectionate regard for the children and each loudly demands them."[77]

Officials of the bureau thus found themselves thrown into the midst of quarrels of profound significance within black communities that demanded they determine which parent had the right to, or perhaps most needed or deserved, custody and control of freedchildren. And although in the end neither parent necessarily secured a right to freedchildren by virtue of gender alone, agents' northern beliefs about free labor and domesticity as well as their preconceived notions of both black and female dependence again factored into the resolution of these disputes. Thus while Maria Richardson did not win her battle—bureau headquarters in Florida offered an "unadorned" directive in her case declaring that "the father of the children shall have the control of them"—other freedmothers would as they found favor with local bureau agents in the postwar South. Black mothers who emphasized their position as dependents—both as wives and mothers—in custody disputes with former partners, whether knowingly or not, strengthened their position considerably with agents interested in seeing them provided for by sources other than bureau relief or public charity.

Freedmothers battling black fathers benefited too from agents' at-times paternalistic reluctance to acknowledge black men as citizens fully prepared to head their own independent households. Again, the gendered assumptions and expectations of those employed by the bureau worked both for and against freedmothers attempting to assert their own understandings of parental rights and responsibilities in freedom.

Clashes between black mothers and fathers over the care and control of their children were certainly not uncommon in the early Reconstruction South. Bureau agents everywhere recorded complaints between parents over freedchildren and, like the agent in Florida, sought guidance from superior officers as they attempted to settle such disputes. As a matter of policy, the bureau instructed agents to settle custody disputes in favor of parents who could provide a "stable" home—meaning, to Reconstruction-era policy makers, a male-headed household in which freedpersons "living as man and wife before emancipation and *who mutually desire[d] to continue in that relation*" had "legalize[d] their marriage"—and demonstrate an ability to support their children. At the same time, however, bureau policy makers in Texas, like those in other states, also told agents, "The Mother has the first claim to her child" and "interference with this right will not be tolerated."[78] The result was that, optimistic and straightforward proclamations aside, bureau support in custody disputes between black parents was diverted at times by ever-pragmatic local agents who came to regard black mothers as more deserving of, entitled to, or in need of their children's labor than black fathers. The agent in Baton Rouge provided a somewhat typical bureau response to cases of parents who chose to separate after emancipation. "Where both parents of the child are living but not living together," he explained, "I have given it to the mother in preference to the father [while] in other cases I have given it to the party who in my opinion is best able to support and educate it."[79]

What mattered to bureau officials settling cases between African American parents was a multitude of factors, certainly, but one that appeared repeatedly in local agents' decision-making process was a belief that black mothers somehow had more right to their children than former slave fathers. Such a notion was founded in some interrelated assumptions. First, some bureau officials argued that because women had been the primary caregivers in slavery, they had earned custody of their children more so than black fathers. The remarks of bureau agent William Fowler in North Carolina perhaps best demonstrated this sentiment. "When husband and wife lived on separate plantations and were owned by separate masters the children went with the mother, who had the entire care and support of them, and," he explained in the summer of 1866, "the father cannot be regarded as having borne any of the responsibilities or having assumed any of the duties of a parent." As a result, this agent, like others, decided that freedmothers were more deserving of the right to control their children's labor.[80] Second, bureau agents relied on their own understandings of dependency and the responsibilities of free labor and domesticity to deny custody of freedchildren to black fathers who refused to work or to provide for their families. And lastly, bureau officials and agents used the laws and customs of slavery to deny parental rights to African American men after emancipation, with the unintended consequence that black women benefited.

Black mothers who could demonstrate that they had long provided for their children without the assistance of fathers tended to find a sympathetic ear in agents of the bureau who considered their cases. Freedwoman Molly Coleman relayed the frustration of many black mothers in the first years of freedom as she turned to the bureau for help when her former husband, now a freedman and citizen, contested her right to their child. "I being in trouble," she wrote to bureau officials in Mississippi, "I want your advice." The anxious freedmother went on to explain: "I have bin married. My husband has left me. We had but one child. he being married again wants to take the child from me to aggravate me. He cares nothing for the child and has never don anything for it since we parted." Continuing, Coleman stressed both her desire and her ability to keep the child by maintaining: "I am not willing to give it up. I am able to support the child."[81] Responding positively to this kind of appeal from a similarly situated freedmother, the bureau in Houston readily awarded Barbara Alfred custody of her daughter when it found that her former partner had "failed to give her any assistance in raising and supporting" their child ever since she was four years old.[82] Like Coleman and Alfred, Georgia freedwoman Julian Battle had raised and cared for her sixteen-year-old son "all his life while his father ha[d] done nothing for him" and, as a result, regained custody after the father, in the bureau's opinion, seized the child unjustly.[83] Mississippi freedwoman Ellen Riley likewise retained custody of her son after demonstrating to the bureau there that she "had raised the boy at her own expense and had always had him with her."[84] If African American mothers could show a continued ability to support their children, the bureau usually defended their right to custody and control of freedchildren.

In most cases, bureau officials simply proved unwilling to deprive freedmothers of the labor of children whom they had "worked hard to raise," in the words of freedmother Mary Winder. Appearing before the local freedmen's court in Yorktown, Virginia, in 1867, Winder fought to defend her custodial rights as a mother and, in doing so, discovered that her case hinged on her longtime care and support of her children. It seems that the father of her children, John Burbridge, brought suit to take "charge" of their children in hopes of making "good" indentures for them. Together some fifteen years earlier as slaves, but of course not legally married, Winder and Burbridge had two children. Insisting to the court that he had "offered to take her back since the war but she refused to live with me," Burbridge hoped to claim custody and control of the two children now old enough to work. Winder, however, was not going to give her children up willingly or easily. "John [has] never done anything for me," she retorted angrily to his testimony before the court. Indeed, she informed the tribunal, "I could not live with him, as he was always drunken and worthless." Moreover, she insisted, the father had not "done anything towards the support of the children since we parted." Clearly, Winder believed Burbridge had been a negligent parent. But perhaps more important—to both this freedmother and members of the freedmen's court—was Winder's assertion that the "children are all the support I have." "I have worked hard to raise these children," she explained, and "they are now at an age that they can help me." "I do not know what would become of me if they were taken away from me," the mother pleaded. The court responded favorably to Winder's passionate appeal. In a unanimous decision, it awarded custody of the children to their mother, flatly declaring that Burbridge, the father, "has no claim to them whatever." Because the mother had continued to bear the primary responsibilities of caring for and supporting the children, the bureau court concluded, she deserved control of her children and their labor.[85]

The gendered nature of nineteenth-century dependency also influenced officials and agents of the bureau to award custody of black children to mothers when black men failed as providers. In short, because they themselves were dependents—although dependents outside the marriage relation—freedmothers, bureau officials decided, needed the children and their labor more than black fathers. With little hesitation, Georgia agent John Knox, for instance, demanded that one black father return two grown sons to their mother, Patsey, whom he had abandoned and who was "unable to support herself without [their] assistance." Indeed, the agent warned the father to "not again interfere with them." In yet another case, this same agent provided freedwoman Hannah David with an order expressly prohibiting her husband, Dick, from taking any of their children should he ever leave her. The agent instructed Hannah to proceed immediately to the bureau office if he did. Although unlikely to protect the freedwoman's rights to the children if he left, the order nonetheless revealed the domestic sentiments of the official who wrote it. Determined to see that black men fulfill their duties as free men and fathers, Agent Knox even went so far as to uphold a grandmother's right to the children she had raised in the absence of her own son. Forbidding George Marshall from taking custody of his older children, who were now old enough to work and earn good wages, this agent ordered the freedman not only to allow them to remain with their grandmother but also to begin to "take care of your mother as in duty you are morally bound." In contrast, the bureau in Texas chose a somewhat different approach in the custody dispute between freedwoman Maria Scaggs and the father of her two eldest children. Although recognizing that the children "had always been with her," the bureau expressed concern that Scaggs and her present husband would not be able to support both children along with six others. Not willing to deny her parental rights completely, however, agents ordered the father to "keep the boy," and the mother, the girl. In the end, these bureau men supported the appeals of freedwomen who, without the assistance and support of their older children, stood poised to fall further into the clutches of poverty.[86]

Freedwomen who came to the bureau in defense of their rights as mothers also benefited, for better or for worse, from agents' gendered expectations for freedmen as heads of households and free laborers. Bureau policy makers believed that to make the federal agency's free labor experiment work, African American men in particular had to reject vagrancy and idleness by assuming responsibility for their individual households and working to earn a living. "A homeless child! Why the angel of mercy weeps over it. And who so exposed, so unhappy, as a woman who has no home!" Assistant Commissioner Fisk had proclaimed in his *Plain Counsels*. "Heretofore, you had no opportunity to provide homes for yourselves and families," Fisk told freedmen as he went on to instruct them in the prerequisite of work to making a home. "But," he cautioned, "all that is now changed." Thus, as Paul Cimbala has suggested more generally, when bureau officials settled disputes between black parents, their actions "went beyond looking for the simplest resolution of an aggrieved spouse's complaint." Rather, their decisions reflected the agency's stance that the South's new free labor society was dependent upon freedmen internalizing "the individual responsibility and personal discipline necessary" to make it a success." When freedmen failed to do so, bureau agents were quick to cast judgment and, among other things, prevent them from regaining their children from former partners or white southerners.[87]

In settling custody disputes, the legacy of slavery—and, in particular, the laws and customs that held that slave fathers had no right to children born out of wedlock—bore heavily on agents' decisions. Susan Hardy, a freedwoman from Georgia, found this to be a great advantage in her struggle to reclaim custody of her eleven-year-old daughter. In a complex series of events, it seems that the father, William Hunter, had laid claim to her child by "contending that he had the control of the child by law." Not knowing "any better," Hardy had allowed Hunter to take the girl but, in doing so, informed her former partner that "it was against her will." Despite having "promised to keep the child himself & not to bind her out," Hunter soon apprenticed their daughter without Hardy's consent. In considering the complaint, the bureau recognized many problems with the indenture, including, most notably, the absence of the mother's consent. In the end, however, the resolution of the complaint—the bureau annulled the apprenticeship agreement and gave custody of the child to her mother—hinged more on Hardy's character and position as a free laborer than any assertion of her parental rights per se. She was, the local agent explained, "a very respectable negress of some attainments" who taught at a school and enjoyed "a good reputation."[88]

Bureau officials' notions of proper family relations and the responsibilities of parenthood could work against freedwomen too. Agents of the federal agency in Algiers, Louisiana, for instance, found freedwoman Catherine Martin ill prepared for the responsibilities of motherhood and, as a result, undeserving of custody of her child. Faced with conflicting stories from Martin and the alleged father of her daughter, officials evaluated the evidence presented by witnesses to the couple's relationship. Although Martin asserted otherwise, the father of the freedgirl whose custody was in question claimed to be legally married to the freedwoman. Indeed, the father insisted, his wife had unjustly abandoned him. Witnesses, including Martin's father, confirmed the freedman's claims and described him as a responsible husband and father who supported, and did not mistreat, his family. On the other hand, these same witnesses portrayed Martin as a freedwoman who needed frequent chastisement and as an adulterer who had abandoned her husband for no apparent reason. In the end, bureau officials had little difficultly in ordering Martin to sacrifice custody of her child. Similarly, the wife of freedman Phillip Lay promptly lost custody of her son when the bureau discovered that she had married another man. In marrying another man before lawfully absolving her former relationship, the agent in Athens, Georgia, concluded, this mother forfeited her right to the minor child. Like those who committed adultery and bigamy (at least in bureau officials' understanding), freedwomen who engaged in prostitution—as well as those merely accused of doing so—also suffered the loss of their children at the hands of these federal policy makers intent on reconstructing black families in freedom.[89] However much understandings of marriage and family relations and the domestic responsibilities inherent to each may have differed among the bureau men who considered their custody complaints, freedwomen nonetheless encountered in agents' gendered assumptions a strong weapon that could either safeguard or, as these examples reveal, endanger their parental rights.

Finally, in settling both custody and apprenticeship disputes, bureau officials considered the wishes and status of the individual freedchildren in question.

Indeed, the struggle to reclaim former slave children did not always end even when African American mothers or fathers successfully asserted a right to their children before the bureau. At times black children resisted reuniting with their parents, especially if it meant leaving the only constancy they had ever known. Slavery and freedom created a peculiar fate for former slave children in the Reconstruction South. In the immediate postemancipation mission to reunite families, the whereabouts of parents and children often remained unknown for some time, if not forever. Yet despite the seemingly impossible journey, as Jennie Hill, a former slave from Missouri, later remembered, once "Lincoln freed the slaves," children looked for parents "sold 'down the river,'" and parents likewise "searched frantically for their children." Once found—if found—confusion and uncertainty followed. Hill struggled to explain the loss of identity that children, in particular, experienced in slavery. In "the majority of cases," she insisted, "the children of slaves lost their identity when they were taken from the place of their birth into a new county."[90]

Frankie Goole, only a child as the Civil War ended, understood this legacy of slavery that haunted African American children after emancipation. In the first days of freedom, a judge asked the young child to identify her mother. Her response was simple and straightforward: "I dunno, she sez she ez." Decades later Goole would describe the confusion she felt as a freedchild who had little —if any—memory of parents lost in slavery: "W'at did I know ob a mammy dat wuz tuk fum me at six weeks ole." Sarah Debro, also a child at the time of emancipation, experienced similar ambivalence toward the mother who reclaimed her as "the Yankees was all around." Despite the daughter's cries to remain with her former mistress, Miss Polly, her resolute mother dragged her away. Angrily reminding her former mistress—who also pleaded with her to allow Debro to stay—of the grief she felt years ago, the black mother snapped: "You took her away from me and didn't pay no mind to my crying. We's now free, Miss Polly, we ain't going to be slaves no more to nobody." That night, as Debro lay on a bed of straw and looked through the cracks in the ceiling of their "stick-and-mud house," all she could think was how much she wanted to return to Miss Polly and the clean dresses, aprons, and sheets she had left behind.[91]

Unlike Goole and Debro, other African American children resisted returning to the custody and control of their parents so much that federal officials, including bureau agents, refused to force them. For bureau officials and agents across the South, such actions most often tended to be the case when the children in question were older and could readily support themselves, and agents recognized them as having a right to control their own labor. Jane, the thirteen-year-old daughter of freedwoman Margaret Wesendonck, for instance, proved especially adamant in her desire to remain with her former mistress in Richmond. "My daughter Jane . . . has refused to come back to me," the equally determined freedmother informed the bureau official in Christiansburg, Virginia, in August 1866. Continuing, Wesendonck asserted what she believed were her parental rights and duties. "Now it is my earnest wish and Will for my daughter Jane to return to me," she explained, "as I have a good home here where I can take care of her. . . . The separation now makes me most unhappy, and I hope the day not far off, to see Jane return to me, and I claim this of her, as my right as Mother and her duty as a child." In this instance, however, the bureau disagreed and upheld the free labor rights of the child by allowing Jane to remain.[92]

Certainly factors beyond the stated wishes of black children influenced agents of the Freedmen's Bureau to resist black women's assertion of parental rights. It was not uncommon for children to be deceived, cajoled, intimidated, threatened, or forced by white employers to reject their parents' claims. Yet in instances where the bureau allowed children to remain, agents presented a great deal more justification for doing so—although, often, even that was not enough. Attempting to defend his own right to two freedchildren now claimed by their mother, one white Georgian and civilian agent of the bureau, John Calvin Johnson, insisted that the "children [were] horrified at the idea of leaving" to go with such an "idle and profligate" woman. He went on to establish that the father was a thief who had abandoned his children—he had fled the county after being accused of hog stealing—and to depict the mother as unfit. Not married to the father of the children, and now abandoned by him, the freedwoman had chosen to marry an "improvident" man—indeed, a depraved "vagabond"—according to the bureau official. Johnson used notions of African Americans' allegedly innate inferiority to bolster the legitimacy of the apprenticeship agreements in question. His tactics did not work, however. Johnson's superior officers in the bureau concluded that his claims asserting the mother was unfit proved insufficient. Declaring that the bureau had no authority to deny the legal rights of a mother—even if a child would be better off in a white home—the bureau assistant commissioner returned the children to the care and custody of their mother. Harkening back to their own beliefs in the promise of free labor or the natural state of dependence of African Americans, agents sometimes nonetheless supported freedchildren's desire to remain with one parent or the other or, more devastating to black parents, their former masters, by offering justifications for their actions that insisted children had "a good home," were "well fed and clothed," and received instruction in "reading and other studies" and asserting that freedmothers were "miserable and unthrifty creature[s]," "loose," "drunkard," "common thie[ves]," or simply "worthless."[93]

Black mothers—especially those freedwomen who, according to bureau officials, had "put forth almost superhuman efforts to regain their children"—looked to the Freedmen's Bureau as their advocate in the assertion of parental rights in the postwar South.[94] And in the end, they discovered that bureau men could be a useful ally or a fierce adversary in the struggle for the custody and control of black children. As a matter of policy, the federal agency worked to disallow white southerners' use of apprenticeship as a tool to reassert control over blacks, and this response to the practice aided black parents. The bureau expressed grave reservations about the worst abuses perpetrated by the system of apprenticeship, especially when they involved fraud and intimidation or were inflicted upon black families that could support themselves. But the federal agency's response to the practice of binding out freedchildren varied widely, especially at the local level, and readily supported the indenture of poor and orphaned black children. Poor black mothers and those who lacked the support of husbands thus proved particularly at risk of losing their children to apprenticeship at the hands of both civil and bureau authorities. Having borne, according to law, "illegitimate" or "bastard" children "out of wedlock," former slave women fought a losing battle against apprenticeship laws that gave courts limitless authority over "orphan" (often meaning, in practice, "fatherless") black children. Free but faced with propertylessness, few employment prospects, and extraordinary deprivation, poor black mothers—particularly the "unproductives," unmarried mothers who bore the "encumbrance" of young children—also encountered bureau agents and civil authorities with unrestricted powers to bind out the children of mothers (black or white) who did not have the resources or ability to support them. Thus while the bureau ultimately challenged apprenticeship's use as a system of racial control, the federal agency accepted, and even employed, the practice as a way to restrict the parental rights of mothers.

Freedwomen who presented themselves as autonomous individuals whose rights had been violated did not stand the best chance of putting a stop to external claims to their children—whether by white southerners, the Freedmen's Bureau, or former partners and fathers. Claims like that of the "ragged" South Carolina freedwoman who insisted to the bureau that she "has a right to hev" her daughter were all too often cast aside with indifference.[95] Rather, bureau agents and officials most readily came to the defense of former slave women who appealed either to principles of free labor or to their middle-class domestic ideals as dependent wives—that is, as married women who, together with husbands, could support and care for their children—fighting capricious apprenticeship laws and practices. Similarly, agents of the bureau also supported freedwomen who presented themselves as devoted—although still dependent—mothers in custody battles against black fathers who, they believed, were unprepared to become responsible patriarchs. That is, they sided often with freedwomen, declaring that mothers, instead of black fathers, were entitled to control the labor (and profits) of freedchildren in the postwar South. Despite proclamations asserting black men's "sacred right and privilege" to their families and to the fortuitous benefit of former slave women, bureau officials at times proved unable, in the words of Karin Zipf, "to escape the quicksand of assumptions that prescribed African Americans' dependence" or to rise above "the paradox in which society celebrated paternal rights yet denied those rights to African American men."[96] These agents and officials thus at times disregarded black fathers' parental rights and determined that black mothers could not be robbed of their children. Without the labor of their children, these dependent women, such pragmatic local agents of the bureau perhaps rightly feared, would fall further into the clutches of extreme poverty and all the evils—including a need for public charity—to which it gave rise.

Whatever the intentions of Freedmen's Bureau policy makers, freedwomen remained intent on claiming what they understood as fundamental rights of freedom—the reestablishment of their families and control of their children's labor. Even in the face of hostile courts, deceptive and malicious white southerners, rights-driven black fathers, and a bureau that sometimes wavered in its commitment to freedwomen, black mothers objected to what they considered unjust claims to their children and fought back. Turning to the bureau was one way they sought to reclaim their children and assert the bond between mother and child. And some former slave women were successful as they put their faith in the hands of bureau men. But when agents dismissed their complaints and, "by dint of ridicule, coaxing, and arguing," sought to convince them that their children were better off with others, black mothers did not hesitate to take matters into their own hands. But despite great effort, they faced overwhelming obstacles—the law, the bureau, black fathers, former masters, threats of violence, actual violence, and so much more—as they attempted to reclaim their children. And, certainly, freedwomen discovered in the midst of battles over freedchildren that their gender alone failed to assure them custody and control of their children. While in part because women's protected but unequal position in American society was still a matter of contest—that is, white women did not possess the rights that these former slave mothers sought—black women nonetheless remained insistent that their womanhood and dependency did not dictate the surrender of parental authority and, even "by stealth," dared to retrieve their children, whatever the trial.[97] "We were delighted when we heard that the Constitution set us free," Lucy Lee, a freedwoman from Baltimore,

Maryland, exclaimed in 1865. "[B]ut God help us, our condition is bettered but little; free ourselves but deprived of our children," the former slave mother declared as she fought, unsuccessfully in the end, to regain custody of her daughter. "It was on their account that we desired to be free," she had protested. "Give us our children," this dispirited mother pleaded, "and don't let them be raised in the ignorance we have."[98]

Freedwomen's resolve that their gender did not require the unconditional surrender of rights, authority, or indeed a public voice would also be visible as they pursued justice in the emancipation-era South. For as they attempted to claim, exercise, and protect their rights over their own bodies and within their own households by making formal public complaint, black women again turned to the Freedmen's Bureau to demand that their particular gendered needs be acknowledged and defended by its agents. But here too bureau men wavered. And the recognition of freedwomen as women and as dependents certainly shaped how they came to mediate southern justice. The frustration of former slave women's expectations for freedom especially would be apparent as they found yet again that their gender did not always secure them the protections and benefits they so desired.

5

"strict justice for every man, woman, and child"

Gender, Justice, and the Freedmen's Bureau

The reason why I think the negro has so little chance for justice at the hands of Mississippians is, that into whatever place I go—the street, the shop, the house, the hotel, the steamboat—I everywhere hear the people talk in a way that indicates, that public sentiment has not come to the attitude in which it can conceive of the negro having any rights at all.

Describing the state of affairs in Mississippi in the autumn of 1865, Assistant Commissioner Samuel Thomas expressed little hope that former slave women and men could ever obtain justice in his state. "Men, who are honorable in their dealings with their white neighbors," he explained, "will cheat a negro without feeling a single twinge of their honor; to kill a negro they do not deem murder; to debauch a negro woman they do not think fornication; to take property away from a negro they do not consider robbery." Clearly discouraged and frustrated, the assistant commissioner insisted that the "reason" for this behavior was "simple and manifest." White Mississippians, like other southern whites, "esteem the negro the property of the white man by natural right." In spite of emancipation, they "still have the ingrained feeling that the black people at large belong to the whites at large." In the end, Thomas concluded, "the white people cannot, as yet, feel that he [the freedman] has any rights that should prevent them [from] treating him just as their profit, caprice, or passion may dictate."[1]

Prospects for securing justice for African Americans certainly did not look good to bureau officials like Thomas in the immediate postemancipation South. Yet even in the face of "denunciations, jeers, and threats of assassination," bureau policy makers pledged "to protect the freedpeople in their rights." Placing their faith in the agency's demand for "justice before the laws" and, for the short time it existed, a system of freedmen's courts, these men worked to secure the blessings of liberty for former slaves and trusted that the federal government, as Assistant Commissioner Clinton Fisk wrote to Commissioner Howard in early 1866, would "insist upon strict justice for every man, woman, and child who through the Red sea of civil strife has marched from slavery to freedom."[2]

The judicial policy of the bureau, perhaps somewhat predictably, followed the same prescription as other agency undertakings with its insistence that former slaves needed "to be trained with a firm and vigorous yet kind hand" as emergent citizens. But it was similar too in that enforcement again exposed bureau men's desire to implement northern white notions of free labor and domesticity. Operating at best with a belief that freedmen and women required "a guardian rather than a jailor or hangman," as an agent in Georgia put it in early 1866, bureau men worked not only to defend the rights of African Americans against racial discriminations but also to enforce the obligations of freedom as they mediated southern justice. Freedmen, as this federal official explained, "need to be encouraged, to have their manhood appealed to. They need to have praise judiciously mixed with blame." They must "be protected in their rights as well as punished for their misdeeds, to be instructed in their duties and treated as men with immortal souls rather than as beasts of burden or machines for pulling cotton." Freedwomen also needed to be guided in their rights and duties as well as treated "in the eyes of the law," the bureau asserted, as women "entitled to the same priveleges and immunities and the same protection . . . accorded to" their white counterparts. They too were emergent citizens, bureau men acknowledged, but not in the same way or with the same rights as African American men.[3]

As bureau men faced the daily deluge of disputes brought by freedpeople determined to "realize their rights in practice" and hard-nosed white southerners equally determined to negate those rights, northern ideologies guided the effort to adjudicate southern justice. But so too did freedwomen resolved to play a role in the reconstruction of rights and justice that came in the postemancipation South. For the "complaints," as the federal agency called them, brought to the bureau by freedwomen insistent that they had been "rouged out of [their] rites" were many. Beyond labor disputes and clashes over their children, African American women also initiated complaints that revealed their desire to claim rights within their own households and over their own bodies.[4] But in this fight for strict justice for themselves, freedwomen would have to negotiate the terms of these rights with bureau officials—as well as white southerners and black men—who brought their own beliefs about gender, race, and rights to the table. To bureau men, dispensing justice meant in the end enforcing racial equality before the law and extending civil rights to African Americans rather than fighting gender discriminations. Thus as it mediated legal disputes involving freedpeople, the bureau again claimed the opportunity to impress upon former slaves the rights and obligations of free labor and contract as well as northern notions of household relations, an independent manhood, and a dependent womanhood. When freedwomen's demands for rights within their households and over their bodies were in keeping with these efforts, they benefited from the bureau's brand of justice. But when that was not the case—when they appeared to agents as less-than-respectable women or sought rights and safeguards that white women did not yet possess—freedwomen lost out in their judicial encounters with the bureau.

Bureau policy makers understood that they, as well as the men who served in the agency's offices scattered far too sparsely across the South, were to play a role in what historians today call "the broad revolution in American citizenship that defined the period of Reconstruction."[5] The extent and broad contours of that revolution, however, were not yet clear to bureau men in 1865 and 1866. The Union may have declared victory and Congress may have abolished slavery, but it was still undecided as to what justice and rights for freedpeople meant in the immediate postemancipation South. The outcome of emancipation was far too tentative. Congress had not yet delivered the formal constitutional promises of color-blind citizenship or, for African American men, suffrage. Perhaps the only certainty that the men who staffed the bureau had in the first days of freedom was that any rights the former slaves did possess as free laborers or emergent citizens would require protection.

"The work of my officers in obtaining recognition of the negro as a man instead of a chattel before the civil and criminal courts," Commissioner Howard later insisted, "took the lead" as the agency moved into the South. "[U]nder the title of justice," the Reconstruction-era policy maker maintained, the bureau assumed "the initiative in influencing the South in its transition into the new order of things" and inaugurated "the first active endeavor to put the colored man or woman on a permanent basis on a higher plane." But what did it mean to recognize freedmen and women as something more than "chattel" before the courts? And what was the "higher plane" that Howard sought for them?[6]

Bureau men believed that Union victory and President Abraham Lincoln's proclamation of emancipation, and in due course the Thirteenth Amendment, had secured freedom for African Americans. And this freedom, they reasoned, guaranteed former slaves certain rights (even before the civil and political rights that would come in federal legislation and constitutional amendments). To them, freedom included the absolute rights laid out in the nation's founding documents and accepted by nineteenth-century Americans as human rights—life, liberty, and property. As part of their freedom too the now-former slaves, bureau policy makers agreed, also had the right to expect equal protection of the laws as well as equal standing in the courtroom. "Few things stand out as positively in the records of the Freedmen's Bureau," the historian James Oakes maintains, "as the commitment of its agents to the principle of equal justice under the law." But beyond legal rights were still other rights, according to the bureau. Operating with a broad understanding of justice and influenced by northern notions of free labor and domesticity as well as, for some, abolitionists' call for an expansive definition of rights that included "the sacred rights of the weak," those who led and served the agency insisted that emancipation had brought, at the very least, government protection for the rights to self-ownership, to movement, to the fruit of one's labor, and to lawful marriage and familial relations. "The government has set the slaves free and bound itself to make that freedom an indisputable fact," Howard declared in his first annual report. It was the job of his bureau to make that happen. The formidable work before the Freedmen's Bureau was to, "everywhere," in the commissioner's estimation, "declare and protect their freedom" by securing to freedpeople "equal justice and the same personal liberty" enjoyed by "other citizens and inhabitants" of the nation.[7]

Until southern courts recognized African Americans' changing status and the growing rights that came with it, the Freedmen's Bureau took temporary charge of administering justice. Beginning in its first days in 1865, the bureau backed a judicial policy that placed jurisdiction over disputes involving freedpeople in the hands of federal officials (both military and bureau) stationed across the former Confederacy. Commissioner Howard addressed the issue of justice in his first policy directives. In the "rules and regulations" for assistant commissioners issued on 30 March, for example, he ordered those in "places where there is an interruption of civil law, or in which local courts, by reason of old codes . . . disregard the negro's right to justice before the law" to "adjudicate . . . all difficulties arising between negroes themselves or between negroes and whites or Indians, except those in military service . . . and not taken cognizance of by other tribunals, civil or military, of the United States." Bureau jurisdiction was limited. Policy makers called for agents to refer serious offenses such as felonies or capital crimes to federal courts, provost courts, or—if they ensured blacks' rights to testify and bring suit—state courts. Federal authorities, as the historian Donald Nieman explains, "were unwilling to permit individual officers and agents, most of whom had no legal training, to try such serious matters as grand larceny, burglary, arson, rape, assault with intent to kill, and murder." Bureau men could, and did, arrest persons accused of these kinds of serious offenses against freedpeople, but holding to mid-nineteenth-century understandings of federalism, they surrendered offenders to other authorities when the evidence warranted prosecution. In the end, what federal officials like Commissioner Howard wanted from bureau judicial policy was a way to force southern states to recognize African Americans' emergent citizenship and to cede the civil rights—in particular, to bring suit and to testify in court—that would enable them to protect their own interests once the agency was no more. These Reconstruction-era policy makers did not yet comprehend that equality before the law might not be enough to sustain a meaningful freedom for African Americans in the postwar South.[8]

Howard and his assistant commissioners soon built upon the 30 March policy circular to create an interim system for mediating southern justice. Perhaps most striking in this effort to promote equal justice under the law was the bureau's establishment of freedmen's courts in late 1865. Addressing a crowd of disgruntled white planters in Virginia in September, Commissioner Howard offered these courts a solution to what they regarded as an untenable situation: "Gentlemen, no one of us alone is responsible for emancipation. The negro *is free*. This is a fact." "Now," the commissioner-turned-diplomat asked, "cannot we blue-eyed Anglo-Saxons devise some method by which we can live with him as a free man?" The answer, Howard suggested, was the creation of a system of informal tribunals in which "every interest will be fairly represented." Handling only "minor" cases, these courts, he told them, would be administered by a panel of three community members—one to represent planters, another to represent the freedpeople, and the third a bureau agent to represent the federal government. Though the commissioner's intent was not necessarily to appease white southerners with these courts, he certainly did not say so to this audience. Even so, Howard hoped that the freedmen's courts, as they came to be known, would give former slaves "protection . . . against small personal persecutions and the hostility of white juries." That is, they offered African Americans legal recourse for the "small, endless, mean little injustice of every day" life as well as courtrooms free from the prejudiced judges and juries in state and local courts.[9]

As it evolved, the judicial policy of the bureau allowed for great divergence among local agents who adjudicated legal complaints involving freedmen and women. Official policy had restricted its men and its tribunals to sitting in judgment of "minor" cases. But the meaning of "minor" and thus the extent of bureau assertions of jurisdiction over freedpeople's legal claims varied from state to state. Bureau officials in Mississippi, for instance, offered agents perhaps the most unambiguous guidance, telling them to try "petty cases such as theft, disobedience and breach of the peace," "cases of cruelty and abuse of freedmen," and "cases between Freedmen and Freedmen, and between employers and . . . negroes." In contrast, assistant commissioners in North Carolina and Tennessee provided only vague policy directives, instructing agents to resolve "differences between freedmen and others (or between themselves)" with "counsel and arbitration." Punishments—that is, if agents could enforce them—also fluctuated widely enough that Howard eventually would step in to limit sentences dispensed by the bureau to fines, "in no case exceeding one hundred dollars," and imprisonment of no more than thirty days. Damages in civil cases would be limited similarly. Even the freedmen's courts themselves took on different forms. Although ideally consisting of three officials—a bureau agent and two community representatives, one chosen by local freedpeople and the other by area whites—the bureau's system of arbitration more often looked far different from this model. Most closely resembling what Howard had proposed to planters was the three-judge system created in Virginia by Assistant Commissioner Orlando Brown. Elsewhere, especially in states where bureau officials were fewer in number, assistant commissioners allowed local agents to hear cases on their own or created other kinds of single-judge courts (some even with civilian magistrates). In South Carolina, where military provost courts commandeered cases involving freedpeople, bureau courts would not even exist until June 1866. Finally, it must be remembered that, even though its agents would remain thoroughly involved in blacks' pursuit of justice as "next friends, attorneys, arbitrators, and information gatherers," bureau-run judicial efforts were short lived. The bureau began restoring jurisdiction over cases involving freedpeople to state civil authorities, as had always been intended by its creators and leaders, beginning in late 1865. As southern states relented and passed laws that at least outwardly offered blacks equal access to the law, the agency started to step away from its more formal judicial involvement and turned all but the "petty" cases over to civil authorities. It did, however, reserve the right to reassert itself judicially—which it would do—when states violated blacks' growing civil rights. All things considered—from the difference in crimes considered, punishments handed down, and makeup to their brief existence—the consequences of bureau formal judicial activities were great. They offered an avenue and a public space to pursue claims for justice, even if only for a brief moment, to freedpeople who otherwise would have had access to none.[10]

Bureau efforts to secure equal justice for former slaves, at least as a matter of principle and law, would gain ground in the midst of Congress's expansion of African Americans' rights and enactment of military reconstruction in 1866 and 1867. As a consequence of passage of the black codes by southern legislatures and nonstop bureau reports of "outrages" perpetrated against former slaves, Republicans in Congress came together in February 1866 to preserve the Freedmen's Bureau and to expand its authority. Although still insistent that the agency was but a temporary necessity, authors of the second Freedmen's Bureau bill broadened federal power in the South by extending its life for two years. The legislation also proposed several legal safeguards for African Americans by ordering rebel states to grant them the civil rights "belonging to white persons," to provide blacks "full and equal benefit of all laws and proceedings for security of person and estate," and to end racially discriminatory practices in the punishment of criminals. And to enforce these provisions, Congress empowered the bureau to punish recalcitrant state officials (with fines of as much as $1,000 and imprisonment up to one year) and to assume jurisdiction of cases involving freedpeople if state officials refused to recognize their rights. President Andrew Johnson, desirous of a swift restoration of southern states, vehemently opposed the legislation and charged that Congress lacked the power to force southern states to afford equal rights to former slaves. He vetoed the bill. Congress eventually would override the veto, along with Johnson's strategy to direct Reconstruction alone, however. After months of conflict, the Freedmen's Bureau Act became law without presidential approval in July 1866. Passage of the Military Reconstruction Acts in 1867 would combine with the expanded legal authority of the bureau to give the appearance of a federal government prepared to reassert military control over southern justice.[11]

Beyond granting the bureau renewed life and expanding federal legal authority, Congress further aided the cause of equal justice in the postemancipation South by making African Americans citizens. Passage of the Civil Rights Act of 1866 promised both citizenship and equal rights in state law to former slaves. Indeed, it guaranteed basic civil rights—the right to contract, sue and be sued, testify in court, and own and convey property, for example—to African Americans nationwide. The federal law also declared that no state could deny the "full and equal benefit of all laws and proceedings for the security of person and property" to any citizen, regardless of race. Perhaps most important to the role of the bureau as an arbitrator of southern justice, it also authorized federal authorities to prosecute in federal court any person who deprived another of these rights. In 1868, ratification of the Fourteenth Amendment would augment the rights defined in the Civil Rights Act. Securing African Americans the rights of citizenship, it declared: "All persons born or naturalized in the United States, and subject to the jurisdiction thereof, are citizens of the United States and of the State wherein they reside. No State shall make or enforce any law which shall abridge the privileges and immunities of citizens of the United States; nor shall any State deprive any person of life, liberty, or property, without due process of law; nor deny to any person within its jurisdiction the equal protection of the laws." Although not available for use by the Freedmen's Bureau, the Fourteen Amendment's principle of equal justice before the law was an indispensable part of the agency's judicial efforts nonetheless.[12]

Historians have long concluded that, even with the law on its side, bureau judicial policy and practice ultimately fell short in the postemancipation South. As Robert Kaczorowski explains, the "efforts of Bureau agents to protect and enforce freedmen's rights were insufficient and ineffective." While they "exercised sufficient civil legal authority to secure the civil rights and personal safety of the freedmen of the South," bureau men encountered "virtually insurmountable practical obstacles to civil rights enforcement." Their failure was not, in other words, attributable to an "insufficiency" in bureau authority or even to the lack of civil rights law but rather, he writes, resulted from the "hopeless conditions that impeded, if not precluded," bureau men from enforcing civil rights in Reconstruction. Their president was intent on impeding any effectiveness of the agency. Their mission was often frustrated by the limits of official policy that at once seemed to offer much legal discretion and yet told them to concede that discretion to military authorities or to restore jurisdiction to civil courts. And when they did issue commands, they found it near impossible to enforce them, given the limited number of federal troops and federal courts in their sizeable districts. Bureau men were operating in communities that paid no heed to law and order, rejected their (indeed all federal) authority, and generally subverted justice and backed lawlessness in heretofore unthinkable ways. The courts and judicial efforts of the Freedmen's Bureau were just not enough and, in consequence, diminished significantly through 1867 and, by the end of 1868, ended altogether.[13]

Even if a "splendid failure," as W. E. B. Du Bois once described Reconstruction, and even if only for a short time, the courts and the agents of the Freedmen's Bureau that meted out southern justice from 1865 to 1868 played an important role in shaping African Americans' demand for rights as emergent citizens. The bureau offered an opening and a space for freedpeople to fight racial injustice under the new laws of freedom, as well as an ally. Long denied access to the legal system but familiar nonetheless with the process of localized law, as the historian Laura Edwards has demonstrated with particular precision, freedwomen and men became an incredibly litigious people in the immediate postemancipation years.[14] And, for a great many, their first experiences with law, the judicial process, and the assertion of rights came in the field offices of the Freedmen's Bureau. There, bureau men offered former slaves a broad concept of justice as well as entry to a place—whether that meant a freedmen's court, a bureau field office, an individual agent, a military tribunal, or the civil courts—that promised recognition of their legal standing and expanding rights. Laying before the bureau complaints that touched upon every aspect of their lives, former slaves would come to regard the agency as a partner in their pursuit of justice until its last days. Still "everyday," an agent stationed in Athens,

Georgia, would report in 1868, bureau offices were "crowded with freedmen women and children . . . demanding justice."[15] And just as they had in so many other instances, freedwomen looked to the bureau as an ally to assert rights within their own households and over their own bodies.

In countless ways, African American women in the immediate postemancipation years endeavored to "throw off the badge of servitude" and, in doing so, claim the dignity, self-respect, and self-determination commensurate with their new legal status. Perhaps the greatest promise of freedom lay in the possibility of reclaiming families, reconstructing households, and establishing domestic relations that, at last, would be protected by law. "If I'm really free I must go and find my husband," explained one former slave woman to her former master in the aftermath of Confederate defeat. Weeping with joy as she located a former partner from the days of slavery, another freedwomen underscored some of the most intimate complexities that slavery and emancipation had wrought upon slaves-turned-freedpeople and their families. "'Twas like a stroke of death to me," she proclaimed upon seeing the freedman for the first time after their emancipation. "We threw ourselves into each others arms and cried," she remembered. "His wife looked and was jealous, but she needn't have been. My husband is so kind, I shouldn't leave him, but I ain't happy." Oh how the former slave damned those responsible for her pain: "White folks got a heap to answer for the way they've done to colored folks!" To freedwomen, the end of slavery had given birth to rights previously unimaginable. At last they could be women who, as the historian Thavolia Glymph explains, were "mothers, workers, friends, and companions" with rights, they believed, "to citizenship and dignity." "In their eyes," as a bureau agent explained about the black mothers and children he encountered while stationed in South Carolina, "the work of emancipation was incomplete until the families which had been dispersed by slavery were reunited."[16] Without question, the reconstruction of black families was not just a paramount concern to the Freedmen's Bureau in these first days of freedom.

Neither was lawful marriage. For many former slave women and men, legally sanctioned marriage offered a visible sign of their new status. It conferred legitimacy to their most intimate relationships as well as offered security for their domestic lives that had been unknown in slavery. "*I praise God for this day!* I have long been praying for it. The Marriage Covenant is at the foundation of all our rights," a black Union soldier in Virginia declared in 1866 after the bureau superintendent of marriage for the area read a policy circular on marriage. "In slavery we could not have *legalised* marriage: *now* we have it," he proclaimed. "Let us conduct ourselves worthy of such a blessing—and all the people will respect us—God will bless us, and we shall be established as a people." An emancipation celebration in 1866 among freedpeople in Georgia expressed similar sentiments—sentiments that had to sound good to bureau men who promoted northern understandings of domesticity: "This is a day of gratitude for the freedom of matrimony. Formerly there was no security for domestic happiness. Our ladies were insulted and degraded with or without their consent. Our wives were sold and husbands bought, children were begotten and enslaved by their fathers, we therefore were polygamists by virtue of our condition. But now we can marry and raise our children and teach them to fear God, O! black age of dissipation, thy days are nearly numbered." Just as the denial of marriage to slaves had "underscored their dependent position and the precariousness of their family ties," marriage under the laws of the land, as Laura Edwards explains, confirmed much to black men in particular about their changed status. It proved their freedom. It embodied their absolute rejection of slavery. It demonstrated their manhood and worth as citizens. To former slaves, lawful marriage and the legitimized families that it created symbolized the rights of freedom.[17]

But African Americans understood that marriage and family went beyond rights to convey to them obligations. Although not necessarily recognized by the bureau in the ways that they wanted, freedwomen and men generally embraced certain gender distinctions in their familial obligations. Black men, for example, accepted public authority over families and strived to provide for them with the fruits of their labor. Black women, on the other hand, took up domestic responsibilities as well as working as needed outside the home to help support their families. In accepting these gendered roles and responsibilities, however, former slave women and men were not simply trying to emulate the ideal of the northern white, middle-class nuclear family promoted by bureau men. Rather, they welcomed them as a sign of their dignity and status as emergent citizens. Moreover, freedmen and freedwomen made clear that just as they accepted these roles, so too could they reject them. In particular, while many freedwomen encouraged black men's assertion of their manhood as heads of household and granted familial authority to them, that did not mean they relinquished their own authority. Instead, as the historians Nancy Bercaw, Elsa Barkley Brown, Noralee Frankel, and Susan O'Donovan, among others, have demonstrated, African American women in the Reconstruction-era South "took their place as citizens alongside men" and came to recognize benefits to freedmen's authority in public spaces. Still, some—like freedwoman Mary Bennett, who spat in her husband's face when he brought her before the bureau, insisted she "would not obey his orders," and told him that she was "her own woman"—would forcefully reject any attempt by others, even black men, to assert control over them.[18]

The complaints involving domestic discord brought by freedwomen to the Freedmen's Bureau confirm that they, like freedmen and bureau men, understood marriage and family both as symbolic of their changed status and as relationships that came with obligations. They also confirm that black women were prepared to make use of the bureau's interest in transforming the black family when their familial needs went unmet or when domestic discord arose. By proceeding to local bureau offices to settle disputes over child custody (as seen in Chapter 4), abandonment and desertion, and marital discord involving infidelity, familial support—both for their children and themselves—and violence, freedwomen attempted to defend their own place and authority in black families. But just as they did in other instances, they sought bureau involvement in domestic affairs on their own terms, accepted its support when it was to their benefit, and rejected it when the wishes of the federal government differed from their own.[19]

With the bureau's help, freedwomen attempted to hold black men accountable to the obligations of marriage and family life as they understood them. Perhaps the most common domestic complaint brought to the bureau by African American women involved freedmen's failure to perform as responsible husbands and fathers. They complained when husbands abandoned them and left them, and their children, without support.[20] They made charges too against black husbands who committed adultery or were unfaithful in some other way.[21] Such was the case for Sarah Runnels, a Texas freedwoman who complained to the agent in Boston that her husband of twelve or fourteen years had deserted her and their children "without cause." Clearly unhappy, she also reported that he had taken up with another woman. Freedwoman Matilda Strafford found herself in comparable circumstances, reporting to the bureau that her husband had abandoned her, forcing her "to labor to support herself and her child." Virginia freedwoman Ann Marie Brown complained of a husband who had gone off to Maryland but would "send her no money" so that she might join him. In Mississippi, freedwoman Caroline Denby reported to the bureau in Yazoo City that her "husband had left her and lives with another woman." As if that were not enough, she also lamented that the freedman had "sold the house over her head and taken away her marriage papers." So bad was abandonment in his district in Albemarle County, Virginia, that Agent William Tidball insisted that black men were "frequently" changing their names "to escape detection, and almost invariably live with other women in adultery." Complaints of desertion and infidelity were not limited to freedwomen, however. Although significantly fewer, freedmen also brought suit against wives who had violated the conjugal bonds of matrimony. Indeed, when freedmen entered domestic complaints with the bureau, it almost always involved charges that wives had committed infidelity. Freedman Jerry Ellis, for instance, complained to the bureau official in Charlottesville, Virginia, that his wife, Molly, had "deserted him, and refuses to live with him." Similarly, Mississippi freedman John Taylor complained that "his wife Martha has left his 'bread and board' and taken away his child with her, and is now living in adultery with Peter Clark." Regardless of who initiated the formal complaint to the bureau, the point was clear. Both black women and black men expected spouses to uphold certain obligations of marriage and family in freedom.[22]

Guided by seemingly uncompromising notions about the obligations of free labor and domesticity, bureau men offered little support to freepersons—male or female—who refused to marry, deserted spouses, entered into adulterous relationships, or failed to support their families. Neither they nor God, as Assistant Commissioner Fisk put it, would "wink at adultery and fornication among" those who, he insisted, "should be married according to law, as soon as possible." The bureau showed little empathy for sexual liaisons outside marriage. This was especially apparent when black women petitioned the bureau to hold accountable men who had "seduced" them, made "promises" of marriage, or left them after they had lived together without being formally married. Freedwoman Jane Pace, for instance, came to the bureau complaining that a freedman had "ruined her character by sleeping with her" and now wanted the bureau "to make him pay." The agent showed no compassion for the woman, who had been, according to the bureau at least, "careless in [her] morals." Rather, he informed Pace that she had had "no business sleeping with him" and that, because she was not lawfully married, the bureau "had no power to make him pay." Similarly, when asked about the "cases where freedmen having lived for years with women . . . lately have deserted them and taken up with other women," the assistant commissioner of Mississippi, Alvan Gillem, replied steadfastly that "where the parties are legally married the civil law provides for such cases." Having issued what Nancy Bercaw has called a crackdown "on what he defined as promiscuous behavior," Gillem worked with civil courts to enforce marriage laws in black communities. "The courts alone," he insisted, "can establish a radical cure." But for those not legally married, he concluded, "this Bureau has no authority to make the people live together." Not all bureau men agreed, however. Officials in Charlottesville, Virginia, for example, took a different approach. Insisting to freedman Belfield Johnson that even though he and his "wife" had not been "married by a clergyman" he was not at liberty to leave, the bureau ordered that the freedman "must not try to escape" his marital obligations. Most often, and although they decided cases of domestic discord on an individual basis, bureau men did so with notions about the duties of black men foremost in mind. After all, "every right minded freeman," bureau policy in Virginia had declared from the outset in July 1865, "will work to keep his Father, Mother, Brother, Sister, Wife or children out of a place where they must live on alms given by strangers." Freedom demanded that black husbands and fathers "*work like men* who know what it is to be FREE."[23]

Claims for economic support often accompanied freedwomen's complaints of desertion, adultery, and seduction, and they too benefited from the support of bureau men insistent that black men—rather than the federal government or public charity—should support black wives and children.[24] Even before their child was born, freedwoman Mary Johnson asked the bureau to force the father, Frank, to "furnish a Physician during child birth and some one to take care of her afterward." The agent proceeded to "see" Frank, obtained his consent to do so, and then took the opportunity to advise the freedman to "drop" this "Sweetheart business" and accept his obligations as a free man and lawfully marry Johnson. Facing more dire circumstances, freedwoman Mathilda Smith complained to the bureau in Albany, Georgia, that her husband of six years had abandoned her and their two children. Reporting that he had "not done anything whatever . . . [in] assisting her in feeding & clothing those children," she pleaded for help in obtaining some kind of support. And agents were most likely to respond to freedwomen like Smith who presented themselves as devoted mothers. Demonstrating a degree of sympathy for abandoned freedwomen, but more likely influenced by the desire to promote a southern free labor society and northern notions of family, bureau men readily forced freedmen to accept their familial responsibilities—especially in terms of economic support—whenever possible. The agent in Algiers, Louisiana, echoed the responses of many agents when he commanded freedman John Capus to pay the mother of his child $4 per week.[25] So intent that freedwomen and children not become wards of the federal government were some agents that they went so far as to hold white men financially accountable for children born to black women.[26]

Freedwomen also used the bureau to intercede into their domestic relations when they became the target of abuse by husbands.[27] For some women, the acceptance of black men as heads of households had not come without cost. As evident in the complaint records of the bureau, African American men at times seized the power granted to them by emancipation to abuse their wives, to control and even kidnap their children, and to plunder wages meant to support their families. In the worst cases, black men relegated wives and children to the status of slaves in their own homes. The appeal of a Georgia freedman who went to a local bureau official for help forcing the return of his abused—and now runaway—wife made this abundantly clear. The husband wanted her back because she was, as the agent recorded, "the only nigger he had." Mississippi freedwoman Anna Hayden expressed a similar sentiment as she described her abusive and unequal marriage to federal pension authorities in 1905. "Me and my boy Henry were his slaves more than anything else and he took our wages." In South Carolina, Laney complained to the bureau that she had been "beat about 30 lashes, with a leather strap, over her back and shoulders, by her husband Cesar." In Louisiana, freedwoman Sarah was beaten "shamefully" for refusing to dance with Henry Jackson. In Texas, Dollina Williams and Emma Matthews reported husbands who drank heavily and abused them. The extent of domestic violence in the homes of former slaves during Reconstruction is hard to know, but, as the historian Dorothy Sterling notes, it was widespread enough that freedwomen picking cotton in the Carolina Sea Islands sang: "Black men beat me, White men cheat me, Won' get my hundud all day."[28]

As they considered black women's complaints of domestic abuse, bureau men again were guided by the gendered ideologies that demanded black husbands reject the brutality of slavery, assume the household obligations of free men, and care for their families with restraint. And, indeed, freedwomen who appealed to the bureau to stop domestic abuse as lawful, dutiful wives found an ally. Such was the case for freedwoman Silvia, who appealed to the bureau in Georgia for protection from an abusive husband—a man who "beats her brutally & without provocation." Judy Barnett made similar complaint and obtained a comparable response from the bureau. Reporting that her husband "beat her severely with a broom," she wanted not only to see him punished "severely" but also "to part from him forever, never to live with him again." The agent agreed and separated the couple "forever." Bureau inquiries into the complaints of some freedwomen, however, did not always garner such benefits. Lucy Ann King found out as much when she complained to the bureau in Texas that her husband, Wesley King, not only beat her but also owed her money and had deserted her. Reporting that the couple was not lawfully married and that the alleged Mrs. King was a "desperate character, having attempted to poison her master and mistress, also having been in jail for bad conduct," the agent refused to investigate further. By and large, however, freedwomen anxious to end violence against them benefited from agents willing to do what they could to protect them as dependent women.[29]

There were limits to the justice that bureau men could bestow upon African American women who tried to assert their rights within black households, however. Certainly the Georgia freedwoman who returned repeatedly to the bureau in an effort to stop her husband's abuse understood that. Having had the freedman arrested twice already, she faced his wrath yet again, and yet again she threatened to report him to the bureau field office in Chatham County. Undeterred, however, the husband responded forcefully, telling her: "[D]amn the Freedmen's Bureau—I'll cuss you before them." The enraged man, in her words, then "came to my room, took all his things, some four linen sheets & .... tore up two nice dresses of mine." He also tellingly informed his wife that "he would rather keep a woman than be married—because she could not carry him to the law and I could." Freedwoman Susan Akins was another who discovered the threshold of federal authority in black homes. Reporting that her husband, Malice Akins, "cursed and beat her and . . . damned her soul," the woman appealed to the local agent in Athens, Georgia, for redress. Having little patience with his wife or the bureau, for that matter, the freedman announced his plans to leave her for another woman, insisting that neither she nor the bureau could stop him.[30]

As these cases illustrate, bureau resolution of cases involving domestic strife at times could involve more talk than action. Orders, directives, and lectures could do only so much in the Reconstruction-era South. Although in some instances they called on civil authorities to prosecute cases of domestic discord or white employers to counsel disgruntled couples in "the duties of man and wife," most often bureau officials relied on lectures imbued with lessons in northern domesticity and free labor. Thus bureau men responded most often with modest steps that offered advice, guidance, and at times threats to resolve marital and familial disputes. Instead of disciplinarians, they paternalistically declared themselves teacher and marriage counselor. Upon hearing one complaint of spousal abuse, Agent Charles Rauschenberg in Albany, Georgia, responded with what was a rather typical instruction to black men about their roles and responsibilities as free men, husbands, and citizens. "Your wife complains to me, that you are in the habit of whipping & beating her," the agent asserted disapprovingly to the black husband. Continuing, he explained:

[A]s you like many other freedpeople are ignorant of the law I think it proper to inform you that the law of the State gives no . . . husband the right to whip his wife under any circumstances. You are free and have to obey the law as much as anybody else or submit to the same punishment if you violate it, besides that you should think of yourself, your wife and your freedom to act like a brute and beat your wife. Do you want any body to beat you, when you do not do to their notion? If not, why do you think it proper to beat your wife, is she not quite as good as you are? You better learn to act like a free man and a good man & make it your business to learn how to act as a free man & show yourself worthy of your freedom instead of acting the negro any longer. If you do not quit this conduct towards your wife I shall as soon as complaint is made again put the law in force against you and it will cost you time & money & you will probably be imprisoned for your conduct. You have neither to spare, but if you can not profit by advice you must by experience.

Bureau intervention and resolution in cases of domestic discord came often in the form of lectures similar to that of this Georgia agent. Approached with a case of quarrelling and infidelity, a South Carolina agent dealt a similar but more dismissive response. Sending both the husband and wife away, he told the couple "to forget their little troubles, forgive and forget, work hard; lay up something for a rainy day, and they won't have much time or inclination to quarrel, and above all be honest, industrious, and virtuous."[31]

Unsatisfied with lectures on the values of free labor and domesticity, freedwomen's complaints of desertion, adultery, lack of financial support, and spousal abuse at times culminated in demands for separation or divorce. While many freedpeople continued the practice of "quitting," bureau policy makers repeatedly instructed them that the laws of the land and of God required them, as free men and women, to end one relationship before beginning another. Thus, at least to bureau men, with the right of legal marriage came the obligation of legal divorce when parties desired to end a relationship. "You cannot at your pleasure part and take up with another," demanded one Mississippi official. "To have two wives or two husbands," he informed former slaves, "is one of the highest and disastrous offenses that can be committed against human or divine law." Bureau men did not take divorce and separation lightly and in many cases dodged these kinds of complaints altogether by sending black couples to civil authorities. When they did act to settle requests for the dissolution of marriage, however, bureau men were influenced by the broader goals of Reconstruction. Take the case of Sarah Jenkins, a freedwoman in Georgia, for instance. Jenkins appealed to the bureau for separation from her husband, Alford, in consequence of "ill-treatment." Alford, protested his wife, regularly made threats of violence, existed in a state of drunkenness, and did not "provide any thing for suport of herself and child." Indeed, because of his "bad conduct," the black wife now feared that she would lose her job as a cook for a white family. Although in most cases agents lectured the parties on familial responsibility and sent them on their way "to live together peaceably," under these circumstances the agent did not think that wise. Clearly guided by a desire to promote free labor and to punish black men who rejected their "duties and responsibilities as free men & as husbands and fathers," this bureau man supported Mrs. Jenkins's appeal, granted the separation, and even allowed her to retain custody of the couple's child.[32]

In the exceptional cases that bureau officials consented to separations and divorces, they also negotiated settlements. Such was the case as Albert Matthews and his wife, Mary Bennett, came before the bureau in Athens, Georgia. Concluding that Bennett and Matthews were never going to be able to live together "peaceablely," the local agent ordered the two "forever seperated" and for Matthews to pay Bennett support in the sum of $50 at Christmas. The freedmen's court in Richmond, Virginia, encountered a more complicated case when Rebecca and Henry Woodson appeared before it. Having brought suit against her husband for failing to fulfill his marital obligations, the Mrs. Woodson demanded economic support for herself and three children (whom she also requested custody of) as well as a legal divorce. Clearly more sympathetic to the freedwoman's cause, the court ordered the couple "divorced *a mensa et thore*" and "enjoined" the freedman from "molesting" his former wife. It also commanded the freedman to pay the exorbitant sum of $25 per month toward her support. Not completely indifferent to the husband's status, however, the court ruled that the Mr. Woodson could "have exclusive control of the boat and mule . . . so long as he performs this judgement without fault."[33]

For freedwomen, lawful marriage—whether embraced as a right of freedom or decreed for them by southern laws and bureau men who demanded it—was, according to the legal historian Norma Basch, "a mixed blessing." They had been "liberated from the bonds of slavery" only to be told by federal policy makers "to submit to the bonds of matrimony."[34] To bureau men, lawful marriage and the families that it created promised peace and social order to the nation and "the civil rights of married persons" to former slaves, who could now make their "children [their] legal heirs."[35] Without question, those who led and served the bureau expected freedwomen, like freedmen, to enter lawful marriages, take their domestic obligations seriously, and create nuclear families with male heads of household. And freedwomen and men took note of these expectations and the many proclamations that promoted marriage as a right and a duty in freedom. Claiming the rights of marriage and family relations especially, freedpeople grasped the power of bureau policy and, as they had in other aspects of their postemancipation lives, attempted to use the agency's interests in domestic relations to their benefit. Thus just as marriage was a mixed blessing for freedwomen, so too was the bureau. For those who presented themselves as virtuous women, dutiful wives, and devoted mothers in domestic complaints against freedmen who had fallen short in their obligations as free men, responsible husbands, and worthy citizens, the federal agency could be a useful ally. For those who did not, however, the bureau and its men were at best a condescending intermediary that disregarded their domestic claims and at worst a foe that dealt devastating gendered blows.

Freedwomen also turned to the Freedmen's Bureau in protest of racial violence against them. Such violence of course was not new to the women and men who had endured vast cruelties in slavery. What was different in Reconstruction, however, was that African American women understood that they, like black men, had the right to combat white assaults against them as well as the backing of federal authorities, who had a stake in protecting these rights. To the men who led and served the bureau, in particular, the "outrages" perpetuated against freedwomen were part of the larger difficulty of racial violence and lawlessness in the South—a problem that had national implications as it challenged social order, federal authority, and the very experiment of Reconstruction. Freedwomen, like freedmen, also understood white southerners' violent assaults on them as part of a broader attempt to reassert racial control and to void former slaves' recently acquired rights. Thus freedwomen confronted acts of racial violence by going to the bureau (and later by offering testimony in congressional hearings) in an effort to protect their families and communities and to defend a collective meaning of freedom. But by challenging those who tied them up by their thumbs and beat, flogged, raped, maimed, and otherwise abused them, African American women also attempted to assert autonomy over their lives as free women, as respectable women, and, in their minds, as emergent citizens in their own right. Intent on reclaiming, controlling, and protecting their own bodies, they declared a right to self-ownership and, by turning to the bureau, found an ally that was willing (though for reasons different from their own) to recognize them as women, in the historian Hannah Rosen's words, "worthy of equal protection under the law, of bodily integrity, and of voice."[36]

The records of the Freedmen's Bureau are satiated with horrific crimes committed with savagery and depravity against freedpeople in the immediate postemancipation South. Reporting the "outrages" committed in their districts became a routine task for agents, and quite often their reports resembled that of P. Bonesteel. A special inspector employed by the bureau to investigate the condition of freedpeople in Kentucky and Tennessee, Bonesteel reported some sixty cases of outrage "unparalleled in their atrocity and fiendishness" in a period of one month—March 1866—alone. Careful to note that these cases "constituted but a portion of the catalogue of cruelties," he reported:

> I have classified these outrages as follows: Twenty-three cases of severe and inhumane beating and whipping of men; four of beating and shooting; two of robbing and shooting; three of robbing; five men shot and killed; two shot and wounded; four beaten to death; one beaten and roasted; three women assaulted and ravished; four women beaten; two women tied up and

whipped until insensible; two men and their families beaten and driven from their homes, and their property destroyed; two instances of burning of dwellings, and one of the inmates shot. Of these victims, twelve men were Union soldiers, and three women the wives of Union soldiers.[37]

The extent to which whites countered emancipation, blacks' expanding rights, and the presence of federal authority in the South with violence shocked bureau men. "In the more remote districts, where bureau agents are 50 or 100 miles apart, and stations of troops still further, freedmen do not dare or presume to act in opposition to the will of their late masters," the assistant commissioner of Texas reported in 1868. Perhaps more troubling to this bureau policy maker, however, was the fact that the freedpeople "make no effort to exercise rights conferred upon them by the acts of Congress, and few even of Union men are brave enough, or rather foolhardy enough, to advise them" to do otherwise. Just as appalling was the harsh reality that civil authorities paid no heed when whites assaulted or murdered freedmen and women. "Lawless violence and ruffianism have prevailed," the assistant commissioner in Arkansas declared as the bureau prepared to close its doors. In just one day, the agent in Jackson, Mississippi, reported that a white man had shot and "severely if not fatally wounded" a freedman, "another colored man came in from the country severally wounded in the arm by a knife in the hand of his employer," and the city's former mayor had whipped a freedwomen. Indeed, one local law enforcement official had even praised the former mayor's actions, insisting "he was sorry he had not whipped the woman more severely."[38]

Freedwomen were particularly vulnerable to violence in the aftermath of emancipation, and the catalog of abuses they brought to the bureau attests to that fact.[39] As demonstrated in Chapter 3, freedwomen suffered great cruelty at the hands of white employers. But like the former slave woman whipped in Jackson, they also endured horrendous acts of violence at the hands of whites who were not their employers and for reasons far beyond defiance in the workplace. In Georgia, a pregnant freedwoman named Caroline, for instance, "received 350 lashes on her bare legs & shoulders." In Texas, freedwoman Elvira Hammones was struck "several times . . . in her face, left eye and left temple, so that she lay senseless a whole day and night." In New Orleans, freedwoman Lucy Smith was murdered by a group of white men who "cut off her breast, then disemboweled and decapitated her." Even age did not protect black women. In an instance in Virginia, a young freedgirl endured unbridled savagery as she walked to school. The cause of her assault by a white boy? "[S]he was singing, 'Uncle Sam is rich enough to send us all to school,'" reported the local bureau agent in Lexington. The bureau's log of racial violence attests to black women's strength as well as their intense desire that freedom not resemble slavery in any way.[40]

Sexual violence was perhaps the most degrading, but by no means unfamiliar, abuse experienced by freedwomen. As in slavery, black women in freedom suffered the indignities of sexual assaults ranging from "whispered words on the street and attempted seductions to mutilations and gang rapes." Emancipation, as Hannah Rosen, among others, has demonstrated, heightened this violence against freedwomen as southern white men ritualized a gendered script for racial dominance that denied African Americans' legal equality gained in emancipation and the public policy of early Reconstruction. In both their rhetoric and actions, white men desecrated black homes, discredited black women's "potential identities as honorable wives and daughters," and denied the ability of black men to act as heads of household able to protect their families. Rape and other forms of sexual assault thus became part of a gendered instrument of terror employed by southern white men to exact racial control and to negate the promises and laws of freedom.[41]

African American women's testimonies regarding rape before the bureau and other federal authorities demonstrated, perhaps more than any other act in Reconstruction, their intense desire to reject the legacies of slavery and to assert a right to self-ownership. Southern law had long excluded black women from the legal understanding of rape and thus did not acknowledge their sexual violation as a crime. Now possessing the right to marry and with it, according to the bureau, a right to protect their virtue, freedwomen used the bureau as a forum to claim a womanhood of their own and to define as rape the sexual abuse they suffered at the hands of white men.[42] Though not rare in bureau records, complaints of rape against white men are certainly fewer than other grievances filed by freedwomen. Frances Thompson and Lucy Smith were but two former slave women who testified to having endured extreme brutality and degradation during the Memphis riot of 1866,[43] a confrontation between black militia men and white policeman that gave way to an angry white mob ravaging the city's black community. After seven men (two of whom were policemen) burst into Thompson's house and demanded "supper," the men informed her and Smith that "they wanted some women to sleep with." The women resisted, responding that they "were not that sort of women." But that mattered little to these men, for as Thompson recounted,

> They said "that didn't make a damned bit of difference." One of them hit me on the side of my face and, holding my throat, choked me. Lucy tried to get out of the window when one of them knocked her down. They drew their pistols and said they would shoot us and fire the house if we did not

let them have their way with us. All seven of the men violated us. Four of them had to do with me, and the rest with Lucy.[44]

Smith offered a similar recollection of the experience. "They tried to take advantage of me, and did," she told the federal authorities investigating the riot. Continuing, she explained:

> I told them I did not do such things, and would not. One of them said he would make me, and choked me by the neck. My neck was swollen up [the] next day, and for two weeks I could not talk to anyone. After the first man had connexion with me, another got hold of me and tried to violate me, but I was so bad he did not. He gave me a lick with his fist and said that I was so damned near dead he would not have anything to do with me.[45]

Similar reports made their way to the agents and records of the Freedmen's Bureau.[46] No longer slaves, freedwomen resisted having their bodies treated as the property of white men and pleaded that justice be done. Freedwoman Laura Sanders, for instance, went to the Mississippi bureau after several white men broke into her house and "ravished her and otherwise mistreated her." Louisiana freedwoman Mary Jane Forrest likewise complained to the agent in Baton Rouge after she was "thrust . . . against the fence and beat" for refusing a man's demand to "to s——k his privates." Ignoring the threat that her throat would be "cut from ear to ear," Maryland freedwoman Margaret Warner reported the "most brutal" violation of her thirteen-year-old daughter.[47] In a particularly egregious case reported to the Freedmen's Bureau in Georgia, freedwoman Rhoda Ann Childs suffered as many other wives of black Union soldiers had. In her affidavit to the bureau, Childs reported that eight white men had taken her from her home when her husband was away. She testified to the repulsive details of her experience:

> They then Seized me and took me Some distance from the house, where they "bucked" me down across a log, Stripped my clothes over my head, one of the men Standing astride my neck, and two men holding my legs. In this position I was beaten with a strap until they were tired. Then they turned me parallel with the log, laying my neck on a limb which projected from the log, and one man placing his foot upon my neck, beat me again on my hip and thigh. Then I was thrown upon the ground on my back, one of the men Stood upon my breast, while the two other took hold of my feet and stretched my limbs as far apart as they could, while the man Standing upon my breast applied the Strap to my private parts until fatigued into

stopping, and I was more dead than alive. Then a man, I suppose a Confederate Soldier . . . fell upon me and ravished me. During the whipping, one of the men ran his pistol into me, and said he "had a hell of a mind to pull the trigger," and Swore they ought to Shoot me, as my husband had been in the "God damned Yankee Army," and Swore they meant to kill every black Son-of-a-bitch they could find that had ever fought against them. They then went to the house, seized my two daughters and beat them, demanding their father's pistol, and upon failure to get that, they entered the house and took Such articles of clothing as Suited their fancy and decamped.[48]

With such acts of sexual domination, white men in the South employed, in the historian Gerda Lerner's words, "an instrument of oppression of the entire race." Rape demonstrated to freedwomen that white men still considered them property to be used at their disposal, it demonstrated to freedmen that emancipation had not granted them the ability to protect their women without cost, and it demonstrated to the black community as a whole that white southerners intended to uphold the southern system of racial exploitation and white supremacy by whatever means necessary.[49]

By 1868, white vigilante groups such as the Ku Klux Klan had perfected its campaign of widespread terror and employed rape as a gendered tool for racial control directed at upending the consequences of emancipation. As the historian Lou Faulkner Williams has skillfully demonstrated in her study of the Ku Klux Klan trials in South Carolina, although "the Klan was largely political in its purposes and the typical outrage consisted of breaking into a black Republican's home, stealing or destroying his gun, dragging him outside and whipping him unmercifully, then warning him never again to vote the Republican ticket, many of the Klan's most brutal atrocities were crimes against women and children, who could not vote." Louisiana freedwoman Julia Brown certainly understood the viciousness to which some white men would resort to prevent black men from participating in politics and public life as free men. Accompanied by a uniformed police officer from New Orleans, a band of white men entered her home and threatened "to shoot her unless she told where her husband's registration papers were kept." A Mississippi freedwoman and her husband similarly experienced the full fury of white southerners. In an act that was not uncommon, the men concealed their identities with "faces blackened," violently whipped the woman and her husband, and raped her three times. Freedwomen Harriet Simril suffered such cruelty at the hands of Klansmen in South Carolina. Blinded by spit and dirt thrown into her eyes, she was carried into the street, raped in succession by three men, and then left for dead. Not long after, the men returned to burn her home to the ground. The Klan, as another freedwoman later explained to Congress, "took the spite out on the women." The sexual oppression of black women in Reconstruction was, as Williams explains, "more than a matter of sadistic lust, more than a crime against women. It was layered with social and political meaning directed primarily against the assertion of black male political power rather than against women per se."[50]

Defying white demands for silence, fear, and Victorian notions of modesty, freedwomen and men protested acts of violence, sexual and otherwise, against them and their communities by lodging complaints and testimony with the bureau (and, when the bureau was no more, with federal military authorities, congressional committees, and civil authorities). The bureau responded as best it could. It turned to proclamations condemning racial violence just as it had with violence that occurred as part of labor disputes. It attempted to hold offenders accountable within the limits that the law and military authorities allowed, ordering fines of up to $150 and short imprisonments for offenses of rape and other acts of violence against women. It also referred cases to civil authorities, monitored the cases, and acted as "next friends, attorneys, arbitrators, and information gatherers" for African American women and men who sought to defend their rights and to hold their offenders accountable. But as it did so, and as was the case in the bureau's long-standing demands for "strict justice for every man, woman, and child," their efforts were frustrated by seemingly insurmountable obstacles—not the least of which were civil authorities intent on obstructing federal authority and African American rights.[51]

The experiences of Texas freedwoman Harriet Hampton underscored the great difficulties that black women encountered in the system of justice in the postemancipation South. Hampton endured serious repercussions for having reported an assault and battery to the local bureau office—the man she accused of having abused her beat her twice again, once in the bureau office while the agent "was gone to dinner" and again on her way home. Shocked by the blatant disregard for her rights and his authority as a federal officer, the bureau agent vowed to see that Hampton received justice. He charged the man on several counts of assault and turned the matter over to civil authorities, as was called for by federal policy. The agent then monitored the case, offered his own testimony, and aided the freedwoman in filing "an affidavit before the magistrate." But all his efforts seemed for naught. When the busy life of an agent took him away on other business, the effort to secure justice for Hampton was frustrated. While he was away, a local judge "sent after" the freedwoman to inform her that her ally—the local bureau agent—had been sent "to Galveston to be decapitated" and that he "would never officiate in this town again." Instead, the white southern judge warned Hampton that "he . . . or some other of his kind, would succeed" the bureau there to adjudicate a new brand of justice. Indeed, he proclaimed, "the bureau [is] as good as dead" and "the niggers there might look out." The civil magistrate "then and there" proceeded to get Hampton "to believe that she was only signing a paper that merely showed her willingness to drop the suit against" her abuser. Imagine Hamton's surprise when the agent returned. "No one appeared to know where I came from, and looked it," he later told his superiors. Yet even with his return and despite his success at getting a new trial for Hampton, in the end, her "victory" was but one dollar and "one cent" in damages.[52] Access to rights and even to courts did not mean either equality or justice in the immediate postemancipation South.

Yet that was not the end. Freedwomen (and men) continued to report the "outrages" committed against them to the bureau even as doing so brought devastating consequences and justice that fell short. That freedwomen continued to register complaints challenging violence against them—even when they knew the great dangers and limited results that would come—demonstrated their intense desire to assert a right to self-ownership and to a public voice. Even without justice, freedwomen's protests against violence were a brave political act. In their demands that freedom impart justice, black women desired the recognition of their womanhood for the respectability, integrity, and protection it could provide against violence, sexual or otherwise. By turning to the bureau, freedwomen also revealed their recognition of the federal agency and its men as an ally critical to the preservation of their rights.[53] And the men who led and served the bureau worked on behalf of equal justice under the law. They condemned white southerners' use of violence against freedwomen. They acknowledged African American women's right to be protected by law. They demanded that civil courts punish offenders and offered what limited support they could provide. But for freedwomen to obtain legal redress for acts of violence committed against them and for offenders to be held legally accountable, bureau men believed state and local courts had to recognize African Americans' rights and be willing to impart a justice that did not discriminate based on race.[54] And when that did not happen—as was the case in the years between 1865 and 1868—bureau men continued to catalog and report the many "outrages" committed against freedwomen as part of a larger narrative intent on challenging racial injustice and promoting an expanded federal presence and authority in the South. That narrative presented freedwomen as virtuous victims who protested senseless racial brutality that came at the hands of dishonorable men. Such violence against freedwomen, they wanted to believe, would be remedied with the removal of racial distinctions in the letter of the law and the enforcement of justice without regard to race. That is, once white southerners treated freedwomen as citizens equal to their white wives and daughters, all would be well. This understanding was made clear in the words of the assistant commissioner of Georgia upon the occasion of a particularly egregious case in which a freedwoman was brutalized in the streets of Macon and the black community there had risen in protest. "Nobody could doubt," the bureau policy maker perceptively noted, "that if a white woman was taken through the streets of Macon in the manner described it would certainly lead to serious difficulty."[55]

Justice could be hard to find in the age of emancipation. Without question, the Freedmen's Bureau failed in its efforts to secure lasting rights for freedmen and women in the postemancipation South. With no legal training, no precedent to follow, limited means of enforcement, and competing directives giving broad judicial authority yet ordering them to cede jurisdiction to other federal authorities or to restore it to civil authorities, and surrounded by recalcitrant whites set on negating blacks' rights, bureau men understood that even their best efforts were limited in the kind of justice they could provide African Americans. "Public sentiment is such that even should the laws be made impartial, the negro *could not obtain redress* for wrongs done him in person or property," a bureau inspector had reported at the close of 1865.[56] Three years later, in 1868, with legal equality secured and as bureau men prepared to leave their posts, not many federal officials would have disagreed with this disappointing assessment of southern justice.[57]

"Society is demoralized," an agent in Georgia warned his superiors as he prepared to leave his post for home in late 1868, and the "conditions of the Blacks is going from bad to worse, assassinations and murders stalks abroad, law and equity set at defiance and nothing but the strong military arm of the government can restore peace and order."[58] Agents elsewhere made similar reports. The freedpeople "all say that should the Bureau be withdrawn before the state is reconstructed," an agent in Virginia insisted, "the justice that is now given . . . would certainly be withdrawn."[59] Freedwomen and men "have but little if any chance before the law, as things now stand," explained yet another agent in the fall of 1868.[60] W. E. B. Du Bois agreed. "Despite compromise, war, and struggle, the Negro is not free," he would write in 1901. Whatever rights had been granted, the situation of African Americans was bleak as Congress dismantled the bureau. "Negroes are a segregated servile caste, with restricted rights and privileges," Du Bois reported. "That," the historian concluded more than a century ago, "is largely the legacy of the Freedmen's Bureau, the work it did not do because it could not."[61]

But the bureau let freedwomen down with its efforts to provide "equal justice" for reasons that went beyond race, white southern recalcitrance, and the flawed enforcement of law and order in the postemancipation South. Certainly there had been legal gains. Bureau men offered a broad concept of justice and access to spaces to use the new laws of freedom to challenge racial inequality. They allied with freedwomen (and men) to fight racially motivated violence against them. They proclaimed violence unacceptable in a free labor society. They punished offenders within the limits of bureau policy. They backed efforts to bring suit in federal, state, and local courts against those who violated their growing rights. And they cataloged and reported "outrages" against former slave women as part of a larger narrative intent on promoting an expanded federal authority and the extension of suffrage to African American men in the still unreconstructed South. The bureau's role as a partner in the pursuit of justice went only so far for freedwomen, however. Rather than underscoring the civil and political gains made by African Americans in the wake of emancipation, the legal alliance of freedwomen and the Freedmen's Bureau reveals something different. When freedwomen asserted themselves as virtuous women and protested violence against them as citizens with rights, bureau men combated it in a way that sought to secure racial rather than gender equality. Similarly, when freedwomen demanded rights within their own households, the bureau was not always willing to help. Bureau men extended protections and benefits to them because they were women, but so too did the federal agency disregard them and their domestic complaints as trivial and of lesser importance than the instruction of men in their rights as citizens. Bureau men's efforts to promote northern ideologies of free labor and domesticity—filled with images of manly independence, female dependency, and nuclear families—had collided with freedwomen's demands for justice in a way that both helped and hurt them. "My impression is that the freed people are going to have pretty hard times," Agent Daniel Losey in Georgia asserted as he prepared to leave his bureau post in the summer of 1868. His impression was certainly correct. But the freedwoman's persistence in claiming a meaningful freedom did not wane even as white southerners continued to insist that they may have "acknowledged her freedom," but they did "not acknowledge her right to do as she wishes." Long after the bureau was gone, African American women would continue to march on as free women and citizens intent on claiming "strict justice" and, with it, the right to do as they wished.[62]

Conclusion

"the unpardonable sin"

With varying degrees of success, African American women encountered, trusted, challenged, and used the Freedmen's Bureau in their efforts to shape the outcome of emancipation. These interactions did not come without consequence. With defiant words and actions, the freedwomen who complained to federal authorities, in the words of a local bureau official in Virginia in 1866, committed "the unpardonable sin." Although to this agent their complaints only served to "widen the breach between whites and blacks," to the women who made them, they were part of what would become a lengthy battle to define and defend freedom, womanhood, and a newfound citizenship for African Americans on their own terms. By dragging matters that others, including bureau agents and officials, hoped would be relegated to the private sphere across the line into the political arena as well as by challenging notions of their proper "place" as women, as African Americans, as workers, and as emergent citizens in a reconstructed southern society, these former slave women demonstrated the interconnectedness of public policy and private lives in a tumultuous time. Indeed, the very act of making a complaint—whatever the complaint—to the Freedmen's Bureau was a courageous political act in the age of emancipation. Underscoring this reality, one official commented, "[I]t is only the bolder ones who bring their grievances to the notice of the Bureau Agent, the others are overawed and intimidated by the whites." Freedwomen's voice, actions, and agency exhibited a resolve to participate in the private and public, domestic and political, debates that would shape the outcome of emancipation and the contours of citizenship in the post–Civil War South.[1]

The interaction between the Freedmen's Bureau and freedwomen reveals the many ways in which both northern gender ideology and freedwomen themselves acted to shape the political culture of Reconstruction. Although the policies, orders, and dictates of the bureau often espoused a design for remaking the South into a free labor society without regard to gender, their interpretation, alteration, and implementation demonstrated agents' willingness to acknowledge a gendered difference between freedwomen and men. In their treatment of freedwomen, local bureau agents in particular discovered that the federal agency's rigid policies did not translate easily into practice. And all too often in their dealings with former slave women, agents found themselves making recommendations similar to those of the bureau official in Augusta, Georgia, who had advised in 1866: "[T]he present is an instance where the rule above alluded to should not be enforced."[2] While enforcement of its policies often varied little when it came to freedmen, the same simply cannot be said of the bureau's treatment of African American women. What developed were bureau policies that, when implemented, applied to freedmen without seeming exception and to freedwomen in varying degrees according to their marital and parental status, character, and perceived worthiness. The Freedmen's Bureau thus was a federal agency that dealt not only with freed-*people* but with freed*men* and freed*women*, and it did so with different results and significant consequences.

In so many ways as they endeavored to enforce the agency's many policies and dictates, bureau officials proved conscious of a freedperson's gender as well as their own assumptions about the proper place and role of black women and black men in a southern free labor society. The Freedmen's Bureau championed unmistakable expectations for both freedmen and freedwomen from the first days of emancipation and, in doing so, came to award benefits to African American women not available to black men, and vice versa. Bureau officials supported evolving cultural and social ideals of domesticity and womanhood—especially a Victorian gender ideology that revered the dutiful wife and, increasingly, the devoted mother—that, notwithstanding significant legal and political limitations, allowed agents to bestow certain "privileges" on freedwomen. Disregarding increasingly restrictive bureau relief policies, local agents, in practice, expanded definitions of the deserving poor in a way that allowed them to continue providing relief to the neediest and most worthy able-bodied freedwomen. Altering too the agency's harsh labor policies that called for all able-bodied freedpeople to enter contracts or face prosecution as vagrants, local officials came to enforce them differently against freedwomen and freedmen. However much local agents regarded freedwomen as workers, as both federal officials in Washington and whites across the South wanted, they simply did not ignore the fact that they were also women and, as such, dependents. Moreover, even while holding fast to the belief that the black woman's obligation to labor had not ended with emancipation, these agents encountered freedwomen who insisted upon working on their own terms and demanded that their particular gendered needs be met. Complicating matters still further was an employment landscape that devalued women's labor, suffered disparity in labor supply and labor demand, and made it difficult for freedmen, let alone freedwomen, to find work in some parts of the South. In the end, local bureau officials proved unwilling to categorically arrest and punish as vagrants all freedwomen who did not enter contracts, work regularly outside their own households, or possess some visible—and acceptable—means of employment. While jobless black men were vagrants, the same simply did not always hold true for black women.

But freedwomen's gender did not always garner the bureau's largesse. Indeed, and in part because women's protected but unequal status was disputed in the postwar United States and white women did not enjoy many of the rights and privileges that freedwomen demanded the federal government protect, southern black women encountered a bureau that also worked against their efforts to secure control over the fruits of their labor, their families (especially their children), and even their own bodies. The federal agency encouraged black men to control (and contract) the labor of all family members, including that of wives and children. Despite at times defending freedwomen's rights as mothers to claim children illegally apprenticed, bureau officials endorsed harsh apprenticeship practices for parents—most notably poor single mothers—who could not meet appropriate standards of parental fitness and thus seemingly had broken the contractual terms of parenthood. And, as it refereed freedwomen's demands for justice, the bureau sought justice for these women but did so against racial wrongs and only as its agents could enforce the obligations of freedom, the ideals of free labor and contract, black manhood, and northern principles of domesticity and household governance.

Certainly, freedwomen did not always benefit in their encounters with the Freedmen's Bureau, and they could pay a heavy price for turning to its agents for help. Martha, a freedwoman from North Carolina, was but one of many former slaves who discovered the worst of the consequences for making a complaint to the bureau. As she made her way to the local agent's office, Martha endured the wrath of a white neighbor determined to stop her from committing "the unpardonable sin." The man put one end of a rope around the freedwoman's neck and the other around the neck of his mule and then dragged her more than two miles.[3] Certainly, too, some freedwomen blatantly resisted bureau interference into their lives and labors. The local agent in Cuthbert, Georgia, found out as much when he, in attempting to get a freedwoman back to work, was met with the ready assertion that "all the Bureau out" could not "make her work." As the "impertinent" woman "damned the Bureau" for interfering in her life, the agent, responding with perhaps some naïveté but nonetheless in keeping with mid-nineteenth-century notions of family governance, refused to deal with her and ordered the woman's husband to control his wife and keep her "in subjection." Simultaneously encouraging black manhood, promoting a modified patriarchy of domesticity in black households, and enforcing bureau labor policies, this practiced agent removed the federal agency from a contentious corner.[4] In the wake of emancipation, freedwomen thus encountered a bureau determined to apply the ideologies of free labor and contract in the South (and to keep them in the workforce in the process), but also to institute a social reconstruction of their world that advanced northern middle-class notions of domesticity and familial relationships. White federal authorities, white southerners, and black men alike instructed freedwomen to submit to their husbands. Upholding Victorian ideas of true womanhood as well as the gendered nature of dependency in nineteenth-century America, bureau policy thus recognized black men's manhood and their emerging status as citizens by viewing them as heads of households in charge of their wives and children.

In the face of such gendered assertions of public policy, freedwomen boldly encountered and contested the right of others—whether agents of the federal government, their former owners, or freedmen—to mediate the outcome of their emancipation. That so many freedwomen turned to local bureau offices in the effort to define and defend freedom—even if it was "only the bolder ones"—attests to the fact that they considered the Freedmen's Bureau "the government" in the age of emancipation. Former slave women placed hope in the federal agency as they committed "the unpardonable sin" and barraged the bureau with complaints both "*trivial* and of no moment" and substantial and of great consequence.[5] Perhaps that hope was well placed. The agency provided federal relief to thousands of freedpeople, a disproportionate number of whom were women and children, in the immediate aftermath of emancipation. It assisted freedwomen and men in reuniting families torn apart by slavery and the war with its transportation and relocation efforts. It aided southern blacks in their transition from slaves to free laborers and in doing so protected some freedwomen—for instance, married women in productive male-headed households and virtuous mothers unable to find work because of the "weight of circumstances" they encountered in the immediacy of emancipation—as they sought to define for themselves when, where, and how they labored. It prevented, as best it could and at least temporarily, masters-turned-employers from negating the effects of emancipation by using capricious apprenticeship laws and practices to return African American children to a condition that resembled slavery in all but name. And it provided the former slaves a forum for redress where they could assert the rights and privileges of free women and men, free laborers, and emergent citizens in a changing nation.

But perhaps too freedwomen's hope in the bureau was misplaced. To be sure, both freedwomen and men had their doubts about the bureau, and at times that doubt was well deserved. For freedwomen, the bureau's recognition of their gender did not always garner the protections and benefits that they so desired in the wake of emancipation. Without question, and in both policy and action, the bureau continued to regard them as workers and employed a variety of efforts designed to get them back to work in the fields and white households of the South. It promoted an understanding of manhood and the family too that recognized black men as the heads of household and viewed freedwomen as dependents under the mantel of Victorian domesticity. And it fought the racial, but not the gendered, discriminations evident in Reconstruction-era apprenticeship practices, and southern justice more generally, that recognized a limited, indeed gendered, citizenship for them not unlike that of white women. Yet, and in spite of these many inadequacies, African American women, much like African American men, persisted in turning to this temporary federal agency as "something of a snug harbor amid stormy seas" and resisted its departure from their communities.[6] Freedwomen looked to the Freedmen's Bureau as the protector, guardian, and ally that could—although at times it did not and, perhaps, could not or would not—secure and sustain the bountiful promises of emancipation.

Notes

Introduction: "a long time in want of a bureau"

1. Oliver Otis Howard, *Autobiography of Oliver Otis Howard* (New York: Baker and Taylor, 1907), 2:199–200. For a similar account, though presented in a far more disparaging style, see John William De Forest, *A Union Officer in the Reconstruction*, ed. James H. Croushore and David Morris Potter (New Haven, Conn.: Yale University Press, 1948; reprint, Baton Rouge: Louisiana State University Press, 1976), 25.

2. The bureau was most active in the years 1865–67. Between 1868 and 1872, the presence and authority of the bureau diminished significantly across the South. In 1868, Congress directed the bureau to withdraw its officers by year's end and limited its activities to facilitating educational opportunities for freedpeople and administering bounties and military claims for black veterans and their heirs. *Statutes at Large of USA* 15 (1868): 193. By mid-1870, the bureau had rid itself of remaining school properties and relinquished even its supervisory educational efforts to the individual states. Thus, bureau work ended for all intents and purposes in 1870, when all the southern states had been "restored" to the Union and white southerners regarded its powers as all but dead. Congress officially dismantled the bureau, effective 30 June 1872, on 10 June 1872. *Statutes at Large of USA* 17 (1870): 366.

3. Testimony of Susan McIntosh, in Federal Writers' Project, ed., *Slave Narratives: A Folk History of Slavery in the United States from Interviews with Former Slaves* (Washington D.C.: Works Progress Administration, 1941), vol. 4 (Ga.), pt. 3, 86.

4. For the most recent historiographical considerations of Freedmen's Bureau scholarship, see Robert Harrison, "New Representations of a 'Misrepresented Bureau': Reflections on Recent Scholarship on the Freedmen's Bureau," *American Nineteenth Century History* 8 (June 2007): 205–29; John David Smith, "'The Work It Did Not Do Because It Could Not': Georgia and the 'New' Freedmen's Bureau Historiography," *Georgia Historical Quarterly* 82 (1998): 331–49. Although more dated, the historiographical essays by both Barry A. Crouch and LaWanda Cox offer valuable, and still relevant, insight on bureau scholarship. See Barry A. Crouch, *The Freedmen's Bureau and Black Texans* (Austin: University of Texas Press, 1992), 1–11; LaWanda Cox, "From Emancipation to Segregation: National Policy and Southern Blacks," in *Interpreting Southern History: Historiographical Essays in Honor of Sanford W. Higginbotham*, ed. John B. Boles and Evelyn Thomas Nolan (Baton Rouge: Louisiana State University Press, 1987), 224–28. See also references to bureau literature in the historiographical essays in Thomas J. Brown, ed., *Reconstructions: New Perspectives on the Postbellum United States* (New York: Oxford University Press, 2006), 93, 108–9, 163.

5. "An Act to establish a Bureau for the Relief of Freedmen and Refugees," 3 March 1865, *Statutes at Large of USA* 13 (1866): 507–9; Paul A. Cimbala, *Under the Guardianship of the Nation: The Freedmen's Bureau and the Reconstruction of Georgia, 1865–1870* (Athens: University of Georgia Press, 1997), xviii–xix. On the background and creation of

the Freedmen's Bureau, see Paul A. Cimbala, *The Freedmen's Bureau: Reconstructing the American South after the Civil War* (Malabar, Fla.: Krieger, 2005), 3–25; George R. Bentley, *A History of the Freedmen's Bureau* (Philadelphia: University of Pennsylvania, 1955), 1–49; Herman Belz, *A New Birth of Freedom: The Republican Party and Freedmen's Rights, 1861–1866* (Westport, Conn.: Greenwood Press, 1976), 69–112; Randall M. Miller, "The Freedmen's Bureau and Reconstruction: An Overview," in *The Freedmen's Bureau and Reconstruction: Reconsiderations*, ed. Paul A. Cimbala and Randall M. Miller (New York: Fordham University Press, 1999), xiii–xxxii.

Despite the sweeping reassessment of Reconstruction by historians in the last two decades, Bentley's book remains the starting point for most contemporary understandings of the bureau. Although *A History of the Freedmen's Bureau* remains useful for its bureaucratic details, Cimbala's brief account, *The Freedmen's Bureau*, uses the most recent scholarship to reject Bentley's interpretation of the bureau as an agency that "tried to do too much" for African Americans by acting on behalf of Radical Republicans intent on exploiting the former Confederacy. Cimbala's account, like much of the new Freedmen's Bureau historiography, offers an interpretation that presents the bureau as an agency whose agents and officials acted as guardians of the freedpeople and worked earnestly to secure the promise of emancipation as they understood it. Mary Farmer-Kaiser, review of *The Freedmen's Bureau: Reconstructing the American South after the Civil War*, by Paul A. Cimbala, *H-Net Reviews in the Humanities and Social Sciences*, Nov. 2007, http://www.h-net.org/reviews/showrev.php?id=13850. The accounts by both Cimbala and Bentley far surpass Paul Skeels Peirce's *The Freedmen's Bureau: A Chapter in the History of Reconstruction* (Iowa City: University of Iowa Press, 1904; reprint, St. Clair Shores, Mich.: Scholarly Press, 1970).

6. W. E. B. Du Bois, "Reconstruction and Its Benefits," *American Historical Review* 15 (1910): 783. Du Bois castigated his fellow historians in another piece with his insistence that "Above all, nothing is more convenient than to heap on the Freedmen's Bureau all the evils of that evil day, and damn it utterly for every mistake and blunder that was made." W. E. B. Du Bois, "The Freedmen's Bureau," *Atlantic Monthly*, March 1901, 362. Peirce offered the first book-length overview of the bureau in 1904 with his *The Freedmen's Bureau*. His assessments that "the authority of the bureau was widely exercised for political profit, that it served as a convenient political machine for the organization and management of the Negroes, that it was an important factor in maintaining republican principles at a time most trying in the history of that party, and that it was made a prominent political issue by the democrats of the north" (*The Freedmen's Bureau*, 170, 171) are akin to those offered in Bentley's 1955 study. Bentley concludes that the bureau and its political benefactors, the Radical Republicans, "might have helped him [the freedman] much more than they did. As it was, they sought too much for the Negro too soon—and not so much for his own sake as for the benefit of a faction of a party bent on the economic and political exploitation of the states where the Negroes lived. Thus the Freedmen's Bureau had fed the flame of race hostility and had canceled out much of the good it had otherwise accomplished for the Negro and the nation" (*A History of the Freedmen's Bureau*, 214). For historiographical consideration of scholarship published before the 1960s, see Vernon Lane Wharton, "Reconstruction," in *Writing Southern History: Essays in Historiography in Honor of Fletcher M. Green*, ed. Arthur S. Link and Rembert W. Patrick (Baton Rouge: Louisiana State University Press, 1965), 295–315.

7. Harrison, "New Representations," 206–9 (quotations on 206, 208). See also Cox, "From Emancipation to Segregation," 226; Crouch, *The Freedmen's Bureau and Black Texans*, 136–37 nn. 11 and 12. Examples of this scholarship, which Harrison labels "postrevisionist," include William S. McFeely, *Yankee Stepfather: General O. O. Howard and the Freedmen* (New Haven, Conn.: Yale University Press, 1968); John A. Carpenter, *Sword and Olive Branch: Oliver Otis Howard* (Pittsburgh: University of Pittsburgh Press,

1964); Martin Abbott, *The Freedmen's Bureau in South Carolina, 1865–1872* (Chapel Hill: University of North Carolina Press, 1967); Howard A. White, *The Freedmen's Bureau in Louisiana* (Baton Rouge: Louisiana State University Press, 1970); Louis S. Gerteis, *From Contraband to Freedman: Federal Policy toward Southern Blacks, 1861–1865* (Westport, Conn.: Greenwood Press, 1973), 183–92; Leon F. Litwack, *Been in the Storm So Long: The Aftermath of Slavery* (New York: Alfred A. Knopf, 1979; reprint, New York: Vintage Books, 1980), 364–86. Historians of this generation did offer more concessions to the obstacles faced by the agency even if they concluded that the bureau was, as Harrison explains, "[r]epressive rather than liberating, racist rather than liberal, [and] sympathiz-[ing] more often with white planters than with its white charges" ("New Representations," 207). Carpenter, for instance, concedes that given what it faced, the agency "performed near miracles" (*Sword and Olive Branch*, 156). Calling the South Carolina bureau a "qualified failure," Abbott admits that its presence "made an intangible yet important contribution towards helping the Negro to walk in greater dignity as a free man" and, pointing to the many barriers faced by the bureau, concludes that the bureau "could do little more than approximate the potential that lay within it for advancing the general welfare of the freedmen" (*The Freedmen's Bureau in South Carolina*, 131–33). In his state study, White similarly grants that the bureau put the "concept of freedom and dignity in the hearts" of blacks in Louisiana (*The Freedmen's Bureau in Louisiana*, 165). McFeely concludes that the fate of Howard's bureau, although criticized for "misplaced morality," was the result of "naïveté and misunderstanding, timidity, misplaced faith, disloyalty to subordinates who were loyal to the freedmen, and an attempt to diminish the Negroes' aspirations" (*Yankee Stepfather*, 8–9).

8. Harrison, "New Representations," 212; Du Bois, "The Freedmen's Bureau," 364–65; Barbara Jeanne Fields, *Slavery and Freedom on the Middle Ground: Maryland during the Nineteenth Century* (New Haven, Conn.: Yale University Press, 1985), 149. See also, on the "splendid failure" of Reconstruction and the bureau, Michael W. Fitzgerald, *Splendid Failure: Postwar Reconstruction in the American South* (Chicago: Ivan R. Dee, 2007); W. E. B. Du Bois, *Black Reconstruction in America, 1860–1880* (New York: Harcourt, Brace, 1935; reprint, New York: Atheneum, 1992), 708.

Some of the most prominent examples of this new bureau historiography are Donald G. Nieman, *To Set the Law in Motion: The Freedmen's Bureau and the Legal Rights of Blacks, 1865–1868* (Millwood, N.Y.: KTO Press, 1979); Crouch, *The Freedmen's Bureau and Black Texans*; Randy Finley, *From Slavery to Uncertain Freedom: The Freedmen's Bureau in Arkansas, 1865–1869* (Fayetteville: University of Arkansas Press, 1996); Cimbala, *Under the Guardianship of the Nation*; and the essays in *The Freedmen's Bureau and Reconstruction*, edited by Cimbala and Miller.

As early as 1953, historians John Cox and LaWanda Cox concluded that "even the most friendly studies of the Bureau [had] exaggerated its weaknesses and minimized its strength." Historians, they insisted, had failed to recognize the "constructive achievements" of a "Misrepresented Bureau"—an agency that had become "the symbol and substance of military occupation, a hateful or at best an unwelcome power of restraint to those under its shadow and to all men who believe in liberty." John Cox and LaWanda Cox, "General O. O. Howard and the 'Misrepresented Bureau,'" *Journal of Southern History* 19 (1953): 428–29. See also Crouch, *The Freedmen's Bureau and Black Texans*, 136–37 n. 11; Harrison, "New Representations," 209–12, 215; Smith, "The Work It Did Not Do."

Following the lead of Cox and Cox, the new bureau historiography presents a more nuanced appraisal of the agency. Unwilling to see the bureau as a complete failure, Nieman, for instance, maintains that the "fact that Bureau officials, at the conclusion of their work, were able to boast of little success resulted not only from their own attitudes and assumptions, but also from the political, economic, and institutional constraints under which they labored." He concludes that "Bureau officials' fear of social disorder and their faith in human rationality and the inevitability of progress led them to act in ways that were sometimes detrimental to the interests of the freedmen" (*To Set the Law in Motion*, 221, ix). Placing the agency into a broader context, Crouch assesses the bureau within the confines of nineteenth-century America and concludes in his state study of the agency in Texas that "the quality of freedom and independence may not be what was envisioned for black Texans, but the Texas Freedmen's Bureau did what was humanly possible" (*The Freedmen's Bureau and Black Texans*, 131). In his state study of the bureau in Arkansas, Randy Finley finds that blacks there "were aided by the Freedmen's Bureau, at other times they co-opted it, and sometimes they were manipulated by planters, the white majority, or the bureau" (*From Slavery to Uncertain Freedom*, 170). Arriving at similar conclusions in another state study and arguing that Georgia freedpeople saw the bureau as an "ally in their efforts to secure rights commensurate with their new status," Cimbala argues that these federal officials "realistically acknowledged the Bureau's limitations while recognizing the fact that black and white Georgians would be working out their problems without the oversight of the agency within a very short time" (*Under the Guardianship of the Nation*, 219, 223). More critical of the bureau are Reconstruction scholars who criticize the agency for failing to do enough and conclude, as does Foner, that "Perhaps the greatest failing of the Freedmen's Bureau was that it never quite comprehended the depths of racial antagonism and class conflict in the postwar South." Eric Foner, *Reconstruction: America's Unfinished Revolution, 1863–1877* (New York: Harper & Row, 1988), 170. See also Paul A. Cimbala, "Reconstruction's Allies: The Relationship of the Freedmen's Bureau and the Georgia Freedmen," in Cimbala and Miller, *The Freedmen's Bureau and Reconstruction*, 315–35; Barry A. Crouch, "Guardian of the Freedpeople: Texas Freedmen's Bureau Agents and the Black Community," *Southern Studies* 3 (1992): 185–201; Foner, *Reconstruction*, 142–52; Litwack, *Been in the Storm So Long*, 379–86; Richard Lowe, "The Freedmen's Bureau and Local Black Leadership," *Journal of American History* 80 (1993): 989–98; Richard Lowe, "The Freedmen's Bureau and Local White Leaders in Virginia," *Journal of Southern History* 64 (1998): 455–72.

9. There are two notable exceptions to this critique of bureau scholars' lack of attention to black women. See, for example, early examinations of freedwomen and black families in Texas by Barry Crouch and James Smallwood: Barry A. Crouch, "The 'Chords of Love': Legalizing Black Marital and Family Rights in Postwar Texas," *Journal of Negro History* 79 (1994): 334–51; Barry A. Crouch, "Seeking Equality: Houston Black Women during Reconstruction," in *The Dance of Freedom: Texas African Americans during Reconstruction*, ed. Larry Madaras (Austin: University of Texas Press, 2007), 69–89; Barry A. Crouch and Larry Madaras, "Reconstructing Black Families: Perspectives from the Texas Freedmen's Bureau Records," *Prologue* 18, no. 2 (1986): 109–22; James Smallwood, "Black Freedwomen after Emancipation: The Texas Experience," *Prologue* 27, no. 4 (1995): 302–17; James Smallwood, "Emancipation and the Black Family: A Case Study in Texas," *Social Science Quarterly* 57 (1977): 849–57.

10. Until the late 1980s—with the notable exceptions of Anne Firor Scott's *The Southern Lady: From Pedestal to Politics, 1830–1930* (Chicago: University of Chicago Press, 1972); Suzanne Lebsock's "Radical Reconstruction and the Property Rights of Southern Women," *Journal of Southern History* 43 (May 1977): 195–216; and the valuable document collections edited by Gerda Lerner, *Black Women in White America: A Documentary History* (New York: Vintage Books, 1973), and Dorothy Sterling, *The Trouble They Seen: The Story of Reconstruction in the Words of African Americans* (New York: Da Capo Press, 1976) and *We Are Your Sisters: Black Women in the Nineteenth Century* (New York: W. W. Norton, 1984)—women remained hard to find in histories of Reconstruction. Building upon the work of Deborah Gray White, Jacqueline Jones led the challenge to the absence

of black women during this pivotal era by insisting that freedwomen constructed a distinct form of womanhood intrinsically linked to their postwar labors. Allowing freedmen to represent the black family in the public world, she argues, former slave women understood "freedom to mean not a release from back-breaking labor, but rather the opportunity to labor on behalf of their own families and kin within the protected spheres of household and community." Jacqueline Jones, *Labor of Love, Labor of Sorrow: Black Women, Work, and the Family from Slavery to the Present* (New York: Basic Books, 1985), 78. See also Deborah Gray White, *Ar'n't I a Woman? Female Slaves in the Plantation South*, 2nd ed. (New York: W. W. Norton, 1999), chaps. 1, 3, 4. For other scholarship that presents freedwomen as interpreting freedom familially rather than individually, see, for example, Elsa Barkley Brown, "Negotiating and Transforming the Public Sphere: African American Political Life in the Transition from Slavery to Freedom," *Public Culture* 7 (1994): 107–46; Laura F. Edwards, "Sexual Violence, Gender, Reconstruction, and the Extension of Patriarchy in Granville, North Carolina," *North Carolina Historical Review* 68, no. 3 (1991): 237–60; Laura F. Edwards, *Gendered Strife and Confusion: The Political Culture of Reconstruction* (Urbana: University of Illinois Press, 1997); Noralee Frankel, *Freedom's Women: Black Women and Families in Civil War Era Mississippi* (Bloomington: Indiana University Press, 1999); James Smallwood, "Black Freedwomen after Emancipation"; Ira Berlin and Leslie S. Rowland, eds., *Families and Freedom: A Documentary History of African-American Kinship in the Civil War Era* (New York: New Press, 1997); Peter W. Bardaglio, *Reconstructing the Household: Families, Sex, and the Law in the Nineteenth-Century South* (Chapel Hill: University of North Carolina Press, 1995); Karin L. Zipf, *Labor of Innocents: Forced Apprenticeship in North Carolina, 1715–1919* (Baton Rouge: Louisiana State University Press, 2005). Challenging notions that black women always defined womanhood and the domestic arena in a way that placed their status as wives and mothers above all else, much recent scholarship (including some of the works cited in note 13) acknowledges that black women often defined womanhood in ways that contrasted starkly to that of white women and at times rejected signs of black patriarchal authority.

On the increasingly controversial historiographical debate on black agency, its meaning, and whether historians have overstated the ability of former slaves to possess it, see John C. Rodrigue, "Black Agency after Slavery," in *Reconstructions: New Perspectives on the Postbellum United States*, ed. Thomas Brown (New York: Oxford University Press, 2006), 41–42; Susan Eva O'Donovan, *Becoming Free in the Cotton South* (Cambridge, Mass.: Harvard University Press, 2007), 3–5, 277 n. 3; Peter A. Coclanis, "The Captivity of a Generation," review of *Generations of Captivity: A History of African-American Slaves*, by Ira Berlin, *William and Mary Quarterly* 61 (2004): 544–55; Peter A. Coclanis, "Slavery, African-American Agency, and the World We Have Lost," *Georgia Historical Quarterly* 79 (1995): 873–84; Walter Johnson, "On Agency," *Journal of Southern History* 37 (2003): 113–24; Wilma A. Dunaway, *The African-American Family in Slavery and Emancipation* (Cambridge: Cambridge University Press, 2003), 4–5, 278; Barbara Jeanne Fields, "Whiteness, Racism, and Identity," *International Labor and Working Class History* 60 (2001): 48–56.

11. Foner, *Reconstruction*, 142, 143. Bureau historians largely agree with Foner on this point; see, for example, Cimbala, "Reconstruction's Allies," 315. For the best discussion of the gradations in bureau understanding of free labor, see James D. Schmidt, *Free to Work: Labor Law, Emancipation, and Reconstruction, 1815–1880* (Athens: University of Georgia Press, 1999), chap. 4. See also Heather Cox Richardson, *West from Appomattox: The Reconstruction of America after the Civil War* (New Haven, Conn.: Yale University Press, 2007), 39–77; Nieman, *To Set the Law in Motion*, 59–61; Amy Dru Stanley, *From Bondage to Contract: Wage Labor, Marriage, and the Market in the Age of Slave Emancipation* (Cambridge: Cambridge University Press, 1998), 36–37; Cimbala, *Under the Guardianship of the Nation*, 8–9; Peter W. Bardaglio, response to "Negotiating the Boundaries

of Freedom: White and Black Women in the Reconstruction South," Fifth Southern Conference on Women's History, Richmond, Va., 15–17 June 2000, unpublished commentary in author's possession.

12. For a gendered critique of Foner's *Reconstruction*, see Nell Irvin Painter's review, "A Prize-Winning Book Revisited," *Journal of Women's History* 2, no. 3 (1991): 126–34.

13. Nancy D. Bercaw, *Gendered Freedoms: Race, Rights, and the Politics of the Household in the Delta, 1861–1875* (Gainesville: University Press of Florida, 2003); Jane Turner Censer, *The Reconstruction of White Southern Womanhood, 1865–1895* (Baton Rouge: Louisiana State University Press, 2003); Edwards, *Gendered Strife and Confusion*; Laura F. Edwards, *Scarlett Doesn't Live Here Anymore: Southern Women in the Civil War Era* (Urbana: University of Illinois Press, 2000); Carol Faulkner, *Women's Radical Reconstruction: The Freedmen's Aid Movement* (Philadelphia: University of Pennsylvania Press, 2004); Frankel, *Freedom's Women*; Tera W. Hunter, *To 'Joy My Freedom: Southern Black Women's Lives and Labors after the Civil War* (Cambridge, Mass.: Harvard University Press, 1997); Thavolia Glymph, *Out of the House of Bondage: The Transformation of the Plantation Household* (Cambridge: Cambridge University Press, 2008), O'Donovan, *Becoming Free*; Hannah Rosen, *Terror in the Heart of Freedom: Citizenship, Sexual Violence, and the Meaning of Race in the Postemancipation South* (Chapel Hill: University of North Carolina Press, 2009); Julie Saville, *The Work of Reconstruction: From Slave to Wage Laborer in South Carolina, 1860–1870* (New York: Cambridge University Press, 1994); Leslie A. Schwalm, *A Hard Fight for We: Women's Transition from Slavery to Freedom in South Carolina* (Urbana: University of Illinois Press, 1997); Stanley, *From Bondage to Contract*; LeeAnn Whites, *The Civil War as a Crisis in Gender: Augusta, Georgia, 1860–1890* (Athens: University of Georgia Press, 1995); Zipf, *Labor of Innocents*.

Other scholarship that has transformed the historiography of former slave women in the postwar South includes articles like Karin L. Zipf's "Reconstructing 'Free Woman': African-American Women, Apprenticeship, and Custody Rights during Reconstruction," *Journal of Women's History* 12 (2000): 8–31; Hannah Rosen's "'Not That Sort of Women': Race, Gender, and Sexual Violence during the Memphis Riot of 1866," in *Sex, Love, Race: Crossing Boundaries in North American History*, ed. Martha Elizabeth Hodes (New York: New York University Press, 1999), 267–93; Leslie A. Schwalm's "'Sweet Dreams of Freedom': Freedwomen's Reconstruction of Life and Labor in Lowcountry South Carolina," *Journal of Women's History* 9 (1997): 9–38; James Smallwood's "Black Freedwomen after Emancipation"; Catherine Clinton's "Reconstructing Freedwomen," in *Divided Houses: Gender and the Civil War*, ed. Catherine Clinton and Nina Silber (New York: Oxford University Press, 1992), 306–19, which is an adaptation of her article "Bloody Terrain: Freedwomen, Sexuality and Violence during Reconstruction," *Georgia Historical Quarterly* 76 (1992): 313–32; Barry A. Crouch's "Seeking Equality"; Noralee Frankel's "The Southern Side of 'Glory': Mississippi African-American Women during the Civil War," *Minerva: Quarterly Report on Women and Military* 8 (1990): 28–37; Willard G. Gatewood Jr.'s "'The Remarkable Misses Rollin': Black Women in Reconstruction South Carolina," *South Carolina Historical Magazine* 92 (1991): 172–88; Susan A. Mann's "Slavery, Sharecropping, and Sexual Inequality," *Signs: A Journal of Women in Culture and Society* 14, no. 4 (1989): 774–98; and Edmund L. Drago's "Militancy and Black Women in Reconstruction Georgia," *Journal of American Culture* 1 (1978): 838–44.

Some important dissertations that have not yet been published as monographs but further our understanding of African American women's experiences during Reconstruction considerably are Katherine Masur, "Reconstructing the Nation's Capital: The Politics of Race and Citizenship in the District of Columbia, 1862–1878" (Ph.D. diss., University of Michigan, 2001); Michelle Ann Krowl, "Dixie's Other Daughters: African American Women in Virginia, 1861–1868" (Ph.D. diss., University of California, Berkeley, 1998); Antoinette G. van Zelm, "On the Front Lines of Freedom: Black and White

Women Shape Emancipation in Virginia, 1861–1890" (Ph.D. diss., College of William and Mary, 1998).

14. Mary P. Ryan, *Mysteries of Sex: Tracing Women and Men through American History* (Chapel Hill: University of North Carolina Press, 2006), 128; Glymph, *Out of the House of Bondage*, 1. On historians' challenge to the separate spheres paradigm, see Glymph, *Out of the House of Bondage*, 2–12; Linda K. Kerber, "Separate Spheres, Female Worlds, and Woman's Place: The Rhetoric of Women's History," *Journal of American History* 75 (1988): 9–39; Nancy A. Hewitt, "Beyond the Search for Sisterhood: American Women's History in the 1980s," *Social History* 10 (1985): 229–31. Noralee Frankel makes this point clear when she insists that for freedpeople determined to achieve autonomy from white interference in Reconstruction, "practically everything considered private became a public issue: marriage, mobility, parenthood, housing, and control over African American women's sexuality" (*Freedom's Women*, x). For works that bring together the political and social history of Reconstruction to demonstrate the extraordinary blurring of any notion of a public and a private sphere while also offering a context that considers race, see, for example, Peter W. Bardaglio, *Reconstructing the Household*; Elsa Barkley Brown, "Negotiating and Transforming the Public Sphere," and "Uncle Ned's Children: Negotiating Community and Freedom in Postemancipation Richmond, Virginia" (Ph.D. diss., Kent State University, 1994); Katherine M. Franke, "Becoming a Citizen: Reconstruction Era Regulation of African American Marriages," *Yale Journal of Law and the Humanities* 11 (1999): 251–309; Frankel, *Freedom's Women*; Thavolia Glymph, "Freedpeople and Ex-masters: Shaping a New Order in the Postbellum South, 1865–1868," in *Essays on the Postbellum Southern Economy*, ed. Thavolia Glymph and John J. Kushma (College Station: Texas A&M University Press, 1985), 48–72; Thomas Holt, "'An Empire over the Mind': Emancipation, Race, and Ideology in the British West Indies and the American South," in *Region, Race and Reconstruction: Essays in Honor of C. Vann Woodward*, ed. J. Morgan Kousser and James McPherson (New York: Oxford University Press, 1982), 283–313; Stephanie McCurry, *Masters of Small Worlds: Yeoman Households, Gender Relations, and the Political Culture of the Antebellum South Carolina Low Country* (New York: Oxford University Press, 1995); Ada Hurtado, "Relating to Privilege: Seduction and Rejection in the Subordination of White Women and Women of Color," *Signs: A Journal of Women in Culture and Society* 14 (1989): 833–55.

15. Scholarship focusing exclusively on freedwomen's interactions with the Freedmen's Bureau is small in number and incomplete in its analysis of the relationship between the federal agency and former slave women. Much of this scholarship has focused specifically on freedwomen's responses to bureau endorsement of southern apprenticeship laws and practices. See, for example, Zipf, *Labor of Innocents*, especially chap. 4, and "Reconstructing 'Free Woman'"; Rebecca Scott, "The Battle over the Child: Child Apprenticeship and the Freedmen's Bureau in North Carolina," *Prologue* 10, no. 2 (1978): 101–13. Other works that focus on the interactions of freedwomen with the bureau include Faulkner, *Women's Radical Reconstruction*, especially chaps. 5 and 7; Sara Rapport, "The Freedmen's Bureau as a Legal Agent for Black Men and Women in Georgia, 1865–1868," *Georgia Historical Quarterly* 73 (1989): 26–53; LaVonne Roberts Jackson, "Freedom and Family: The Freedmen's Bureau and African American Women in Texas in the Reconstruction Era, 1865–1872" (Ph.D. diss., Howard University, 1996); and my own work: "'With a Weight of Circumstances Like Millstones about Their Necks': Freedwomen, Federal Relief, and the Benevolent Guardianship of the Freedmen's Bureau," *Virginia Magazine of History and Biography* 115, no. 3 (2007): 412–42; "'Are They Not in Some Sorts Vagrants?' Gender and the Efforts of the Freedmen's Bureau to Combat Vagrancy in the Reconstruction South," *Georgia Historical Quarterly* 89, no. 1 (2004): 25–49; and "'Because They Are Women': Gender and the Virginia Freedmen's

Bureau's 'War on Dependency,'" in Cimbala and Miller, *The Freedmen's Bureau and Reconstruction*, 161–92.

16. Some exceptions include the work of Barry Crouch, LaVonne Roberts Jackson, and James Smallwood.

17. Clinton, "Reconstructing Freedwomen," 309.

18. For scholarship that reveals freedwomen's use of the Freedmen's Bureau, see, for example, Crouch, "Seeking Equality"; Crouch and Madaras, "Reconstructing Black Families," 117–19; Bercaw, *Gendered Freedoms*, 146–47, 150–57; Edwards, *Scarlett Doesn't Live Here Anymore*, 143; Frankel, *Freedom's Women*, 101–2, 104–7, 111–12, 128, 135, 135–37, 144, 154–56, 179; Jackson, "Freedom and Family"; Krowl, "Dixie's Other Daughters," chaps. 3, 5, 7; O'Donovan, *Becoming Free*, 134–35, 168–70, 196–99, 203–5; Rapport, "The Freedmen's Bureau as a Legal Agent"; Schwalm, *A Hard Fight for We*, 173–79, 234–68; Scott, "The Battle over the Child," 107; Smallwood, "Black Freedwomen after Emancipation," 305–11, 313–15; Zipf, *Labor of Innocents*, chap. 4.

19. On the specific kinds of complaints made by freedwomen, see, for example, Bercaw, *Gendered Freedoms*, 146–47, 150–57; Frankel, *Freedom's Women*, 179; Jones, *Labor of Love*, 53–54; O'Donovan, *Becoming Free*, 135–36, 196–99, 203; Schwalm, *A Hard Fight for We*, 148, 235, 244, 260–66; Stanley, *From Bondage to Contract*, 51–52. Frankel, for instance, asserts that freedwomen and men "rarely" appealed to the bureau "in cases of marital discord" and that those who made such complaints did so for reasons other than to buttress their application for relief, as Clinton has suggested (*Freedom's Women*, 179).

20. Linda K. Kerber, *No Constitutional Right to Be Ladies: Women and the Obligations of Citizenship* (New York: Hill and Wang, 1998), 67.

21. Stanley, *From Bondage to Contract*, 188–89. For other historical analyses of the gendered nature of free labor and contract ideals espoused by the bureau during Reconstruction, see, for example, Schwalm, *A Hard Fight for We*, chap. 7; Stanley, *From Bondage to Contract*, 36–37, 40–46, 51, 123–29, 188–89, 192; Amy Dru Stanley, "'We Did Not Separate Man and Wife, but All Had to Work': Freedom and Dependence in the Aftermath of Slave Emancipation," in *Terms of Labor: Slavery, Serfdom, and Free Labor*, ed. Stanley L. Engerman (Stanford, Calif.: Stanford University Press, 1999), 188–212; Zipf, *Labor of Innocents*, chap. 3; and Schmidt, *Free to Work*, especially 175–93.

22. Schwalm, *A Hard Fight for We*, 267. For scholarship that discusses the gendered consequences of bureau efforts, see, for example, Nancy F. Cott, *Public Vows: A History of Marriage and the Nation* (Cambridge, Mass.: Harvard University Press, 2000), 84–94; Frankel, *Freedom's Women*, 86–87, 107–9, 115, 128–29, 134–35; Kerber, *No Constitutional Right to Be Ladies*, chap. 2; O'Donovan, *Becoming Free*, 167–70, 179–83, 195, 196–99; Schwalm, *A Hard Fight for We*, 234–68; Stanley, *From Bondage to Contract*, 37, 45–46, 49, 51–52, 188–90, 192; Zipf, *Labor of Innocents*, chaps. 3, 4.

23. Edwards, *Scarlett Doesn't Live Here Anymore*, 133; Zipf, "Reconstructing 'Free Woman,'" 19; Schwalm, *A Hard Fight for We*, 148, 168–69, 238; Clinton, "Reconstructing Freedwomen," 309; Hunter, *To 'Joy My Freedom*, 23. See also, for other examples of scholarship that sees the bureau as limited in its assistance to freedwomen, Bercaw, *Gendered Freedoms*, 122–38, 145–57; Clinton, "Bloody Terrain"; Edwards, *Gendered Strife and Confusion*, 49–50, 63–64, 92–94; Edwards, *Scarlett Doesn't Live Here Anymore*, 133–34; Frankel, *Freedom's Women*; O'Donovan, *Becoming Free*, 115–17, 166–70, 220–22, 243, 267; Schwalm, *A Hard Fight for We*, 167–73, 173–79, 234–68; Scott, "The Battle over the Child"; Zipf, "Reconstructing 'Free Woman'," and *Labor of Innocents*, chap. 4.

24. Certainly, the bureau records have their faults. Agents and the bureau itself, rather than freedwomen and men, take center stage in the drama of Reconstruction recorded in this institutional archive. Because of the very nature of the bureau, too, complaints tend to be the focal point of the records; thus, of African Americans whose

lives continued uninterrupted or who endured the deficiencies of emancipation without protest, these records are silent. Moreover, the complaints of freedwomen were considered trivial to some bureau officials and thus at times the only historical record of African American women who came to the Freedmen's Bureau consists of brief notations and questions posed by agents with little or no follow-up. Without question, historians will want to know more about many of the freedwomen who showed up in bureau offices across the South and will be frustrated when the records do not reveal the outcomes of their cases. Nonetheless, for valuable overviews of bureau manuscript records, see, in particular, Reginald Washington, "Sealing the Sacred Bonds of Holy Matrimony: Freedmen's Bureau Marriage Records," *Prologue* 37, no. 1 (2005): 58–65; Reginald Washington, "Spotlight on NARA: The Freedmen's Bureau Preservation Project," *Prologue* 34, no. 2 (2002): 144–48; Katherine Masur, "The Price of the Past: Preserving the Freedmen's Bureau Papers," *Perspectives: American Historical Association Newsletter* 38, no. 7 (2000): 9–11; Elaine C. Everly, "Freedmen's Bureau Records: An Overview," *Prologue* 29, no. 2 (1997): 95–99; Joseph P. Reidy, "Slave Emancipation through the Prism of Archives Records," *Prologue* 29, no. 2 (1997): 105–11; Noralee Frankel, "From Slave Women to Free Women: The National Archives and Black Women's History in the Civil War Era," *Prologue* 29, no. 2 (1997): 100–104. See also Bercaw, *Gendered Freedoms*, 102.

25. Launched in 1976, the Freedmen and Southern Society Project at the University of Maryland draws heavily from bureau records to document the history of emancipation. For a helpful description of the project and its publications, see the project Web site, www.history.umd.edu/Freedmen, and "Documenting the History of Emancipation: The Freedmen and Southern Society Project," *Annotation: The Newsletter of the National Historical Publications and Records Commission* 26, no. 2 (1998): 15–16.

26. It should be noted that, as Carol Faulkner demonstrates in her important study of female abolitionists and feminists in the post–Civil War freedmen's aid movement, the Freedmen's Bureau did employ a few women to work, in particular, with its employment and relocation efforts. It also at times employed women in hospitals and schools that it supported. Such female employment opportunities tended to come in bureau operations located in urban settings, like Washington, D.C., which is the setting for Faulkner's study. But whatever their capacity or location, females paid directly by the bureau were rare. Indeed, in 1865, Griffing was the only female employed by the bureau. Steven Hahn and others, eds., *Land and Labor, 1865*, series 3, vol. 1, of *Freedom: A Documentary History of Emancipation, 1861–1867* (Chapel Hill: University of North Carolina Press, 2008), 177. Most often, women were connected with, as opposed to working for, the bureau in less official ways as teachers or through their work with freedmen's aid societies. Bureau field agents—that is, the officials designated in the agency's bureaucratic language as superintendents, assistant superintendents, subcommissioners, or assistant subassistant commissioners who worked at the district or county level with freedpeople and ex-masters and dealt daily with labor contracts and disputes, violence, and so forth—were male rather than female. All the assistant commissioners were white males.

On female civilians employed by the bureau, especially Josephine Griffing, see Faulkner, *Women's Radical Reconstruction*, 31–32, 84–85, 92–96, 119; Bentley, *A History of the Freedmen's Bureau*, 77–78; Keith E. Melder, "Angel of Mercy in Washington: Josephine Griffing and the Freedmen, 1864–1872," *Records of the Columbia Historical Society* 45 (1965): 243–72; James M. McPherson, *The Struggle for Equality: Abolitionists and the Negro in the Civil War and Reconstruction* (Princeton, N.J.: Princeton University Press, 1964), 389–92. On the men who staffed the agency, see Cimbala, *The Freedmen's Bureau*, 19–22; Paul A. Cimbala, "On the Front Line of Freedom: Freedmen's Bureau Officers and Agents in Reconstruction Georgia, 1865–1868," *Georgia Historical Quarterly* 76 (1993): 577–611; Crouch, "Guardian of the Freedpeople"; Randy Finley, "The Personnel of the Freedmen's Bureau in Arkansas," in Cimbala and Miller, *The Freedmen's Bureau and Reconstruction*, 94, 99–113; James Smallwood, "Charles E. Culver, a Reconstruction Agent in Texas: The Work of Local Freedmen's Bureau Agents and the Black Community," *Civil War History* 27 (1981): 350–61.

27. Cott, *Public Vows*, 92. On this point, see Brown, "Negotiating and Transforming the Public Sphere."

28. Bercaw, *Gendered Freedoms*, 34.

29. Jones, *Labor of Love*, 70; case no. 121, 16 Sept. 1867, register of complaints, entry 859, vol. 238 (Cuthbert, Ga.), BRFAL-FO; F. E. Grossmann to [bureau headquarters in Lake City, Fla.], 1 Oct. 1866, reproduced in Ira Berlin, Steven F. Miller, and Leslie S. Rowland, eds., "Afro-American Families in the Transition from Slavery to Freedom," *Radical History Review* 42 (1988): 98. See also Lawrence N. Powell, *New Masters: Northern Planters during the Civil War and Reconstruction* (New Haven, Conn.: Yale University Press, 1980), 109; John Richard Dennett, *The South As It Is, 1865–1866*, ed. Henry M. Christman (New York: Viking Press, 1965; reprint, Athens: University of Georgia Press, 1986), 292; Elizabeth Ware Pearson, ed., *Letters from Port Royal: Written at the Time of the Civil War* (Boston: W. B. Clarke, 1906), 53, 88.

30. Foner, *Reconstruction*, 143–44; Stanley, *From Bondage to Contract*, 36–37, 40–46, 122–29, 139–41, 188–90.

31. O'Donovan, *Becoming Free*, 4.

32. On the Freedmen's Bureau's role in black education, see Heather Andrea Williams, *Self-Taught: African American Education in Slavery and Freedom* (Chapel Hill: University of North Carolina Press, 2007); Robert F. Engs, *Educating the Disfranchised and Disinherited: Samuel Chapman Armstrong and Hampton Institute, 1839–1893* (Knoxville: University of Tennessee Press, 1999); Ronald E. Butchart, *Northern Schools, Southern Blacks, and Reconstruction: Freedmen's Education, 1862–1875* (Westport, Conn.: Greenwood Press, 1980); Cimbala, *The Freedmen's Bureau*, 77–90; Paul A. Cimbala, "Making Good Yankees: The Freedmen's Bureau and Education in Reconstruction Georgia, 1865–1870," *Atlanta Historical Journal* 29 (1985): 5–18; Barry A. Crouch, "Black Education in Civil War and Reconstruction Louisiana: George T. Ruby, the Army, and the Freedmen's Bureau," *Louisiana History* 38 (1997): 287–308; Jacqueline Jones, *Soldiers of Light and Love: Northern Teachers and Georgia Blacks, 1865–1873* (Chapel Hill: University of North Carolina Press, 1980); Robert C. Morris, *Reading, 'Riting, and Reconstruction: The Education of Freedmen in the South, 1861–1870* (Chicago: University of Chicago Press, 1981). For scholarship that begins to explore the intersections of race and gender in the education of freedpeople in the Reconstruction-era South, see, for example, Wakako Araki, "Historicising the Ideas of Separate Spheres in the South Carolina Sea Islands, 1862–77," in *Historicising Whiteness: Transnational Perspectives on the Construction of an Identity*, ed. Leigh Boucher, Jane Carey, and Katherine Blinghaus (Melbourne: RMIT Publishing in association with the School of Historical Studies, University of Melbourne, 2007), 190–200.

1. "that the freed-women ... may rise to the dignity and glory of true womanhood": The Men, Purpose, and Gendered Freedom of the Freedmen's Bureau

1. Clinton B. Fisk, *Plain Counsels for Freedmen: In Sixteen Brief Lectures* (Boston: American Tract Society, 1866), 25–26, 61. Excerpts of Fisk's lectures can be found in Dorothy Sterling, ed., *We Are Your Sisters: Black Women in the Nineteenth Century* (New York: W. W. Norton, 1984), 319–20. On Fisk's background and career beyond the bureau, see introduction to *Plain Counsels*; Alphonso A. Hopkins, *The Life of Clinton Bowen Fisk with a Brief Sketch of John A. Brooks* (New York: Funk & Wagnalls, 1888); Paul A. Cimbala, *The Freedmen's Bureau: Reconstructing the American South after the*

Civil War (Malabar, Fla.: Krieger, 2005), 12; George R. Bentley, *A History of the Freedmen's Bureau* (Philadelphia: University of Pennsylvania, 1955), 60; William S. McFeely, *Yankee Stepfather: General O. O. Howard and the Freedmen* (New Haven, Conn.: Yale University Press, 1968), 67.

2. On the "cult of true womanhood" and domesticity, see Barbara Welter's pathbreaking article, "The Cult of True Womanhood, 1820–1860," *American Quarterly* 18 (1966): 151–74. See also Mary Louise Roberts, "True Womanhood Revisited," *Journal of Women's History* 14 (2002): 150–55. On the ideals of true womanhood as they applied to white women, see Nancy F. Cott, *The Bonds of Womanhood: "Woman's Sphere" in New England, 1780–1835* (New Haven, Conn.: Yale University Press, 1977); Carroll Smith-Rosenberg, *Disorderly Conduct: Visions of Gender in Victorian America* (New York: Oxford University Press, 1985); and Thavolia Glymph, *Out of the House of Bondage: The Transformation of the Plantation Household* (Cambridge: University of Cambridge Press, 2008). On the ideals of womanhood as understood by black communities, see Hannah Rosen, *Terror in the Heart of Freedom: Citizenship, Sexual Violence, and the Meaning of Race in the Postemancipation South* (Chapel Hill: University of North Carolina Press, 2009), 55–60, 76–79, 81; Martha S. Jones, *All Bound up Together: The Woman Question in African American Public Culture, 1830–1900* (Chapel Hill: University of North Carolina Press, 2007), especially chap. 4; Shirley Carlson, "Black Ideals of Womanhood in the Late Victorian Era," *Journal of Negro History* 77 (1992): 61–73.

3. Fisk, *Plain Counsels*, 26–27.

4. Roberts, "True Womanhood Revisited," 150; Mary P. Ryan, *Mysteries of Sex: Tracing Women and Men through American History* (Chapel Hill: University of North Carolina Press, 2006), 128; Thomas Holt, "'An Empire over the Mind': Emancipation, Race, and Ideology in the British West Indies and the American South," in *Region, Race and Reconstruction: Essays in Honor of C. Vann Woodward*, ed. J. Morgan Kousser and James McPherson (New York: Oxford University Press, 1982), 288; James D. Schmidt, *Free to Work: Labor Law, Emancipation, and Reconstruction, 1815–1880* (Athens: University of Georgia Press, 1999), 59. On the values of northern free labor society, see LaWanda Cox, "From Emancipation to Segregation: National Policy and Southern Blacks," in *Interpreting Southern History: Historiographical Essays in Honor of Sanford W. Higginbotham*, ed. John B. Boles and Evelyn Thomas Nolan (Baton Rouge: Louisiana State University Press, 1987), 228. On the possibilities of Reconstruction, see LaWanda Cox, "Reflections on the Limits of the Possible," in *Freedom, Racism, and Reconstruction: Collected Writings of LaWanda Cox*, ed. Donald G. Nieman (Athens: University of Georgia Press, 1997), 243–78.

5. Roberts, "True Womanhood Revisited," 151. William McFeely asserts that Fisk was "the most ambitious and certainly the most frank" of the assistant commissioners (*Yankee Stepfather*, 67).

6. Testimony of Susan McIntosh, in Federal Writers' Project, ed., *Slave Narratives: A Folk History of Slavery in the United States from Interviews with Former Slaves*, (Washington D.C.: Works Progress Administration, 1941), vol. 4 (Ga.), pt. 3, 86; *Freedmen's Advocate*, 1 June 1865, 16; Oliver Otis Howard, *Autobiography of Oliver Otis Howard* (New York: Baker and Taylor, 1907), 2:203; William T. Sherman to O. O. Howard, 17 May 1865, in *The War of the Rebellion: A Compilation of the Official Records of the Union and Confederate Armies*, series 1, vol. 47, pt. 3 (Washington, D.C.: Government Printing Office, 1895), 515. On Howard's appointment, see General Orders No. 91, War Department, Adjutant General's Office, 12 May 1865, in U.S. House of Representatives, "Report of the Commissioner of the Bureau of Refugees, Freedmen, and Abandoned Lands [n.d. Dec. 1865]," 39th Cong., 1st sess., House Executive Document 11 (Serial 1255), 40; Howard, *Autobiography*, 2:206–12. On Howard, see Cimbala, *The Freedmen's Bureau*, 11–12; John Cox and LaWanda Cox, "General O. O. Howard and the 'Misrepresented

Bureau,'" *Journal of Southern History* 19 (1953): 427–56; Bentley, *A History of the Freedmen's Bureau*, 52; McFeely, *Yankee Stepfather*, 26, 85; John A. Carpenter, *Sword and Olive Branch: Oliver Otis Howard* (Pittsburgh: University of Pittsburgh Press, 1964), 90–92.

7. Howard, *Autobiography*, 2:245, 217. On the organization of the bureau, see U.S. House of Representatives, "Report of the Commissioner [1865]," 24–32; Cimbala, *The Freedmen's Bureau*, chap. 2; Bentley, *A History of the Freedmen's Bureau*, chap. 5; McFeely, *Yankee Stepfather*, chap. 4.

8. Cimbala, *The Freedmen's Bureau*, 13; James Oakes, "A Failure of Vision: The Collapse of the Freedmen's Bureau Courts," *Civil War History* 25 (1979): 66–67; O. O. Howard, "Address at Augusta, Maine," quoted in Carpenter, *Sword and Olive Branch*, 97. Howard insisted that in selecting the assistant commissioners, he "took generally those who had been long in the work" and men "who were earnest in securing the rights of the freedmen." "When I was compelled to go beyond this class," he said, "I took those whom I knew to be men of integrity and with Christian hearts" (quoted in Carpenter, *Sword and Olive Branch*, 97). On the assistant commissioners, see Howard, *Autobiography*, 2:215–18; Cimbala, *The Freedmen's Bureau*, 12–17; Schmidt, *Free to Work*, 125–45; Bentley, *A History of the Freedmen's Bureau*, 56–61; McFeely, *Yankee Stepfather*, 67–68, 71–72, 78–83; Carpenter, *Sword and Olive Branch*, 96–97.

9. Howard, *Autobiography*, 2:216, 218; Thomas Conway's description of Samuel Thomas quoted in Cimbala, *The Freedmen's Bureau*, 15. See also Cimbala, *The Freedmen's Bureau*, 12–17; Schmidt, *Free to Work*, 125–45; Michael W. Fitzgerald, "Wager Swayne, the Freedmen's Bureau, and the Politics of Reconstruction in Alabama," *Alabama Review* 48 (1995): 188–232; Bentley, *A History of the Freedmen's Bureau*, 56–61; McFeely, *Yankee Stepfather*, 67–68, 71–72, 78–83; Carpenter, *Sword and Olive Branch*, 96–97.

10. Howard, *Autobiography*, 2: 228. For the Freedmen's Bureau laws, see *Statutes at Large of USA* 13 (1865): 507–9; 14 (1866): 174–79; 15 (1868): 193; 17 (1872): 366. On President Johnson's opposition to the bureau, see Hans L. Trefousse, "Andrew Johnson and the Freedmen's Bureau," in *The Freedmen's Bureau and Reconstruction: Reconsiderations*, ed. Paul A. Cimbala and Randall M. Miller (New York: Fordham University Press, 1999), 29–92; John Cox and LaWanda Cox, "Andrew Johnson and His Ghost Writers: An Analysis of the Freedmen's Bureau and Civil Rights Veto Messages," *Mississippi Valley Historical Review* 48 (1961): 460–79.

11. Quotations from the Steedman-Fullerton report in Cimbala, *The Freedmen's Bureau*, 14. On the Steedman-Fullerton investigation, see Cimbala, *The Freedmen's Bureau*, 14–17; Trefousse, "Andrew Johnson and the Freedmen's Bureau," 38–39; Schmidt, *Free to Work*, 125–45; Bentley, *A History of the Freedmen's Bureau*, 125–33.

12. The first assistant commissioners replaced included Conway in Louisiana (replaced by Colonel Joseph Fullerton, one of Johnson's inspectors, in October 1865), Saxton in South Carolina (replaced by Brevet Major General Robert Scott in January 1866), Thomas in Mississippi (replaced by Major General Thomas Wood in April 1866), Gregory in Texas (replaced by Brevet Major General Joseph Barr Kiddoo in April 1866), and Whittlesey in North Carolina (replaced by General Thomas Ruger in May 1866). Fisk too was replaced in Kentucky in June 1866 (by Major General Jeff C. Davis) and in Tennessee in September 1866. In Kentucky, Howard appointed Brevet Brigadier General John Randolph Lewis, a man who would remain just as committed as his predecessor to protecting the interests of freedpeople. On the replacement of Howard's initial assistant commissioner appointees, see Cimbala, *The Freedmen's Bureau*, 14–15; Trefousse, "Andrew Johnson and the Freedmen's Bureau," 33; Steven Hahn and others, eds., *Land and Labor, 1865*, series 3, vol. 1, of *Freedom: A Documentary History of Emancipation, 1861–1867* (Chapel Hill: University of North Carolina Press, 2008), 192–95; Schmidt, *Free*

to Work, 127–36; McFeely, *Yankee Stepfather*, 292–94; Bentley, *A History of the Freedmen's Bureau*, 215–16.

13. O. O. Howard to W. D. Kelley, 11 Sept. 1866, quoted in McFeely, *Yankee Stepfather*, 294.

14. Cimbala, *The Freedmen's Bureau*, 12. On the kind of variation of bureau policy among assistant commissioners, see, for example, Schmidt, *Free to Work*, 124–64.

15. Myrta Lockett Avary, *Dixie after the War: An Exposition of Social Conditions Existing in the South, during the Twelve Years Succeeding the Fall of Richmond* (New York: Doubleday, Page, 1906), 211.

16. Eileen Boris and Peter Bardaglio, "The Transformation of Patriarchy: The Historic Role of the State," in *Families, Politics, and Public Policy: A Feminist Dialogue on Women and the State*, ed. Irene Diamond (New York: Longman, 1983), 71–72.

17. Comments of Commissioner O. O. Howard quoted in Cox and Cox, "General O. O. Howard and the 'Misrepresented Bureau,'" 427; W. E. B. Du Bois, "The Freedmen's Bureau," *Atlantic Monthly*, March 1901, 360. See Eric Foner, *Reconstruction: America's Unfinished Revolution, 1863–1877* (New York: Harper & Row, 1988), 143–44. On bureau field agents, see Randy Finley, "The Personnel of the Freedmen's Bureau in Arkansas," in Cimbala and Miller, *The Freedmen's Bureau and Reconstruction*, 94, 99–113; Cimbala, *The Freedmen's Bureau*, 19–22, 26–29, 31–38; Barry A. Crouch, *The Freedmen's Bureau and Black Texans* (Austin: University of Texas Press, 1992), chap. 4; Leon F. Litwack, *Been in the Storm So Long: The Aftermath of Slavery* (New York: Alfred A. Knopf, 1979; reprint, New York: Vintage Books, 1980), 379–86; Paul A. Cimbala, "On the Front Line of Freedom: Freedmen's Bureau Officers and Agents in Reconstruction Georgia, 1865–1868," *Georgia Historical Quarterly* 76 (1993): 577–611; Barry A. Crouch, "Guardian of the Freedpeople: Texas Freedmen's Bureau Agents and the Black Community," *Southern Studies* 3 (1992): 185–201; J. Thomas May, "The Freedmen's Bureau at the Local Level: A Study of a Louisiana Agent," *Louisiana History* 9 (1968): 5–19; James Smallwood, "Charles E. Culver, a Reconstruction Agent in Texas: The Work of Local Freedmen's Bureau Agents and the Black Community," *Civil War History* 27 (1981): 350–61.

18. Hahn and others, *Land and Labor, 1865*, 19–20; Donald G. Nieman, "The Freedmen's Bureau and the Mississippi Black Code," *Journal of Mississippi History* 40 (1978): 114; Elizabeth Bethel, "The Freedmen's Bureau in Alabama," *Journal of Southern History* 14 (1948): 63; Foner, *Reconstruction*, 143; Donald G. Nieman, ed., *The Freedmen's Bureau and Black Freedom*, vol. 2 of *African American Life in the Post-emancipation South, 1861–1900* (New York: Garland, 1994), viii–ix; Randall M. Miller, "The Freedmen's Bureau and Reconstruction: An Overview," in Cimbala and Miller, *The Freedmen's Bureau and Reconstruction*, xxix; Bentley, *A History of the Freedmen's Bureau*, 136.

19. John Richard Dennett, *The South As It Is, 1865–1866*, ed. Henry M. Christman (New York: Viking Press, 1965; reprint, Athens: University of Georgia Press, 1986), 110 (see also 54–55); *Washington Chronicle*, 13 Aug. 1866; Foner, *Reconstruction*, 142–43; J. Davis to W. W. Deane, 4 June 1866, unregistered letters received, reel 26, BRFAL-GA; Suzanne Stone Johnson and Robert Allison Johnson, eds., *Bitter Freedom: William Stone's Record of Service in the Freedmen's Bureau* (Columbia: University of South Carolina Press, 2008), 30; Cimbala, *The Freedmen's Bureau*, 38.

20. John William De Forest, *A Union Officer in the Reconstruction*, ed. James H. Croushore and David Morris Potter (New Haven, Conn.: Yale University Press, 1948; reprint, Baton Rouge: Louisiana State University Press, 1976), 39, 41–42; Marcus Hopkins to James Johnson, 15 Jan. 1866, enclosed in O. Brown to O. O. Howard, 25 Jan. 1866, letters received, reel 25, BRFAL (M752). See also James Ashworth to James A. Bates, 28 Feb. 1866, monthly narrative reports of operations and conditions from January through

June 1866, reports of operations and conditions, reel 44, BRFAL-VA; Dennett, *The South As It Is*, 109–10, 221.

21. In September 1865, President Johnson effectively ended bureau efforts to distribute lands to black southerners by commanding Howard to issue Circular No. 15, which rescinded earlier land circulars and ordered the return of land to owners pardoned by the president. See Cimbala, *The Freedmen's Bureau*, 52–55.

22. *Statutes at Large of USA* 13 (1865): 507. See also Donald G. Nieman, *To Set the Law in Motion: The Freedmen's Bureau and the Legal Rights of Blacks, 1865–1868* (Millwood, N.Y.: KTO Press, 1979), xv; Foner, *Reconstruction*, 69–70; Harold M. Hyman, *A More Perfect Union: The Impact of the Civil War and Reconstruction on the Constitution* (New York: Alfred A. Knopf, 1973), 286–87.

23. Thomas D. Eliot in U.S. Congress, *Congressional Globe*, 38th Cong., 1st sess., 567–73; Edward Atkinson, "The Future Supply of Cotton," *North American Review* 98, no. 203 (1864): 497. On the ideological limitations of the bureau, see Nieman, *To Set the Law in Motion*, xiii–xvi; Foner, *Reconstruction*, 68–70; Nieman, *The Freedmen's Bureau and Black Freedom*, vii–x; Cimbala, *The Freedmen's Bureau*, 91–94; Herman Belz, *A New Birth of Freedom: The Republican Party and Freedmen's Rights, 1861–1866* (Westport, Conn.: Greenwood Press, 1976), 100—105.

24. North Carolina bureau officer quoted in Litwack, *Been in the Storm So Long*, 382. See also Ira Berlin and others, "The Terrain of Freedom: The Struggle over the Meaning of Free Labor in the U.S. South," *History Workshop Journal* 22 (1986): 109; Cimbala, *The Freedmen's Bureau*, 62–67; Foner, *Reconstruction*, 54–60; Ira Berlin and others, eds., *The Wartime Genius of Free Labor: The Lower South*, series 1, vol. 3, of *Freedom: A Documentary History of Emancipation, 1861–1867* (Cambridge: Cambridge University Press, 1990), 2–8.

25. *New Orleans Tribune*, 6 Nov. 1865, quoted in Foner, *Reconstruction*, 77.

26. Eric Foner, *The Story of American Freedom* (New York: W. W. Norton, 1998), xv; Glymph, *Out of the House of Bondage*, 17. On the divergent meanings of freedom, see Foner, *The Story of American Freedom*, chap. 5; Eric Foner, "The Meaning of Freedom in the Age of Emancipation," *Journal of American History* 81, no. 2 (1994): 435–60; Litwack, *Been in the Storm So Long*, 219–20, 221–91, 296–97, 310–11, 331–35, 338–40, 345–47. For historical analyses that consider gendered interpretations of African American expectations for postemancipation life, see, for example, Nancy D. Bercaw, *Gendered Freedoms: Race, Rights, and the Politics of the Household in the Delta, 1861–1875* (Gainesville: University Press of Florida, 2003); Laura F. Edwards, *Gendered Strife and Confusion: The Political Culture of Reconstruction* (Urbana: University of Illinois Press, 1997); Noralee Frankel, *Freedom's Women: Black Women and Families in Civil War Era Mississippi* (Bloomington: Indiana University Press, 1999), 178–80; Glymph, *Out of the House of Bondage*, chaps. 5–6; Tera W. Hunter, *To 'Joy My Freedom: Southern Black Women's Lives and Labors after the Civil War* (Cambridge, Mass.: Harvard University Press, 1997), especially chap. 2; Susan Eva O'Donovan, *Becoming Free in the Cotton South* (Cambridge, Mass.: Harvard University Press, 2007), especially chap. 4; Rosen, *Terror in the Heart of Freedom*; Leslie A. Schwalm, *A Hard Fight for We: Women's Transition from Slavery to Freedom in South Carolina* (Urbana: University of Illinois Press, 1997).

27. "The Freedmen's Bureau," *Harper's Weekly*, 25 July 1868, 467; remarks of bureau agent in Tennessee quoted in Foner, *Reconstruction*, 155.

28. Howard, *Autobiography*, 2:220–21.

29. Fisk, *Plain Counsels*, 34; Atkinson, "The Future Supply of Cotton," 497.

30. Howard, *Autobiography*, 2:225; McFeely, *Yankee Stepfather*, 131. For an exceptional discussion of the evolving meanings of free labor as they relate to Reconstruction and the Freedmen's Bureau, see Schmidt, *Free to Work*. On free labor's divergent meanings in a broader context, see Eric Foner, *Free Soil, Free Labor, Free Men: The Ideology of the*

Republican Party before the Civil War (New York: Oxford University Press, 1970; reprint, with a new introduction, New York: Oxford University Press, 1995); Robert J. Steinfield, "Changing Legal Conceptions of Free Labor," in *Terms of Labor: Slavery, Serfdom, and Free Labor*, ed. Stanley L. Engerman (Stanford, Calif.: Stanford University Press, 1999), 137–67. On the postwar free labor ideology and the policies of the army and the Freedmen's Bureau, see Paul A. Cimbala, *Under the Guardianship of the Nation: The Freedmen's Bureau and the Reconstruction of Georgia, 1865–1870* (Athens: University of Georgia Press, 1997), chap. 6; Hahn and others, *Land and Labor, 1865*, 3, 12–14, 178–80; Berlin and others, "The Terrain of Freedom"; Louis S. Gerteis, *From Contraband to Freedman: Federal Policy toward Southern Blacks, 1861–1865* (Westport, Conn.: Greenwood Press, 1973); Eric Foner, *Politics and Ideology in the Age of the Civil War* (New York: Oxford University Press, 1980), chap. 6; David Montgomery, *Beyond Equality: Labor and the Radical Republicans, 1862–1872* (New York: Alfred A. Knopf, 1967), chaps. 1–3; Foner, *Reconstruction*, chap. 4; McFeely, *Yankee Stepfather*, 149–65.

31. Fisk, *Plain Counsels*, 40–42, 34; "To the Freedmen of Virginia," issued by O. Brown, 1 July 1865, orders and circulars issued, reel 41, BRFAL-VA.

32. "To the Freedmen of Virginia," issued by O. Brown, 1 July 1865, orders and circulars issued, reel 41, BRFAL-VA. See also circular issued by O. Brown, 4 Nov. 1865, orders and circulars issued, reel 41, BRFAL-VA; Holt, "An Empire over the Mind," 288; Foner, *Reconstruction*, 153–70.

33. E. Whittlesey, "Summary Report of North Carolina," 15 Oct. 1865, in U.S. Congress, *Report of the Joint Committee on Reconstruction* (Washington, D.C.: Government Printing Office, 1866), 189; circular issued by Orlando Brown, 4 Nov. 1865, in U.S. House of Representatives, "Freedmen's Bureau. Letter from the Secretary of War, in answer to A resolution of the House of March 8, transmitting a report, by the Commissioner of the Freedmen's Bureau, of all orders issued by him or any assistant commissioner," 39th Cong., 1st sess., House Executive Document 70 (Serial 1256), 139; "Meeting at Augusta, Me., in Behalf of the Freedmen—Speech of Gen. Howard," *National Freedman*, Aug. 1865, quoted in Amy Dru Stanley, *From Bondage to Contract: Wage Labor, Marriage, and the Market in the Age of Slave Emancipation* (Cambridge: Cambridge University Press, 1998), 36; Hahn and others, *Land and Labor, 1865*, 178. On contract and northern free labor ideology, see Stanley, *From Bondage to Contract*, chaps. 1–2, 5; Schmidt, *Free to Work*, chaps. 1, 3–4. On the bureau's use of contract, see Foner, *Reconstruction*, chap. 4; Hahn and others, *Land and Labor, 1865*, 178–79, chap. 3; McFeely, *Yankee Stepfather*, chap. 8; Nieman, *To Set the Law in Motion*, chap. 5; Schmidt, *Free to Work*, chaps. 3–4; Stanley, *From Bondage to Contract*, 35–40.

34. Stanley, *From Bondage to Contract*, 2, 35, 36; "Preliminary Report Touching the Condition and Management of Emancipated Refugees," 30 June 1863, in *The War of the Rebellion: A Compilation of the Official Records of the Union and Confederate Armies*, series 3, vol. 3 (Washington, D.C.: Government Printing Office, 1899), 437, 442, 432, 431; "Final Report of the American Freedmen's Inquiry Commission to the Secretary of War," 15 May 1864, in *The War of the Rebellion: A Compilation of the Official Records of the Union and Confederate Armies*, series 3, vol. 4 (Washington, D.C.: Government Printing Office, 1900), 382. On the Union army's use of contract labor, see Willie Lee Rose, *Rehearsal for Reconstruction: The Port Royal Experiment* (New York: Bobbs-Merrill, 1964; reprint, New York: Oxford University Press, 1976).

35. Fisk, *Plain Counsels*, 47.

36. Although the bureau did not always recognize it, freedmen and freedwomen too recognized lawful marriage as a visible sign of their changed status. On this point, see Chapter 5 of this work; Bercaw, *Gendered Freedoms*, 99–116; Ira Berlin and Leslie S. Rowland, eds., *Families and Freedom: A Documentary History of African-American Kinship in the Civil War Era* (New York: New Press, 1997), 155–91; Edwards, *Gendered Strife and*

Confusion, 45–54; Frankel, *Freedom's Women*, 79–122; Herbert G. Gutman, *The Black Family in Slavery and Freedom, 1750–1925* (New York: Pantheon Books, 1976), 412–18, 425–30; Schwalm, *A Hard Fight for We*, 239–44.

37. H. H. Moore to S. L. McHenry, 12 June 1865, letters received, reel 16, BRFAL (M752); General Orders No. 8, "Marriage rules," issued by R. Saxton, 11 Aug. 1865, in U.S. House of Representatives, "Freedmen's Bureau," 108, 111; Fisk, *Plain Counsels*, 31. The historian Leslie Schwalm argues that lawful marriage served "as a means of raising freedpeople to a new level of civilization" for federal authorities. It offered stability in that "by establishing legitimate heirs, it helped order and regulate the transfer of property between generations; it institutionalized men's privileges and obligations as heads of household, and assured their entitlement to the unpaid labor of women on behalf of the household; it also established the legally normative subordinate status of married women in Northern society by subsuming their legal identities under those of their husbands. Civil marriage regulated female sexuality and ordered the family in ways that many Northern middle-class and elite whites considered to be essential to social stability and civilization itself" (Schwalm, *A Hard Fight for We*, 239). On the anti-slavery rhetoric and culture that condemned slavery's disregard of slave families and contributed to the northern gender ideology that bureau officials carried south, see especially Elizabeth B. Clark, "'The Sacred Rights of the Weak': Pain, Sympathy, and the Culture of Individual Rights in Antebellum America," *Journal of American History* 82, no. 2 (1995): 463–93. On marriage and family as a stabilizing source, see Michael Grossberg, *Governing the Hearth: Law and the Family in Nineteenth-Century America* (Chapel Hill: University of North Carolina Press, 1985), 18–19, 130; Elizabeth Regosin, *Freedom's Promise: Ex-slave Families and Citizenship in the Age of Emancipation* (Charlottesville: University Press of Virginia, 2002), 9–10, 80–82; Bercaw, *Gendered Freedoms*, 2–7, 15, 118. On the role of the state in defining marriage, see Nancy F. Cott, *Public Vows: A History of Marriage and the Nation* (Cambridge, Mass.: Harvard University Press, 2000); Norma Basch, "Marriage and Domestic Relations," in *The Cambridge History of Law in America*, vol. 2, *The Long Nineteenth Century (1789–1920)*, ed. Michael Grossberg and Christopher Tomlins (New York: Cambridge University Press, 2008), 245–79; Boris and Bardaglio, "The Transformation of Patriarchy."

38. General Orders No. 8, "Marriage rules," issued by R. Saxton, 11 Aug. 1865, in U.S. House of Representatives, "Freedmen's Bureau," 108, 111; "The Marriage Institution among the Southern Negroes," *New York Times*, 26 Aug. 1866; Circular No. 5, issued by O. O. Howard, 30 May 1865, reel 7, BRFAL (M742); Special Orders No. 15, issued by John Eaton, superintendent of contrabands, Department of Tennessee and Arkansas, quoted in introduction, BRFAL (M1875), 3.

39. General Orders No. 8, "Marriage rules," issued by R. Saxton, 11 Aug. 1865, in U.S. House of Representatives, "Freedmen's Bureau," 111.

40. For an overview of official bureau policy on marriage and the variation among assistant commissioners' orders, see Reginald Washington, "Sealing the Sacred Bonds of Holy Matrimony: Freedmen's Bureau Marriage Records," *Prologue* 37, no. 1 (2005): 58–65; Elaine C. Everly, "Marriage Registers of Freedmen," *Prologue* 5, no. 3 (1973): 150–54. For examples of bureau marriage records, see BRFAL (M1875).

41. Regosin, *Freedom's Promise*, 9; Fisk, *Plain Counsels*, 31. On the bureau's use of marriage to regulate black families, see Cimbala, *Under the Guardianship of the Nation*, 193–94; Cott, *Public Vows*, 83–94; Barry A. Crouch, "The 'Chords of Love': Legalizing Black Marital and Family Rights in Postwar Texas," *Journal of Negro History* 79 (1994): 334–51; Edwards, *Gendered Strife and Confusion*, 18–23, 24–29, 34–40, 64–65; Regosin, *Freedom's Promise*, 9–10, 81–82, 154–57; Schwalm, *A Hard Fight for We*, 239–48; Stanley, *From Bondage to Contract*, 36–37, 44–46, 48–49, 51, 188–89.

42. Basch, "Marriage and Domestic Relations," 270. See also Steven Hahn, *A Nation under Our Feet: Black Political Struggles in the Rural South from Slavery to the Great Migration* (Cambridge, Mass.: Belknap Press of Harvard University Press, 2003), 169.

43. Johnson and Johnson, *Bitter Freedom*, 9 (first and last quotations); McFeely, *Yankee Stepfather*, 131; James Hutchinson to J. T. Kirkman, 1 April 1867, quoted in Crouch, "The 'Chords of Love,'" 340.

44. Bureau assistant superintendent to James A. Bates, 30 April 1866, reports of operations and conditions, reel 44, BRFAL-VA; J. Gregg to O. O. Howard, 16 July 1865, letters received, reel 15, BRFAL (M752); remarks of Representative William D. Kelley in U.S. Congress, *Congressional Globe*, 1 Feb. 1864, 38th Cong., 1st sess., 774, quoted in Cott, *Public Vows*, 82; "Extract from a Speech by Hon. Judge Kelly to the Colored People in Charleston, S.C., April, 1865," in L. Maria Child, ed., *The American Negro: His History and Literature* (New York: Arno Press and the New York Times, 1968), 262–63; remarks of John Kasson in U.S. Congress, *Congressional Globe*, 10 and 11 Jan. 1865, 38th Cong., 2nd sess., 193, 215, quoted in Foner, "The Meaning of Freedom," 455–56.

45. Circular letter issued by C. C. Richardson, 17 Jan. 1866, letters sent, entry 1036, vol. 379 (Thomasville, Ga.), BRFAL-FO; W. W. Deane to M. P. Mayfield, 23 Jan. 1866, reel 1, BRFAL-GA; Circular No. 1, issued by E. Whittlesey, 1 July 1865, in U.S. House of Representatives, "Freedmen's Bureau," 2; "Marriage rules," issued by R. Saxton, 11 Aug. 1865, in U.S. House of Representatives, "Freedmen's Bureau," 110. See Hahn and others, *Land and Labor, 1865*, 13–14; Stanley, *From Bondage to Contract*, chap. 4; Cott, *Public Vows*, 81–82, 92–94; Carol Faulkner, *Women's Radical Reconstruction: The Freedmen's Aid Movement* (Philadelphia: University of Pennsylvania Press, 2004), 3–4.

46. Fisk, *Plain Counsels*, 18, 23–24, 33; Clinton B. Fisk to the "Freedmen of Kentucky," 26 Dec. 1865, in U.S. House of Representatives, "Freedmen's Bureau," 232; "The Marriage Institution among the Southern Negroes," *New York Times*, 26 Aug. 1866. See also Cott, *Public Vows*, 84–85.

47. E.A., "Free Labor," *Freedmen's Record*, March 1865, 45; "Extract from a Speech," in Child, *The American Negro*, 262; Fisk, *Plain Counsels*, 25; Angelina E. Grimké, *Appeal to the Christian Women of the South* (New York, 1836), quoted in Stanley, *From Bondage to Contract*, 29.

48. Fisk, *Plain Counsels*, 24, 33–34, 26–27, 61.

49. Hopkins, *The Life of Clinton Bowen Fisk*, 99.

50. De Forest, *A Union Officer in the Reconstruction*, 94; Johnson and Johnson, *Bitter Freedom*, 9; Welter, "The Cult of True Womanhood," 158. See also Amy Dru Stanley, "'We Did Not Separate Man and Wife, but All Had to Work': Freedom and Dependence in the Aftermath of Slave Emancipation," in Engerman, *Terms of Labor*, 199. On freedwomen who were perceived by whites as trying to "play the lady" and bureau responses, see Chapter 3 of this work; Gymph, *Out of the House of Bondage*, especially 213–26; Stanley, "We Did Not Separate Man and Wife," 188–212; Schwalm, *A Hard Fight for We*, 204–7, 211–14, 234–35.

51. Susie King Taylor, *Reminiscences of My Life in Camp: With the 33d United States Colored Troops Late 1st S.C. Volunteers* (Boston: Author, 1904); Glymph, *Out of the House of Bondage*, 10; Frederick Douglass, *The Life and Writings of Frederick Douglass*, ed. Philip S. Foner (New York: International Publishers, 1950–55), 3:293.

52. Johnson and Johnson, *Bitter Freedom*, 15.

53. Evelyn Brooks Higginbotham, "African-American Women's History and the Metalanguage of Race," *Signs: A Journal of Women in Culture and Society* 17, no. 21 (1992): 257; Nina Silber, *The Romance of Reunion: Northerners and the South, 1865–1900* (Chapel Hill: University of North Carolina Press, 1993), 24. See also Ryan, *Mysteries of Sex*, 124–36; Schwalm, *A Hard Fight for We*, 234–68; Silber, *The Romance of Reunion*, 21, 24–38; Mary McIntosh, "The State and the Oppression of Women," in *Feminism and*

Materialism: Women and the Modes of Production, ed. Annette Kuhn and Ann Marie Wolpe (Boston: Routledge and Kegan Paul, 1978), 259; Joan Wallach Scott, "Gender: A Useful Category of Historical Analysis," in *Gender and the Politics of History* (New York: Columbia University Press, 1988), 28–50; Varda Burstyn, "Masculine Dominance and the State," *Socialist Register* 20 (1983): 59–62; Jeanne Boydston, *Home and Work: Housework, Wages, and the Ideology of Labor in the Early Republic* (New York: Oxford University Press, 1990).

54. [Assistant subassistant commissioner Augusta, Ga.] to William Whigham, 7 March 1866, letters sent, entry 753, vol. 150 (Augusta, Ga.), BRFAL-FO.

55. On slave women's rejection of white southern domesticity and its differences from northern domesticity, see Glymph, *Out of the House of Bondage*, especially chap. 3.

56. Laura F. Edwards, *Scarlett Doesn't Live Here Anymore: Southern Women in the Civil War Era* (Urbana: University of Illinois Press, 2000), 148. On freedwomen's expectations for freedom, see, for example, Bercaw, *Gendered Freedoms*, especially 48–50, 99–102, 110–16; Edwards, *Gendered Strife and Confusion*, 198–210; Edwards, *Scarlett Doesn't Live Here Anymore*, 126–48; Darlene Clark Hine and Kathleen Thompson, *A Shining Thread of Hope: The History of Black Women in America* (New York: Broadway Books, 1998), chap. 6; Schwalm, *A Hard Fight for We*, especially 173–78.

2. "a weight of circumstances like millstones about their necks to drag and keep them down": Freedwomen, Federal Relief, and the Freedmen's Bureau

1. Samuel C. Armstrong to Orlando Brown, 30 June 1866, letters received, reel 10, BRFAL-VA; Samuel C. Armstrong to Orlando Brown, 12 Jan. 1867, letters received, reel 45, BRFAL (M752).

2. Samuel C. Armstrong to Orlando Brown, 12 Jan. 1867, letters received, reel 45, BRFAL (M752); Commissioner O. O. Howard quoted in Edith Armstrong Talbot, *Samuel Chapman Armstrong: A Biographical Study* (New York: Doubleday, Page, 1904), 136; Paul A. Cimbala, *The Freedmen's Bureau: Reconstructing the American South after the Civil War* (Malabar, Fla.: Krieger, 2005), 28. On Samuel Chapman Armstrong and, in particular, his role in the promotion of industrial education as an answer to the deficiencies of freedom, see Robert Francis Engs, *Educating the Disfranchised and Disinherited: Samuel Chapman Armstrong and Hampton Institute, 1839–1893* (Knoxville: University of Tennessee Press, 1999). For an interesting analysis of Armstrong, Booker T. Washington, and evolving ideologies of American masculinity, see Maurice O. Wallace, *Constructing the Black Masculine: Identity and Ideality in African American Men's Literature and Culture, 1775–1995* (Durham, N.C.: Duke University Press, 2002), 101–4.

3. Samuel C. Armstrong to Orlando Brown, 12 Jan. 1867, letters received, reel 45, BRFAL (M752). In September 1865, President Andrew Johnson effectively ended any effort by the bureau to provide black southerners with land by commanding Commissioner Howard to issue Circular No. 15, which rescinded earlier bureau land circulars and ordered the return of confiscated land to former owners who had sworn their loyalty to the federal government or had been pardoned by the president. See Oliver Otis Howard, *Autobiography of Oliver Otis Howard* (New York: Baker and Taylor, 1907), 2:229–44; U.S. House of Representatives, "Report of the Commissioner of the Bureau of Refugees, Freedmen, and Abandoned Lands [n.d. Dec. 1865]," 39th Cong., 1st sess., House Executive Document 11 (Serial 1255), 4–5; Foner, *Reconstruction: America's Unfinished Revolution, 1863–1877* (New York: Harper & Row, 1988), 187–95.

4. Howard, *Autobiography*, 2:351. The bureau's insistence that the "able poor" were undeserving of assistance was not new. As Michael B. Katz points out, since the early nineteenth century, Americans have fought "a war" against the able-bodied poor, endeavoring to "to define, locate, and purge them from the roles of relief." Michael B. Katz, *In the Shadow of the Poorhouse: A Social History of Welfare in America* (New York:

Basic Books, 1986), 18. On bureau relief policies, see Robert Harrison, "Welfare and Employment Policies of the Freedmen's Bureau in the District of Columbia," *Journal of Southern History* 72 (2006): 75–110; Cimbala, *The Freedmen's Bureau*, 39–51; Ira C. Colby, "The Freedmen's Bureau: From Social Welfare to Segregation," *Phylon* 46, no. 3 (1985): 219–30; Robert H. Bremner, *The Public Good: Philanthropy and Welfare in the Civil War Era* (New York: Alfred A. Knopf, 1980), 117–21; Howard N. Rabinowitz, "From Exclusion to Segregation: Health and Welfare Services for Southern Blacks, 1865–1890," *Social Service Review* 48, no. 3 (1974): 327–54; John Hope Franklin, "Public Welfare in the South during the Reconstruction Era, 1865–1880," *Social Service Review* 44, no. 4 (1970): 379–92; Victoria Olds, "The Freedmen's Bureau: A Nineteenth-Century Federal Welfare Agency," *Social Casework* 44 (1963): 247–54. See also the following works, which consider bureau relief efforts as part of a larger study: Chad Alan Goldberg, *Citizens and Paupers: Relief, Rights, and Race, from the Freedmen's Bureau to Workfare* (Chicago: University of Chicago Press, 2007), chap. 2; Jim Downs, "The Other Side of Freedom: Destitution, Disease, and Dependency among Freedwomen and Their Children during and after the Civil War," in *Battle Scars: Gender and Sexuality in the American Civil War*, ed. Catherine Clinton and Nina Silber (New York: Oxford University Press, 2006), 78–103; Carol Faulkner, *Women's Radical Reconstruction: The Freedmen's Aid Movement* (Philadelphia: University of Pennsylvania Press, 2004), chap. 5; Elna C. Green, *This Business of Relief: Confronting Poverty in a Southern City, 1740–1940* (Athens: University of Georgia Press, 2003), chap. 5; Linda Faye Williams, *The Constraint of Race: Legacies of White Skin Privilege* (University Park: Pennsylvania State University Press, 2003), chap. 1; Paul A. Cimbala, *Under the Guardianship of the Nation: The Freedmen's Bureau and the Reconstruction of Georgia, 1865–1870* (Athens: University of Georgia Press, 1997), chap. 4; Martin Abbott, *The Freedmen's Bureau in South Carolina, 1865–1872* (Chapel Hill: University of North Carolina Press, 1967), 37–51; George R. Bentley, *A History of the Freedmen's Bureau* (Philadelphia: University of Pennsylvania, 1955), 76–79, 139–44, 209; Elizabeth Wisner, *Social Welfare in the South: From Colonial Times to World War I* (Baton Rouge: Louisiana State University Press, 1970), 67–85.

5. S. P. Ryland to O. Brown, 16 Oct. 1866, letters received, box 3, BRFAL-VA; S. C. Armstrong to O. Brown, 30 June 1866, registered letters received, reel 10, BRFAL-VA. For examples of the preponderance of freedwomen and children on bureau relief rolls, see reports of indigent refugees and freedmen from subordinate officers, reel 32, BRFAL-LA; received and retained reports relating to rations, lands, and bureau personnel, reels 29–31, BRFAL-TX; records relating to destitute freedmen and refugees, reel 57, BRFAL-VA; monthly reports of destitutes requiring rations, entry 1503 (Baton Rouge, La.), BRFAL-FO; applications for rations, entry 1615 (Franklin, La.), BRFAL-FO; reports of indigents and helpless, entry 1773 (Natchitoches, La.), BRFAL-FO; applications for rations, entry 1797 (New Iberia, La.), BRFAL-FO; register of ration returns approved, entry 4080 (Lynchburg, Va.), BRFAL-FO; register of persons receiving rations, entry 4099 (Manchester, Va.), BRFAL-FO; records relating to the issuance of rations, entry 4110 (Fort Monroe, Va.), BRFAL-FO; registers of destitutes receiving rations, entry 4130 (Fort Monroe, Va.), BRFAL-FO; registers of freedmen receiving rations, entry 4167 (Norfolk, Va.), BRFAL-FO; register of soldiers' families and destitutes receiving rations in Portsmouth, entry 4168 (Norfolk, Va.), BRFAL-FO; register of ration returns, entry 4213 (Petersburg, Va.), BRFAL-FO; lists of indigent persons and loyal refugees to whom rations were issued, entry 4255 (Richmond, Va.), BRFAL-FO; register of freedmen and refugees receiving rations, entry 4319 (Winchester, Va.), BRFAL-FO; registers of persons receiving ration tickets, entry 4353 (Yorktown, Va.), BRFAL-FO; registers of infirm and destitute freedmen, entry 4355 (Yorktown, Va.), BRFAL-FO; G. Cook to W. S. How, 3 May 1866, report of operations and conditions, box 37, BRFAL-VA; T. P. Jackson to A. S. Flagg, 19 April 1866, registered letters received, reel 13, BRFAL-VA; S. C. Armstrong to

O. Brown, 4 May 1866, registered letters received, reel 10, BRFAL-VA. On the refusal of white planters to hire "unproductives" or, in the words of historian Susan O'Donovan, "the pregnant, the recently pregnant, the potentially pregnant, and the very young," see Frank P. Crandon, "Report of Freedmen Able to Work and for whom Employment Cannot be Found in the 4th District Va. Bureau R. F. and A. Lands on the 31st January 1866," 31 Jan. 1866, registered letters received, reel 12, BRFAL-VA; Susan Eva O'Donovan, *Becoming Free in the Cotton South* (Cambridge, Mass.: Harvard University Press, 2007), 158–61 (quotation in note on 159); Nancy D. Bercaw, *Gendered Freedoms: Race, Rights, and the Politics of the Household in the Delta, 1861–1875* (Gainesville: University Press of Florida, 2003), 113, 121–24; Noralee Frankel, *Freedom's Women: Black Women and Families in Civil War Era Mississippi* (Bloomington: Indiana University Press, 1999), 72–74; Lynda J. Morgan, *Emancipation in Virginia's Tobacco Belt, 1850–1870* (Athens: University of Georgia Press, 1992), 153, 174–75; Jacqueline Jones, *Labor of Love, Labor of Sorrow: Black Women, Work, and the Family from Slavery to the Present* (New York: Basic Books, 1985), 53.

6. For application of the term "war on dependency" to bureau relief activities, see Foner, *Reconstruction*, 152. On the expanding definitions of dependency and the deserving poor, see Faulkner, *Women's Radical Reconstruction*, 83–99; Carol Faulkner, "A Nation's Sin: White Women and U.S. Policy toward Freedpeople," in *Gender and Slave Emancipation in the Atlantic World*, ed. Pamela Scully and Diana Paton (Durham, N.C.: Duke University Press, 2005), 121–40; Nancy Fraser and Linda Gordon, "A Genealogy of *Dependency*: Tracing a Keyword of the U.S. Welfare State," *Signs: A Journal of Women in Culture and Society* 19, no. 2 (1994): 309–36; Laura F. Edwards, *Gendered Strife and Confusion: The Political Culture of Reconstruction* (Urbana: University of Illinois Press, 1997), 67–80; Megan J. McClintock, "Civil War Pensions and the Reconstruction of Union Families," *Journal of American History* 83 (1996): 456–58; Elizabeth Regosin, *Freedom's Promise: Ex-slave Families and Citizenship in the Age of Emancipation* (Charlottesville: University Press of Virginia, 2002), 157–73; Leslie A. Schwalm, *A Hard Fight for We: Women's Transition from Slavery to Freedom in South Carolina* (Urbana: University of Illinois Press, 1997), chap. 7; Theda Skocpol, *Protecting Soldiers and Mothers: The Political Origins of Social Policy in the United States* (Cambridge, Mass.: Belknap Press of Harvard University Press, 1992), 87–88, 92–96, 102–51; Amy Dru Stanley, *From Bondage to Contract: Wage Labor, Marriage, and the Market in the Age of Slave Emancipation* (Cambridge: Cambridge University Press, 1998), chap. 3; Michael B. Katz, *The Undeserving Poor: From the War on Poverty to the War on Welfare* (New York: Pantheon Books, 1989), 5, 7–8, 9–15.

7. Testimony of Violet Guntharpe, in George P. Rawick, ed., *The American Slave: A Composite Autobiography* (Westport, Conn.: Greenwood Press, 1972–79), vol. 2 (S.C.), pt. 2, 216; testimony of Sarah Debro, in Norman R. Yetman, ed., *Life under the "Peculiar Institution": Selections from the Slave Narrative Collection* (New York: Holt, Rinehart and Winston, 1970), 100. Debro's account can also be found in Belinda Hurmence, ed., *My Folks Don't Want Me to Talk about Slavery: Twenty-one Oral Histories of Former North Carolina Slaves* (Winston-Salem, N.C.: John F. Blair, 1984), 59. See also Cimbala, *The Freedmen's Bureau*, 39.

8. Faulkner, *Women's Radical Reconstruction*, 3; Faulkner, "A Nation's Sin"; Keith E. Melder, "Angel of Mercy in Washington: Josephine Griffing and the Freedmen, 1864–1872," *Records of the Columbia Historical Society* 45 (1965): 251–52, 255–562. On the activities of the freedmen's aid movement, see Bremner, *The Public Good*, 98–100, 129–33; Faulkner, *Women's Radical Reconstruction*; Jacqueline Jones, *Soldiers of Light and Love: Northern Teachers and Georgia Blacks, 1865–1873* (Chapel Hill: University of North Carolina Press, 1980), 14–30; James M. McPherson, *The Struggle for Equality: Abolitionists and the Negro in the Civil War and Reconstruction* (Princeton, N.J.: Princeton University

Press, 1964), 160–77, 393–405; Joe M. Richardson, *Christian Reconstruction: The American Missionary Association and Southern Blacks, 1861–1890* (Athens: University of Georgia Press, 1986); Willie Lee Rose, *Rehearsal for Reconstruction: The Port Royal Experiment* (New York: Bobbs-Merrill, 1964; reprint, New York: Oxford University Press, 1976).

9. Howard, *Autobiography*, 2:363, 365, 226, 312, 364. While northern states and southern states had long since expanded public relief efforts beyond that of private charity, especially in the decade before the Civil War, this kind of distribution of material aid by the federal government was unprecedented. Cimbala, *The Freedmen's Bureau*, 8, 39; Howard A. White, *The Freedmen's Bureau in Louisiana* (Baton Rouge: Louisiana State University Press, 1970), 64–85; Abbott, *The Freedmen's Bureau in South Carolina*, 37–51; Colby, "The Freedmen's Bureau," 219; June Axinn and Herman Levin, *Social Welfare: A History of the American Response to Need* (New York: Longman, 1982), 94–95; Wisner, *Social Welfare in the South*, 72–74, 76–77, 85; Walter I. Trattner, *From Poor Law to Welfare State: A History of Social Welfare in America*, 2nd ed. (New York: Free Press, 1979).

10. Howard, *Autobiography*, 2:256; U.S. House of Representatives, "Report of the Commissioner of the Bureau of Refugees, Freedmen, and Abandoned Lands [20 Oct. 1869]," 41st Cong., 2nd sess., House Executive Document 1, pt. 2 (Serial 1412), 430; Howard, *Autobiography*, 2:214.

11. According to the historian Ira C. Colby, in 1860 there were 3,653,870 African Americans in the South (slave and free), yet by 1870, that number had grown to 3,939,033. "Comparing the rations data to the 1870 population," he argues, ".76 of the freedmen took part in this program during its peak use" ("The Freedmen's Bureau," 227). See also Bentley, *A History of the Freedmen's Bureau*, 141; U.S. House of Representatives, "Report of the Commissioner [1869]," 6–7.

12. Cimbala, *The Freedmen's Bureau*, 44; William Armstrong, president of the Board of Overseers of the Poor in Stafford County, Virginia, in Hector Sears to Orlando Brown, 28 Feb. 1866, letters received, reel 30, BRFAL (M752).

13. For a discussion of southern public relief efforts during the period of Reconstruction, see Franklin, "Public Welfare in the South"; Rabinowitz, "From Exclusion to Segregation," 327–48; Colby, "The Freedmen's Bureau," 219–30; Elna C. Green, ed., *Before the New Deal: Social Welfare in the South, 1830–1930* (Athens: University Press of Georgia, 1999); Peter Wallenstein, *From Slave South to New South: Public Policy in Nineteenth-Century Georgia* (Chapel Hill: University of North Carolina Press, 1987), 88, 137–38; Crandall A. Shifflett, *Patronage and Poverty in the Tobacco South: Louisa County, Virginia, 1860–1900* (Knoxville: University of Tennessee Press, 1982); Wisner, *Social Welfare in the South*, 47–52, 67–85, 102–4.

14. U.S. House of Representatives, "Report of the Commissioner of the Bureau of Refugees, Freedmen, and Abandoned Lands [1 Nov. 1866]," 39th Cong., 2nd sess., House Executive Document 1 (Serial 1285), 651; U.S. House of Representatives, "Report of the Commissioner of the Bureau of Refugees, Freedmen, and Abandoned Lands [1 Nov. 1867]," 40th Cong., 2nd sess., House Executive Document 1 (Serial 1323), 23; U.S. House of Representatives, "Report of the Commissioner of the Bureau of Refugees, Freedmen, and Abandoned Lands [24 Oct. 1868]," 40th Cong., 3rd sess., House Executive Document 1 (Serial 1367), 501; Howard, *Autobiography*, 2:365. See also U.S. House of Representatives, "Report of the Commissioner [1869]"; U.S. House of Representatives, "Report of Bureau Expenditures [20 Oct. 1869]," 41st Cong., 2nd sess., House Executive Document 142 (Serial 1417), 6–7; *Statutes at Large of USA* 15 (1867–69): 28; Bremner, *The Public Good*, 121–22; Cimbala, *The Freedmen's Bureau*, 39–51.

15. Arguing that it was indeed a "question of life and death," Assistant Commissioner Wager Sawyne reported that the devastation required the issuance of some 25,000 rations a week in May 1866. Wager Swayne to O. O. Howard, 25 May 1866, letters received, BRFAL (M752). See also Orville H. Browning, *The Diary of Orville Hickman*

Browning (Springfield: Trustees of the Illinois State Historical Library, 1933), 2:95; Bentley, *A History of the Freedmen's Bureau*, 122.

16. Reports of Assistant Commissioners O. Brown (Va.) and Wager Swayne (Ala.) in U.S. Senate, "Reports of the Assistant Commissioners of the Bureau of Refugees, Freedmen, and Abandoned Lands and Laws in Relation to the Freedmen [1866]," 39th Cong., 2nd sess., Senate Executive Document 6 (Serial 1276). Analyses of variance—statistical tests of the difference of means for two or more groups known as ANOVA—assessing the disbursement of relief to freedpeople (men, women, and children) during the spring of 1866 in Virginia districts support these conclusions by revealing an agency clearly disposed to aiding black women and children, but not black men. The findings indicate that the gender or age of a freedperson significantly influenced whether the Virginia bureau provided federal relief. Moreover, the analyses show that agents' aversion to distributing rations to freedmen and general endorsement of the issue of relief to freedwomen and children was not simply a development in one district but rather was statewide.

17. Circular No. 16, 18 June 1866, issuances and rosters of bureau personnel, reel 19, BRFAL-TX; W. Pease to J. Kirkman, 18 May 1867, letters sent, entry 3716, vol. 102 (Houston, Tex.), BRFAL-FO; Barry A. Crouch, "Seeking Equality: Houston Black Women during Reconstruction," in *The Dance of Freedom: Texas African Americans during Reconstruction*, ed. Larry Madaras (Austin: University of Texas Press, 2007), 76; U.S. House of Representatives, "Report of the Commissioner [1867]," 22–32. See also James Smallwood, "Black Freedwomen after Emancipation: The Texas Experience," *Prologue* 27, no. 4 (1995): 308–9.

18. F. A. Massey to S. C. Armstrong and M. S. Reed to S. C. Armstrong, 11 Sept. 1866, as cited in Robert F. Engs, *Freedom's First Generation: Black Hampton, Virginia, 1861–1890* (Philadelphia: University of Pennsylvania Press, 1979), 118. See, in general, records relating to destitute freedmen and refugees, reel 57, BRFAL-VA; register of ration returns approved, entry 4080 (Lynchburg, Va.), BRFAL-FO; register of persons receiving rations, entry 4099 (Manchester, Va.), BRFAL-FO; records relating to the issuance of rations, entry 4110 (Fort Monroe, Va.), BRFAL-FO; registers of destitutes receiving rations, entry 4130 (Fort Monroe, Va.), BRFAL-FO; registers of freedmen receiving rations, entry 4167 (Norfolk, Va.), BRFAL-FO; register of soldiers' families and destitutes receiving rations at Portsmouth, entry 4168 (Norfolk, Va.), BRFAL-FO; register of ration returns, entry 4213 (Petersburg, Va.), BRFAL-FO; lists of indigent persons and loyal refugees to whom rations were issued, entry 4255 (Richmond, Va.), BRFAL-FO; register of freedmen and refugees receiving rations, entry 4319 (Winchester, Va.), BRFAL-FO; registers of persons receiving ration tickets, entry 4353 (Yorktown, Va.), BRFAL-VA; registers of infirm and destitute freedmen, entry 4355 (Yorktown, Va.), BRFAL-FO. For other states, see reports of indigent refugees and freedmen from subordinate officers, reel 32, and reports of indigent refugees and freedmen from subordinate officers, reel 32, BRFAL-LA; monthly reports of destitutes requiring rations, entry 1503 (Baton Rouge, La.) BRFAL-FO; applications for rations, entry 1615 (Franklin, La.), BRFAL-FO; reports of indigents and helpless, entry 1773 (Natchitoches, La.), BRFAL-FO; applications for rations, entry 1797 (New Iberia, La.), BRFAL-FO; received and retained reports relating to rations, lands, and bureau personnel, reels 29–31, BRFAL-TX. See also Herbert G. Gutman, *The Black Family in Slavery and Freedom, 1750–1925* (New York: Pantheon Books, 1976), 235.

19. Reports of George B. Carse, 3 Feb. 1868 and 13 April 1868, and J. H. Durkee to A. H. Jackson, 8 July 1868, letters received, bureau records for Florida, quoted in Bentley, *A History of the Freedmen's Bureau*, 137 and 142.

20. Circular No. 7, issued by Samuel Thomas, 29 July 1865, in U.S. House of Representatives, "Freedmen's Bureau. Letter from the Secretary of War, in answer to A resolution of the House of March 8, transmitting a report, by the Commissioner of the

Freedmen's Bureau, of all orders issued by him or any assistant commissioner," 39th Cong., 1st sess., House Executive Document 70 (Serial 1256), 155 (first and third quotations); comments of Assistant Commissioner Clinton Fisk, Aug. 1865, quoted in Cimbala, *The Freedmen's Bureau*, 42 (second quotation); Mrs. J. S. Griffing to Commissioner O. O. Howard, 23 May 1868, letters received, reel 53, BRFAL (M752) (last quotation). See also Bentley, *A History of the Freedmen's Bureau*, 77; Green, *Before the New Deal*; Katz, *In the Shadow of the Poorhouse*, 18–19.

The only widespread exception to the restrictive nature of bureau relief policies came in 1867 when Congress authorized the bureau to use any portion of its existing appropriation to prevent extreme suffering among "any and all classes of destitute or helpless persons." In the wake of widespread droughts followed by intense flooding and crops besieged with caterpillars, bollworms, and other insects, as well as rampant fears of a cholera epidemic, the only apparent limitation placed on this congressional expenditure was that it forbade the issuance of relief to those living on land still under cultivation. Qualified adults—both black and white—were eligible to receive a bushel of corn and eight pounds of meat per month; children under the age of fourteen were issued half of this ration. On the congressional appropriation of 1867, see Bentley, *A History of the Freedmen's Bureau*, 140–41; Cimbala, *The Freedmen's Bureau*, 45; White, *The Freedmen's Bureau in Louisiana*, 69–76; Paul A. Cimbala, *Under the Guardianship of the Nation*, 95–98; W. Martin Hope and Jason H. Silverman, *Relief and Recovery in Post–Civil War South Carolina* (Lewiston, N.Y.: Edwin Mellen Press, 1997), 5–10.

For further discussion of assumptions regarding how relief undermined manly independence and resulted in vagrancy, see Chapter 3 of this work; James D. Schmidt, *Free to Work: Labor Law, Emancipation, and Reconstruction, 1815–1880* (Athens: University of Georgia Press, 1999), 59–61, 122–64; Paul David Phillips, "A History of the Freedmen's Bureau in Tennessee" (Ph.D. diss., Vanderbilt University, 1964), 125; Linda K. Kerber, *No Constitutional Right to Be Ladies: Women and the Obligations of Citizenship* (New York: Hill and Wang, 1998), 47–80.

21. Comments of Clinton B. Fisk, assistant commissioner of Kentucky and Tennessee, quoted in Cimbala, *The Freedmen's Bureau*, 41; comments of Mississippi assistant commissioner Samuel Thomas, April 1866, quoted in Cimbala, *The Freedmen's Bureau*, 40; Bercaw, *Gendered Freedoms*, 105. My analysis of dependency draws upon work on domestic dependency, free labor ideology, and nineteenth-century labor and family relations. See in particular Laura F. Edwards, "The Problem of Dependency: African Americans, Labor Relations, and the Law in the Nineteenth-Century South," *Agricultural History* 72, no. 2 (1998): 313–40; Fraser and Gordon, "A Genealogy of *Dependency*"; Bercaw, *Gendered Freedoms*, chap. 4, especially 102–6; Edwards, *Gendered Strife and Confusion*; Faulkner, *Women's Radical Reconstruction*, chap. 1, 83–84, 87–88, 94, 99; Stanley, *From Bondage to Contract*, 10–11, 16–17, 34, 48–49, 58–59, 129–35, 140, 143–48, 151–54, 188–92, 197–200. See also Victoria E. Bynum, *Unruly Women: The Politics of Social and Sexual Control in the Old South* (Chapel Hill: University of North Carolina Press, 1992); Nancy F. Cott, *Public Vows: A History of Marriage and the Nation* (Cambridge, Mass.: Harvard University Press, 2000), 81–82, 91–94; William F. Forbath, "The Ambiguities of Free Labor: Labor and Law in the Gilded Age," *Wisconsin Law Review* 4 (1985): 767–817; Harrison, "Welfare and Employment Policies," 106–7; O'Donovan, *Becoming Free*, 165–70; Amy Dru Stanley, "Beggars Can't Be Choosers: Compulsion and Contract in Postbellum America," *Journal of American History* 78 (1992): 1265–93; Peter W. Bardaglio, *Reconstructing the Household: Families, Sex, and the Law in the Nineteenth-Century South* (Chapel Hill: University of North Carolina Press, 1995).

22. Selden N. Clark to C. H. Howard, 4 Jan. 1868, letters received, reel 10, BRFAL-DC.

23. Feby (also spelled "Phobe" and "Pheobe") Leach (Waynesboro, Va.) to Thomas P. Jackson, 15 June 1867, registered letters received, entry 4269, box 55 (Staunton, Va.), BRFAL-FO; W. A. Sharp to J. Cromie, 23 Feb. 1867, unregistered letters received, entry 1766 (Natchitoches, La.), BRFAL-FO. See also Cimbala, *The Freedmen's Bureau*, 46–51.

24. John William De Forest, *A Union Officer in the Reconstruction*, ed. James H. Croushore and David Morris Potter (New Haven, Conn.: Yale University Press, 1948; reprint, Baton Rouge: Louisiana State University Press, 1976), 94; Edwards, *Gendered Strife and Confusion*, 158. On black women's notions of womanhood and domesticity in the late nineteenth-century South, see Bercaw, *Gendered Freedoms*; Bynum, *Unruly Women*; Edwards, *Gendered Strife and Confusion*; Frankel, *Freedom's Women*; Glenda Elizabeth Gilmore, *Gender and Jim Crow: Women and the Politics of White Supremacy in North Carolina, 1896–1920* (Chapel Hill: University of North Carolina Press, 1996); Tera W. Hunter, *To 'Joy My Freedom: Southern Black Women's Lives and Labors after the Civil War* (Cambridge, Mass.: Harvard University Press, 1997); Jones, *Labor of Love*; Hannah Rosen, "'Not That Sort of Women': Race, Gender, and Sexual Violence during the Memphis Riot of 1866," in *Sex, Love, Race: Crossing Boundaries in North American History*, ed. Martha Elizabeth Hodes (New York: New York University Press, 1999), 267–93; O'Donovan, *Becoming Free*; Schwalm, *A Hard Fight for We*. On bureau efforts to combat the "evil of female loaferism," as John William De Forest called freedwomen's perceived withdrawal from the fields, see Chapter 3 of this work.

25. J. DeGray to A. F. Hayden, 14 July 1866, entry 1546, vols. 245–48 (Clinton, La.), BRFAL-FO; case of Mrs. Martin Randale (also spelled "Motin Ramsel") in letter and endorsement on J. H. Boring to J. G. Van Gilder, 22 Aug. 1865, letters received, reel 14, BRFAL (M752); R. Folles to F. H. Sterling, 24 April 1868, registered letters received, entry 1452, box 2 (Algiers, La.), BRFAL-FO; J. R. Lyle to T. F. Forbes, 12 Sept. 1866, unregistered letters received, reel 27, BRFAL-GA; J. O. O'Neill to O. Brown, 25 Dec. 1866, monthly narrative reports of operations and conditions, reel 46, BRFAL-VA; Horace James, *Annual Report of the Superintendent of Negro Affairs in North Carolina, 1864. With an Appendix, Containing the History and Management of Freedmen in this Department up to June 1st 1865* (Boston: W. F. Brown, 1865), 55, quoted in Patricia C. Click, *Time Full of Trial: The Roanoke Island Freedmen's Colony, 1862–1867* (Chapel Hill: University of North Carolina Press, 2001), 146. For sentiments similar to those of the Reverend James, see F. Sargent Free to Samuel Thomas, 1 Nov. 1865, letters received, reel 22, BRFAL (M752). For other examples of bureau support to soldiers' wives, see, for example, P. H. Sheridan to A. P. Ketchum, 1 Oct. 1866, letters received, reel 38, BRFAL (M752); E. Whittlesey to [O. O. Howard], 15 Oct. 1865, letters received, reel 23, BRFAL (M752); Circular No. 7, issued by O. O. Howard, 13 June 1865, orders and circulars received, entry 4349, box 67, BRFAL-FO; endorsement of Samuel C. Armstrong in agent in Elizabeth City County at Fortress Monroe to Samuel C. Armstrong, 12 July 1866, letters and orders received, entry 4349, box 67, BRFAL-FO; register of soldiers, families, and destitutes receiving rations at Portsmouth, March–July 1865, entry 4168, vol. 401 (Norfolk, Va.), and registers of freedmen receiving rations, 1865–67, entry 4167, vol. 354 (Norfolk, Va.), both in BRFAL-FO.

26. O'Donovan, *Becoming Free*, 159, 161.

27. J. F. James to H. S. Merrill, 11 Oct. 1865, letters received, entry 4239, vol. 404 (Richmond, Va.), BRFAL-FO; John Durdin to Gilbert L. Eberhart, 5 July 1866, unregistered letters received, reel 26, BRFAL-GA; D. B. Graham to D. Tillson, 25 May 1866, unregistered letters received, reel 27, BRFAL-GA; W. Tidball to J. A. Bates, 31 July 1866, monthly narrative reports of operations and conditions, reel 45, BRFAL-VA; General Orders No. 16, issued by Stuart Barnes, 15 Sept. 1865, entry 4198 (Petersburg, Va.), BRFAL-FO; B. C.

NOTES 197

Cook to J. A. McDonald, 31 Oct. 1866, monthly narrative reports of operations and conditions, reel 45, BRFAL-VA; agent in Elizabeth City County at Fortress Monroe to Samuel C. Armstrong, and accompanying endorsements, 12 July 1866, letters and orders received, entry 4349, box 67 (Yorktown, Va.), BRFAL-FO.

28. Howard, *Autobiography*, 2:226; remarks of the bureau subassistant commissioner at Albany, Georgia, in 1867, quoted in O'Donovan, *Becoming Free*, 170.

29. S. C. Armstrong to O. Brown, 28 March 1866, letters received, reel 10, BRFAL-VA. On bureau ambivalence to relief activities, see, for example, Foner, *Reconstruction*, 152–53; Rose, *Rehearsal for Reconstruction*, 375–76. See also Fraser and Gordon, "A Genealogy of *Dependency*," 314–20.

30. J. Gregg to O. O. Howard, 16 July 1865, letters received, reel 15, BRFAL (M752); Clinton B. Fisk, *Plain Counsels for Freedmen: In Sixteen Brief Lectures* (Boston: American Tract Society, 1866), 32; Circular Letter No. 33, issued by E. M. Gregory, 17 Oct. 1865, letters sent, reel 1, BRFAL-TX; Edwin Lyon to Orlando Brown, 31 May 1866, reports of operations and conditions, reel 44, BRFAL-VA. Almost the same word for word, the statute passed by the Texas legislature in 1866 read: "All labor contracts shall be made with the heads of families; they shall embrace the labor of all the members of the family named therein able to work, and shall be binding on all minors of said families." "Laws in Relation to Freedmen," in U.S. Senate, "Reports of the Assistant Commissioners of the Bureau of Refugees, Freedmen, and Abandoned Lands and Laws in Relation to the Freedmen [1866]," 39th Cong., 2nd sess., Senate Executive Document 6 (Serial 1276), 223. See *The General Laws of the Regular Session of the Eleventh Legislature of the State of Texas* (Austin, 1866), chaps. 80, 77; Kerber, *No Constitutional Right to Be Ladies*, 53–55, 63–64.

31. The number of abandoned women, particularly those with children, who came to the bureau seeking assistance was great. For examples of such complaints and bureau responses, see R. C. Scott to O. O. Howard, 26 March 1868, letters received, reel 55, BRFAL (M752); Stephen R. Palmer to J. D. G. Cotting, 2 Feb. 1868, entry 759, box 9 (Augusta, Ga.), unregistered letters received, BRFAL-FO; J. M. Cochran to provost marshal, 6 Nov. 1866, unregistered letters received, entry 1602 (Franklin, La.), BRFAL-FO; J. W. McConanghey to W. H. Sinclair, 28 March 1866, letters received, reel 7, BRFAL-TX; W. A. McNulty to [bureau agent in Leesburg, Va.], 16 Aug. 1866, letters received, entry 3850, vol. 85 (Alexandria, Va.), BRFAL-FO; Ameilia Maynard v. Charles Maynard, 6 April 1867, Louisa Grandison v. Wallace Grandison, 29 Sept. 1868, Martha Pry v. Smith Pry, 11 Jan. 1867, all in register of complaints, entry 3868, vol. 98 (Alexandria, Va.), BRFAL-FO; Bunney v. Burden, 22 May 1865, Walhop v. Dennis, n.d., and Binney v. Binney, 20 Aug. [1866], proceedings of the freedmen's court, entry 3959 (Drummondtown, Va.), BRFAL-VA; Brown v. Brown, 13 June [1866], Young v. Young, 25 June [1866], Richardson v. Richardson, 4 July [1866], Tarray v. Tarray, 28 July [1866], Johnson v. Johnson, 1 Aug. [1866], Hatten v. Hatten, 9 Aug. [1866], Whendleton v. Whendleton, 9 Aug. [1866], Storers v. Jones, 9 Aug. [1866], Brown v. Coles, 11 Aug. [1866], Commodore v. Commodore, 15 Aug. [1866], Spinner v. Spinner, 27 Aug. [1866], all in register of complaints, entry 3924, vol. 131 (Charlotte Courthouse, Va.), BRFAL-FO; B. C. Cook to A. McDonnell, 26 June 1866, unregistered letters received, entry 4240 (Richmond, Va.), BRFAL-FO; J. A. Bates to C. B. Wilder, 23 Nov. 1866, and [F. I. Massey] to S. C. Armstrong, 28 Jan. 1867, letters sent, entry 4346, vol. 500 (Yorktown, Va.) BRFAL-FO; J. O. Hollis to S. Barnes, 15 Dec. 1865, letters sent, reel 11, BRFAL-VA.

32. Alvan C. Gillem to O. O. Howard, 31 March 1868, letters received, reel 54, BRFAL (M752) (first quotation); Fred. Palmer to J. W. Groesbeck, 13 Feb. 1867, letters received, reel 44, BRFAL (M752) (second quotation); General Orders No.12, issued by the military headquarters in Lynchburg, Virginia, 26 May 1865, published in the *Daily Lynchburg Virginian*, 1 June 1865 (third quotation); General Orders No. 1, issued by the military

commander of the Department of South Carolina, 1 Jan. 1866, printed in the *Charleston Daily Courier*, 23 Jan. 1866, cited in Schwalm, *A Hard Fight for We*, 256–57. See also Wm. Tidball to James A. Bates, 31 July 1866, monthly narrative reports of operations and conditions, reel 45, BRFAL-VA.

33. It is difficult to determine to what extent such orders were enforced—if, in fact, they could be enforced at all. Judging from the registers of complaints kept by local bureau agents and summaries of the freedmen's courts' proceedings in Virginia, orders and enforcement efforts varied widely and according to individual agents' personal views and interests as well as the circumstances and policies they encountered. Moreover, ordering freedmen to return and/or support their abandoned wives and children usually proved easier than exacting compliance from them. More often, local agents and the courts found themselves relying on sermons instructing complainants and deserters in their marital obligations and urging them to "live together peaceably." For examples, see cases cited in note 31 and Dorothy Sterling, ed., *We Are Your Sisters: Black Women in the Nineteenth Century* (New York: W. W. Norton, 1984), 341.

34. Case of Lucinda Molley in M. McKennel to J. Joyes, 9 March 1866, letters received, reel 12, BRFAL-VA; case of Rebecca Woodson v. Henry Woodson, 24 Nov. 1865, proceedings of the freedmen's court, entry 4246, vol. 415 (Richmond, Va.), BRFAL-FO; J. M. Cochran to provost marshal, 6 Nov. 1866, unregistered letters received, entry 1602 (Franklin, La.), BRFAL-FO; case of Ann Marie Brown v. James Brown, 13–14 June 1866, register of complaints, entry 3924, vol. 131 (Charlotte Courthouse, Va.), BRFAL-FO.

35. The certificate read: "I hereby certify on honor, that . . . has a family of (here state number of adults and children) dependent upon . . . for support, that he (or she) owns no Real Estate or any Description, nor personal property of any kind, beyond a limited amount of Household furniture, Tools of Trade and agriculture implements, nor does any member of said family own any, that said . . . is entirely destitute and has no possible means of subsisting and is a proper subject of charity." Certificate in Office of Ch. C. S., Dept. of Va., Richmond, to [?], 14 Aug. 1865, contracts, bonds, court records, and miscellaneous reports and lists, 1865–68, entry 3905, box 9 (Buckingham Courthouse, Va.), BRFAL-FO. See also General Orders No. 11, issued by Maj. Genl. Hartsuff, U.S. Forces Headquarters, Petersburg, Va., 24 April 1865, BRFAL-FO.

36. Lewis Kooker to M. T. Donohoe, 4 May 1865, vol. 19/58 24AC, 159, letters sent, series 7000, 1st Brigade 3rd Division, 24th Army Corps, Records of the U.S. Army Continental Commands, pt. 2, no. 478, RG 393, National Archives; "314B: Commander of Department of Virginia to the Commander of the District of Eastern Virginia," in Ira Berlin, Joseph P. Reidy, and Leslie S. Rowland, eds., *The Black Military Experience*, series 2 of *Freedom: A Documentary History of Emancipation, 1861–1867* (Cambridge: Cambridge University Press, 1982), 721 (Richmond quotations). See also Chas. H. Millar to Geo. S. Darling, 15 Dec. 1864, vol. 299 DG, 756, letters sent, series 1839, provost marshal, Department of the Gulf, Records of the U.S. Army Continental Commands, pt. 1, RG 393, National Archives; Kerber, *No Constitutional Right to Be Ladies*, 63, 67; Jones, *Labor of Love*, 45, 53.

37. Case of Anne Virginia Brown in George A. Arnes to John F. Marsh, 6 Sept. 1865, letters received, entry 3853, box 1 (Alexandria, Va.), BRFAL-FO. See also Harrison, "Welfare and Employment Policies," 89–93, 106.

38. For the best description of bureau relocation policies and the organization of employment agents that resulted from them, see William Cohen, *At Freedom's Edge: Black Mobility and the Southern White Quest for Racial Control, 1861–1915* (Baton Rouge: Louisiana State University Press, 1991), chap. 3 and 78–96. See also Harrison, "Welfare and Employment Policies," 93–107; Bentley, *A History of the Freedmen's Bureau*, 97, 124–25; Donald G. Nieman, *To Set the Law in Motion: The Freedmen's Bureau and the Legal Rights of Blacks, 1865–1868* (Millwood, N.Y.: KTO Press, 1979), 37.

39. Orlando Brown, "Summary Report," 30 Nov. 1865, enclosed in Max. Woodhull to Orlando Brown, 11 Dec. 1865, letters received, BRFAL-VA; Orlando Brown to O. O. Howard, 4 Oct. and [n.d.] Dec. 1865, letters received, BRFAL (M752); Assistant Adjutant General to Orlando Brown, 25 July 1865, letters sent, reel 1, BRFAL (M742); O. O. Howard to Orlando Brown, 31 May 1865, letters sent, reel 1, BRFAL (M742). See also Cohen, *At Freedom's Edge*, 46; Bentley, *A History of the Freedmen's Bureau*, 97.

40. S. C. Armstrong to O. Brown, 28 March 1866, registered letters received, reel 10, BRFAL-VA. See also the annual reports of Commissioner Howard, which indicate the number of destitute refugees and freedpeople provided with transportation by the Freedmen's Bureau. These reports show that from May 1865 to September 1868, the bureau relocated some 29,402 African Americans. While this number appears substantial, the historian William Cohen maintains that "there is good reason to believe that it substantially undercounts the number who received such assistance." Indeed, he argues that the discrepancies evident in bureau records make it plausible that "the number transported by the bureau may have been double the number reported, that is, perhaps fifty or sixty thousand freedmen in the period from May 30, 1865, to September 30, 1868" (*At Freedom's Edge*, 59 n. 34). For official transportation records of the Freedmen's Bureau, see U.S. House of Representatives, "Report of the Commissioner [1865]," especially comments regarding General Orders No. 138, on 14; U.S. House of Representatives, "Report of the Commissioner [1866]"; U.S. House of Representatives, "Report of the Commissioner [1867]"; "Report of the Commissioner [1868]"; U.S. House of Representatives, "Report of the Commissioner [1869]."

41. Petition for transportation by Charity Cox in M. McKennel to J. Joyes, 9 March 1866, registered letters received, reel 12, BRFAL-VA; Sarah Sanford (thru Mrs. A. J. Reynolds) to O. O. Howard, 27 July 1869, letters received, reel 63, BRFAL (M752). Unfortunately, Sarah Sanford appealed to the bureau too late. Her request was returned with the endorsement: "Respectfully returned . . . with the information that the Bureau has no longer power to grant transportation to Refugees and Freedmen."

42. The bureau approved her request for transportation "if upon inquiry it be found that her husband is able and willing to provide for her." H. Catley to M. G. Gallagher, 14 May 1868, letters received, entry 767, box 10, BRFAL-FO.

43. William Cohen estimates that from 1865 to 1868, the bureau relocated more than 9,000 freedpeople from the Washington, D.C., area alone and another 522 from Virginia to northern cities (*At Freedom's Edge*, 83, 95).

44. Rev. J. N. Glouchester to [O. Brown], 2 Jan. 1866, registered letters and telegrams received, reel 13, BRFAL-VA. On bureau involvement in transporting freedpeople north, see Harrison, "Welfare and Employment Policies," 99–110; Faulkner, *Women's Radical Reconstruction*, 117–31; Cohen, *At Freedom's Edge*, 78–96; Bentley, *A History of the Freedmen's Bureau*, 124–25.

45. E. H. Smith to O. Brown, 24 June 1865, and P. S. Evans to A. S. Flagg, 11 July 1865, letters sent, reel 1, BRFAL-VA. On the bureau's use of free transportation, see also circular issued by O. O. Howard, 15 June 1865, in U.S. House of Representatives, "Freedmen's Bureau," 120; "Report of the Assistant Commissioner for the District of Columbia," 15 Dec. 1865, in U.S. House of Representatives, "Freedmen's Bureau," 381; Bentley, *A History of the Freedmen's Bureau*, 97, 124–25; Cohen, *At Freedom's Edge*, 44, 51–52, 54–55, chap. 4.

46. *New York Herald*, 26 Feb. 1866; *Washington Chronicle*, 15 May 1866, [O. O. Howard] to O. Brown, 10 Feb. 1866, letters received, box 11, BRFAL-VA; C. H. Howard to J. S. Griffing, 15 Oct. 1866, letters sent, reel 1, BRFAL-DC; Tillson quoted in O'Donovan, *Becoming Free*, 169. On bureau threats to discontinue rations, see *Washington Chronicle*, 15 May 1866; F. I. Massey to O. Brown, 22 June 1866, registered letters and telegrams received, reel 10, BRFAL-VA; Clark to P. Davis, 20 March 1867, letters sent,

reel 1, BRFAL-DC; Clark to John J. W. Vanderburgh, 20 Jan. 1868, letters sent, reel 2, BRFAL-DC.

47. Faulkner, *Women's Radical Reconstruction*, 126; S. C. Armstrong to O. Brown, 5 Aug. 1866, letters received, quoted in Bentley, *A History of the Freedmen's Bureau*, 124; *Columbus Daily Sun*, 11 Nov. 1866, quoted in Alan Conway, *The Reconstruction of Georgia* (Minneapolis: University of Minnesota Press, 1966), 79 n. 73; Anna Earle to C. H. Howard, 12 Oct. 1867 and 24 Jan. 1867, quoted in Faulkner, *Women's Radical Reconstruction*, 127. See also the reports of Samuel C. Armstrong, superintendent of bureau operations at Fortress Monroe, Virginia, "List of Colored Persons Going North," miscellaneous records, entry 4113 (Fort Monroe, Va.), and register of freedmen sent to New England, entry 4141, vol. 198 (Fort Monroe, Va.), both in BRFAL-FO; Cohen, *At Freedom's Edge*, 57–58, 65–66, 80–81; O'Donovan, *Becoming Free*, 168–69; Melder, "Angel of Mercy in Washington," 258–59. On the generally bad experiences of the bureau with private employment agents and complaints issued by freedpeople, see Cohen, *At Freedom's Edge*, 57–58, 65, 69–71; Faulkner, *Women's Radical Reconstruction*, 119–20, 126–30; Harrison, "Welfare and Employment Policies," 105.

48. Endorsement of James A. Bates on B. C. Cook to J. A. Bates, 27 Nov. 1866, letters received, reel 11, BRFAL-VA. For similar actions in other states, see also Circular No. 3, 14 Oct. 1865, and Circular No. 6, 9 April 1866, both issued by Assistant Commissioner Davis Tillson (Ga.), orders and circulars, reel 34, BRFAL-GA. On the use of apprenticeship by the bureau, see Chapter 4 of this work; Karin L. Zipf, *Labor of Innocents: Forced Apprenticeship in North Carolina, 1715–1919* (Baton Rouge: Louisiana State University Press, 2005), 78–83; Mary Niall Mitchell, *Raising Freedom's Child: Black Children and Visions of the Future after Slavery* (New York: New York University Press, 2008), 144–45, 153–62; Barry A. Crouch, "'To Enslave the Rising Generation': The Freedmen's Bureau and the Texas Black Code," in *The Freedmen's Bureau and Reconstruction: Reconsiderations*, ed. Paul A. Cimbala and Randall M. Miller (New York: Fordham University Press, 1999), 265–78; Richard Paul Fuke, "Planters, Apprenticeship, and Forced Labor: The Black Family under Pressure in Post-emancipation Maryland," *Agricultural History* 62 (1988): 57–74; Rebecca Scott, "The Battle over the Child: Child Apprenticeship and the Freedmen's Bureau in North Carolina," *Prologue* 10, no. 2 (1978): 101–13; Cimbala, *Under the Guardianship of the Nation*, 193–203; Bardaglio, *Reconstructing the Household*, 79, 98, 104, 161; Barbara Jeanne Fields, *Slavery and Freedom on the Middle Ground: Maryland during the Nineteenth Century* (New Haven, Conn.: Yale University Press, 1985), 139–42; Karin L. Zipf, "Reconstructing 'Free Woman': African-American Women, Apprenticeship, and Custody Rights during Reconstruction," *Journal of Women's History* 12 (2000): 8–31.

49. Endorsement on J. F. Wilcox to R. S. Lacey, 14 Dec. 1865, letters received, entry 3948, box 14 (Danville, Va.), BRFAL-FO; G. Pillsbury to O'Brien, 22 Aug. 1866, testimony, reports, and other records relating to court cases, entry 3284 (Moncks Corner, S.C.), BRFAL-FO; *Washington Chronicle*, 15 May 1866; W. H. Sinclair to Philip Howard, 17 April 1866, letters sent, reel 1, BRFAL-TX. See also J. W. Throckmorton (Governor, Tex.) to Griffin, 4 March 1867, letters received, reel 9, BRFAL-TX; Mart. W. Wagner to Gregory, 15 March 1866, letters received, reel 9, BRFAL-TX; E. Whittlesey to O. O. Howard, 15 Jan. 1866, letters received, reel 23, BRFAL (M752). For examples of bureau men desirous of parental consent in apprenticeship of freedchildren, see Circular No. 4, issued by E. Whittlesey, reel 20, BRFAL-NC; B. C. Cook to J. A. Bates, 27 Nov. 1866, letters sent, reel 1, BRFAL-VA; J. F. Wilcox to R. S. Lacey, 13 Dec. 1865, letters received, entry 3948, box 14 (Danville, Va.), BRFAL-FO; G. P. Sherwood to J. O. O'Neill, 27 July 1866, letters sent, entry 4328, vol. 2 (Wytheville, Va.), BRFAL-FO; W. W. Deane to W. H. Pritchell, 30 April 1866, letters sent, reel 2, BRFAL-GA; W. W. Deane to L. Campbell, 23 April 1866, letters sent, reel 2, BRFAL-GA. See also Crouch, "To Enslave the Rising

Generation," 265–67, 269–71; Fuke, "Planters, Apprenticeship, and Forced Labor," 72–74; Scott, "The Battle over the Child," 101–4, 107–8; Schwalm, *A Hard Fight for We*, 252; Zipf, *Labor of Innocents*, 74–76.

50. For a short introduction to apprenticeship law in the context of the nineteenth-century United States, more broadly, see Michael Grossberg, *Governing the Hearth: Law and the Family in Nineteenth-Century America* (Chapel Hill: University of North Carolina Press, 1985), 259–73. On the practice of apprenticeship and its "almost nonexistent" status in the North by the time of the Civil War, see Schmidt, *Free to Work*, 62–63; Zipf, *Labor of Innocents*, 40–41.

51. C. Cilley to E. Whittlesey, 19 Nov. 1865, letters received, reel 7, BRFAL-NC; A. F. Hayden to J. W. Keller, 14 June 1866 and 3 Nov. 1866, unregistered letters received, entry 1602 (Franklin, La.), BRFAL-FO; Georgia order described and enclosed in Davis Tillson to John B. Walker, 20 Nov. 1865, letters sent, reel 1, BRFAL-GA; case of Sylvia Darden in Jesse Aycock to N. Sellers Hill, 27 May 1867, letters received, entry 933, box 21 (Macon, Ga.), BRFAL-FO; case of Virginia Berry in [F. A. E. Gaebel] to S. A. McLenden, 14 June 1866, letters received and miscellaneous papers relating to complaints, entry 883, box 18 (Fort Gaines, Ga.), BRFAL-FO. It is not known whether Louisiana freedwoman Phillis recovered her daughter.

52. Wm. L. Van Derliss to E. Whittlesey, 19 Dec. 1868, and endorsement of Harry L. Haskell, 4 Jan. 1869, letters received, reel 62, BRFAL (M752); freedwoman Lucinda quoted in Faulkner, *Women's Radical Reconstruction*, 25–26; C. H. Howard to Anna Lowell, 14 Dec. 1866, letters sent, reel 1, BRFAL-DC; G. Cook to W. S. How, 3 May 1866, report of operations and conditions, box 37, BRFAL-VA; Thomas P. Jackson to A. S. Flagg, 8 Feb. 1866, reports of operations and conditions, box 37, reel 44, BRFAL-VA; F. I. Massey to S. C. Armstrong, 7 Oct. 1866, letters received, box 4, BRFAL-VA. On the determination of freedwomen to leave the plantation and their refusal to return to the countryside, see, for example, W. S. How to O. Brown, 8 Aug. 1865, letters received, box 2, and E. B. Townsend to H. S. Merrell, 31 Jan. 1866, letters received, box 8, BRFAL-VA; Wm. P. Austin to J. M. Schofield, 3 Sept. 1866, letters received, reel 10, BRFAL-VA; S. C. Armstrong to O. Brown, 5 Aug. 1866, letters received, box 3, BRFAL-VA; F. I. Massey to S. C. Armstrong, 9 Sept. 1866 and 7 Oct. 1866, letters received, box 4, BRFAL-VA. On the difficulties of encouraging freedwomen to go to homes in the North, see, for example, A. F. Williams to O. O. Howard, n.d. [rec'd 16 Jan. 1867], letters received, reel 45, BRFAL (M752); A. F. Williams to O. O. Howard, 20 Jan. 1867, letters received, reel 42, BRFAL (M752); B. F. Partridge to O. O. Howard, 9 Oct. 1865, letters received, reel 23, BRFAL (M752); J. S. Griffing to E. Whittlesey, 29 Aug. 1868, letters received, reel 58, BRFAL (M752); F. I. Massey to O. Brown, 22 June 1866, letters received, reel 11, BRFAL-VA; S. C. Armstrong to O. Brown, 30 June 1866, letters received, reel 10, BRFAL-VA; C. H. Howard to O. O. Howard, 22 Oct. 1866, letters sent, BRFAL-DC; J. S. Griffing to C. H. Howard, 20 Oct. 1866, letters received, reel 7, BRFAL-DC. For examples of threats to discontinue rations, see F. I. Massey to O. Brown, 22 June 1866, registered letters and telegrams received, reel 10, BRFAL-VA; Clark to P. Davis, 20 March 1867, letters sent, reel 1, BRFAL-DC; C. H. Howard to J. S. Griffing, 15 Oct. 1866, letters sent, reel 1, BRFAL-DC; Clark to John J. W. Vanderburgh, 20 Jan. 1868, letters sent, reel 2, BRFAL-DC; Cohen, *At Freedom's Edge*, 80–81; Faulkner, *Women's Radical Reconstruction*, 119. See also William A. Poillon to Wager Swayne, [n.d.] Nov. 1865, letters received, BRFAL-AL; William T. Alderson, "The Influence of Military Rule and the Freedmen's Bureau on Reconstruction Virginia, 1865–1870" (Ph.D. diss., Vanderbilt University, 1952), 282–84; Engs, *Freedom's First Generation*, 116–19; Harrison, "Welfare and Employment Policies," 93–94, 96–98, 101–5; Peter Kolchin, *First Freedom: The Response of Alabama's Blacks to Emancipation and Reconstruction* (Westport, Conn: Greenwood Press, 1972), 10; Robert Manson Myers, ed., *Children of Pride: A True Story of Georgia and the Civil War* (New

Haven, Conn.: Yale University Press, 1972), 1263, 1292; Leon F. Litwack, *Been in the Storm So Long: The Aftermath of Slavery* (New York: Alfred A. Knopf, 1979; reprint, New York: Vintage Books, 1980), 304–35.

53. S. C. Armstrong to O. Brown, 30 June 1866, letters received, reel 10, BRFAL-VA (first quotation); F. I. Massey to O. Brown, 22 June 1866, BRFAL-VA (second quotation); C. B. Wilder to O. Brown, 18 Jan. 1866, BRFAL-VA (third quotation); testimony of Abram Colby, 28 Oct. 1871, in *Testimony taken by the Joint Select Committee to Inquire into the Condition of Affairs in the Late Insurrectionary States* (Washington, D.C.: Government Printing Office, 1872), 2:700 (fourth quotation); C. B. Wilder to O. Brown, 18 Jan. 1866, registered letters sent, reel 20, BRFAL-VA (last quotation). See also Hunter, *To 'Joy My Freedom*, 22–26; Schwalm, *A Hard Fight for We*, 151–52; Litwack, *Been in the Storm So Long*, 304–16.

54. For examples of children sent away without parental consent, see Harrison, "Welfare and Employment Policies," 105 n. 71; Faulkner, *Women's Radical Reconstruction*, 126–29. On the significance of motherhood to freedwomen, see Bercaw, *Gendered Freedoms*, 58, 153–54, 176–77; Edwards, *Gendered Strife and Confusion*, 157–58, 160–61; Frankel, *Freedom's Women*, 72–74; Jones, *Labor of Love*, chap. 2; Deborah Gray White, *Ar'n't I a Woman? Female Slaves in the Plantation South*, 2nd ed. (New York: W. W. Norton, 1999), 105–18, 159–60, 170–72, 180–81. On blacks' criticism of bureau transportation policies, see Faulkner, *Women's Radical Reconstruction*, 126–31; Harrison, "Welfare and Employment Policies," 104–5. On the bureau and apprenticeship, see Chapter 4 of this work.

55. Thomas T. Tredway to O. Brown, 21 Dec. 1865, unregistered letters received, entry 3972 (Farmville, Va.), BRFAL-FO; testimony of William F. Taylor, 14 and 16 Jan. 1867, in the Investigation of the Government of Maryland [1867], RG 233, National Archives, Washington, D.C.

56. B. C. Cook to J. A. Bates, 27 Nov. 1866, and endorsement, letters sent, reel 1, BRFAL-VA (first and second quotations); D. M. White to A. W. Preston, 14 Feb. 1867, letters received, reel 43, BRFAL (M752) (last quotation). See also W. P. Austin to J. M. Schofield, 3 Sept. 1866, letters received, reel 10, BRFAL-VA; Zipf, *Labor of Innocents*, chap. 4; Fuke, "Planters, Apprenticeship, and Forced Labor," 58–59, 65–68; Scott, "The Battle over the Child," 101–2; Hunter, *To 'Joy My Freedom*, 35–38; Schwalm, *A Hard Fight for We*, 252–54, 254–60.

57. On this point, see Harrison, "Welfare and Employment Policies," 106.

58. S. C. Armstrong to Orlando Brown, 12 Jan. 1867, letters received, reel 45, BRFAL (M752).

3. "The women are the controlling spirits": Freedwomen, Free Labor, and the Freedmen's Bureau

1. J. D. Harris to Davis Tillson, 23 July 1866, unregistered letters received, reel 27, BRFAL-GA.

2. Francis W. Loring and C. F. Atkinson, *Cotton Culture and the South Considered with Reference to Emigration* (Boston: A. Williams, 1869), 4. For similar assertions by white southerners, see 5, 9, 13–16, 20, 22, 24, 72–75, 103, 109, and 137. This work is an analysis of data collected in an 1868 survey of southern labor and economic conditions that focuses on the cotton-producing regions of the South. See also John William De Forest, *A Union Officer in the Reconstruction*, ed. James H. Croushore and David Morris Potter (New Haven, Conn.: Yale University Press, 1948; reprint, Baton Rouge: Louisiana State University Press, 1976), 94.

Drawing from the plethora of contemporary complaints about freedwomen's work habits as well as the conclusions of the quantitative analysis of census data in the cotton-producing regions of the South noted above, many historians have likewise asserted that freedwomen withdrew from agricultural production and, to a lesser extent, domestic work in the immediate postemancipation South. The reasons given for this vary. Some scholars contend that freedwomen gladly yielded to the demands of their husbands and fathers to abandon field labor and voluntarily accepted freedmen's claims to the rights and privileges of the patriarchal family advocated by whites. Others argue that freedwomen not only accepted but emulated white behavior, claiming the right to "play the lady" in the wake of emancipation. Still other scholars maintain that freedwomen's withdrawal from agricultural labor—or perhaps, more appropriately, redistribution of their labor—was a defining act of freedom by which they claimed control over themselves, their labor, and their families. See, in particular, Roger L. Ransom and Richard Sutch, who offered the first quantitative analysis of freedwomen's withdrawal from the fields in *One Kind of Freedom: The Economic Consequences of Emancipation* (Cambridge: Cambridge University Press, 1977), 44–47, 232–36; Herbert G. Gutman, *The Black Family in Slavery and Freedom, 1750–1925* (New York: Pantheon Books, 1976), 167–68; Leon F. Litwack, *Been in the Storm So Long: The Aftermath of Slavery* (New York: Alfred A. Knopf, 1979; reprint, New York: Vintage Books, 1980), 244–47; Lawrence N. Powell, *New Masters: Northern Planters during the Civil War and Reconstruction* (New Haven, Conn.: Yale University Press, 1980), 108–9; Jacqueline Jones, *Labor of Love, Labor of Sorrow: Black Women, Work, and the Family from Slavery to the Present* (New York: Basic Books, 1985), 58–63; Gerald David Jaynes, *Branches without Roots: Genesis of the Black Working Class in the American South, 1862–1882* (New York: Oxford University Press, 1986), 229–31; Eric Foner, *Reconstruction: America's Unfinished Revolution, 1863–1877* (New York: Harper & Row, 1988), 84–87.

The most recent scholarship on African American women in Reconstruction recognizes that freedwomen, particularly those in productive family units with male heads of household, performed less labor in southern agricultural fields and white households than they had in slavery. But this "withdrawal" by former slave women, as the historian Steven Hahn notes, was "not so much from field labor in general as from *full-time* field labor under the supervision of white employers and managers." Steven Hahn, *A Nation under Our Feet: Black Political Struggles in the Rural South from Slavery to the Great Migration* (Cambridge, Mass.: Belknap Press of Harvard University Press, 2003), 171. On freedwomen's continued labors, see, for example, Thavolia Glymph, *Out of the House of Bondage: The Transformation of the Plantation Household* (Cambridge: Cambridge University Press, 2008), especially chap. 6; Susan Eva O'Donovan, *Becoming Free in the Cotton South* (Cambridge, Mass.: Harvard University Press, 2007), especially chap. 4; Nancy D. Bercaw, *Gendered Freedoms: Race, Rights, and the Politics of the Household in the Delta, 1861–1875* (Gainesville: University Press of Florida, 2003), 36–40, 113, 121–28, 167, 185–86; Leslie A. Schwalm, *A Hard Fight for We: Women's Transition from Slavery to Freedom in South Carolina* (Urbana: University of Illinois Press, 1997), especially 194–233; Noralee Frankel, *Freedom's Women: Black Women and Families in Civil War Era Mississippi* (Bloomington: Indiana University Press, 1999), chap. 3.

3. Robert Manson Myers, ed., *Children of Pride: A True Story of Georgia and the Civil War* (New Haven, Conn.: Yale University Press, 1972), 1310; J. D. Harris to Davis Tillson, 23 July 1866, unregistered letters received, reel 27, BRFAL-GA.

4. J. D. Harris to Davis Tillson, 23 July 1866, unregistered letters received, reel 27, BRFAL-GA.

5. W. St. J. Mazyck to Col. Smith, 4 Feb. 1866, letters received, series 2392, Fourth Subdistrict, Military District of Charleston, Records of the U.S. Army Continental Commands, 1821–1920, pt. 2, no. 142, RG 393, quoted in Schwalm, *A Hard Fight for We*, 268. On the bureau and free labor, see Chapter 1 of this work; Foner, *Reconstruction*, 143–44, 155–56; Donald G. Nieman, *To Set the Law in Motion: The Freedmen's Bureau and the Legal Rights of Blacks, 1865–1868* (Millwood, N.Y.: KTO Press, 1979), 34–66.

6. Remarks of bureau agent in Tennessee quoted in Foner, *Reconstruction*, 155; James Davison to Davis Tillson, 8 Jan. 1866, in U.S. Senate, "Reports of the Assistant Commissioners of the Bureau of Refugees, Freedmen, and Abandoned Lands [1865–66]," 39th Cong., 1st sess., Senate Executive Document 27 (Serial 1238), 90; J. W. Alvord (inspector of schools and finances) to O. O. Howard, 1 Jan. 1866, in U.S. Senate, "Reports of the Assistant Commissioners [1865–66]," 120; Circular No. 2, 19 May 1865, letters sent, reel 2, BRFAL (M742); Circular No. 5, 30 May 1865, orders and circulars sent, reel 7, BRFAL (M742). See also O. O. Howard to William Hayward, 23 Dec. 1865, Oliver Otis Howard Papers, Bowdoin College Library, quoted in Nieman, *To Set the Law in Motion*, 56; "Letter of Advice to Assistant Commissioners," 14 June 1865, letters sent, reel 1, BRFAL (M742); Orlando Brown to H. S. Merrell, 15 June 1865, letters received, reel 13, BRFAL (M752); Oliver Otis Howard, *Autobiography of Oliver Otis Howard* (New York: Baker and Taylor, 1907), 2:220.

7. Charles Nordhoff, *Freedmen of South Carolina: Some Account of Their Appearance, Character, Condition and Peculiar Customs* (New York: C. T. Evans, 1863), 7–8.

8. Testimony of Elsie Reece, in Ronnie C. Tyler and Lawrence R. Murphy, eds., *The Slave Narratives of Texas* (Austin, Tex.: Encino Press, 1974), 116; testimony of Julia Francis Daniels, in Tyler and Murphy, *The Slave Narratives of Texas*, 120; testimony of M. Fowler, in George P. Rawick, ed., *The American Slave: A Composite Autobiography* (Westport, Conn.: Greenwood Press, 1972–79), suppl., series 1, vol. 1 (Ala.), 161. See also testimony of Annie Greigg, in B. A. Botkin, ed., *Lay My Burden Down: A Folk History of Slavery* (Chicago: University of Chicago Press, 1945), 246. For similar examples of freedwomen who chose to remain with former owners, see testimonies of Mandy Hadnot, Mattie Gilmore, and John McCoy, in Tyler and Murphy, *The Slave Narratives of Texas*, 124, 125, 126; James Oakes to J. Kirkman, 30 May 1867, letters sent, entry 3653, vol. 49 (Austin, Tex.), BRFAL-FO; O'Donovan, *Becoming Free*, 119–21, 140–41, 161.

9. Erastus W. Everson to H. W. Smith, 30 May 1866, reel 9, Records of the Assistant Commissioner for the State of South Carolina, BRFAL, RG 105, Microfilm Publication M869, NARA, quoted in Julie Saville, *The Work of Reconstruction: From Slave to Wage Laborer in South Carolina, 1860–1870* (New York: Cambridge University Press, 1994), 99–100.

10. Quoted in Litwack, *Been in the Storm So Long*, 416. Historians have demonstrated that freedwomen sought, with varying degrees of success, to define and defend the boundaries of freedom by determining for themselves the number of hours they and their families would spend in the fields, demanding days off, employing collective work slowdowns and strikes, bargaining for better wages and contractual terms as well as rejecting those considered unreasonable, refusing to labor under the watchful eye of hated overseers and former slave drivers, insisting that they alone could determine the difference between slave and free labor, rejecting particularly hated tasks of field labor as well as work that went beyond the tasks jointly agreed upon by employer and employee, restricting their labor in the fields to the "busy seasons," and asserting other demands and restrictions on the terms and conditions of their labors—seeking to balance their paid and unpaid work—at times even going so far as to reject work in the plantation fields altogether. On the collective action of freedwomen, see, in particular, Glymph, *Out of the House of Bondage*, 152; O'Donovan, *Becoming Free*, 241–42; Laura F. Edwards, *Scarlett Doesn't Live Here Anymore: Southern Women in the Civil War Era* (Urbana: University of Illinois Press, 2000), 135–36; Schwalm, *A Hard Fight for We*, 161–64, 173–76, 183–86, 194–208, 257–58; Frankel, *Freedom's Women*, 56–78; Saville, *The Work of Reconstruction*, 59–62, 69–70, 86–87, 99–101, 140, 147, 177–78, 186, 193; Tera W. Hunter, *To 'Joy My Freedom: Southern Black Women's Lives and Labors after the Civil War* (Cambridge, Mass.: Harvard University Press, 1997), 70–73, 74–97; Lynda J. Morgan, *Emancipation in Virginia's Tobacco Belt, 1850–1870* (Athens: University of Georgia Press, 1992), 193; Jones,

Labor of Love, 56–57; Philip S. Foner, *Women and the American Labor Movement: From Colonial Times to the Eve of World War I* (New York: Free Press, 1979), 124–25; C. Peter Ripley, *Slaves and Freedmen in Civil War Louisiana* (Baton Rouge: Louisiana State University Press, 1976), 22–23; Dorothy Sterling, ed., *We Are Your Sisters: Black Women in the Nineteenth Century* (New York: W. W. Norton, 1984), 355–58.

11. Testimony of Betty Jones recalling the experiences of her grandmother, Sarah, in Workers of the Writers' Program of the Work Projects Administration in the State of Virginia, comps., *The Negro in Virginia* (Winston-Salem, N.C.: John F. Blair, 1994), 232; Edward Ehrlich to D. C. Dunn, 27 Dec. 1865, letters sent, entry 1473, vol. 203 (Amite City, La.), BRFAL-FO; Mrs. Nicholas Ware Eppes [Susan Bradford Eppes], *The Negro of the Old South: A Bit of Period History* (Chicago: Joseph G. Branch, 1925), 128, 130–31. For additional examples of freedwomen who left their former masters in the first days of freedom, see testimony of Molly Harrell and Tempie Cummins, in Tyler and Murphy, *The Slave Narratives of Texas*, 115, 125; Litwack, *Been in the Storm So Long*, chap. 6; O'Donovan, *Becoming Free*, 77, 90–91.

12. Amelia Edith Huddleston Barr, *All the Days of My Life: An Autobiography* (New York: D. Appleton, 1913), 251–52; Myers, *Children of Pride*, 1241, 1371, 1405, 1412; testimony of Mary Lindsay, in Rawick, *The American Slave*, vol. 7 (Okla.), 184–85.

13. Labor contract with James Shipman, 12 Jan. 1867, labor contracts, June 1865–June 1868, reel 50, BRFAL-MS; account of Venus William, 7 Jan. 1867, freedmen's accounts, entry 2336 (Starkville, Miss.), BRFAL-FO; contract between Emmie, "a freedwoman," and I. A. Gray, 22 Feb. 1867, reprinted in Sterling, *We Are Your Sisters*, 327–28; J. M. Dill to Davis Tillson, 29 May 1866, letters received, reel 13, BRFAL-GA; Alice Palmer to [My Dear Hattie], 20 July and 2 Aug. 1865, and 19 Sept. 1866, Palmer Family Papers, South Caroliniana Collection, University of South Carolina, quoted in Schwalm, *A Hard Fight for We*, 210; Jacob E. Yoder, 2 May 1866 diary entry, Jacob E. Yoder Diaries, 1861–70, acc. 27680 (b), Library of Virginia, Richmond, quoted in Michelle Ann Krowl, "Dixie's Other Daughters: African American Women in Virginia, 1861–1868" (Ph.D. diss., University of California, Berkeley, 1998), 140. On freedwomen's negotiation of contractual obligations, see, for example, Glymph, *Out of the House of Bondage*, 149–66; O'Donovan, *Becoming Free*, 184–85, 188–92, 201–2, 266; Schwalm, *A Hard Fight for We*, 199–211; Noralee Frankel, "From Slave Women to Free Women: The National Archives and Black Women's History in the Civil War Era," *Prologue* 29, no. 2 (1997): 100–104; Hunter, *To 'Joy My Freedom*, 26–28; Litwack, *Been in the Storm So Long*, 394–95, 432–37.

14. Henry L. Swint, ed., *Dear Ones at Home: Letters from Contraband Camps* (Nashville, Tenn.: Vanderbilt University Press, 1966), 233; E. Whittlesey to O. O. Howard, 15 Oct. 1865, in U.S. Senate, "Reports of the Assistant Commissioners [1865–66]," 163; O. Hawks Howard to M. Frank Gallagher, 19 Sept. 1868, letters sent, entry 690, vol. 123 (Cuthbert, Ga.), BRFAL-FO. On the kinds of employment-related complaints brought by freedwomen, see, for example, Sterling, *We Are Your Sisters*, chap. 18; James D. Schmidt, *Free to Work: Labor Law, Emancipation, and Reconstruction, 1815–1880* (Athens: University of Georgia Press, 1999), 177–78; Barry A. Crouch, "Seeking Equality: Houston Black Women during Reconstruction," in *The Dance of Freedom: Texas African Americans during Reconstruction*, ed. Larry Madaras (Austin: University of Texas Press, 2007), 77–79; O'Donovan, *Becoming Free*, 133–36, 177–78, 203–5; Bercaw, *Gendered Freedoms*, 146–47, 150–57; Jones, *Labor of Love*, 53–54; Amy Dru Stanley, *From Bondage to Contract: Wage Labor, Marriage, and the Market in the Age of Slave Emancipation* (Cambridge: Cambridge University Press, 1998), 51–52. For other complaints for nonpayment of wages involving freedwomen, see, for example, John J. Knox to Mrs. Cook, 13 April 1867, letters sent, entry 718, vol. 169 (Athens, Ga.), BRFAL-FO; complaint of Phillis, 12 Feb. 1867, register of complaints, entry 723, vol. 174 (Athens, Ga.), BRFAL-FO; Howell C. Flourney to Joe. McWhorter, 16 May 1868 and 23 July 1868, letters sent, entry 725, vol.

172 (Athens, Ga.), BRFAL-FO; case nos. 11, 13, 21, 24, 35, 50, 51, 58, 67, 69, 86, 89, 92, 96, 102, 107, 108, 109, 110, and 113, register of complaints, entry 771, vol. 156 (Augusta, Ga.), BRFAL-FO; complaints of Alice, 18 May 1867, and Candice Boon, 7 June 1867, journal, entry 840, vol. 226 (Columbus, Ga.), BRFAL-FO.; affidavits of Sarah Dixon, 18 March 1868, Hester Beek, 25 June 1868, and Ella Lafton, 13 July 1868, affidavits of freedmen, entry 858, vol. 239 (Cuthbert, Ga.), BRFAL-FO; Amy Burney v. M. S. Cheshire, 11 June 1867, register of complaints, entry 859, vol. 238 (Cuthbert, Ga.), BRFAL-FO; Andrew B. Clark to Mark Husan, 23 Nov. 1868, letters sent, entry 873, vol. 251 (Dawson, Ga.), BRFAL-FO.; Emily Batts v. Elija Gaddy, 27 Dec. 1867, and George Reynolds v. V. Clegg, 8 June 1868, register of complaints, entry 877, vol. 368 (Dawson, Ga.), BRFAL-FO; Dina Roberts v. Ben Collier, 6 July 1867, Mary Gilmore v. John Matthis, 6 July 1867, and Margaret Wilson v. Sam Howell, 9 July 1867, register of complaints, entry 884, vol. 193 (Fort Gaines, Ga.), BRFAL-FO; Dina Roberts v. Ben Collier, 6 July 1867, Mary Gilmore v. John Matthis, 6 July 1867, Betsy Slaten v. A. Slaten, 26 Sept. 1867, and Catherine Sutton v. Bill Smith, 29 Nov. 1867, register of cases tried in freedmen's court, entry 885, vol. 260½ (Fort Gaines, Ga.), BRFAL-FO; N. Sellers Hill to Mrs. Frame and N. Sellers Hill to Mrs. Julia Davis, 2 April 1866, register of complaints, entry 935, vol. 299 (Macon, Ga.), BRFAL-FO; passim, register of complaints, entry 1019, vols. 351–52 (Savannah, Ga.), BRFAL-FO; passim, register of complaints, entry 1044, vol. 385 (Thomasville, Ga.), BRFAL-FO; U.S. v. J. C. M. Branch, Charlotte, 13 Oct. 1866, register of court trials, entry 1466, vol. 197 (Algiers, La.), BRFAL-FO; U.S. v. Olive Runnier, Manuel Thomas, 6 Nov. 1866, register of court trials, entry 1466, vol. 197 (Algiers, La.), BRFAL-FO; complaint of Phebe Brown, 16 May 1868 and 5 June 1868, journal of business transacted, entry 1469, vol. 199 (Algiers, La.), BRFAL-FO; Lucinda Keith v. Mrs. Redman, 7 Nov. 1868, journal of business transacted, entry 1469, vol. 200 (Algiers, La.), BRFAL-FO; J. F. P. Richardson to F. B. Sturgis, 20 May 1867, letters sent, vol. 48, entry 3653 (Austin, Tex.), BRFAL-FO.; passim, register of complaints, vol. 52, entry 3657 (Austin, Tex.), BRFAL-FO; Matilda Dinna v. W. C. Collins, 19 May 1867, register of complaints, vol. 62, entry 3661 (Bastrop, Tex.), BRFAL-FO; Chas. Smith to James Oakes, 7 Nov. 1867 and 17 Nov. 1867, letters sent, vol. 53, entry 3663 (Belton, Tex.), BRFAL-FO; passim, register of complaints, vols. 54–55, entry 3665 (Belton, Tex.), BRFAL-FO; William B. Kirkman to Chas. F. Rand, 9 Jan. 1868, letters sent, vol. 68, entry 3666 (Boston, Tex.), BRFAL-FO; passim, register of complaints, vol. 58, entry 3680 (Bryan, Tex.), BRFAL-FO; J. Ernest Goodman to Mrs. Elizabeth Turner, 17 May 1866, letters sent, vol. 72, entry 3694 (Columbus, Tex.), BRFAL-FO; Louis W. Stevenson to Col. Webb, 6 March 1868, press copies of letters sent, vol. 74, entry 3695 (Columbus, Tex.), BRFAL-FO; passim, register of complaints, vol. 75, entry 3699 (Columbus, Tex.), BRFAL-FO; I. C. DeGress to John Cherry, 11 Dec. 1865, letters sent, vol. 100, entry 3716 (Houston, Tex.), BRFAL-FO; passim, register of complaints, vols. 107–9, entry 3720 (Houston, Tex.), BRFAL-FO; passim, register of complaints, vol. 136, entry 3746 (Marshall, Tex.), BRFAL-FO; passim, letters sent, vols. 143–44, entry 3755 (Richmond, Tex.), BRFAL-FO; passim, endorsements sent, vol. 147, entry 3756 (Richmond, Tex.), BRFAL-FO; passim, register of complaints, vol. 160, entry 3775 (Sumpter, Tex.), BRFAL-FO; Lucy Robinson v. George Jacobs, 29 Jan. 1867, Precilla Campbell, Midwife v. George Nelson, 27 Jan. 1867, Josephine Johnson v. Wilkes Brooks, 13 Feb. 1867, Julia Ann Ball v. Mrs. Hetty Kline, 20 Feb. 1867, Matilda Lee v. Fanny Walker, Virginia Patterson, 2 March 1867, and Laura Mills v. P. H. Smith, n.d., register of complaints, entry 5868, vol. 98 (Alexandria, Va.), BRFAL-FO; and Jenny Walker v. J. N. Ragsdale, 8 July 1867, and Mary Davis v. P. Robertson, 23 Sept. 1867, proceedings of the freedmen's court, entry 3912, vol. 288 (Burkesville, Va.), BRFAL-FO.

15. Fanny M. Clinton v. James Ainsley, 9 Aug. 1867, register of complaints, entry 859, vol. 238 (Cuthbert, Ga.), BRFAL-FO; F. A. H. Gaebel to W. W. Dean, 15 June 1866, letters sent, entry 690, vol. 234 (Cuthbert, Ga.), BRFAL-FO.

16. Howell C. Flourney to Ed. Grisham, 11 June 1867, letters sent, entry 725, vol. 171 (Athens, Ga.), BRFAL-FO; Robert Campbell to J. R. Lewis, 15 Aug. 1867, and endorsement of D. A. Newsom, 17 Sept. 1867, letters received, reel 17, BRFAL-GA.

17. Complaint of A. J. Wharton, 12 Feb. 1867, register of complaints, entry 723, vol. 174 (Athens, Ga.), BRFAL-FO; Mrs. Byers v. Mahala Williams, 25 June 1867, and Lucinda Runnells v. David Ferguson, 2 July 1867, register of complaints, entry 859, vol. 238 (Cuthbert, Ga.), BRFAL-FO; 14 March 1866 and 10 and 11 April 1866 diary entries, Diary of Richard Eppes, 1 Sept. 1865–4 July 1867, sec. 47, Eppes Family Papers, 1722–1948, Mss1Ep734d, Virginia Historical Society, Richmond; Whitelaw Reid, *After the War: A Tour of the Southern States, 1865–1866* (Cincinnati: Moore, Wilstach & Baldwin, 1866; reprint, New York: Harper & Row, 1965), 530; Edward Fonaine to Alvan Gillem, 14 Oct. 1867, registered letters received, reel 21, BRFAL-MS.

18. Alice Palmer to [My Dear Hattie], 19 Sept. 1866, Palmer Family Papers, South Caroliniana Collection, University of South Carolina, quoted in Schwalm, *A Hard Fight for We*, 210; J. W. McConaughy to W. H. Sinclair, 9 July 1866, letters sent, entry 3785, vol. 172 (Wharton, Tex.), BRFAL-FO. See also J. W. McConaughy to Wm. H. Sinclair, 8 July 1866, letters received, reel 7, BRFAL-TX; and H. R. Casey to Geo. R. Campbell, 23 Nov. 1865, unregistered letters received, entry 759, box 9 (Augusta, Ga.), BRFAL-FO.

19. Mary Magruder v. Alex Crawford, 4 Aug. 1868, register of complaints, entry 859, vol. 238 (Cuthbert, Ga.), BRFAL-FO; S. M. Ivey v. Angeline Sealy, 9 Sept. 1867, register of complaints, entry 859, vol. 238 (Cuthbert, Ga.), BRFAL-FO.

20. [Bureau agent in Lee and Dougherty counties, Ga.] to John P. Thomas, 13 May 1867, affidavits of freedmen and charges and specifications against citizens and military personnel, entry 695, vol. 237 (Albany, Ga.), BRFAL-FO; [bureau agent in Lee and Dougherty counties, Ga.] to G. M. Byne, 7 May 1867, affidavits of freedmen and charges and specifications against citizens and military personnel, entry 695, vol. 237 (Albany, Ga.), BRFAL-FO; Bryon Porter to C. C. Morse, 5 Jan. 1866, letters sent, entry 3716, vol. 100 (Houston, Tex.), BRFAL-FO; Bryon Porter [by order of Assistant Commissioner Gregory] to Mrs. Ann Grant, 20 Dec. 1865, letters sent, entry 3716, vol. 100 (Houston, Tex.), BRFAL-FO; Eugene Pickett to A. M. McIver, 6 Feb. 1867, letters sent, reel 5, BRFAL-GA. See also Norma Basch, "Marriage and Domestic Relations," in *The Cambridge History of Law in America*, vol. 2, *The Long Nineteenth Century (1789–1920)*, ed. Michael Grossberg and Christopher Tomlins (Cambridge University Press, 2008), 270; Stanley, *From Bondage to Contract*.

21. [Bureau agent in Lee and Dougherty counties, Ga.] to Meril Calloway, 13 May 1867, affidavits of freedmen and charges and specifications against citizens and military personnel, entry 695, vol. 237 (Albany, Ga.), BRFAL-FO; [bureau agent in Dougherty, Lee, and Terrell counties, Ga.] to Mr. Seth Wilson, 9 Aug. 1867, letters sent, entry 697, vol. 127 (Albany, Ga.), BRFAL-FO; Harrison Hugan v. W. J. Gaines, 21 July 1868, journal of business transacted, entry 1469, vol. 200 (Algiers, La.), BRFAL-FO. See also [subassistant commissioner of Houston, Tex.] to Dan Roberts, 5 July 1867, letters sent, entry 3716, vol. 102 (Houston, Tex.), BRFAL-FO.

22. F. A. H. Gaebel to W. W. Deane, 7 June 1866, unregistered letters received, reel 27, BRFAL-GA; W. W. Deane to F. A. H. Gaebel, letters sent, reel 3, BRFAL-GA; George G. Gladwin to James H. Bowman, 19 Dec. 1865, letters sent, entry 3716, vol. 100 (Houston, Tex.), BRFAL-FO; order issued by Bryon Porter [by order of Assistant Commissioner Gregory], 24 Jan. 1866, letters sent, entry 3716, vol. 100 (Houston, Tex.), BRFAL-FO; Bryon Porter to Bradford Deaton, 23 April 1866, letters sent, entry 3716, vol. 100 (Houston, Tex.), BRFAL-FO.

23. W. B. Stickney to T. W. Conway, 2 July 1865, registered letters and telegrams received, reel 12, BRFAL-LA.

24. Complaint of Mary Connor, 20 April 1867, register of complaints, entry 2180 (Grenada, Miss.), BRFAL-FO; Bettie Kelson v. Curtis Grines, 9 March 1867, register of complaints, entry 5868 (Alexandria, Va.), BRFAL-FO; case of Dilsey and son quoted in Krowl, "Dixie's Other Daughters," 187; James Hough to Dr. J. J. Overstreet, 27 Aug. 1867, letters sent, entry 1473, vol. 203 (Amite City, La.), BRFAL-FO; George Haller, July 1868, narrative reports from subordinate officers, reel 33, BRFAL-MS; case no. 109, 18 June 1868, register of complaints, entry 771, vol. 158 (Augusta, Ga.), BRFAL-FO; "Document 146: Affidavit of a Georgia Freedwoman [Josephine Lamkins]," in Steven Hahn and others, eds., *Land and Labor, 1865*, series 3, vol. 1, of *Freedom: A Documentary History of Emancipation, 1861–1867* (Chapel Hill: University of North Carolina Press, 2008), 146; J. Yeckley to A. A. A. G., 29 May 1866, report of operations and conditions, box 37, BRFAL-VA; case of Sarah Bolton v. Dr. Henry Biquon, 1 May 1868, register of complaints, entry 771, vol. 156 (Augusta, Ga.), BRFAL-FO. On the continued reliance on violence to enforce labor force discipline, see, for example, Hahn and others, *Land and Labor, 1865*, 40–41, 80–81 83–84, 183–84, 497–98, 917; Litwack, *Been in the Storm So Long*, 277, 289, 303, 372–76; Foner, *Reconstruction*, 119–23; Glymph, *Out of the House of Bondage*; Crouch, "Seeking Equality," especially 80–82; Hannah Rosen, *Terror in the Heart of Freedom: Citizenship, Sexual Violence, and the Meaning of Race in the Postemancipation South* (Chapel Hill: University of North Carolina Press, 2009), 51, 52; O'Donovan, *Becoming Free*, 136–38, 214–18, 247, 268; Schwalm, *A Hard Fight for We*, 178, 188, 219–22, 252–53; Saville, *The Work of Reconstruction*, 125–27.

25. John J. Knox to J. W. Arnold, 1 April 1867, letters sent, entry 718, vol. 169 (Athens, Ga.), BRFAL-FO; Rufus Saxton to O. O. Howard, 15 Jan. 1866, in U.S. Senate, "Reports of the Assistant Commissioners [1865–66]," 21–22; case of Mrs. Tyrell in Bercaw, *Gendered Freedoms*, 154; W. P. Carlin to O. O. Howard, 11 Sept. 1867, letters received, reel 51, BRFAL (M752); Harriet Murray v. David Porter, Nov. 1867, letters sent, entry 2326, vol. 252 (Sardis, Miss.), BRFAL-FO. For other incidents of violence at the hands of employers, see, for example, H. R. Casey to Geo. R. Campbell, 23 Nov. 1865, unregistered letters received, entry 759, box 9 (Augusta, Ga.), BRFAL-FO; N. Sellers Hill to W. W. Deane, 17 May 1866, letters sent, entry 931, vol. 296 (Macon, Ga.), BRFAL-FO; complaints of Harriet Green, 1 Aug. 1865, Elizabeth Moore, 18 Aug. 1865, Patsey Clay, 25 Aug. 1865, register of complaints, entry 1479, vol. 204 (Amite City, La.), BRFAL-FO; J. W. McConaughy to Squire McMasters, 28 May 1866, letters sent, entry 3785, vol. 172 (Wharton, Tex.), BRFAL-FO.

26. William Sims Tidball to Jacob Van Doran, 24 Oct. 1866, letters sent, entry 3921, vol. 128 (Charlottesville, Va.), BRFAL-FO; Samuel S. Sumner to Thomas Schokleford, 12 Sept. 1867, letters sent, entry 2195 (Jackson, Miss.), BRFAL-FO.

27. W. B. Pease to Judge B. P. Fuller, 8 March 1867, letters sent, entry 3716, vol. 101 (Houston, Tex.), BRFAL-FO.

28. O. H. Howard to the Honorable William Newson, 5 July 1867, letters sent, entry 695, vol. 122 (Albany, Ga.), BRFAL-FO. For a similar expression of disgust, see S. K. Wood to John M. Sharp, 14 March 1866, register of complaints, entry 935, vol. 299 (Macon, Ga.), BRFAL-FO.

29. J. W. Barney to J. Scott, 15 May 1868, letters sent, entry 8181, vol. 211 (Carnesville, Ga.), BRFAL-FO; S. S. Sumner to Thomas Schokleford, 12 Sept. 1867, letters sent, entry 2195 (Jackson, Miss.), BRFAL-FO. See also Frankel, *Freedom's Women*, 70. On the influences of antebellum northern notions of sympathy and abolitionist rhetoric and imagery, see Elizabeth B. Clark, "'The Sacred Rights of the Weak': Pain, Sympathy, and the Culture of Individual Rights in Antebellum America," *Journal of American History* 82, no. 2 (1995): 463–93, especially 490–93.

30. Fred. Mosebach to Eugene Pickett, 14 Feb. 1866, letters sent, entry 832, vol. 222 (Columbus, Ga.), BRFAL-FO; James Hough to Dr. J. J. Overstreet, 27 Aug. 1867, letters

sent, entry 1472, vol. 203 (Amite City, La.), BRFAL-FO; Chas A. Vernon to [?], 17 Aug. 1868, letters sent, entry 3755, vol. 145 (Richmond, Tex.), BRFAL-FO. The number of freedwomen who experienced violence at the hands of employers is far too great to document, but for other bureau reports and efforts to hold employers accountable for such actions, see, for example, Hahn and others, *Land and Labor, 1865*, documents 14, 26, 39, 43, 90, 125, 137, 146, 161; statement of Eliza Jane House, 15 Aug. 1865, affidavits and statements, entry 3545 (provost marshal of freedmen, Memphis, Tenn.), BRFAL-FO; statement of Jane Coleman, 26 Aug. 1865, entry 3545 (provost marshal of freedmen, Memphis, Tenn.), BRFAL-FO; Byron Porter to Charles F. Allen, 22 May 1866, letters sent, entry 3716, vol. 100 (Houston, Tex.), BRFAL-FO; Emily Matthews v. H. F. Mathews, 7 June 1867, entry 3720, vol. 108 (Houston, Tex.), BRFAL-FO; Selina Parker v. Michael Linney, 22, 26 Jan. 1866, Milly Graham v. Louisa Thompson, 2 May 1866, both in register of complaints, entry 3720, vol. 109 (Houston, Tex.), BRFAL-FO. See also Crouch, "Seeking Equality," especially 80–82; Rosen, *Terror in the Heart of Freedom*, 51, 52; O'Donovan, *Becoming Free*, 136–38, 214–18, 247, 268; Schwalm, *A Hard Fight for We*, 178, 188, 219–22, 252–53; Saville, *The Work of Reconstruction*, 125–27.

31. J. Kearney Smith to Daniel E. Roberts, 7 July 1866, letters sent, entry 1008, vol. 347 (Savannah, Ga.), BRFAL-FO; Bryon Porter to Mr. Bradford Deaton, 23 April 1866, letters sent, entry 3716, vol. 100 (Houston, Tex.), BRFAL-FO.

32. Circular issued by Orlando Brown, 4 Nov. 1865, in U.S. House of Representatives, "Freedmen's Bureau. Letter from the Secretary of War, in answer to A resolution of the House of March 8, transmitting a report, by the Commissioner of the Freedmen's Bureau, of all orders issued by him or any assistant commissioner," 39th Cong., 1st sess., House Executive Document 70 (Serial 1256), 139. See also Howard, *Autobiography*, 2:213; Circular No. 7, issued by Stuart Eldridge, 29 July 1865, in U.S. House of Representatives, "Freedmen's Bureau," 155. On wartime labor policies of the Union army, see, in general, Ira Berlin and others, *Slaves No More: Three Essays on Emancipation and the Civil War* (Cambridge: Cambridge University Press, 1992), chap. 2; Ira Berlin and others, "The Terrain of Freedom: The Struggle over the Meaning of Free Labor in the U.S. South," *History Workshop Journal* 22 (1986): 108–30; Eric Foner, *Politics and Ideology in the Age of the Civil War* (New York: Oxford University Press, 1980), chap. 6; Louis S. Gerteis, *From Contraband to Freedman: Federal Policy toward Southern Blacks, 1861–1865* (Westport, Conn.: Greenwood Press, 1973); J. Thomas May, "Continuity and Change in the Labor Program of the Union Army and the Freedmen's Bureau," *Civil War History* 17 (1971): 245–54; Bell Irvin Wiley, *Southern Negroes, 1861–1865* (New Haven, Conn.: Yale University Press, 1938), 175–344. See also George R. Bentley, *A History of the Freedmen's Bureau* (Philadelphia: University of Pennsylvania, 1955), 1–29.

33. Howard, *Autobiography*, 2:247.

34. William Cohen, *At Freedom's Edge: Black Mobility and the Southern White Quest for Racial Control, 1861–1915* (Baton Rouge: Louisiana State University Press, 1991), 46; E. M. Gregory to O. O. Howard, 31 Jan. 1866, in U.S. Senate, "Reports of the Assistant Commissioners [1865–66]," 78; O. Brown to O. O. Howard, 31 Nov. 1865, in U.S. Senate, "Reports of the Assistant Commissioners [1865–66]," 77–79, 145–47.

35. See, for example, [assistant subassistant commissioner in Augusta, Georgia] to William Whigham, 7 March 1866, letters sent, entry 753, vol. 150 (Augusta, Ga.), BRFAL-FO.

36. Special Orders No. 15, 31 Jan. 1866, enclosed in T. W. Osborne to O. O. Howard, 19 Feb. 1866, letters received, reel 23, BRFAL (M752); Clinton B. Fisk, *Plain Counsels for Freedmen: In Sixteen Brief Lectures* (Boston: American Tract Society, 1866), 33; Robert K. Scott to O. O. Howard, 22 April 1868, letters received, reel 55, BRFAL (M752).

37. M. C. Fulton to Davis Tillson, 17 April 1866, unregistered letters received, reel 26, BRFAL-GA; J. W. Sharp to O. Brown, 28 Feb. 1866, F. M. Kimball to S. Barnes, 28 Feb.

1866, William Smith to O. Brown, 1 May 1866, Dr. Dennis to [Edwin Lyon], 25 April 1866, all in reports of operations and conditions, reel 44, BRFAL-VA; J. Jordon to J. Stone, 26 Oct. 1866, reports of operations and conditions, reel 45, BRFAL-VA; De Forest, *A Union Officer in the Reconstruction*, 94. For similar complaints of bureau men about freedwomen, see Louis Aherns to Alfred H. Terry, 1 May 1866, Edwin Lyon to O. Brown, 30 April, 29 May, and 30 May 1866, and George Buffum to O. Brown, 30 March 1866, reports of operations and conditions, reel 44, BRFAL-VA; James W. Jordan to John Schofield, 27 Feb. 1867, reports of operations and conditions, reel 46, BRFAL-VA; and Robert Cullen to John M. Schoefield, 31 Aug. 1866, reports of operations and conditions, reel 45, BRFAL-VA. See also Barbara Jeanne Fields, "Ideology and Race in American History," in *Region, Race, and Reconstruction: Essays in Honor of C. Vann Woodward*, ed. J. Morgan Kousser and James M. McPherson (New York: Oxford University Press, 1982), 165–66; Jones, *Labor of Love*, 45; Gutman, *The Black Family*, 167–68.

38. M. C. Fulton to Davis Tillson, 17 April 1866, unregistered letters received, reel 26, BRFAL-GA. For similar complaints from southern planters, see also Loring and Atkinson, *Cotton Culture and the South*, 4, 5, 9, 13–16, 20, 22, 24, 72–75, 103, 109, 137

39. De Forest, *A Union Officer in the Reconstruction*, 94. On the gendered nature of vagrancy in the antebellum United States, see also Schmidt, *Free to Work*, 59–61. On vagrancy and freedwomen, see also Mary Farmer-Kaiser, " 'Are They Not in Some Sorts Vagrants?' Gender and the Efforts of the Freedmen's Bureau to Combat Vagrancy in the Reconstruction South," *Georgia Historical Quarterly* 89, no. 1 (2004): 25–49; Linda K. Kerber, *No Constitutional Right to Be Ladies: Women and the Obligations of Citizenship* (New York: Hill and Wang, 1998), chap. 2.

40. E. Lyon to O. Brown, 31 May 1866, reports of operations and conditions, reel 44, BRFAL-VA; case no. 29, R. M. Johnson v. Mary Miller, 30 May 1868, register of complaints, entry 859, vol. 238 (Cuthbert, Ga.), BRFAL-FO. On the promotion of lawful marriage by the bureau, see Chapters 1 and 5 of this work; Schwalm, *A Hard Fight for We*, 234–35, 239–48, 266–67; Stanley, *From Bondage to Contract*, 36–37, 44–46, 48–49, 51, 188–89; Nancy F. Cott, *Public Vows: A History of Marriage and the Nation* (Cambridge, Mass.: Harvard University Press, 2000), 84–94; Reginald Washington, "Sealing the Sacred Bonds of Holy Matrimony: Freedmen's Bureau Marriage Records," *Prologue* 37, no. 1 (2005): 58–65; Barry A. Crouch, "The 'Chords of Love': Legalizing Black Marital and Family Rights in Postwar Texas," *Journal of Negro History* 79 (1994): 334–51; Basch, "Marriage and Domestic Relations," 270; Laura F. Edwards, "Civil War and Reconstruction," in *The Cambridge History of Law in America*, vol. 2, *The Long Nineteenth Century (1789–1920)*, ed. Michael Grossberg and Christopher Tomlins (New York: Cambridge University Press, 2008), 333, 340; Laura F. Edwards, *Gendered Strife and Confusion: The Political Culture of Reconstruction* (Urbana: University of Illinois Press, 1997), 47; Frankel, *Freedom's Women*, 86–87, 106–8; Bercaw, *Gendered Freedoms*, 109–12, 164.

41. Loring and Atkinson, *Cotton Culture and the South*, 13; J. L. Thorp (also spelled "Tharp") to John Tyler, 30 April 1867, reports of bureau operations, reel 25, Records of the Assistant Commissioner for the State of Arkansas, BRFAL, RG 105, Microfilm Publication M979, NARA; E. Lyon to O. Brown, 31 May 1866, reports of operations and conditions, reel 44, BRFAL-VA; A. N. Murtagh to S. W. Purchase, 20 Aug. 1867, registered letters received, entry 1601 (Franklin, La.), BRFAL-FO.

42. J. Jordan to J. Stone, 26 Oct. 1866, reports of operations and conditions, reel 45, BRFAL-VA. On the conflict over women's labor in black households, see O'Donovan, *Becoming Free*, 7, 184–85, 192–93, 199; Frankel, *Freedom's Women*, 70–78, 104–9; Schwalm, *A Hard Fight for We*, 247, 260–66; Bercaw, *Gendered Freedoms*.

43. Circular Letter No. 33, issued by E. M. Gregory, 17 Oct. 1865, letters sent, reel 1, BRFAL-TX; Circular No. 25, issued by J. B. Kiddoo, 21 Dec. 1866, letters received, reel

44, BRFAL (M752); remarks of Assistant Commissioner E. M. Gregory, *Houston Telegraph*, 17 Jan. 1866. Bureau officials in other states acted in like manner by promoting, or requiring in some instances, family contracts in which the head of household contracted with an employer for the entire household. For example, although a Florida agent maintained that "[o]ne great mistake has been made by the planters; that is, in binding several persons in one contract, all said persons being adults. In my opinion, those contracts are illegal, and I have instructed the judge . . . to cancel all such documents, and have separate contracts made for each person," he made one exception— contracts made with male "heads of families, who are the proper guardians of" their family members and who "have a right to contract for them." Andrew Mahony to T. W. Osborn, 30 Jan. 1866, in U.S. Senate, "Reports of the Assistant Commissioners [1865–66]," 57. Beginning in 1866, southern state legislatures in areas where laborers were in short supply responded similarly. Louisiana law, for example, mandated that contracts "shall embrace the labor of all the members of the family able to work, and shall be binding on all minors of said families." The Texas statute similarly stated: "All labor contracts shall be made with the heads of families; they shall embrace the labor of all the members of the family named therein able to work, and shall be binding on all minors of said families." See "Laws in Relation to Freedmen," in U.S. Senate, "Reports of the Assistant Commissioners of the Bureau of Refugees, Freedmen, and Abandoned Lands and Laws in Relation to the Freedmen [1866]," 39th Cong., 2nd sess., Senate Executive Document 6 (Serial 1276), 182, 223; "An Act Regulating Contracts for Labor," labor contract, Legislature of Texas, n.d., letters received, reel 44, BRFAL (M752); James Smallwood, "Black Freedwomen after Emancipation: The Texas Experience," *Prologue* 27, no. 4 (1995): 306; Foner, *Reconstruction*, 87; Stanley, *From Bondage to Contract*, 188–89; and O'Donovan, *Becoming Free*, 199–205. Susan O'Donovan argues that women benefited, especially in terms of wages, "when husbands and fathers got involved" (*Becoming Free*, 199).

44. Circular No. 4, issued by Rufus Saxton, 12 Oct. 1865, in U.S. House of Representatives, "Freedmen's Bureau," 95. See also Stanley, *From Bondage to Contract*, 127.

45. S. C. Armstrong to Orlando Brown, 27 May 1867, letters sent, reel 48, BRFAL (M752); S. C. Armstrong to Orlando Brown, 1 April 1867, monthly lists of unemployed freedmen, reel 58, BRFAL-VA; Benjamin C. Cook to Orlando Brown, 30 Nov. 1868, monthly lists of unemployed freedmen, reel 58, BRFAL-VA. See also O'Donovan, *Becoming Free*, 158–60, 166–70; Catherine Clinton, "Bloody Terrain: Freedwomen, Sexuality and Violence during Reconstruction," *Georgia Historical Quarterly* 76 (1992): 320.

46. Kerber, *No Constitutional Right to Be Ladies*, 51. On this point, see also Schmidt, *Free to Work*, 59–61. On the post-Reconstruction use of vagrancy laws to combat prostitution, see also Stanley, *From Bondage to Contract*, chap. 6.

47. W. E. Dougherty to Louis E. Granger, 22 Aug. 1865, registered letters received, entry 1452, box 2 (Algiers, La.), BRFAL-FO; R. E. Folles to A. F. Hayden, 12 Nov. 1866, letters sent, entry 1447, vol. 187 (Algiers, La.), BRFAL-FO; [acting subassistant commissioner in Cuthbert, Ga.] to S. A. McLendan, 14 June 1866, letters received and miscellaneous papers relating to complaints, entry 883, box 18 (Fort Gaines, Ga.), BRFAL-FO. See also R. E. Folles to W. H. Sterling, 20 Oct. 1866, letters sent, entry 1447, vol. 187 (Algiers, La.), BRFAL-FO.

48. James W. Sunderland to Leathy, Jane, and Ester, 4 April 1866, letters sent, entry 2246 (Meridian, Miss.), BRFAL-FO; W. E. Griffin to F. A. H. Gaebel, 13 June 1866, unregistered letters received, entry 694, box 2 (Albany, Ga.), BRFAL-FO; F. A. H. Gaebel to W. W. Dean, 5 March [1866], letters sent, entry 690, vol. 234 (Cuthbert, Ga.), BRFAL-FO. See also Circular No. 1, issued by the Subdistrict of Memphis, Tenn., 13 July 1865, orders and circulars received, entry 1015, box 29 (Savannah, Ga.), BRFAL-FO.

49. S. A. McLenden to F. A. H. Gaebel, 16 April 1866, unregistered letters received, entry 694, box 2 (Albany, Ga.), BRFAL-FO.

50. [Subassistant commissioner of Houston, Tex.] to J. B. Fuller, 24 June 1867, letters sent, entry 3716, vol. 102 (Houston, Tex.), BRFAL-FO; Maria Widgeon v. Maria Handy, Nancy Bundy, Sally Bundy, Leah Colburn, Kitty Joins, 4 May 1865, proceedings of the freedmen's court, entry 3959, vol. 153 (Drummondtown, Va.), BRFAL-FO; case of Agnes Ann Gunter, 8 May 1865, proceedings of the freedmen's court, entry 3959, vol. 153 (Drummondtown, Va.), BRFAL-FO. The day after their arrest, Nancy Bundy and Sally Bundy paid their fines and were released from jail. No mention is made on the release of Maria Handy or Leah Colburn.

51. People v. Laura Elliot and Caroline Young, 8 March 1866, proceedings of the freedmen's court, entry 4139, vol. 211 (Fort Monroe, Va.), BRFAL-FO; People v. Phillis Barber, 18 July 1866, proceedings of the freedmen's court, entry 4139, vol. 211 (Fort Monroe, Va.), BRFAL-FO; Edw. C. Anderson to J. Kearney Smith, 9 Aug. 1866, and endorsement of J. Kearney Smith to W. W. Deane, letters sent, entry 1008, vol. 347 (Savannah, Ga.), BRFAL-FO.

52. Cases of Cherry Frances, Harriett Hanberry, Lavinia White, May Williams, Alma White, 12 July 1865, proceedings of the freedmen's court, entry 4160, vol. 352 (Norfolk, Va.), BRFAL-FO; case of Mary Edwards, 1 Nov. 1865, proceedings of the freedmen's court, entry 4246, vol. 415 (Richmond, Va.), BRFAL-FO. Unlike her counterparts, Cherry Frances was found innocent of "Walking the streets." For punishments, see, for example, the charges and sentences in "List of Prisoners in Military Prison," proceedings of the freedmen's court, entry 4139, vol. 211 (Fort Monroe, Va.), BRFAL-FO; Brevet Major G. E. Head v. Francis White, Timpy Liggins, Mary Wilson, 6 Feb. 1866, proceedings of the freedmen's court, entry 4139, vol. 211 (Fort Monroe, Va.), BRFAL-FO. See also case of Lizzy Gray, 8 Nov. 1865, proceedings of the freedmen's court, entry 4246, vol. 415 (Richmond, Va.), BRFAL-FO.

53. All three women pleaded guilty and were identified in the records as "public prostitutes and vagrants" by witnesses. Brevet Major G. E. Head v. Francis White, Timpy Liggins, Mary Wilson, 6 Feb. 1866, proceedings of the freedmen's court, entry 4139, vol. 211 (Fort Monroe, Va.), BRFAL-FO.

54. See note 2.

55. De Forest, *A Union Officer in the Reconstruction*, 94.

56. Freedwoman Lizzie, "Extracts from Letters from Mississippi," *American Freedman*, July 1869, 20.

57. Testimony of Sallie Carder, in Rawick, *The American Slave*, vol. 7 (Okla.), 29.

58. Freedwoman Lizzie, "Extracts from Letters from Mississippi," *American Freedman*, July 1869, 20; wife of freedman Daniel Bell quoted in Frankel, *Freedom's Women*, 129. See also Randall M. Miller, "The Freedmen's Bureau and Reconstruction: An Overview," in *The Freedmen's Bureau and Reconstruction: Reconsiderations*, ed. Paul A. Cimbala and Randall M. Miller (New York: Fordham University Press, 1999), xxv.

4. "to put forth almost superhuman efforts to regain their children": Freedwomen, Parental Rights, and the Freedmen's Bureau

1. John Eaton to O. O. Howard, 15 Dec. 1865, in U.S. Senate, "Reports of the Assistant Commissioners of the Bureau of Refugees, Freedmen, and Abandoned Lands [1865–66]," 39th Cong., 1st sess., Senate Executive Document 27 (Serial 1238), 151–52.

2. John Eaton to O. O. Howard, 15 Dec. 1865, in U.S. Senate, "Reports of the Assistant Commissioners [1865–66]," 151–52.

3. On black parents' efforts to reclaim freedchildren in the immediacy of emancipation, see, in particular, Mary Niall Mitchell, *Raising Freedom's Child: Black Children and Visions of the Future after Slavery* (New York: New York University Press, 2008), chap.

4; Karin L. Zipf, *Labor of Innocents: Forced Apprenticeship in North Carolina, 1715–1919* (Baton Rouge: Louisiana State University Press, 2005), chap. 4; Nancy D. Bercaw, *Gendered Freedoms: Race, Rights, and the Politics of the Household in the Delta, 1861–1875* (Gainesville: University Press of Florida, 2003), 101; Noralee Frankel, *Freedom's Women: Black Women and Families in Civil War Era Mississippi* (Bloomington: Indiana University Press, 1999), 138–43; Ira Berlin and Leslie S. Rowland, eds., *Families and Freedom: A Documentary History of African-American Kinship in the Civil War Era* (New York: New Press, 1997), 193–95; Laura F. Edwards, *Gendered Strife and Confusion: The Political Culture of Reconstruction* (Urbana: University of Illinois Press, 1997), 38–39, 48–54; James Smallwood, "Black Freedwomen after Emancipation: The Texas Experience," *Prologue* 27, no. 4 (1995): 304; Peter W. Bardaglio, *Reconstructing the Household: Families, Sex, and the Law in the Nineteenth-Century South* (Chapel Hill: University of North Carolina Press, 1995), chap. 5; Nell Irvin Painter, "A Prize-Winning Book Revisited," review of *Reconstruction: America's Unfinished Revolution*, by Eric Foner, *Journal of Women's History* 2, no. 3 (1991): 129–30; Jacqueline Jones, *Labor of Love, Labor of Sorrow: Black Women, Work, and the Family from Slavery to the Present* (New York: Basic Books, 1985), 51–58.

4. Black Marylanders quoted in Herbert G. Gutman, *The Black Family in Slavery and Freedom, 1750–1925* (New York: Pantheon Books, 1976), 411. See also Berlin and Rowland, *Families and Freedom*, 194. On the disruption of political conventions posed by freedwomen's assertions of parental rights, see in particular Zipf, *Labor of Innocents*, 85, 89–93.

5. Circular No. 1, issued by E. Whittlesey, 16 Feb. 1866, letters received, reel 29, BRFAL (M752).

6. For two exceptional analyses of southern apprenticeship laws and their use by an elite white patriarchy to assert class, racial, and gender controls in the mid-nineteenth century, see Zipf, *Labor of Innocents*, and Mitchell, *Raising Freedom's Child*, chap. 4. See also Peter Bardaglio's important examination of apprenticeship and its racial and patriarchal makeup in the southern legal context in *Reconstructing the Household*, 23–36, 97–107, 161–65. For an introduction to apprenticeship law in the context of the nineteenth-century United States more broadly, see Michael Grossberg, *Governing the Hearth: Law and the Family in Nineteenth-Century America* (Chapel Hill: University of North Carolina Press, 1985), 259–73. On the practice of apprenticeship and its "almost nonexistent" status in the North by the time of the Civil War, see James D. Schmidt, *Free to Work: Labor Law, Emancipation, and Reconstruction, 1815–1880* (Athens: University of Georgia Press, 1999), 62–63; Zipf, *Labor of Innocents*, 40–41. On the use of apprenticeship by southern whites in the immediate aftermath of emancipation, see Gutman, *The Black Family*, 402–12; Eric Foner, *Reconstruction: America's Unfinished Revolution, 1863–1877* (New York: Harper & Row, 1988), 40–41, 201–2; Richard Paul Fuke, *Imperfect Equality: African Americans and the Confines of White Racial Attitudes in Post-emancipation Maryland* (New York: Fordham University Press, 1999), chap. 4; Karin L. Zipf, "Reconstructing 'Free Woman': African-American Women, Apprenticeship, and Custody Rights during Reconstruction," *Journal of Women's History* 12 (2000): 8–31.

7. On the black codes in general, see Donald G. Nieman, *To Set the Law in Motion: The Freedmen's Bureau and the Legal Rights of Blacks, 1865–1868* (Millwood, N.Y.: KTO Press, 1979), 72–98; Barry A. Crouch, "'All the Vile Passions': The Texas Black Code of 1866," *Southwestern Historical Quarterly* 97 (1993): 13–34; Donald G. Nieman, "The Freedmen's Bureau and the Mississippi Black Code," *Journal of Mississippi History* 40 (1978): 91–118; Joe M. Richardson, "Florida Black Codes," *Florida Historical Quarterly* 47 (1969): 365–79; Theodore Brantner Wilson, *The Black Codes of the South* (University: University of Alabama Press, 1965); Wayne K. Durrill, "The South Carolina Black

Code," in *True Stories from the American Past*, ed. William Graebner (New York: McGraw-Hill, 1993), 1–15.

8. W. H. Sinclair to Kirkman, 26 Feb. 1867, letters received, reel 3, BRFAL-TX. On apprenticeship laws and practices in the antebellum South, see Zipf, *Labor of Innocents*, 2–3, chap. 1; Victoria E. Bynum, "On the Lowest Rung: Court Control over Poor White and Free Black Women," *Southern Exposure* 12 (1984): 40–44; Victoria E. Bynum, *Unruly Women: The Politics of Social and Sexual Control in the Old South* (Chapel Hill: University of North Carolina Press, 1992), 99–109; Edwards, *Gendered Strife and Confusion*, 51; Bardaglio, *Reconstructing the Household*, 97–106; Schmidt, *Free to Work*, 88–86; James W. Ely Jr., "Poor Laws of the Post-revolutionary South, 1776–1800," *Tulsa Law Journal* 21 (1985): 1–22; Ira Berlin, *Slaves without Masters: The Free Negro in the Antebellum South* (New York: Pantheon Books, 1974), 226–27. On Reconstruction-era apprenticeship laws and practices, see Zipf, *Labor of Innocents*, 1–7, chap. 2; Barry A. Crouch, "'To Enslave the Rising Generation': The Freedmen's Bureau and the Texas Black Code," in *The Freedmen's Bureau and Reconstruction: Reconsiderations*, ed. Paul A. Cimbala and Randall M. Miller (New York: Fordham University Press, 1999), 261–87; Fuke, *Imperfect Equality*, chap. 4; Frankel, *Freedom's Women*, 138–43.

9. "An Act to Define the Relative Duties of Master and Apprentice," 23 Feb. 1866, in U.S. Senate, "Reports of the Assistant Commissioners of the Bureau of Refugees, Freedmen, and Abandoned Lands and Laws in Relation to the Freedmen [1866]," 39th Cong., 2nd sess., Senate Executive Document 6 (Serial 1276), 172; "An Act Concerning Negroes and Persons of Color or of Mixed Blood," chap. 5, "Apprentices," 10 March 1866, in U.S. Senate, "Reports of the Assistant Commissioners [1866]," 200; "An Act to Establish and Regulate the Domestic Relations of Persons of Color, and to Amend the Law in Relation to Paupers and Vagrancy," 21 Dec. 1865, *Statutes at Large of South Carolina* [1865], in "Reports of the Assistant Commissioners [1866]," 209; "Negro Apprentices," art. 6, secs. 31–40, *Maryland Code of Public General Laws*, in U.S. Senate, "Reports of the Assistant Commissioners [1866]," 187–88; "An Act to Alter and Amend the Laws of this State [Georgia] in Relation to Apprentices," 17 March 1866, in U.S. Senate, "Reports of the Assistant Commissioners [1866]," 180.

For examples of the postwar laws regulating apprenticeship, see the apprenticeship provisions of the black codes for the states of Alabama, Georgia, Mississippi, North Carolina, South Carolina, and Texas, all reprinted in U.S. Senate, "Reports of the Assistant Commissioners [1866]," 170–230. See also, on the use of apprenticeship by southern whites to control former slaves in the aftermath of emancipation more generally, Zipf, *Labor of Innocents*, chap. 2; Fuke, *Imperfect Equality*, chap. 4; Crouch, "To Enslave the Rising Generation"; Edwards, *Gendered Strife and Confusion*, 39, 43–44; Frankel, *Freedom's Women*, 138–43; Schmidt, *Free to Work*, 130–31. It is important to note that the Maryland code left apprenticeship to the discretion of the orphans' courts and clearly discriminated between black and white apprentices. For example, the code relieved employers from the duty of educating black apprentices and openly permitted courts to transfer black children to employers without parental consent despite the fact that the law prohibited the apprenticing of children whose parents "have the means and are willing to support such child, and keep the same employed, so as to teach habits of industry" and required parents to be present at binding proceedings. "Negro Apprentices," Article 6, sections 31–40, *Maryland Code of Public General Laws*, in U.S. Senate, "Reports of the Assistant Commissioners [1866]," 187–88.

10. William Henry Stiles quoted in Paul A. Cimbala, *Under the Guardianship of the Nation: The Freedmen's Bureau and the Reconstruction of Georgia, 1865–1870* (Athens: University of Georgia Press, 1997), 197; Thomas B. Davis to Judge Hugh L. Bond, 6 Nov. 1864, in Ira Berlin and others, eds., *Free at Last: A Documentary History of Slavery, Freedom, and the Civil War* (New York: New Press, 1992), 371; E. Belcher to C. C. Sibley, 23

Sept. 1867, letters sent, entry 872, vol. 367 (Dawson, Ga.), BRFAL-FO; F. A. H. Gaebel to F. Mosebach, 30 April 1867, letters sent, entry 690, vol. 120 (Albany, Ga.), BRFAL-FO, quoted in Cimbala, *Under the Guardianship of the Nation*, 200. On Edwin Belcher's background and mixed racial heritage, see Cimbala, *Under the Guardianship of the Nation*, 45–46.

On apprenticeship in Maryland, see C. H. Howard to O. O. Howard, 22 Oct. 1866, in U.S. Senate, "Reports of the Assistant Commissioners [1866]," 34; U.S. House of Representatives, "Report of the Commissioner of the Bureau of Refugees, Freedmen, and Abandoned Lands [1 Nov. 1867]," 40th Cong., 2nd sess., House Executive Document 1 (Serial 1323), 41; E. M. Gregory to A. P. Ketchum, 11 April 1867, reports of operations, BRFAL-MD. For similar reports, see S. S. Ashley to Rev. James J. Woolsey (New York), 12 March 1866, letters received, reel 29, BRFAL (M752); E. Whittlesey to O. O. Howard, 16 March 1866, BRFAL (M752); *Freedmen's Record*, July 1865, 105–6; *Washington Chronicle*, 25 Aug. 1865, and 20 July 1866. See also Fuke, *Imperfect Equality*, 70; Barbara Jeanne Fields, *Slavery and Freedom on the Middle Ground: Maryland during the Nineteenth Century* (New Haven, Conn.: Yale University Press, 1985), 153. For additional evidence of the extent to which white southerners used apprenticeship, see Gutman, *The Black Family*, 402–12; Edmund L. Drago, *Black Politicians and Reconstruction Georgia: A Splendid Failure*, 2nd ed. (Athens: University of Georgia Press, 1992), 112, 117; Vernon Lane Wharton, *The Negro in Mississippi, 1865–1890* (New York: Harper & Row, 1965), 91; Zipf, *Labor of Innocents*, 44–46.

11. Mitchell, *Raising Freedom's Child*, 179–86; Fuke, *Imperfect Equality*, 72–74; Rebecca Scott, "The Battle over the Child: Child Apprenticeship and the Freedmen's Bureau in North Carolina," *Prologue* 10, no. 2 (1978): 102; Zipf, *Labor of Innocents*, especially chap. 4.

12. Fuke, *Imperfect Equality*, 72–73; "A List of Names of Children Bound by Justices of the Peace for Kent County," n.d., enclosed in Bartus Trew to James R. Ross, 28 Nov. 1864, and Charlotte Hall to Gen. Ross, 20 Jan. 1865, both in "Communication from Major General Lew Wallace in Relation to the Freedmen's Bureau to the General Assembly of Maryland," *Journal of the Proceedings of the House of Delegates, January Session, 1865* (Annapolis, 1865), document J, 40–46, 90. According to the historian Ervin L. Jordan Jr., more than 185,000 African American men—92,000 from the South—served as soldiers and 30,000 as sailors in the Union army. Ervin L. Jordan Jr., *Black Confederates and Afro-Yankees in Civil War Virginia* (Charlottesville: University Press of Virginia, 1995), 289. See also Adjutant General, Rolls of Maryland Troops, U.S. Colored Troops [1863–64] and Talbot County, Negro Docket, 1855–67, Maryland State Archives, Annapolis.

13. G. M. Conway to Wilcox, 6 Feb. 1866, letters received, entry 3948, box 14 (Danville, Va.), BRFAL-FO; John T. Raper to Edgar M. Gregory, 29 Nov. 1865, unregistered letters received, reel 17, BRFAL-TX. See also Crouch, "To Enslave the Rising Generation," 268–69; Nieman, *To Set the Law in Motion*, 76–82; Frankel, *Freedom's Women*, 138–43; Scott, "The Battle over the Child," 102. For efforts to end apprenticeship abuses by the courts in Mississippi, see Opinion of Attorney General C. E. Hooker in "Orders and Instructions to Subcommissioners," orders and circulars issued, reel 28, BRFAL-MS; Eldridge to Wood, 3 Feb. 1866, letters sent, reel 1, BRFAL-MS; Eldridge to C. E. Yeoman, 23 Feb. 1866, letters sent, reel 1, BRFAL-MS; Thomas to Donaldson, 28 Feb. 1866, letters sent, reel 1, BRFAL-MS; Knox to Eldridge, 28 March 1866, letters received, reel 14, BRFAL-MS; Adam to S. Thomas, 30 April 1866, letters received, reel 13, BRFAL-MS; Wood to Humphreys, 10 May and 4 June 1866, letters sent, reel 1, BRFAL-MS; Adam to Wood, 30 April 1866, letters received, reel 13, BRFAL-MS; Humphreys to Wood, 6 June 1866, letters received, reel 13, BRFAL-MS; [?] to Judge J. B. Thrasher, 10 July 1866,

letters received, reel 14, BRFAL-MS; A. W. Preston to Wilkinson and Bowman, 22 Dec. 1866, letters sent, BRFAL-MS.

14. A. G. Brady to J. M. Foote, 18 June 1866, letters received, entry 2666 (Halifax, N.C.), BRFAL-FO; J. M. Foote to A. G. Brady, 23 June 1866, letters received, entry 2666 (Halifax, N.C.), BRFAL-FO. See also J. M. Foote to A. G. Brady, 23 May 1866, letters received, entry 2666 (Halifax, N.C.), BRFAL-FO; Scott, "The Battle over the Child," 102; Crouch, "To Enslave the Rising Generation," 268–69.

15. *Baltimore American*, 10 Dec. 1866.

16. Thomas T. Tredway to O. Brown, 21 Dec. 1865, unregistered letters received, entry 3972 (Farmville, Va.), BRFAL-FO; affidavit of Rebecca Parsons, 28 April 1867, letters received, reel 15, BRFAL-GA; testimony of William F. Taylor, 14 and 16 Jan. 1867, in the Investigation of the Government of Maryland [1867], RG 233, National Archives, Washington, D.C. See also John G. Mitchell to Lew Wallace, 22 Nov. 1864, in "Communication from Major General Lew Wallace," 23–25.

17. William H. Webster to W. H. Sterling, 30 April 1867, letters sent, entry 1490 (Baton Rouge, La.), BRFAL-FO; H. H. Beadle to E. Whittlesey, 10 Mar. 1866, letters received, reel 7, BRFAL-NC; E. Whittlesey to O. O. Howard, 15 Jan. 1866, letters received, reel 23, BRFAL (M752). On the Freedmen's Bureau and apprenticeship, see Zipf, *Labor of Innocents*, 40–105; Crouch, "To Enslave the Rising Generation"; Scott, "The Battle over the Child"; Fuke, *Imperfect Equality*, 69–87; Cimbala, *Under the Guardianship of the Nation*, 197–203.

18. E. Whittlesey to O. O. Howard, 15 Jan. 1866, letters received, reel 23, BRFAL (M752); W. G. Vance to John T. Spague, 31 Jan. 1867, letters received, reel 42, BRFAL (M752); J. Knox to E. Bamberger, 10 March 1866, registered letters received, entry 2249 (Meridian, Miss.), BRFAL-FO. On Whittlesey, see William S. McFeely, *Yankee Stepfather: General O. O. Howard and the Freedmen* (New Haven, Conn.: Yale University Press, 1968), 78–83.

19. Statement of Bartus Trew, 28 Nov. 1864, in "Communication from Major General Lew Wallace," 40; Circular No. 1, issued by E. Whittlesey, 16 Feb. 1866, letters received, reel 29, BRFAL (M752). See also Zipf, *Labor of Innocents*, 75.

20. J. C. Robinson to J. V. Bomford, 26 Dec. 1866, registered letters received, reel 43, BRFAL (M752); A. H. Mayer to Henry A. Ellis, 24 Nov. 1866, letters sent, entry 3733, vol. 120 (Liberty, Tex.), BRFAL-FO; Samuel C. Sloan to [the assistant commissioner], 1 Jan. 1867, reports of operations and conditions, reel 20, BRFAL-TX; S. N. Clark to J. S. Fullerton, 5 Feb. 1866, letters received, reel 19, BRFAL (M752). On Assistant Commissioner Robinson, see also McFeely, *Yankee Stepfather*, 293.

21. *Kent News*, 17 Dec. 1864, quoted in Fuke, *Imperfect Equality*, 70–71; O. H. P. Garrett to A. J. Hamilton, 11 Dec. 1865, Governor's Papers, Texas State Library, Austin, quoted in Crouch, "To Enslave the Rising Generation," 270; J. Eaton to O. O. Howard, 15 Dec. 1865, U.S. Senate, "Reports of the Assistant Commissioners [1865–66]," 151–52.

22. *New York Times*, 11 Feb. 1866.

23. J. B. Kiddoo to O. O. Howard, Oct. 1886, U.S. Senate, "Reports of the Assistant Commissioners [1866]," 157. On Kiddoo, see Schmidt, *Free to Work*, 127–32. On Johnson's efforts to reshape the bureau, see Cimbala, *The Freedmen's Bureau: Reconstructing the American South after the Civil War* (Malabar, Fla.: Krieger, 2005), 13–16, 23–24; Hans L. Trefousse, "Andrew Johnson and the Freedmen's Bureau," in Cimbala and Miller, *The Freedmen's Bureau and Reconstruction*, chap. 2; John Cox and LaWanda Cox, "Andrew Johnson and His Ghost Writers: An Analysis of the Freedmen's Bureau and Civil Rights Veto Messages," *Mississippi Valley Historical Review* 48 (1961): 460–67.

24. Clinton B. Fisk, *Plain Counsels for Freedmen: In Sixteen Brief Lectures* (Boston: American Tract Society, 1866), 32. On the backgrounds of these assistant commissioners, see McFeely, *Yankee Stepfather*, 67, 68, 71–72, 78–83.

25. Fisk, *Plain Counsels for Freedmen*, 32; Cimbala, *The Freedmen's Bureau*, 17–18, 123–24; comments of Rufus Saxton quoted in Schmidt, *Free to Work*, 126. See also Zipf, *Labor of Innocents*, especially 74–75. On the background and ideological stance of Saxton, see Schmidt, *Free to Work*, 125–27.

26. Circular letter issued by Clinton B. Fisk, [n.d.] 1865, in U.S. House of Representatives, "Freedmen's Bureau. Letter from the Secretary of War, in answer to A resolution of the House of March 8, transmitting a report, by the Commissioner of the Freedmen's Bureau, of all orders issued by him or any assistant commissioner," 39th Cong., 1st sess., House Executive Document 70 (Serial 1256), 45. See also, for similar orders, Circular No. 2, issued by Davis Tillson, 3 Oct. 1865, Circular No. 5, issued by Davis Tillson, 22 Dec. 1865, Circular No. 16, issued by J. W. Sprague, 26 Oct. 1865, circular letter issued by Rufus Saxton, [n.d.] 1865, General Orders No. 8, issued by Rufus Saxton, 11 Aug. 1865, all in U.S. House of Representatives, "Freedmen's Bureau," 59, 64, 78, 90, 110–11; Eliphalet Whittlesey to Asa Teal, 28 July 1865, letters received, entry 2650 (Greensboro, N.C.), BRFAL-FO.

27. Extract of orders issued by O. O. Howard, 4 Oct. 1865, reprinted in Circular No. 25, issued by J. S. Fullerton, 31 Oct. 1865, in U.S. House of Representatives, "Freedmen's Bureau," 28.

28. Circular No. 3, issued by Davis Tillson, 14 Oct. 1865, in U.S. House of Representatives, "Freedmen's Bureau," 60. See also Circular No. 5, issued by Stuart Eldridge, 26 July 1865, and Circular No. 4, issued by Rufus Saxton, 12 Oct. 1865, in U.S. House of Representatives, "Freedmen's Bureau," 94, 153.

29. Circular letter issued by O. O. Howard, 4 Oct. 1865, in U.S. House of Representatives, "Freedmen's Bureau," 137. See also, for example, Circular No. 1, issued by E. Whittlesey, 16 Feb. 1866, letters received, reel 29, BRFAL (M752).

30. O. O. Howard, "Rules and Regulations for Assistant Commissioners," 30 May 1865, in U.S. House of Representatives, "Freedmen's Bureau," 102; David S. Beath to Vernou, 18 Sept. 1868, letters sent, entry 3701, vol. 86 (Cotton Gin, Tex.), BRFAL-FO. See also Circular No. 2, issued by Clinton B. Fisk, 24 July 1865, in U.S. House of Representatives, "Freedmen's Bureau," 49.

31. G. Pillsbury to O'Brien, 22 Aug. 1866, testimony, reports, and other records relating to court cases, entry 3284 (Moncks Corner, S.C.), BRFAL-FO; *Washington Chronicle*, 15 May 1866.

32. Endorsement on J. F. Wilcox to R. S. Lacey, 14 Dec. 1865, letters received, entry 3948, box 14 (Danville, Va.), BRFAL-FO.

33. W. H. Sinclair to Philip Howard, 17 April 1866, letters sent, reel 1, BRFAL-TX. See also J. W. Throckmorton to Griffin, 4 March 1867, letters received, reel 9, BRFAL-TX; Martin W. Wagner to Gregory, 15 March 1866, letters received, reel 9, BRFAL-TX; Edward Miller to J. B. Kiddoo, 11 Jan. 1867, reports of operations and conditions, reel 21, BRFAL-TX; Howard to Kirkman, 13 Aug. 1867, reports of operations and conditions, reel 21, BRFAL-TX; Howard to Garretson, 31 Oct. 1867, reports of operations and conditions, reel 22, BRFAL-TX.

34. Official policy of the bureau in Georgia insisted that only children without guardians and those whose parents consented to their indenture could be apprenticed. Order described and enclosed in Davis Tillson to John B. Walker, 20 Nov. 1865, letters sent, reel 1, BRFAL-GA.

35. E. Whittlesey to O. O. Howard, 15 Jan. 1866, letters received, reel 23, BRFAL (M752). See also Circular No. 4, issued by E. Whittlesey, reel 20, BRFAL-NC. For other examples of agents desirous of parental consent in apprenticeship of freedchildren, see B. C. Cook to J. A. Bates, 27 Nov. 1866, letters sent, reel 1, BRFAL-VA; J. F. Wilcox to R. S. Lacey, 13 Dec. 1865, letters received, entry 3948, box 14 (Danville, Va.), BRFAL-FO; G. P. Sherwood to J. O. O'Neill, 27 July 1866, letters sent, entry 4328, vol. 2 (Wytheville,

Va.), BRFAL-FO; W. W. Deane to W. H. Pritchell, 30 April 1866, letters sent, reel 2, BRFAL-GA; W. W. Deane to L. Campbell, 23 April 1866, letters sent, reel 2, BRFAL-GA. See also Richard Paul Fuke, "Planters, Apprenticeship, and Forced Labor: The Black Family under Pressure in Post-emancipation Maryland," *Agricultural History* 62 (1988): 72–74; Scott, "The Battle over the Child," 101–4, 107–8; Schwalm, *A Hard Fight for We*, 252

36. W. F. White to Stuart Barnes, 12 June 1866, letters sent, vol. 102, entry 3879 (Amelia Courthouse, Va.), BRFAL-FO. See also Ira Berlin, Steven F. Miller, and Leslie S. Rowland, eds., "Afro-American Families in the Transition from Slavery to Freedom," *Radical History Review* 42 (1988): 116–18.

37. This freedwoman, like other black parents in Maryland, turned to military authorities for assistance in reclaiming her children. See statement of Hester Anthony, 5 Dec. 1864, in "Communication from Major General Lew Wallace," 9.

38. Statement of Louisa Foster, 22 Nov. 1864, in "Communication from Major General Lew Wallace," 53. See also 49.

39. J. W. Sprague to O. O. Howard, 7 June 1866, letters received, reel 34, BRFAL (M752).

40. J. Arnold Yeckley to James A. Bates, 19 April 1866, letters received, reel 34, BRFAL (M752).

41. A. F. Hayden to J. W. Keller, 14 June 1866 and 3 Nov. 1866, unregistered letters received, entry 1602 (Franklin, La.), BRFAL-FO. Three months after the agent in Franklin reported Phillis's arrest and incarceration, the bureau concluded that although "by the law the mother is the natural guardian of her child, and can enforce obedience," in this case—because "it appears that in the case mother has done nothing for the support of the child for the last five years"—more "weight should be given to the wishes of the child and the relative advantages of the two places." It is not known whether she recovered her child.

42. Case of Julia Handy in Samuel Sawyer to O. O. Howard, 28 Oct. 1865, reprinted in W. A. Low, "The Freedmen's Bureau and Civil Rights in Maryland," *Journal of Negro History* 37, no. 3 (1952): 235.

43. Statement of Jane Kamper, 14 Nov. 1864, in Berlin and Rowland, *Families and Freedom*, 214. For other examples of freedwomen who "stole" their children back, see complaint of Ann Lewis, 3 Aug. 1867, orders sent to local citizens and register of complaints, entry 739, vol. 103 (Atlanta, Ga.), BRFAL-FO; affidavit of Laura Taylor, 31 July 1866, letters received, BRFAL-AL, in Peter Kolchin, *First Freedom: The Response of Alabama's Blacks to Emancipation and Reconstruction* (Westport, Conn.: Greenwood Press, 1972), 65.

44. J. M. Henderson to W. Swayne, 25 Jan. 1866, letters received, reel 8, BRFAL-AL; statement of Linday Robbins, 29 Oct. 1863, in "Communication from Major General Lew Wallace," 32–33.

45. Remarks of Freedmen's Bureau officer in Annapolis, Md., quoted in U.S. House of Representatives, "Report of the Commissioner [1867]," 41; Schmidt, *Free to Work*, 178.

46. John William De Forest, *A Union Officer in the Reconstruction*, ed. James H. Croushore and David Morris Potter (New Haven, Conn.: Yale University Press, 1948; reprint, Baton Rouge: Louisiana State University Press, 1976), 112–13.

47. Circular No. 1, issued by E. Whittlesey, 16 Feb. 1866, letters received, reel 29, BRFAL (M752). See also Zipf, *Labor of Innocents*, chap. 3; Schmidt, *Free to Work*, 126, 137, 152, 178–93; Fuke, *Imperfect Equality*, especially 77–83.

48. F. A. H. Gaebel to E. Pickett, 3 April 1867, letters received, entry 955, box 1 (Marietta, Ga.), BRFAL-FO; W. G. Vance to John T. Spague, 31 Jan. 1867, letters received, reel 42, BRFAL (M752); L. S. Livermore to R. S. Donaldson, 10 Jan. 1866, registered letters received, entry 2188 (Jackson, Miss.), BRFAL-FO; E. Whittlesey to O. O. Howard, 16

March 1866, letters received, reel 29, BRFAL (M752). For similar bureau complaints, see, for example, Albert Evans to W. H. Sinclair, 18 Jan. 1867, reports of operations and conditions, reel 20, BRFAL-TX; Albert H. Latimer to W. G. Kirkman, 1 June 1867, reports of operations and conditions, reel 21, BRFAL-TX; S. N. Clark to J. S. Fullerton, 5 Feb. 1866, letters received, reel 19, BRFAL (M752); Thomas J. Wood to O. O. Howard (Washington), 13 July 1866, letters received, reel 34, BRFAL (M752); L. S. Livermore to R. S. Donaldson, 10 Jan. 1866, registered letters received, entry 2188 (Jackson, Miss.), BRFAL-FO.

49. L. S. Livermore to R. S. Donaldson, 10 Jan. 1866, registered letters received, entry 2188 (Jackson, Miss.), BRFAL-FO; J. C. de Graffereid to W. W. Deane, 14 Aug. 1866, unregistered letters received, reel 26, and T. F. Forbes to J. C. de Graffereid, 29 Aug. 1866, letters sent, reel 3, BRFAL-GA; "Deposition of Grace Jenkins," 6 Oct. 1866, letters received, reel 8, BRFAL-NC; Mary Porter to O. O. Howard, 19 June 1867, letters received, reel 47, BRFAL (M752); affidavit of Dina Williams, [n.d.] June 1867, letters received, entry 693, box 1 (Albany, Ga.), BRFAL-FO; L. S. Livermore to R. S. Donaldson, 10 Jan. 1866, registered letters received, entry 2188 (Jackson, Miss.), BRFAL-FO. For additional instances of freedwomen who were forced to comply with apprenticeship, see, for example, Thomas Smith to Francis Goodwin, 10 Feb. 1866, letters sent and received, entry 2194 (Jackson, Miss.), BRFAL-FO; Thomas Norton, 30 July 1867, registered letters received, entry 2219 (Lauderdale, Miss.), BRFAL-FO; O. D. Greene, 14 Sept. 1867, registers of letters received, reel 7, BRFAL-MS.

50. Case of Basil Croudy in S. N. Clark to C. H. Howard, 16 June 1866, letters received, entry 2013, box 11 (Annapolis, Md.), BRFAL-FO; "d——d head" quote in Fields, *Slavery and Freedom on the Middle Ground*, 139–40; Maria Nichols to O. O. Howard, 11 Oct. 1866, letters received, entry 1961, vol. 1, BRFAL-MD.

51. Howard quoted in *Baltimore Sun*, 24 July 1865, reprinted in Fuke, *Imperfect Equality*, 79; comments of Maryland bureau agents in U.S. House of Representatives, "Report of the Commissioner [1867]," 40; Swayne to Mrs. Thomas Harrell, 18 April 1866, letters sent, reel 1, BRFAL-AL.

52. Phillis Peebles v. Dr. Milner, 2 Aug. 1867, register of complaints, entry 3665, vol. 54 (Belton, Tex.), BRFAL-FO; J. Kearney Smith to W. W. Deane, letters sent, entry 1008, vol. 347 (Savannah, Ga.), BRFAL-FO; Frederick Mosebach, to J. S. N. Waldrop, 22 Oct. 1867, letters sent, entry 729, vol. 99 (Atlanta, Ga.), BRFAL-FO. For other cases in which the bureau expressly rejected apprenticeship agreements made without the consent of parents, see, for example, J. F. Wilcox to R. S. Lacey, 28 Dec. 1865, letters received, entry 3948, box 14 (Danville, Va.), BRFAL-FO; G. P. Sherwood to O. Brown, 23 July 1866, letters sent, entry 4328, vol. 489 (Wytheville, Va.), BRFAL-FO; [A. G. Malloy] to J. S. Kirkman, 2 Sept. 1867, letters sent, entry 3743, vol. 134 (Marshall, Tex.), BRFAL-FO. For a case in which the bureau encouraged obtainment of consent from family members for the indenture of orphans, see, for example, G. P. Sherwood to J. O. O'Neill, 27 July 1866, letters sent, entry 4328, vol. 489 (Wytheville, Va.), BRFAL-FO. For another case in which the bureau overturned its own indenture, see, for example, complaint of Belle Nellson, 1 June 1867, journal of business, entry 1870, vol. 465 (St. Joseph, La.), BRFAL-FO.

53. C. Cilley to E. Whittlesey, 19 Nov. 1865, letters received, reel 7, BRFAL-NC; endorsement of Cilley in G. Hawley to W. A. Wieget, 3 July 1866, quoted in Scott, "The Battle over the Child," 108. It should be noted here that Cilley, a Democrat, was the sole bureau official in North Carolina to gain "approval" in the Steedman-Fullerton report, which had been ordered by President Johnson and had resulted in the removal of Assistant Commissioner Whittlesey from his post in 1866. See McFeely, *Yankee Stepfather*, 252–53.

54. Case of Eliza Elder in John J. Knox to Young Elder, 8 April 1867, letters sent, entry 718, vol. 169 (Athens, Ga.), BRFAL-FO; affidavit of Annie Gibbs, 16 July 1866, and endorsement of Davis Tillson, 16 July 1866, letters received, entry 732, box 7 (Augusta,

Ga.), BRFAL-FO; case of Edna Chapman in James DeGrey to Mr. Chapman, 20 May 1867, letters sent, entry 1546, vol. 245 (Clinton, La.), BRFAL-FO; L. Jolissaint to Paul Faust, 13 June 1867, letters sent, entry 1802, vol. 401 (New Orleans, La.), BRFAL-FO.

For other cases in which freedwomen complained of employers who violated apprenticeship contracts, see, for example, Louis W. Stevenson to P. Stevens, 9 March 1868, letters sent, entry 3695, vol. 74 (Columbus, Tex.), BRFAL-FO; William B. Kirkman to Philip Howard, 16 July 1867, letters sent, entry 3666, vol. 67 (Boston, Tex.), BRFAL-FO. For other complaints of abuse or ill treatment, see, for example, Eliza Coleman to Wilson, 1 March 1866, contracts and indentures, orders received, and bills of lading, entry 4005 (Goochland, Va.), BRFAL-FO; complaint of Mary Ann Johnson against Bony Calmus, 27 Aug. 1865, register of complaints, entry 1479, vol. 204 (Amite City, La.), BRFAL-FO; Eliza Wilson v. James Scott, 13 Jan. 1866, proceedings of the freedmen's court, entry 4204, vol. 390 (Petersburg, Va.), BRFAL-FO; J. H. Hastings to Mr. Goldman, 27 Aug. [1866], letters sent, entry 1859, vol. 462 (St. Joseph, La.), BRFAL-FO; complaint of Celeste Doucet, 9 July 1867, journal of business, entry 1799, vol. 449 (New Iberia, La.), BRFAL-FO; complaint, 26 April 1867, journal of business, entry 1799, vol. 449 (New Iberia, La.), BRFAL-FO. For additional complaints in which bureau agents specifically restored custody of children to mothers on account of abuse or ill treatment, see, for example, Ann Calloway v. Aron Price, 23 July 1867, register of complaints, entry 859, vol. 238 (Cuthbert, Ga.), BRFAL-FO; Phillis Peebles v. Dr. Milner, 2 Aug. 1867, register of complaints, entry 3665, vol. 54 (Belton, Tex.), BRFAL-FO. For other complaints by freedwomen regarding nonpayment of wages due for children's services, see, for example, Andrew B. Clark to Edward Skilden, 13 Nov. 1868, letters sent, entry 873, vol. 251 (Dawson, Ga.), BRFAL-FO; Charlotte Logan v. Mrs. Pettus, 15 Jan. 1866, proceedings of the freedmen's court, entry 3945, vol. 147 (Cumberland Courthouse, Va.), BRFAL-FO; Julia Ann Ball v. Mrs. Hetty Kline, 20 Feb. 1867, register of complaints, entry 3869, vol. 98 (Alexandria, Va.), BRFAL-FO; Lucy Whitley v. Enoch Low, 5 April 1867, register of complaints, entry 3869, vol. 98 (Alexandria, Va.), BRFAL-FO; Molly Harris v. Mathey McEwen, 15 Dec. 1868, register of complaints, entry 3869, vol. 98 (Alexandria, Va.), BRFAL-FO; Sarah Stewart v. J. P. Street, 27 May 1867, proceedings of the freedmen's court, entry 3912, vol. 288 (Burkesville, Va.), BRFAL-FO; Nancy Allen v. Rovert Lovett, 19 Sept. 1868, proceedings of freedmen's court, entry 4352, vol. 506 (Yorktown, Va.), BRFAL-FO; complaint of Mary Murry, 6 July 1867, register of complaints, entry 3657, vol. 52 (Austin, Tex.), BRFAL-FO; James Oakes to Byron Porter, 20 Feb. 1868, letters sent, entry 3653, vol. 49 (Austin, Tex.), BRFAL-FO; complaint of Jane Erine, 29 May 1868, register of complaints, entry 1949, vol. 528 (Vidalia, La.), BRFAL-FO; endorsement of B. B. Brown, 25 April [1867], letters sent, entry 1859, vol. 455 (St. Joseph, La.), BRFAL-FO.

55. Schmidt, *Free to Work*, 120 (quotation), 121, 188–93.

56. Circular No. 2, issued by R. Saxton, 16 Aug. 1865, in U.S. House of Representatives, "Freedmen's Bureau," 93; General Orders No. 8, 11 Aug. 1865, issued by order of R. Saxton, BRFAL-FO, 111; Elizabeth Kennard to Col. Ross, 22 Dec. 1864, in "Communication from Major General Lew Wallace," 66–67; Mary Anne Ran quoted in Gutman, *The Black Family*, 409; Ann Maria Tripp to W. E. W. Ross, 21 Dec. 1864, in "Communication from Major General Lew Wallace"; C. C. Sibley to O. O. Howard, 14 Feb. 1866, letters sent, reel 7, BRFAL-GA. See also Berlin and others, "Afro-American Families," 116–19; Edwards, *Gendered Strife and Confusion*, 51–52; McFeely, *Yankee Stepfather*, 131; Joseph P. Reidy, *From Slavery to Agrarian Capitalism in the Cotton Plantation South: Central Georgia, 1800–1880* (Chapel Hill: University of North Carolina Press, 1992), 154–55; Frankel, *Freedom's Women*, 141–42; Gutman, *The Black Family*, 409–10.

57. On the case of *Timmins v. Lacy*, 30 Tex. 115 (1867), see Schmidt, *Free to Work*, 184–86, 190–91. For other examples of freedpeople using apprenticeship as an avenue to secure land, see Scott, "The Battle over the Child," 105, 107, 112.

58. Chief Justice Moore's ruling quoted in Schmidt, *Free to Work*, 190–91.
59. J. C. Robinson to Gov. J. Worth, 30 Oct. 1866, registered letters received, reel 43, BRFAL (M752). By juxtaposing the case presented by Lucy Ross with that of Wiley Ambrose and his wife, Hepsey Saunders, Zipf reveals the decision of bureau officials North Carolina to challenge apprenticeship laws and practices in that state—particularly the racial distinctions inherent to them—by centering a test case on the rights of a freedman rather than an unmarried freedwoman. Zipf, *Labor of Innocents*, chap. 4, especially 97–99. On the *Ambrose* case, see also Schmidt, *Free to Work*, 183–86, 190–91.
60. Affidavit of Lucy Ross, 24 Sept. 1866; affidavit of James Ross, 24 Sept. 1866; affidavit of William James, 24 Sept. 1866; affidavit of Chas. Aubriden, 24 Sept. 1866; A. Rutherford to A. Coats, 13 Sept. 1866, all in registered letters received, reel 43, BRFAL (M752). On Lucy Ross's appeal, see also Zipf, *Labor of Innocents*, 93–99, 103–4.
61. Zipf, *Labor of Innocents*, 97–98; and "Ambrose v. Russell," registered letters received, reel 43, BRFAL (M752). See also Edwards, *Gendered Strife and Confusion*, 42–54; Schmidt, *Free to Work*, 189–90; Scott, "The Battle over the Child," 111–12.
62. J. C. Robinson to Gov. J. Worth, 30 Oct. 1866, registered letters received, reel 43, BRFAL (M752); *Statutes at Large of USA* 14 (1866): 27–30; Zipf, *Labor of Innocents*, 95–99. See also A. Rutherford to A. Coats, 13 Sept. 1866, and J. C. Robinson to Gov. J. Worth, 26 Dec. 1866, both in BRFAL (M752); O. O. Howard to J. C. Robinson, 21 Nov. 1866, letters received, reel 13, BRFAL-NC. For the full text of the Civil Rights Act of 1866, see Edward McPherson, *The Political History of the United States of America during the Period of Reconstruction* (Washington, D.C.: Solomons & Chapman, 1875), 72–84.
63. O. O. Howard to J. C. Robinson, 21 Nov. 1866, letters received, reel 13, BRFAL-NC; Zipf, *Labor of Innocents*, 96–99.
64. *In the Matter of Ambrose and Moore*, 61 N.C. 91 (1867), quoted in Edwards, *Gendered Strife and Confusion*, 44; petition for habeas corpus, *In the Matter of Harriet Ambrose and Eliza Ambrose*, quoted in Zipf, *Labor of Innocents*, 99.
65. "Ambrose v. Russell," registered letters received, reel 43, BRFAL (M752). See also Schmidt, *Free to Work*, 189; Zipf, *Labor of Innocents*, 99–101; Edwards, *Gendered Strife and Confusion*, 43–44.
66. O. O. Howard to J. C. Robinson, 21 Nov. 1866, letters received, reel 13, BRFAL-NC.
67. U.S. House of Representatives, "Report of the Commissioner [1867]," 73.
68. "List of Names of White and Black bound as apprentices," quoted in Zipf, *Labor of Innocents*, 101–2. On bureau agents' responses to *Ambrose* and the cancellations of indentures in North Carolina, see Zipf, *Labor of Innocents*, 61–62, 101–2; Edwards, *Gendered Strife and* Confusion, 50. On African American parents' efforts to use the bureau and the courts to challenge apprenticeship, see, in general, Bardaglio, *Reconstructing the Household*, 162–65; Edwards, *Gendered Strife and Confusion*, 42–54; Fuke, *Imperfect Equality*, 80–82; Gutman, *The Black Family*, 411–12; Nieman, *To Set the Law in Motion*, 78–82, 137–38; Schmidt, *Free to Work*, 175, 178–93; Zipf, *Labor of Innocents*, chaps. 3, 4. For examples of individual apprenticeship cases in southern and, at least in one instance, federal courts, see the cases discussed in Schmidt, *Free to Work*, 175, 178–93, and those included in Apprentice Bonds, Granville County, North Carolina Division of Archives and History, cited in Edwards, *Gendered Strife and Confusion*, 271 n. 68.
69. On Daniel Russell and the continued efforts of Lucy Ross to regain custody of her daughters, see Zipf, *Labor of Innocents*, 103–4.
70. Endorsement of James DeGrey on Cyntha Nickols to Freedmen's Bureau, 19 Jan. 1867, letters received, reel 18, BRFAL-LA.
71. De Forest, *A Union Officer in the Reconstruction*, 114, 115.
72. The official also told the agent: "The girl herself is very decided that she does not wish to change." J. P. Richardson to J. T. [Vinny?], 3 June 1867, letters sent, entry 3653, vol. 49 (Austin, Tex.), BRFAL-FO.

73. De Forest, *A Union Officer in the Reconstruction*, 115 (first and last quotations); comments of Caleby Sibley's adjutant general, Oct. 1867, quoted in Cimbala, *Under the Guardianship of the Nation*, 203; Jas. R. Ferree to O. O. Howard, 19 Sept. 1865, letters received, reel 14, BRFAL (M752). See also Schmidt, *Free to Work*, 188–89; Cimbala, *Under the Guardianship of the Nation*, 202–3.

74. *Public Laws of North Carolina, 1866–67* (Raleigh, N.C.: Wm. E. Pell, State Printer, 1867),10–11; case of Ailsie Merrit quoted in Barry A. Crouch, "Seeking Equality: Houston Black Women during Reconstruction," in *The Dance of Freedom: Texas African Americans during Reconstruction*, ed. Larry Madaras (Austin: University of Texas Press, 2007), 73. On the actions of the North Carolina General Assembly, see Zipf, *Labor of Innocents*, 102–5. For the case of Sylvia Darden, see Jesse Aycock to N. Sellers Hill, 27 May 1867, letters received, entry 933, box 21 (Macon, Ga.), BRFAL-FO. For the case of Virginia Berry, see [F. A. E. Gaebel] to S. A. McLenden, 14 June 1866, letters received and miscellaneous papers relating to complaints, entry 883, box 18 (Fort Gaines, Ga.), BRFAL-FO.

75. A. F. Hayden to J. W. Keller, 14 June 1866 and 3 Nov. 1866, unregistered letters received, entry 1602 (Franklin, La.), BRFAL-FO; De Forest, *A Union Officer in the Reconstruction*, 113. It is not known whether the freedwoman in Franklin, Louisiana, identified only as Phillis in bureau records ever recovered her daughter.

76. C. C. Hubbard to E. Bamberger, 30 Dec. 1865, registered letters received, entry 2200 (Jackson, Miss.), BRFAL-FO; P. F. Duggan to [acting assistant adjutant general], 1 Aug. 1867, reports of operations and conditions, reel 21, BRFAL-TX; I. C. DeGress to D. F. Meyers, 13 Dec. 1865, letters sent, entry 3716, vol. 100 (Houston, Tex.), BRFAL-FO.

77. Richardson to S. C. Plummer, 29 May 1867, letters received, vol. 49 (Prairie Lea, Tex.), BRFAL-FO, quoted in Crouch, "To Enslave the Rising Generation," 271–72; case of Madison Day and Maria Richardson in F. E. Grossmann to [bureau headquarters in Lake City, Fla.], 1 Oct. 1866, reproduced in Berlin and others, "Afro-American Families," 98. On custody disputes between black parents, see Mitchell, *Raising Freedom's Child*, 164–67; Frankel, *Freedom's Women*, 135–37.

78. Orders of the assistant commission's office in Florida quoted in Berlin and others, "Afro-American Families," 97; Texas bureau officials quoted in Crouch, "Seeking Equality," 71.

79. William H. Webster to W. H. Sterling, 30 April 1867, letters sent, entry 1490 (Baton Rouge, La.), BRFAL-FO.

80. William Fowler to Robinson, 22 June 1866, letters received, reel 9, BRFAL-MS; Zipf, *Labor of Innocents*, 80–81.

81. Molly Coalman to General Ord, 20 Jan. 1868, unregistered letters received, reel 27, BRFAL-MS. See also Frankel, *Freedom's Women*, 135–36.

82. M. E. Davis to "Whom It May Concern," 7 Sept. 1868, letters sent, entry 3716, vol. 104 (Houston, Tex.), BRFAL-FO. See also William A. J. Finney to [Danville, Virginia, Freedmen's Bureau], 8 Feb. 1866, letters received, entry 3948, box 14 (Danville, Va.), BRFAL-FO.

83. Julian Battle v. Soloman Hadge, 20 May [1868], register of complaints, entry 877, vol. 368 (Dawson, Ga.), BRFAL-FO.

84. P. P. Bergeoni, "Report of Operations and Conditions for October 1868," narrative reports from subordinate officers, reel 33, BRFAL-MS.

85. John Burbridge (cold.) v. Mary Winder (cold.), 19 June 1867, proceedings of freedmen's court, entry 4352, vol. 506 (Yorktown, Va.), BRFAL-FO. For similar cases in which parents emphasized economic motives to retain custody and control of their children, see, for example, M. W. Wagner to Edgar M. Gregory, 15 March 1866, letters received, reel 9, BRFAL-TX; George Corliss to Edward M. Gresham, 30 Dec. 1867, letters sent, entry 2207 (Lake Station, Miss.), BRFAL-FO; [?] to Wm. M. Este, 26 Nov. 1864, in "Communication from Major General Lew Wallace," 61–62; James Murray to H. H.

Lockwood, 27 Dec. 1867, in "Communication from Major General Lew Wallace," 76–77; Emeline Woolford to Wallace, 22 Dec. 1864, in "Communication from Major General Lew Wallace," 78.

86. John J. Knox to Faus Randall, 27 March 1867, letters sent, entry 718, vol. 169 (Athens, Ga.), BRFAL-FO John J. Knox to Hannah David, 24 Jan. 1868, letters sent, entry 718, vol. 169 (Athens, Ga.), BRFAL-FO; John J. Knox to George Marshall, 20 March 1868, letters sent, entry 718, vol. 169 (Athens, Ga.), BRFAL-FO; Maria Scaggs v. Campbell Frigg, 4 April 1867, register of complaints, entry 3661, vol. 62 (Bastrop, Tex.), BRFAL-FO.

87. Fisk, *Plain Counsels*, 59, 60; Cimbala, *Under the Guardianship of the Nation*, 196. See also Fisk, *Plain Counsels*, 42.

88. Susan Hardy (also spelled "Haley") v. William Hunter, register of complaints, entry 859, vol. 238 (Cuthbert, Ga.), BRFAL-FO.

89. U.S. v. Andrew Jackson, Catherine Martin, 14 Sept. 1866, proceedings before the provost court, entry 1465, box, 3 (Algiers, La.), BRFAL-FO; U.S. v. Henry Johnson [Andrew Jackson], 16 Sept. 1866, register of court trials, entry 1466, vol. 197 (Algiers, La.), BRFAL-FO; Howell C. Flourney to Charles Mason, 25 Jan. 1868, entry 725, vol. 171 (Athens, Ga.), BRFAL-FO; affidavit of Emily Bush, 26 Sept. 1867, letters received, entry 2239 (Macon, Miss.), BRFAL-FO; P. P. Bergeoni, "Report of Operations and Conditions for October 1868," narrative reports from subordinate officers, reel 33, BRFAL-MS. For a similar instance in which the bureau denied custody to a freedwoman based on her character and reputation, see, for example, complaint of P. A. Summy, 16 Feb. 1867, register of complaints, entry 723, vol. 174 (Athens, Ga.), BRFAL-FO.

90. Testimony of Jennie Hill, in John W. Blassingame, ed., *Slave Testimony: Two Centuries of Letters, Speeches, Interviews, and Autobiographies* (Baton Rouge: Louisiana State University Press, 1977), 593. Hill was careful to note that despite even the most Herculean efforts on the part of both parents and children, she recalled only one instance when a family was actually reunited. On bureau consideration of the wants of freedchildren, see also Mitchell, *Raising Freedom's Child*, 74–76. See also James Marten, *The Children's Civil War* (Chapel Hill: University of North Carolina Press, 1998), 189, 195–99, 203.

91. Testimony of Frankie Goole, in George P. Rawick, ed., *The American Slave: A Composite Autobiography* (Westport, Conn.: Greenwood Press, 1972–79), vol. 16 (Tenn.), 19–21; testimony of Sarah Debro, in Belinda Hurmence, ed., *My Folks Don't Want Me to Talk about Slavery: Twenty-one Oral Histories of Former North Carolina Slaves* (Winston-Salem, N.C.: John F. Blair, 1984), 59.

92. Statement of Margaret Wesendonck, 2 Aug. 1866, letters and orders received, entry 3929 (Christiansburg, Va.), BRFAL-FO.

93. J. C. Johnson to D. Tillson, 19 Nov. 1866, unregistered letters received, reel 27, BRFAL-GA; E. Pickett to J. C. Johnson, 26 Nov. 1866, letters sent, reel 4, BRFAL-GA; C. K. Smith to O. O. Howard, 5 Nov. 1867, letters received, reel 17, BRFAL-GA; J. P. Richardson to John M. Davis, 8 Jan. 1868, letters sent, reel 1, BRFAL-TX; Daniel F. Dulany to [?], 1 Sept. 1866, letters received, reel 46, BRFAL (M752); Edmund Scott v. Catherine Pendleton, 30 Jan. 1867, register of complaints, entry 4086, vol. 304 (Lynchburg, Va.), BRFAL-FO; John H. Brough to G. Clements, 11 Dec. 1867, letters sent, entry 1577, vol. 262 (Donaldsonville, La.), BRFAL-FO. Because of his position, John Calvin Johnson forwarded the dispute to Assistant Commissioner Davis Tillson for settlement. For similar cases in which the bureau permitted freedchildren who refused to return to their parents to remain, see, for example, complaint of Dinah Murray, 18 April 1867, register of complaints, entry 763, vol. 157 (Augusta, Ga.), BRFAL-FO; J. T. White to J. M. Lee, 16 Oct. 1867, letters sent, entry 1802, vol. 401 (New Orleans, La.), BRFAL-FO; J. R. Folles to J. M. Lee, 15 Nov. 1869, unregistered letters received, entry 1452, box 2 (Algiers,

La.), BRFAL-FO; complaint, 26 April 1867, journal of business, entry 1799, vol. 449 (New Iberia, La.), BRFAL-FO; complaint of A. Gaudin v. E. Laroix, 6 May 1868, court cases, complaints, and journal of business, entry 1586, vol. 267 (Donaldsonville, La.), BRFAL-FO; John H. Brough to W. H. Sterling, 20 March 1867, letters sent, entry 1577, vol. 262 (Donaldsonville, La.), BRFAL-FO; complaint of Edith Jackson, 15 July 1867, daily journal of business relating to complaints and paperwork, entry 1556, vol. 251 (Clinton, La.), BRFAL-FO; A. Finch to J. A. Mower, 27 Aug. 1867, letters sent, entry 1512 (Bayou Sara, La.), BRFAL-FO; R. G. Rutherford to J. R. Stone, 2 March 1868, letters sent, entry 3906, vol. 122 (Burkesville, Va.), BRFAL-FO; Salina Parker v. Mrs. Smith, 6 May 1867, register of complaints, entry 3869, vol. 98 (Alexandria, Va.), BRFAL-FO; complaint of [?] Henry, 24 Aug. 1867, register of complaints, entry 5868, vol. 98 (Alexandria, Va.), BRFAL-FO; endorsement of J. A. Ross, 14 Sept. 1866, letters received, entry 3850, vol. 85 (Alexandria, Va.), BRFAL-FO; John L. Murphy to Conway, 30 July 1865, registered letters and telegrams received, reel 11, BRFAL-LA; John M. Davis to [bureau], 16 May 1867, letters received, reel 5, BRFAL-TX; J. B. Bostwick to W. H. Sinclair, 23 March 1866, letters received, reel 4, BRFAL-TX; Margaret Kent to [bureau], 26 July 1866, letters received, reel 33, BRFAL (M752); C. Whittlesey to O. Brown, 11 July 1868, letters received, reel 61, BRFAL (M752); F. D. Sewall to O. Brown, 8 Sept. 1868, BRFAL (M752).

94. J. Eaton to O. O. Howard, 15 Dec. 1865, U.S. Senate, "Reports of the Assistant Commissioners [1865–66]," 151.

95. De Forest, *A Union Officer in the Reconstruction*, 112.

96. Circular letter issued by C. C. Richardson, 17 Jan. 1866, letters sent, entry 1036, vol. 379 (Thomasville, Ga.), BRFAL-FO; Zipf, *Labor of Innocents*, 81.

97. De Forest, *A Union Officer in the Reconstruction*, 113; J. Eaton to O. O. Howard, 15 Dec. 1865, U.S. Senate, "Reports of the Assistant Commissioners [1865–66]," 151; statement of Jane Kamper, in Berlin and Rowland, *Families and Freedom*, 214.

98. Lucy Lee to W. E. W. Ross, 10 Jan. 1865, in "Communication from Major General Lew Wallace," 68–69; see also 19. This black mother's pleas went unheard; bound in a legal apprenticeship agreement in 1860, her daughter was required to serve out the indenture.

5. "strict justice for every man, woman, and child": Gender, Justice, and the Freedmen's Bureau

1. Samuel Thomas to O. O. Howard, 21 Sept. 1865, letters received, reel 22, BRFAL (M752).

2. Clinton B. Fisk, "Memorandum of report of General Fisk of January 23, 1866," in U.S. Senate, "Reports of the Assistant Commissioners of the Bureau of Refugees, Freedmen, and Abandoned Lands [1865–66]," 39th Cong., 1st sess., Senate Executive Document 27 (Serial 1238), 12 (first and last quotations); "Rules and Regulations for Assistant Commissioners," Circular No. 5, issued by O. O. Howard, 30 May 1865, in U.S. House of Representatives, "Report of the Commissioner of the Bureau of Refugees, Freedmen, and Abandoned Lands," [n.d.] Dec. 1865, 39th Cong., 1st sess., House Executive Document 11 (Serial 1255), 45; endorsement of Davis Tillson to Judge of County Court, Pike County, 26 Sept. 1866, on E. M. L. Ehlers to W. W. Deane, 3 Sept. 1866, letters received, reel 13, BRFAL-GA.

3. H. B. Sprague to Davis Tillson, 10 Jan. 1866, unregistered letters received, reel 29, BRFAL-GA; W. B. Pease to Judge B. P. Fuller, 8 March 1867, letters sent, entry 3716, vol. 101 (Houston, Tex.), BRFAL-FO. This particular local bureau's pronouncement asserting the rights of freedwomen did not depict the women, referred to as "wenches" throughout, as either virtuous or citizens. Rather, it asserted the rights of women (white and black) only in an effort to demonstrate to a white employer that he could not use corporal punishment against his black female employees. In full, the statement reads: "Any

man who assaults a woman is worse than a brute, for brutes do not bite or injure females of their kind. It may have been well enough in former times for a white man to 'wallup' a wench the state of society prehaps demanded it. But those days are passed and men who now presume to indulge their brutish propensities by beating and kicking women must be taught that in the eyes of the law the wench is entitled to the same privileges and immunities and the same protection that is accorded to the wife of their neighbor or the daughter of the[ir] Mother."

4. Laura F. Edwards, *Scarlett Doesn't Live Here Anymore: Southern Women in the Civil War Era* (Urbana: University of Illinois Press, 2000), 148; Nancy Patten to Mr. Allen, 11 Feb. 1867, letters received, entry 3028 (Abbeville Court House, S.C.), BRFAL-FO, quoted in Julie Saville, *The Work of Reconstruction: From Slave to Wage Laborer in South Carolina, 1860–1870* (New York: Cambridge University Press, 1994), 122–23. Without question, freedwomen's complaints to the bureau about domestic discord and violations of their bodies (aside from those connected to labor disputes) were far fewer in number than those involving their labor and their children. On the nature of freedwomen's complaints, see, besides this work, Leslie A. Schwalm, *A Hard Fight for We: Women's Transition from Slavery to Freedom in South Carolina* (Urbana: University of Illinois Press, 1997), 148, 235, 244, 260–66, 358 n. 86; Nancy D. Bercaw, *Gendered Freedoms: Race, Rights, and the Politics of the Household in the Delta, 1861–1875* (Gainesville: University Press of Florida, 2003), 146–47, 150–57; Susan Eva O'Donovan, *Becoming Free in the Cotton South* (Cambridge, Mass.: Harvard University Press, 2007), 135–36, 196–99, 203; Noralee Frankel, *Freedom's Women: Black Women and Families in Civil War Era Mississippi* (Bloomington: Indiana University Press, 1999), 179; Jacqueline Jones, *Labor of Love, Labor of Sorrow: Black Women, Work, and the Family from Slavery to the Present* (New York: Basic Books, 1985), 53–54.

5. Hannah Rosen, *Terror in the Heart of Freedom: Citizenship, Sexual Violence, and the Meaning of Race in the Postemancipation South* (Chapel Hill: University of North Carolina Press, 2009), 11. See also Rogers Smith, *Civic Ideals: Conflicting Visions of Citizenship in U.S. History* (New Haven, Conn.: Yale University Press, 1997), chap. 10.

6. Oliver Otis Howard, *Autobiography of Oliver Otis Howard* (New York: Baker and Taylor, 1907), 2:251.

7. James Oakes, "A Failure of Vision: The Collapse of the Freedmen's Bureau Courts," *Civil War History* 25 (1979): 67; Elizabeth B. Clark, "'The Sacred Rights of the Weak': Pain, Sympathy, and the Culture of Individual Rights in Antebellum America," *Journal of American History* 82, no. 2 (1995): 487; U.S. House of Representatives, "Report of the Commissioner [1865]," 22, 32, 42. On the rights of freedmen and women in the immediacy of emancipation, see in particular Paul A. Cimbala, *The Freedmen's Bureau: Reconstructing the American South after the Civil War* (Malabar, Fla.: Krieger, 2005), 91–92; Paul A. Cimbala, *Under the Guardianship of the Nation: The Freedmen's Bureau and the Reconstruction of Georgia, 1865–1870* (Athens: University of Georgia Press, 1997), 14–15; Clark, "The Sacred Rights of the Weak," 487–88, 490–92; Laura F. Edwards, *The People and Their Peace: Legal Culture and the Transformation of Inequality in the Postrevolutionary South* (Chapel Hill: University of North Carolina Press, 2009), 286–91; Herman Belz, *Emancipation and Equal Rights: Politics and Constitutionalism in the Civil War Era* (New York: W. W. Norton, 1978), chap. 3; LaWanda Cox, "Reflections on the Limits of the Possible," in *Freedom, Racism, and Reconstruction: Collected Writings of LaWanda Cox*, ed. Donald G. Nieman (Athens: University of Georgia Press, 1997), 257.

8. "Rules and Regulations for Assistant Commissioners," Circular No. 5, issued by O. O. Howard, 30 May 1865, in U.S. House of Representatives, "Report of the Commissioner [1865]," 45; Donald G. Nieman, *To Set the Law in Motion: The Freedmen's Bureau and the Legal Rights of Blacks, 1865–1868* (Millwood, N.Y.: KTO Press, 1979), 4–28 (quotation on 9). See also Oakes, "A Failure of Vision," 66–76; Eric Foner, *Reconstruction:*

America's Unfinished Revolution, 1863–1877 (New York: Harper & Row, 1988), 68–70; Randy Finley, *From Slavery to Uncertain Freedom: The Freedmen's Bureau in Arkansas, 1865–1869* (Fayetteville: University of Arkansas Press, 1996), chap. 6.

9. Howard, *Autobiography*, 2:252, 253; Sidney Andrews, *The South since the War: As Shown by Fourteen Weeks of Travel and Observation in Georgia and the Carolinas* (Boston: Ticknor & Fields, 1866; reprint, Boston: Houghton Mifflin, 1974), 371.

10. General Orders No. 6, 1 Aug. 1865, scrapbook of orders issued and received, reel 29, BRFAL-MS; Whittlesey to Howard, 15 Oct. 1865, letters received, BRFAL (M752); circular letter issued by Clinton B. Fisk, June 1865, in U.S. Senate, "Reports of the Assistant Commissioners [1865–66]," 44; U.S. House of Representatives, "Report of the Commissioner [1865]," 22–23; Cimbala, *The Freedmen's Bureau*, 103. See also Nieman, *To Set the Law in Motion*, 8–9; Oakes, "A Failure of Vision," 68–69; William A. Blair, "Justice versus Law and Order: The Battles over the Reconstruction of Virginia's Minor Judiciary, 1865–1870," *Virginia Magazine of History and Biography* 103 (1995): 166; Sara Rapport, "The Freedmen's Bureau as a Legal Agent for Black Men and Women in Georgia, 1865–1868," *Georgia Historical Quarterly* 73 (1989): 26–53. On the variety of actions taken by the bureau to adjudicate complaints involving blacks, see Howard, *Autobiography*, 2:252–53; George R. Bentley, *A History of the Freedmen's Bureau* (Philadelphia: University of Pennsylvania, 1955), chap. 11; Cimbala, *The Freedmen's Bureau*, 94–106; Nieman, *To Set the Law in Motion*; Oakes, "A Failure of Vision."

By late 1866, Commissioner Howard had reconsidered turning over direct judicial involvement to the states. Using the expanded authority granted by Congress in the second bureau bill in July 1866, Howard discreetly authorized assistant commissioners to reassert jurisdiction of cases involving freedpeople. Although southern states had abandoned racial distinctions in testimony, "impartial justice," he insisted, was "seldom administered." "I am of the opinion," he explained, "that in the Courts of superior jurisdiction, the judges are generally disposed to deal fairly with the negro, but it is notorious that he stands little or no chance before a jury or magistrate of inferior jurisdiction." O. O. Howard to E. M. Stanton, 19 Jan. 1867, letters sent, reel 3, BRFAL (M742). See also O. O. Howard to each assistant commissioner, 19 Sept. 1866, letters sent, reel 2, BRFAL (M742). For a discussion of the secretive nature of Howard's orders to assistant commissioners to reassert judicial authority, see Nieman, *To Set the Law in Motion*, 144–47.

11. Freedmen's Bureau bill quoted in Nieman, *To Set the Law in Motion*, 108. For the full text of the legislation, see Edward McPherson, *The Political History of the United States of America during the Period of Reconstruction* (Washington, D.C.: Solomons & Chapman, 1875), 72–84. See also Nieman, *To Set the Law in Motion*, 108–9, 115, 221; Cimbala, *The Freedmen's Bureau*, 99–103; Oakes, "A Failure of Vision," 75; Brooks D. Simpson, "Ulysses S. Grant and the Freedmen's Bureau," in *The Freedmen's Bureau and Reconstruction: Reconsiderations*, ed. Paul A. Cimbala and Randall M. Miller (New York: Fordham University Press, 1999), 14–20. On President Andrew Johnson's veto, see John Cox and LaWanda Cox, "Andrew Johnson and His Ghost Writers: An Analysis of the Freedmen's Bureau and Civil Rights Veto Messages," *Mississippi Valley Historical Review* 48 (1961): 460–79.

12. *Statutes at Large of USA* 14 (1866): 27–30; U.S. Const. amend. XIV, sec. 1. See also Nieman, *To Set the Law in Motion*, 109; Foner, *Reconstruction*, 243–44; Harold M. Hyman, *A More Perfect Union: The Impact of the Civil War and Reconstruction on the Constitution* (New York: Alfred A. Knopf, 1973), 461–62; Randall M. Miller, "The Freedmen's Bureau and Reconstruction: An Overview," in Cimbala and Miller, *The Freedmen's Bureau and Reconstruction*, xvii.

13. Robert J. Kaczorowski, *The Politics of Judicial Interpretation: The Federal Courts, Department of Justice, and Civil Rights, 1866–1876* (New York: Oceana Publications, 1985;

reprint, with a new introduction, New York: Fordham University Press, 2004), chap. 2 (quotations on 21). On the sufficiency and possibilities of Reconstruction-era federal and constitutional law, see also Laura F. Edwards, "Civil War and Reconstruction," in *The Cambridge History of Law in America*, vol. 2, *The Long Nineteenth Century (1789–1920)*, edited by Michael Grossberg and Christopher Tomlins (New York: Cambridge University Press, 2008), especially 327–44; Cox, "Reflections on the Limits of the Possible."

14. The historian W. E. B. Du Bois concludes his study of Reconstruction with the assessment that "The attempt to make black men American citizens was in a certain sense all a failure, but a splendid failure." W. E. B. Du Bois, *Black Reconstruction in America, 1860–1880* (New York: Harcourt, Brace, 1935; reprint, New York: Atheneum, 1992), 708. On the determination of former slaves to claim rights and to use the legal system to their benefit in Reconstruction, see Edwards, *The People and Their Peace*, 79, 286–91; Laura F. Edwards, *Gendered Strife and Confusion: The Political Culture of Reconstruction* (Urbana: University of Illinois Press, 1997); Laura F. Edwards, "Women and the Law: Domestic Discord in North Carolina after the Civil War," in *Local Matters: Race, Crime, and Justice in the Nineteenth-Century South*, ed. Christopher Waldrep and Donald G. Nieman (Athens: University of Georgia Press, 2001), 125–54; James D. Schmidt, *Free to Work: Labor Law, Emancipation, and Reconstruction, 1815–1880* (Athens: University of Georgia Press, 1999), 177–78; Rosen, *Terror in the Heart of Freedom*, 8–9, 17–18, 38–39, 50–53, 75–82, 204–207, 224–56, 222–41; Barry A. Crouch, "Black Dreams and White Justice," *Prologue* 6, no. 4 (1974): 255–65; Nieman, *To Set the Law in Motion*; Cimbala, *Under the Guardianship of the Nation*, chap. 8; Rapport, "The Freedmen's Bureau as a Legal Agent." On slaves' familiarity with law, see, for example, Edwards, *The People and Their Peace*; Laura F. Edwards, "Enslaved Women and the Law: Paradoxes of Subordination in the Post-revolutionary Carolinas," *Slavery and Abolition* 26 (2005): 305–23; Glenn McNair, "Slave Women, Capital Crime, and Criminal Justice in Georgia," *Georgia Historical Quarterly* 93, no. 2 (2009): 135–58; Timothy S. Huebner, "The Roots of Fairness: *State v. Caesar* and Slave Justice in Antebellum North Carolina," in Waldrep and Nieman, *Local Matters*, 29–52; Judith Kelleher Schafer, "Slaves and Crime: New Orleans, 1846–1862," in Waldrep and Nieman, *Local Matters*, 53–91; Ariela J. Gross, "The Law and the Culture of Slavery: Natchez, Mississippi," in Waldrep and Nieman, *Local Matters*, 92–124; Ariela J. Gross, *Double Character: Slavery and Mastery in the Antebellum Southern Courtroom* (Princeton, N.J.: Princeton University Press, 2000); Judith Kelleher Schafer, *Slavery, the Civil Law, and the Supreme Court of Louisiana* (Baton Rouge: Louisiana State University Press, 1997).

15. H. C. Flourney to T. D. Elliot, 8 Jan. 1868, letters sent, entry 725, vol. 171 (Athens, Ga.), BRFAL-FO. For a similar observation, see John Richard Dennett, *The South As It Is, 1865–1866*, ed. Henry M. Christman (New York: Viking Press, 1965; reprint, Athens: University of Georgia Press, 1986), 54–55.

16. Eliza Frances Andrews, *The War-time Journal of a Georgia Girl* (New York: D. Appleton, 1908), 347; freedwomen responding to emancipation, quoted in Dorothy Sterling, ed., *We Are Your Sisters: Black Women in the Nineteenth Century* (New York: W. W. Norton, 1984), 310, 317–18; Thavolia Glymph, *Out of the House of Bondage: The Transformation of the Plantation Household* (Cambridge: Cambridge University Press, 2008), 17; John William De Forest, *A Union Officer in the Reconstruction*, ed. James H. Croushore and David Morris Potter (New Haven, Conn.: Yale University Press, 1948; reprint, Baton Rouge: Louisiana State University Press, 1976), 36.

17. J. R. Johnson to S. P. Lee, 1 June 1866, unregistered letters received, entry 3853 (Alexandria, Va.), BRFAL-FO, in Ira Berlin, Joseph P. Reidy, and Leslie S. Rowland, eds., *The Black Military Experience*, series 2 of *Freedom: A Documentary History of Emancipation, 1861–1867* (Cambridge: Cambridge University Press, 1982), 672; address commemorating the first anniversary of emancipation on 5 Jan. 1866, reported in the *Colored*

American, 13 Jan. 1866, quoted in Catherine Clinton, "Reconstructing Freedwomen," in *Divided Houses: Gender and the Civil War*, ed. Catherine Clinton and Nina Silber (New York: Oxford University Press, 1992), 307; Edwards, *Gendered Strife and Confusion*, 47. On the importance of marriage to African Americans, see Peter W. Bardaglio, *Reconstructing the Household: Families, Sex, and the Law in the Nineteenth-Century South* (Chapel Hill: University of North Carolina Press, 1995), 132–33; Bercaw, *Gendered Freedoms*, 99–116; Ira Berlin and Leslie S. Rowland, eds., *Families and Freedom: A Documentary History of African-American Kinship in the Civil War Era* (New York: New Press, 1997), 155–91; Cimbala, *Under the Guardianship of the Nation*, 193–94; Edwards, *Gendered Strife and Confusion*, 45–54, 51–53, 95–97; Frankel, *Freedom's Women*, chap. 4; Herbert G. Gutman, *The Black Family in Slavery and Freedom, 1750–1925* (New York: Pantheon Books, 1976), 412–18, 425–30; Schwalm, *A Hard Fight for We*, 239–44; Norma Basch, "Marriage and Domestic Relations," in *The Cambridge History of Law in America*, vol. 2, *The Long Nineteenth Century (1789–1920)*, ed. Michael Grossberg and Christopher Tomlins (New York: Cambridge University Press, 2008), 270. Not all former slaves responded to emancipation by legitimizing unions according to southern law and/or federal policies. On the reluctance of recently emancipated slaves to marry legally, see Ira Berlin, Steven F. Miller, and Leslie S. Rowland, eds., "Afro-American Families in the Transition from Slavery to Freedom," *Radical History Review* 42 (1988): 92, 98; Frankel, *Freedom's Women*, 43, 79–84, 87; Schwalm, *A Hard Fight for We*, 340–44; Edwards, *Gendered Strife and Confusion*, 54–59.

18. Bercaw, *Gendered Freedoms*, 155; complaint of Albert Matthews [against his wife, Mary Bennett], 9 May 1868, register of complaints, entry 723, vol. 174 (Athens, Ga.), BRFAL-FO. On freedwomen's assertions of authority within their own households and their willingness to allow husbands and fathers to represent them in public, see, for example, Elsa Barkley Brown, "Negotiating and Transforming the Public Sphere: African American Political Life in the Transition from Slavery to Freedom," *Public Culture* 7 (1994): 107–46; Bercaw, *Gendered Freedoms*, especially 146–57; O'Donovan, *Becoming Free*, 196–207; Frankel, *Freedom's Women*, especially 124–35.

19. Leslie Schwalm and Susan O'Donovan likewise contend that freedwomen willingly used bureau notions of dependency and domesticity to their advantage. See, for example, Schwalm, *A Hard Fight for We*, 260–66; O'Donovan, *Becoming Free*, 197. For a sampling of the kinds of domestic complaints initiated by freedwomen to the bureau, see, for example, those reprinted in Sterling, *We Are Your Sisters*, 338–42.

20. Examples are abundant, but for some cases in which freedwomen complained of abandonment, see John J. Knox to [bureau subassistant commissioner in Charleston, S.C.], 21 Feb. 1867, letters sent, entry 718, vol. 169 (Athens, Ga.), BRFAL-FO; Stephen R. Palmer to Jno. D. G. Cotting, 29 Feb. 1868, unregistered letters received, entry 759, box 9 (Augusta, Ga.), BRFAL-FO; R. E. Folles to W. H. Sterling, 22 April 1868, letters sent, entry 1447, vol. 187 (Algiers, La.), BRFAL-FO; Lee Ann Anderson v. Josiah Anderson, 20 Dec. 1867, letters sent, entry 1546, vol. 245 (Clinton, La.), BRFAL-FO; Emily Jackson v. Soloman Jackson, 8 June 1867, complaints of Isabella Jones, 4 July 1867, Lena Graham, 6 July 1867, Mary Carter, 16 July 1867, and Amy Thompson, 14 Sept. 1867, daily journal of business relating to complaints and paperwork, entry 1558, vol. 251 (Clinton, La.), BRFAL-FO; J. W. Keller to S. O. Parker, 30 June 1867, letters sent, entry 1598, vol. 274 (Franklin, La.), BRFAL-FO; complaints of Celestine Broussard, 17 Aug. 1867, and Julia Ann, 8 Feb. 1868, journal of business, entry 1799, vol. 499 (New Iberia, La.), BRFAL-FO; L. Jolissaint to W. W. Tyler, 5 Aug. 1867, letters sent, entry 1802, vol. 401 (New Orleans, La.), BRFAL-FO; Diana Jackson v. Joseph Jackson, 13 May 1867, Philomene Morris v. Lacroix, 16 July 1867, Georgiana Singleton v. Henry Levy, 13 Nov. 1867, register of complaints, entry 1807, vol. 404 (New Orleans, La.), BRFAL-FO; J. H. Hastings to Mr.

Thomas Dohan, 22 Oct. 1866, letters sent, entry 1859, vol. 462 (St. Joseph, La.), BRFAL-FO; Kitty Sullivan v. "her husband," 3 May 1866, Julia Davis v. Gilbert, 10 May 1866, and Maria Lankersley v. John Fuller, 21 June 1866, register of complaints, entry 3720, vol. 109 (Houston, Tex.), BRFAL-FO; Mariah Randon v. Lorenzo Randon, 27 May 1867, letters sent, entry 3755, vol. 145 (Richmond, Tex.), BRFAL-FO; Mariah Randon v. Lorenzo Randon, 27 May 1867, Diana Hunter v. Peter Hunter, 29 May 1867, Hettie Hayses v. Ransom Hunter, 30 May 1867, Mariah Burton v. Jack Burton, 4 June 1867, and Martha Williams v. Henry Williams, 4 June 1867, endorsements sent, entry 3756, vol. 147 (Richmond, Tex.), BRFAL-FO; Martha Pry v. Smith Pry, 11 Jan. 1867, Amelia Maynard v. Charles Maynard, 6 April 1867, and Louisa Grandison v. Wallace Grandison, 29 Sept. 1868, register of complaints, entry 3868, vol. 98 (Alexandria, Va.), BRFAL-FO; complaints of Margaret Robins, 14 Aug. 1867, and Catherine Johnson, 6 Nov. 1867, register of complaints, entry 3868, vol. 98 (Alexandria, Va.), BRFAL-FO.

21. For cases in which freedwomen appealed to the Freedmen's Bureau to hold husbands accountable for adultery, see, for example, affidavits of Jane Joung, 23 April 1867, and Ann Martin, 27 May 1867, affidavits of freedmen and charges and specifications against citizens and military personnel, entry 695, vol. 237 (Albany, Ga.), BRFAL-FO; Charles Rauschenberg to Peter Daniel, 31 Aug. 1868, letters sent, entry 697, vol. 124 (Albany, Ga.), BRFAL-FO; John J. Knox to O. H. Howard, 29 April 1868, letters sent, entry 718, vol. 170 (Athens, Ga.), BRFAL-FO; [bureau agent in Cuthbert, Ga.] to S. A. McLenden, 14 June 1866, letters received and miscellaneous papers relating to complaints, entry 883, box 18 (Fort Gaines, Ga.), BRFAL-FO; Wm. Dougherty to M. A. Reno, 24 June 1866, letters received, entry 1452, box 2 (Algiers, La.), BRFAL-FO; Hester Barbee v. Simon Barbee, 21 Dec. 1867, letters sent, entry 1546 (Clinton, La.), BRFAL-FO; complaint of Lena Graham, 23 Aug. 1867, daily journal of business relating to complaints and paperwork, entry 1558, vol. 251 (Clinton, La.), BRFAL-FO; complaint of Caroline Robinson, 20 Aug. 1867, register of complaints, entry 3657, vol. 52 (Austin, Tex.), BRFAL-FO; Jane v. Handy, 12 June 1867, register of complaints, entry 3680, vol. 58 (Bryan, Tex.), BRFAL-FO; Bryon Porter to Jacob, 10 Jan. 1866, letters sent, entry 3716, vol. 100 (Houston, Tex.), BRFAL-FO; W. B. Pease to Jas. P. Hutchinson, 19 March 1867, and W. B. Pease to Edward Miller, 21 March 1867, letters sent, entry 3716, vol. 101 (Houston, Tex.), BRFAL-FO; Milly Barnes v. Alfred Harroll, 24 June 1867, register of complaints, entry 3720, vol. 108 (Houston, Tex.), BRFAL-FO; Maria Flowers v. Wash Sessmms, 3 Feb. 1866, Ester Johnson v. Robert Johnson, 19 May 1866, Annette Caswell v. Caswell Bannister, 12 March 1867, Ann America Grier v. Riley Grier, 27 March 1867, Geo. Lewis v. Nellie Lewis, 23 May 1867, and Eliza Williams v. Sterling Williams, 5 June 1867, register of complaints, entry 3720, vol. 109 (Houston, Tex.), BRFAL-FO; Lilly Johnson v. Belfield Johnson, 20 July and 6 Aug. 1866, register of complaints, entry 3924, vol. 131 (Charlottesville, Va.), BRFAL-FO; Jno. C. Dickson to Davis Tillson, 28 April 1866, unregistered letters received, reel 26, BRFAL-GA. The historian Noralee Frankel argues that freedwomen "rarely complained formally to the Freedmen's Bureau about male adultery on their own behalf" and points out that the few instances of male infidelity that do appear in the records of the bureau in Mississippi came in complaints involving "lack of financial provision for the children" (*Freedom's Women*, 102).

22. Sarah Runnels v. Adam Runnels, 2 Aug. 1867, register of complaints, entry 3672, vol. 70 (Boston, Tex.), BRFAL-FO; Thomas Lee to John D. Moore, 24 July 1867, letters sent, entry 2143 (Corinth, Miss.), BRFAL-FO; complaint of Ann Marie Brown, 13 June [1866], register of complaints, entry 3924 (Charlottesville, Va.), BRFAL-FO; complaint of Caroline Denby, 15 Oct. 1867, register of complaints, entry 2429, vol. 327 (Yazoo City, Miss.), BRFAL-FO; William Tidball to James A. Bates, 31 July 1866, monthly narrative reports of operations and conditions, reel 45, BRFAL-VA; Jerry Ellis v. Molly Ellis, 29 June 1866, register of complaints, entry 3924, vol. 131 (Charlottesville, Va.), BRFAL-FO;

George P. Corliss, report of complaints, 30 Sept. 1867, narrative reports from subordinate officers, reel 30, BRFAL-MS.

For instances in which freedmen appealed to the bureau to hold wives accountable for adultery, see for example [bureau agent in Lee and Dougherty counties, Ga.] to Lee County judge, 27 April 1867, affidavits of freedmen and charges and specifications against citizens and military personnel, entry 695, vol. 237 (Albany, Ga.), BRFAL-FO; Jerry Ellis v. Molly Ellis, 29 and 30 June 1866, and Isaac Scott v. Lucy Scott, 2 and 3 July 1866, register of complaints, entry 3924, vol. 131 (Charlottesville, Va.), BRFAL-FO; J. H. Chapman to James Biddle, 31 Aug. 1868, letters sent, entry 2357, vol. 275 (Vicksburg, Miss.), BRFAL-FO; complaint of Aaron McDonald, [n.d.] Nov. 1868, register of complaints, entry 2245, vol. 194 (Magnolia, Miss.), BRFAL-FO; De Gress to Rhoda Ann Licks, 8 Oct. 1866, and De Gress to Anna Allen, 22 Oct. 1866, both in letters sent, entry 3716, vol. 100 (Houston, Tex.), BRFAL-FO; Moses Jackson v. Carlinda Jackson, 6 July 1867, and Charles Smith v. Lizzie Smith, 24 Aug. 1867, both in registers of complaints, entry 3720, vol. 108 (Houston, Tex.), BRFAL-FO; Smith Welton v. His Wife, 25 May 1866, registers of complaints, entry 3720, vol. 109 (Houston, Tex.), BRFAL-FO. See also Barry A. Crouch, "Seeking Equality: Houston Black Women during Reconstruction," in *The Dance of Freedom: Texas African Americans during Reconstruction*, ed. Larry Madaras (Austin: University of Texas Press, 2007), 75; Frankel, *Freedom's Women*, 104–5.

23. Clinton B. Fisk, *Plain Counsels for Freedmen: In Sixteen Brief Lectures* (Boston: American Tract Society, 1866), 31–32; complaint of Jane Pace, 15 July 1868, register of complaints, entry 723, vol. 174 (Athens, Ga.), BRFAL-FO; Fisk, *Plain Counsels*, 26; remarks of Assistant Commissioner Alvan Gillem quoted in Frankel, *Freedom's Women*, 92; Bercaw, *Gendered Freedoms*, 109; Lilly Johnson v. Belfield Johnson, 20 July and 6 Aug. 1866, register of complaints, entry 3924, vol. 131 (Charlottesville, Va.), BRFAL-FO; "To the Freedmen," issued by O. Brown, 14[?] July 1865, enclosure in W. Storer to O. Brown, 14 July 1865, unregistered letters and telegrams received, BRFAL-VA, reprinted in Steven Hahn and others, eds., *Land and Labor, 1865*, series 3, vol. 1, of *Freedom: A Documentary History of Emancipation, 1861–1867* (Chapel Hill: University of North Carolina Press, 2008), 136–37. See also Bercaw, *Gendered Freedoms*, 111–12.

24. For instances in which freedwomen claimed child support for children abandoned or born out of wedlock, see, for example, [bureau agent in Lee and Dougherty counties, Ga.] to John W. McLennen, 23 April 1867, affidavits of freedmen and charges and specifications against citizens and military personnel, entry 695, vol. 237 (Albany, Ga.), BRFAL-FO; affidavit of Mathilda Dodd, 27 June 1867, letters sent, entry 697, vol. 122 (Albany, Ga.), BRFAL-FO; [bureau agent in Lee, Dougherty, and Terrell counties, Ga.] to Hon. Thomas C. Spicer, 20 July 1867, letters sent, entry 697, vol. 122 (Albany, Ga.), BRFAL-FO; complaints of Mary Johnson, 18 Feb. 1867, Caroline Thomas, 14 May 1868, Lucy Freeman, 4 June 1868, and Martha Steavens, 3 Sept. 1868, register of complaints, entry 723, vol. 174 (Athens, Ga.), BRFAL-FO; Stephen R. Palmer to Jno. D. G. Cotting, 29 Feb. 1868, unregistered letters received, entry 759, box 9 (Augusta, Ga.), BRFAL-FO; affidavit of Franky Ann Worrell, 8 Aug. 1867, orders received, contracts, and miscellaneous court papers, entry 857, box 16 (Cuthbert, Ga.), BRFAL-FO; R. E. Folles to W. H. Sterling, 22 April 1868, letters sent, entry 1447, vol. 187 (Algiers, La.), BRFAL-FO; Capus v. Capus, 6 June 1867, register of court trials, entry 1466, vol. 197 (Algiers, La.), BRFAL-FO; complaints of Helen Williams, 8 June 1867, Catherine Brown, 13 Aug. 1867, daily journal of business relating to complaints and paperwork, entry 1558, vol. 251 (Clinton, La.), BRFAL-FO; L. Jolissaint to Oscar Launuse, 11 June 1867, letters sent, entry 1802, vol. 401 (New Orleans, La.), BRFAL-FO; Diana Jackson v. Joe Jackson, 19 June 1867, register of complaints, entry 1807, vol. 404 (New Orleans, La.), BRFAL-FO; complaints of Martha Pelham, 4 June and 31 Oct. 1867, Betsey Tenny, 23 Aug. 1867, and Elizabeth Wallace, 21 Sept. 1867, register of complaints, entry 3657, vol. 52 (Austin, Tex.),

BRFAL-FO; Fanny Davis v. Charles Davis, 1 Dec. 1868, register of complaints, entry 3680, vol. 58 (Bryan, Tex.), BRFAL-FO; Bryon Porter to Jacob, 10 Jan. 1866, letters sent, entry 3716, vol. 100 (Houston, Tex.), BRFAL-FO; W. B. Pease to A. Doubleday, 15 April 1867, and W. B. Pease to E. Miller, 18 April 1867, letters sent, entry 3716, vol. 101 (Houston, Tex.), BRFAL-FO; Rachel Neal v. Adam Neal, 9 Feb. 1866, register of complaints, entry 3720, vol. 109 (Houston, Tex.), BRFAL-FO; Louisa Grandison v. Wallace Grandison, 29 Sept. 1868, Amelia Maynard v. Charles Maynard, 6 April 1867, complaints of Columbia Tibbs, ex parte, 14 Feb. 1868, Catherine Johnson, 6 Nov. 1867, and Margaret Robins, 14 Aug. 1867, register of complaints, entry 3868, vol. 98 (Alexandria, Va.), BRFAL-FO; Geo. W. Graham to T. P. Jackson, 14 Dec. 1868, letters sent, entry 3895, vol. 142 (Boydton, Va.), BRFAL-FO. See also O'Donovan, *Becoming Free*, 196–98; Frankel, *Freedom's Women*, 102, 111; Crouch, "Seeking Equality," 74–77.

25. Complaint of Mary Johnson, 18 Feb. 1867, register of complaints, entry 723, vol. 174 (Athens, Ga.), BRFAL-FO; Charles Rauschenberg to O. H. Howard, 19 May 1868, letters sent, entry 697, vol. 124 (Albany, Ga.), BRFAL-FO; case no. 70, Capus v. Capus, 6 June 1867, register of court trials, entry 1466, vol.197 (Algiers, La.), BRFAL-FO.

26. See, for example, complaints of Ellen Nesbit, 12 May 1868, Harriet Griffin, 11 and 15 June 1868, Matilda Barry, 22 June 1868, and Harriett Oglebly, 24 and 25 Aug. 1868, register of complaints, entry 723, vol. 174 (Athens, Ga.), BRFAL-FO; Howell C. Flourney to Drew Oglebly, 25 Aug. 1868, and Howell C. Flourney to Jno. S. Scales, 25 Aug. 1868, letters sent, entry 725, vol. 172 (Athens, Ga.), BRFAL-FO; complaints of Emma Hartsfield, 4 June 1867, and Milly, 28 Aug. and 14 Nov. 1867, register of complaints, entry 3657, vol. 52 (Austin, Tex.), BRFAL-FO.

27. Although not a complete record of the complaints brought to the bureau by freedwomen protesting abuse by husbands, see, for example, Charles Rauschenberg to Judge Spicer, 18 Feb. 1868, and Charles Rauschenberg to Ephraim, 20 Oct. 1868, letters sent, entry 697, vol. 124 (Albany, Ga.), BRFAL-FO; Sarah Jenkins v. Alford Jenkins, 13 March 1868, Malinda Jordon v. John Jordon, 21 and 25 July 1868, complaint of Emiline Middlebrook, 20 Aug. 1868, register of complaints, entry 723, vols. 174 and 176 (Athens, Ga.), BRFAL-FO; Emeline Miller v. Wyatt Henry, 9 Aug. 1867, Emeline Williams v. W. Frank Thorton, 26 Aug. 1867, Cinda Dowd v. Henry Dowd, 4 Aug. 1868, and Lina Baldwin v. Perry Owens, 2 Sept. 1867, register of complaints, entry 859, vol. 238 (Cuthbert, Ga.), BRFAL-FO; affidavit of Eliza O'Brien, 31 Aug. 1867, letters sent, entry, 881, vol. 258 (Fort Gaines, Ga.), BRFAL-FO; Eliza O'Brien v. Henry O'Brien, 31 Aug. 1867, register of cases tried in freedmen's court, entry 885, vol. 260½ (Fort Gaines, Ga.), BRFAL-FO; R. E. Folles to Hon. John Brownler, 22 April 1866, letters sent, entry 1447, vol. 187 (Algiers, La.), BRFAL-FO; U.S. v. Primus Seaman, Mrs. Seaman, 29 Aug. 1866, L. Elein v. R. Elein, 28 May 1867, and Heath v. Jackson, 19 June 1867, register of court trials, entry 1466, vol. 197 (Algiers, La.), BRFAL-FO; complaints of Mrs. Louisa Elein, 28 May 1867, and Mary Richardson, 15 June 1867, journal of business transacted, entry 1469, vol. 199 (Algiers, La.), BRFAL-FO; Margaret Story v. Geo. Story, 25 Sept. 1865, register of complaints, entry 1479 (Amite City, La.), BRFAL-FO; Caroline Craig v. Richard Craig, 10 May 1867, and Queen Morrison v. Ed. Morrison, 5 June 1867, complaints, entry 1499, vol. 222 (Baton Rouge, La.), BRFAL-FO; James DeGray to Isaac Doughty, 18 July 1866, James DeGray to Ben Franklin, 10 Aug. 1866, letters sent, entry 1546 (Clinton, La.), BRFAL-FO; complaints of Maria Nichols, 20 June 1867, and Catherine Haines, 10 Sept. 1867, daily journal of business relating to complaints and paperwork, entry 1558, vol. 251 (Clinton, La.), BRFAL-FO; Rachel Penniston v. Joseph Penniston, 25 Nov. 1866, court cases, complaints, journal of business, entry 1586, vol. 267 (Donaldsonville, La.), BRFAL-FO; J. W. Keller to Wm. M. Sterling, 10 and 30 July and 31 Aug. 1867, letters sent, entry 1598 (Franklin, La.), BRFAL-FO; complaint of Susan Robinson, 1 May 1867, journal of business, entry 1799, vol. 499 (New Iberia, La.), BRFAL-FO; Mary Spencer v. Jesse Coulson,

24 Oct. 1867, register of complaints, entry 3661, vol. 62 (Bastrop, Tex.), BRFAL-FO; Mary Jane Bell v. Clark Bell, register of complaints, entry 3680, vol. 58 (Bryan, Tex.), BRFAL-FO; J. C. De Gress to "all whom it may concern," 3 Dec. 1866, letters sent, entry 3716, vol. 100 (Houston, Tex.), BRFAL-FO; Lucy Ann King v. Wesley King, 2 Jan. 1866, Dollina Williams v. Andrew Johnson Williams, 12 Feb. 1866, Emma Matthews v. Frank Matthews, 15 Feb. 1866, Catherine Compton v. "her husband Napoleon," 6 July 1866, Mrs. Oates v. William Oates, 20 Feb. 1867, Mrs. Yell v. Anderson Yell, 22 Feb. 1867, Mrs. Williams v. Husband Sterling, 25 Feb. 1867, Elizabeth Hill v. Henry Hill, 1 April 1867, James Boone v. Maria Boone, 6 April 1867, and Louis Wade v. Mary Wade, 1 May 1867, register of complaints, entry 3720, vol. 109 (Houston, Tex.), BRFAL-FO; complaints of Rebecca Collin, 14 Jan. 1866, and Martha Pinker v. Edward Pinker, 14 Oct. 1866, letters sent, entry 3755, vol. 143 (Richmond, Tex.), BRFAL-FO; Mariah Burton v. Jack Burton, 4 June 1867, and Helen Anderson v. Peter Anderson, 6 June 1867, endorsements sent, entry 3756, vol. 147 (Richmond, Tex.), BRFAL-FO; Saml. Anderson v. James Foulks, 13 March 1866, register of complaints & weekly reports to the superintendent of the 2nd District, entry 3883, vol. 105 (Amelia Courthouse, Va.), BRFAL-FO; Eliza Hackley v. John Hackley, 16 Feb. 1867, and Mary Stanton v. Henry Stanton, 11 Feb. 1867, register of complaints, entry 5868, vol. 98 (Alexandria, Va.), BRFAL-FO.

28. Georgia freedman quoted in O'Donovan, *Becoming Free*, 195; deposition N, Anna Hayden, 15 May 1905, Samuel Hayden claim, widow application 729789, pensions, Records of the Veterans Administration, RG 15, National Archives, Washington, D.C., quoted in Bercaw, *Gendered Freedoms*, 111; case of Laney quoted in Schwalm, *A Hard Fight for We*, 262; Sarah v. Henry Jackson, case no. 20, 18 Feb. 1867, register of court trials, entry 1466 (Algiers, La.), BRFAL-FO; cases of Dollina Williams and Emma Matthews in Crouch, "Seeking Equality," 81; Sterling, *We Are Your Sisters*, 340. The bureau in Louisiana referred the case of Sarah v. Henry Jackson to civil authorities. On spousal abuse in black households during Reconstruction, see Schwalm, *A Hard Fight for We*, 234, 260–66; Bercaw, *Gendered Freedoms*, 111–13, 117, 131, 135–38, 153–54; Frankel, *Freedom's Women*, 106–7; O'Donovan, *Becoming Free*, 195; Linda K. Kerber, *No Constitutional Right to Be Ladies: Women and the Obligations of Citizenship* (New York: Hill and Wang, 1998), 64–65; Mary P. Ryan, *Mysteries of Sex: Tracing Women and Men through American History* (Chapel Hill: University of North Carolina Press, 2006), 128–29.

29. J. B. Davenport to [bureau headquarters in Georgia], 2 July 1867, registers of letters received, reel 12, BRFAL-GA; complaint of Judy Barnett, 10 April 1868, register of complaints, entry 723, vol. 174 (Athens, Ga.), BRFAL-FO; Lucy Ann King v. Wesley King, 2 Jan. 1866, registers of complaints, entry 3720, vol. 109 (Houston, Tex.), BRFAL-FO.

30. Complaint of freedwoman in Chatham County, Georgia, quoted in Sterling, *We Are Your Sisters*, 339; complaint of Susan Akins, 27 April 1868, register of complaints, entry 723, vol. 174 (Athens, Ga.), BRFAL-FO. See also letters sent, entry 718, vol. 2 (Athens, Ga.), p. 2, BRFAL-FO.

31. Jerry Ellis v. Molly Ellis, 29 June 1866, register of complaints, entry 3924, vol. 131 (Charlottesville, Va.), BRFAL-FO; Charles Rauschenberg to Ephraim, 20 Oct. 1868, letters sent, entry 697, vol. 124 (Albany, Ga.), BRFAL-FO; register of complaints, entry 3309, vol. 254 (Orangeburg, S.C.), BRFAL-FO, quoted in Schwalm, *A Hard Fight for We*, 266.

32. E. E. Platt to Mr. Reskey's Hands, 1 July 1866, miscellaneous records, entry 2280 (Natchez, Miss.), BRFAL-FO; Sarah Jenkins v. Alford Jenkins, 13 March 1868, register of complaints, entry 723, vol. 174 (Athens, Ga.), BRFAL-FO; J. Gregg to O. O. Howard, 16 July 1865, letters received, reel 15, BRFAL (M752).

33. Complaint of Albert Matthews, 9 May 1868, register of complaints, entry 723, vol. 174 (Athens, Ga.), BRFAL-FO; Rebecca Woodson v. Henry Woodson, 24 Nov. 1865, proceedings of the freedmen's court, entry 4246, vol. 415 (Richmond, Va.), BRFAL-FO.

34. Basch, "Marriage and Domestic Relations," 270.

35. Clinton, *Plain Counsels*, 31.

36. Rosen, *Terror in the Heart of Freedom*, 225. The role of federal authorities such as agents of the Freedmen's Bureau as partners of freedwomen in combating gendered racial violence is described with particular brilliance in Hannah Rosen's *Terror in the Heart of Freedom*. But on bureau efforts to secure justice for freedwomen in cases of racial violence, see Barry A. Crouch, "A Spirit of Lawlessness: White Violence, Texas Blacks, 1865–1868," *Journal of Social History* 18 (1984): 217–32; Crouch, "Seeking Equality," especially 80–83. For discussions of violence against freedwomen in a context broader than the Freedmen's Bureau, see, for example, Rosen, *Terror in the Heart of Freedom*; Hannah Rosen, "'Not That Sort of Women': Race, Gender, and Sexual Violence during the Memphis Riot of 1866," in *Sex, Love, Race: Crossing Boundaries in North American History*, ed. Martha Elizabeth Hodes (New York: New York University Press, 1999), 267–93; Marek Steedman, "Gender and the Politics of Household in Reconstruction Louisiana, 1865–1878," in *Gender and Slave Emancipation in the Atlantic World*, ed. Pamela Scully and Diana Paton (Durham, N.C.: Duke University Press, 2005), 310–27; Lisa Cardyn, "Sexual Terror in the Reconstruction South," in *Battle Scars: Gender and Sexuality in the American Civil War*, ed. Catherine Clinton and Nina Silber (New York: Oxford University Press, 2006), 140–67; Deborah Gray White, *Ar'n't I a Woman? Female Slaves in the Plantation South*, 2nd ed. (New York: W. W. Norton, 1999), chap. 6; Edwards, *Gendered Strife and Confusion*; Laura F. Edwards, "The Disappearance of Susan Daniel and Henderson Cooper: Gender and Narratives of Political Conflict in the Reconstruction-Era South," *Feminist Studies* 96, no. 2 (1996): 363–86; Laura F. Edwards, "Sexual Violence, Gender, Reconstruction, and the Extension of Patriarchy in Granville, North Carolina," *North Carolina Historical Review* 68, no. 3 (1991): 237–60; Catherine Clinton, "Bloody Terrain: Freedwomen, Sexuality and Violence during Reconstruction," *Georgia Historical Quarterly* 76 (1992): 313–32; Lou Faulkner Williams, *The Great South Carolina Ku Klux Klan Trials, 1871–1872* (Athens: University of Georgia Press, 1996), 34–36, 63; Allen W. Trelease, *White Terror: The Ku Klux Klan Conspiracy and Southern Reconstruction* (New York: Harper & Row, 1971), 232, 322, 341; Gutman, *The Black Family*, 83–84, 395–99.

37. "Inspector's Report of Affairs in Kentucky," P. Bonesteel to O. O. Howard, 5 March 1866, in U.S. House of Representatives, "Freedmen's Bureau. Letter from the Secretary of War, in answer to A resolution of the House of March 8, transmitting a report, by the Commissioner of the Freedmen's Bureau, of all orders issued by him or any assistant commissioner," 39th Cong., 1st sess., House Executive Document 70 (Serial 1256), 201.

38. "Report of Gen. O. O. Howard. Commissioner of Bureau of Refugees, Freedmen, and Abandoned Lands," 24 Oct. 1867, 527 (comments of Texas assistant commissioner J. J. Reynolds), 529 (comments of Arkansas assistant commissioner C. H. Smith); R. S. Donaldson to J. H. Weber, 6 Nov. 1865, quoted in Nieman, *To Set the Law in Motion*, 25. See also Nieman, *To Set the Law in Motion*; Foner, *Reconstruction*, 119–23, 442–44; Rapport, "The Freedmen's Bureau as a Legal Agent," 41–45.

39. Cases filed by freedwomen (or on their behalf) demanding redress for violence against them are far too numerous to list. The following, however, provide some examples of their claims: Susan Robinson to [bureau], 24 July 1866, letters received, reel 13, BRFAL-GA; Wm. F. Martin to W. W. Deane, 15 Oct. 1866, letters received, reel 13, BRFAL-GA; J. A. Arnold to T. W. Conway, 11 Aug. 1865, registered letters received, reel 7, BRFAL-LA; Edward Erlich to D. G. Fenno, 18 Sept. 1865, registered letters received, reel 8, BRFAL-LA; L. S. Barnes to Wm. H. Sinclair, 14 June 1866, letters received, reel 4, BRFAL-TX; J. C. DeGress to J. A. Mower, 13 Nov. 1865, letters received, reel 5, BRFAL-TX; C. C. Millican to Duggen, 26 June 1867, letters received, reel 7, BRFAL-TX; Albert A. Metzner to Wm. H. Sinclair, 19 June 1866, BRFAL-TX; John H. Morrison to Gregory,

2 April 1866, BRFAL-TX; Wm. F. White to O. Brown, 4 July 1866, reports of operations and conditions, box 37, BRFAL-VA; Cornelius Harris & 5 other freedpeople to [bureau], 24 July 1866, letters received, reel 36, BRFAL (M752); affidavit of Ellen Brown, 14 May 1866, letters received, reel 33, BRFAL (M752); G. B. Carse to W. Storer How, [n.d.] March 1866, letters received, reel 30, BRFAL (M752); Geo. W. Rollins to W. H. Sterling, 30 April 1867, letters received, reel 47, BRFAL (M752); Joseph A. Mower, to F. D. Sewell, 12 Aug. 1867, letters received, reel 47, BRFAL (M752); W. P. Carlin to O. O. Howard, 11 Sept. 1867, letters received, reel 51, BRFAL (M752); George Haller to C. H. Smith, [n.d.] 1867, letters received, reel 51, BRFAL (M752); C. D. Gilmore to [BRFAL], 13 April 1868, letters received, reel 53, BRFAL (M752); M. W. Taylor to "Chief Agent of the Freedmen's Bureau and abandoned lands &c.," 24 Dec. 1867, letters received, reel 56, BRFAL (M752); F. A. H. Gaebel to E. Pickett, [n.d.] 1867, letters sent, entry 690, vol. 120 (Albany, Ga.), BRFAL-FO; Howell C. Flourney to Ed. Grisham, 11 June 1867, letters sent, entry 725, vol. 171 (Athens, Ga.), BRFAL-FO; Howell C. Flourney to Jno. J. Knox, 10 Nov. 1868, letters sent, entry 725, vol. 173 (Athens, Ga.), BRFAL-FO; complaints of Sophia Johnson, 27 June 1867, and Henry Stokes, 10 Aug. 1867, journal, entry 840, vol. 226 (Columbus, Ga.), BRFAL-FO; affidavit of Betsey Barber, 15 Sept. 1865, affidavits of freedmen, entry 858, vol. 239 (Cuthbert, Ga.), BRFAL-FO; Lucinda Runnells v. David Ferguson, 2 July 1867, Caroline Nicholson v. John W. Bowden, 6 Aug. 1867, and D. Ann Crawford v. John G. Price, 12 Aug. 1867, register of complaints, entry 859, vol. 238 (Cuthbert, Ga.), BRFAL-FO; affidavit of Sarah Williams, 16 Nov. 1867, letters sent, entry 881, vol. 258 (Fort Gaines, Ga.), BRFAL-FO; N. Sellers Hill to W. W. Deane, 21 April 1866, letters sent, entry 931, vol. 296 (Macon, Ga.), BRFAL-FO; N. Sellers Hill to Jesse Aycock, 9 Aug. 1867, letters sent, entry 931, vol. 297 (Macon, Ga.), BRFAL-FO; Grace Lewis v. Louisa Jackson, 23 Aug., 1866, Easter Powell v. Miss R. Surine, 30 Aug. 1866, Lizzie Smith v. Dinah Johnson, 30 Aug. 1866, and Celia Young v. Mr. Lowenthall, 4 Sept. 1866, register of complaints, entry 1019, vol. 351 (Savannah, Ga.), BRFAL-FO; affidavit of Margaret Washington, 31 Dec. 1865, register of complaints, entry 1044, vol. 385 (Thomasville, Ga.), BRFAL-FO; case no. 4, John Richardson, proceedings before the provost court, entry 1465, box 3 (Algiers, La.), BRFAL-FO; U.S. v. Louise Alger, Wm. Antoine, 6 Nov. 1866, U.S. v. Lear King, John Linton, 22 Nov. 1866, U.S. v. Jane Ellis, Celestine Frank, 26 Jan. and 1 Feb. 1867, Sarah v. Jackson, 18 Feb. 1867, Rose v. Green, 29 March 1867, Davis v. Farnsworth, 4 April 1867, and Johnson v. Burns, 4 June 1867, register of court trials, entry 1466, vol. 197 (Algiers, La.), BRFAL-FO; complaints of Louisa Griffin, 30 May 1867, Mary Taylor, 19 Dec. 1867, Sarah Marshall, 23 May 1868, Mary Tidwill, 26 Aug. 1868, and Julia Brown, Vino Sparks, Ruffin Wilkins, Margaret Brown, Emily Fentus, and Eliza Moon, 10 Oct. [Nov.] 1868, journal of business transacted, entry 1469, vols. 199–200 (Algiers, La.), BRFAL-FO; Emma Morris v. Gill Robert, 9 March 1867, Louisa Call v. John McDaniels, 25 Aug. 1867, and Mary Stratton v. Thomas Christain, 26 Aug. 1867, register of complaints, entry 3661, vol. 62 (Bastrop, Tex.), BRFAL-FO; Adaline Peck v. Mike Rogers, n.d., Lucy Schafer v. Mr. Schafer, 22 Aug. 1867, Jane Washington v. Geo. Chancellors, 20 Dec. 1867, Nelly Davis v. Geo. Chancellors, Aaron Black, and John Wills, 23 Dec. 1867, register of complaints, entry 3665, vol. 54 (Belton, Tex.), BRFAL-FO; William B. Kirkman to Chas. Griffin, 9 July 1867, William B. Kirkman to W. H. Tilson, 11 Sept. 1867, letters sent, entry 3666, vol. 67 (Boston, Tex.), BRFAL-FO; Louisa Moody v. John Steward, 11 Aug. 1868, Margret Augburn v. T. Johnson and Sarah Bailey v. D. Camiel, 29 June [n.d.], James Wood v. Rhoda Ann Fan, 13 Aug. [n.d.], Clariss Dupres v. W. H. Banks, 20 Aug. [n.d.], Mary Boatwright v. David Lawson, 20 Aug. [n.d.], and Mary Freedwoman v. James Boatner, n.d., register of complaints, entry 3680, vol. 58 (Bryan, Tex.), BRFAL-FO; J. W. McConaughy to Squire McMasters, 18 May 1866, letters sent, entry 3785, vol. 171 (Wharton, Tex.), BRFAL-FO; Commonwealth of Virginia v. W. S. Wilson, 9 Sept. 1867, registered letters received, proceedings of freedmen's court in Lunenburg Co. in

which the Commonwealth of Va. was the Complainant, entry 3913, vol. 287 (Burkesville, Va.), BRFAL-FO; Estella Mottley v. Bertt Fulks, 22 June 1867, Sarah White v. Warren Gay, 19 Sept. 1867, Agnes Blackwell v. Bob Mathews, 11 Nov. 1867, Silvia Gee v. Jas. Bishop, 11 Nov. 1867, Ella Whatson v. Wm. C. Tisdale, 12 Nov. 1867, Marie Hurt v. David Hurt, 25 Nov. 1867, Martha Jefferson v. Dr. Wm. H. Robertson, 3 Feb. 1868, Lilly Bush v. William Gibbs, 15 Feb. 1868, Lucinda Miller v. John Bearby, 24 April 1868, Tidelia Fowlkes v. Wm. Gibbs, 25 May 1868, Susan Gregory v. Sonny [or Lonny] Bohanna, 17 July 1868, Anna Bolling v. Thomas, 25 July 1868, and Betsey Taylor v. Rob. Small, 13 Nov. 1868, register of complaints, entry 3914, vol. 124 (Burkesville, Va.), BRFAL-FO; Wm. Sims Tidball to Jacob Can Doran, 24 Oct. 1866, letters sent, entry 3921, vol. 128 (Charlottesville, Va.), BRFAL-FO; John O. Michie to Wm. M. Tidball, 17 July 1866, letters received, entry 3922, box 11 (Charlottesville, Va.), BRFAL-FO.

40. F. A. H. Gaebel to W. W. Deane, 28 Aug. 1866, unregistered letters received, reel 27, BRFAL-GA; Albert A. Metzner to Wm. H. Sinclair, 29 June 1866, letters received, reel 7, BRFAL-TX; case of Lucy Smith in Gilles Vandal, *Rethinking Southern Violence: Homicides in Post–Civil War Louisiana, 1866–1884* (Columbus: Ohio State University Press, 2000), 118; G. B. Carse to W. Storer How, [n.d.] March 1866, letters received, reel 30, BRFAL (M752). See also Crouch, "Seeking Equality," 80–82.

41. Sterling, *We Are Your Sisters*, 353; Rosen, *Terror in the Heart of Freedom*, 182. See also Rosen, *Terror in the Heart of Freedom*, especially chaps. 3–4; Rosen, "Not That Sort of Women"; Cardyn, "Sexual Terror in the Reconstruction South"; Clinton, "Bloody Terrain," 330–31; Barbara Jeanne Fields, *Slavery and Freedom on the Middle Ground: Maryland during the Nineteenth Century* (New Haven, Conn.: Yale University Press, 1985), 143; Gutman, *The Black Family*, 83–84, 395–99.

42. Rosen, "Not That Sort of Women," 267–68.

43. On the Memphis riot of 1866, see Rosen, *Terror in the Heart of Freedom*, especially chap 2.

44. Testimony of Frances Thompson, quoted in Gerda Lerner, ed., *Black Women in White America: A Documentary History* (New York: Vintage Books, 1973), 174. In 1876, Thompson was arrested in Memphis for "being a man and wearing women's clothing." On this "unexpected postscript to the history of freedwomen's testimony about rape during Reconstruction," see Rosen, *Terror in the Heart of Freedom*, 234–41.

45. Testimony of Lucy Smith, quoted in Lerner, *Black Women in White America*, 175.

46. Examples are numerous, but for other cases of rape brought to the Freedmen's Bureau, see, for example, affidavit of Paty Murray, 17 April 1867, affidavits of freedmen and charges and specifications against citizens and military personnel, entry 695, vol. 237 (Albany, Ga.), BRFAL-FO; complaint of Andy Smith, 16 Nov. 1868, register of complaints, entry 723, vol. 176 (Athens, Ga.), BRFAL-FO; complaint of Belsire Chambert, 15 July 1867, complaint of Genny Gile, 24 and 25 March 1868, Pamela Costillio v. McRae, 12 May 1868, journal of business, entry 1799, vol. 385 (New Iberia, La.), BRFAL-FO; J. W. Keller to W. H. Sterling, 10 Aug. 1867, letters sent, entry 1784, vol. 383 (New Iberia, La.), BRFAL-FO; Melissa Hill v. Albert Williams, 13 June 1867, and Alice James v. Peter Smith, 27 June 1867, register of complaints, entry 3720, vol. 108 (Houston, Tex.), BRFAL-FO; complaints of 25 and 30 Dec. 1865, register of complaints, entry 3720, vol. 109 (Houston, Tex.), BRFAL-FO; [Adam G. Malloy] to J. P. Richardson, 31 Aug. 1867, letters sent, entry 3743, vol. 134 (Marshall, Tex.), BRFAL-FO; affidavit of Fanny Whelstone, 21 Nov. 1868, register of complaints, entry 3746, vol. 136 (Marshall, Tex.), BRFAL-FO; Sarah White v. Ballon, 15 Jan. 1866, proceedings of the freedmen's court, entry 3945 (Cumberland Courthouse, Va.), BRFAL-FO; Crockett Jackson to Pope, 20 July 1867, letters received, reel 18, BRFAL-GA; W. P. Carlin to O. O. Howard, 16 May 1867, letters received, reel 44, BRFAL (M752); A. F. Flagg to [asst. adjt. genl, BRFAL], 2 June 1866, letters received, reel 34, BRFAL (M752); report of outrages by R. S. Lacey, in O. Brown to O. O. Howard, 11

Jan. 1866, letters received, reel 25, BRFAL (M752); Edward Hatch to O. O. Howard, 30 Nov. 1868, letters received, reel 63, BRFAL (M752); W. P. Carlin to O. O. Howard, 11 Sept. 1867, letters received, reel 51, BRFAL (M752); register of arrests, entry 4212, vol. 386 (Petersburg, Va.), BRFAL-FO; proceedings of the freedmen's court and register of persons arrested, entry 4085, vol. 303 (Lynchburg, Va.), BRFAL-FO.

47. Report of Lloyd Wheaton, 31 Jan. 1868, narrative reports from subordinate officers, reel 32, BRFAL-MS; complaint of Mary Jane Forrest against Joseph McKitrick quoted in Sterling, *We Are Your Sisters*, 353; A. F. Flagg to [asst. adj. genl., BRFAL], 2 June 1866, letters received, reel 34, BRFAL (M752).

48. Affidavit of Rhoda Ann Childs, 25 Sept. 1867, letters received, reel 14, BRFAL-GA.

49. Lerner, *Black Women in White America*, 172. On the role of rape and sexual oppression as an instrument of terror employed by white southerners in Reconstruction, see Lerner, *Black Women in White America*, 172–73; Clinton, "Bloody Terrain"; Jacqueline Dowd Hall, "'The Mind That Burns in Each Body': Women, Rape, and Racial Violence," in *Powers of Desire: The Politics of Sexuality*, ed. Ann Snitow, Christine Stansell, and Sharon Thompson (New York: Monthly Review Press, 1983), 328–49; Williams, *The Great South Carolina Ku Klux Klan Trials*, 34–36, 63; and Jim Cullen, "'I's a Man Now': Gender and African American Men," in Clinton and Silber, *Divided Houses*, 89.

50. Williams, *The Great South Carolina Ku Klux Klan Trials*, 63, 35; account of Julia Brown in Isaac Stathem to J. M. Lee, 10 Nov. 1868, letters sent, entry 1447 (Algiers, La.), BRFAL-FO; affidavit of John Perkins, n.d., miscellaneous records, entry 2205 (Jackson, Miss.), BRFAL-FO; *Testimony taken by the Joint Select Committee to Inquire into the Condition of Affairs in the Late Insurrectionary States* (Washington, D.C.: Government Printing Office, 1872), 5:1860–62; *Testimony taken by the Joint Select Committee*, 3:586. See also Rosen, *Terror in the Heart of Freedom*, 203–4; Frankel, *Freedom's Women*, 110–12, 128, 174; Clinton, "Bloody Terrain," 315, 317–18, 328–29; Edwards, *Gendered Strife and Confusion*, 208; Edwards, "Sexual Violence, Gender, Reconstruction, and the Extension of Patriarchy," 248; Cardyn, "Sexual Terror in the Reconstruction South," 145–47; Tera W. Hunter, *To 'Joy My Freedom: Southern Black Women's Lives and Labors after the Civil War* (Cambridge, Mass.: Harvard University Press, 1997), 33–34; Leon F. Litwack, *Been in the Storm So Long: The Aftermath of Slavery* (New York: Alfred A. Knopf, 1979; reprint, New York: Vintage Books, 1980), 277, 280; Diane Miller Sommerville, *Rape and Race in the Nineteenth-Century South* (Chapel Hill: University of North Carolina Press, 2004), 147–57.

51. Clinton B. Fisk, "Memorandum of report of General Fisk of January 23, 1866," in U.S. Senate, "Reports of the Assistant Commissioners [1865–66]," 12; Cimbala, *The Freedmen's Bureau*, 103. For examples of cases in which bureau officials fined or imprisoned whites for violence against women, see Albert A. Metzner to Wm. H. Sinclair, 29 June 1866, reel 7, BRFAL-TX; C. C. Millican to Duggen, 26 June 1867, reel 7, BRFAL-TX. See also James Smallwood, "Emancipation and the Black Family: A Case Study in Texas," *Social Science Quarterly* 57 (1977): 851–52; James Smallwood, "Black Freedwomen after Emancipation: The Texas Experience," *Prologue* 27, no. 4 (1995): 302–17; Frankel, *Freedom's Women*, 110–12, 128, 174.

52. W. Longworth to Wm. Sinclair, 13 June 1866, letters received, reel 8, BRFAL-TX. For similar examples, see also Geo. W. Smith to J. T. Krikman, 6 Feb. 1867, reel 8, BRFAL-TX; Susan Robinson to [BRFAL], 24 July 1866, reel 13, BRFAL-GA; B. B. Brown to [?], 29 March 1867, reel 14, BRFAL-LA; R. Folles to J. M. Lee, 19 Dec. 1867, reel 15, BRFAL-LA; affidavit of Ellen Fellows before Howell C. Flourney, 30 July 1868, reel 21, BRFAL-GA; Davis Tillson to U. S. Hill, 23 April [1866], reel 2, BRFAL-GA. On particular, and continued, legal prejudices experienced by freedwomen even after passage of the Civil Rights Act, the Military Reconstruction Acts, and the Fourteenth Amendment, see

Edwards, *Gendered Strife and Confusion*, 198–217; Bardaglio, *Reconstructing the Household*, 190–97; Edwards, "Sexual Violence."

53. See also on this point Rosen, *Terror in the Heart of Freedom*, especially chap. 6, and "Not That Sort of Women," 282.

54. On the efforts of local bureau agents to push a case forward, either to superior officers or to state courts, see Laura F. Edwards, "The Disappearance of Susan Daniel and Henderson Cooper."

55. Davis Tillson to U. S. Hill, 23 April [1866], letters sent, reel 2, BRFAL-GA.

56. C. H. Howard to O. O. Howard, 30 Dec. 1865, in U.S. Senate, "Reports of the Assistant Commissioners [1865–66]," 132.

57. Congress stipulated in July 1868 that the bureau would end all its activities except for its educational work and collection and payment of black soldiers' bounties on 1 January 1869. As a result, most bureau men prepared to leave their posts as 1868 came to a close. See Nieman, *To Set the Law in Motion*, 221; Bentley, *A History of the Freedmen's Bureau*, 201–2.

58. P. J. O'Rourke to G. G. Meade, 10 Feb. 1868, letters received, reel 20, BRFAL-GA; [?] to O. O. Howard, 5 Feb. 1868, letters sent, reel 7, BRFAL-GA; P. J. O'Rourke, 4 Dec. 1868, unregistered letters received, reel 30, BRFAL-GA; E. Whittlesey to J. R. Lewis, 16 Dec. 1868, letters received, reel 23, BRFAL-GA.

59. J. Fincke to O. Brown, 30 Nov. 1868, report of operations and conditions, reel 49, BRFAL-VA.

60. [Bureau agent in Quitman, Ga.], "Contract Report for September 1868," monthly reports of contracts, entry 989, box 26 (Quitman, Ga.), BRFAL-FO. For similar remarks, see also D. Losey, "Contract Reports for November 1868," [n.d.] Dec. 1868, reports, entry 984, box 25 (Perry, Ga.), BRFAL-FO; Charles Rauschenberg to M. F. Gallagher, 15 Oct. 1868, letters received, reel 23, BRFAL-GA; O. H. Howard to C. C. Sibley, 19 Sept. 1868, letters received, reel 58, BRFAL (M752); W. H. Stowell to O. Brown, 30 Nov. 1868, report of operations and conditions, reel 49, BRFAL-VA; Marcus S. Hopkins to O. Brown, 31 Dec. 1868, report of operations and conditions, reel 49, BRFAL-VA.

61. W. E. B. Du Bois, "The Freedmen's Bureau," *Atlantic Monthly*, March 1901, 364–65.

62. D. Losey to C. C. Sibley, 17 June 1868, letters sent, entry 980, vol. 332 (Perry, Ga.), BRFAL-FO; comments of a white southern woman quoted in Sterling, *We Are Your Sisters*, 332.

Conclusion: "the unpardonable sin"

1. J. R. Stone to James A. Bates, 28 Feb. 1866, and James Ashworth to James A. Bates, 28 Feb. 1866, both in monthly narrative reports of operations and conditions, Jan.–June 1866, reports of operations and conditions in Virginia, reel 44, BRFAL-VA. See also John Richard Dennett, *The South As It Is, 1865–1866*, ed. Henry M. Christman (New York: Viking Press, 1965; reprint, Athens: University of Georgia Press, 1986), 54–55.

2. [Assistant subassistant commissioner at Augusta, Georgia] to William Whigham, 7 March 1866, letters sent, entry 753, vol. 150 (Augusta, Ga.), BRFAL-FO.

3. Case of "colored woman, Martha," who was "on her way to the office of the Superintendent of Freedmen" at Salisbury, North Carolina, reported by Dennett in *The South As It Is*, 125.

4. Case No. 29, R. M. Johnson v. Mary Miller, 30 May 1868, register of complaints, entry 859, vol. 238 (Cuthbert, Ga.), BRFAL-FO.

5. J. R. Stone to James A. Bates, 28 Feb. 1866, monthly narrative reports of operations and conditions, Jan.–June 1866, reports of operations and conditions in Virginia, reel 44, BRFAL-VA; J. Davis to W. W. Deane, 4 June 1866, unregistered letters received, reel 26, BFRAL-GA.

6. Joseph P. Reidy, "Slave Emancipation through the Prism of Archives Records," *Prologue* 29, no. 2 (1997): 108. For other assessments of the successes and failures of the bureau, see, for example, Robert Harrison, "New Representations of a 'Misrepresented Bureau': Reflections on Recent Scholarship on the Freedmen's Bureau," *American Nineteenth Century History* 8 (June 2007): 205–29; Randall M. Miller, "The Freedmen's Bureau and Reconstruction: An Overview," in *The Freedmen's Bureau and Reconstruction: Reconsiderations*, ed. Paul A. Cimbala and Randall M. Miller (New York: Fordham University Press, 1999), xxvi–xxx; Paul A. Cimbala, "Reconstruction's Allies: The Relationship of the Freedmen's Bureau and the Georgia Freedmen," in Cimbala and Miller, *The Freedmen's Bureau and Reconstruction*, 315–42; John David Smith, "'The Work It Did Not Do Because It Could Not': Georgia and the 'New' Freedmen's Bureau Historiography," *Georgia Historical Quarterly* 82 (1998): 331–49; Paul A. Cimbala, *Under the Guardianship of the Nation: The Freedmen's Bureau and the Reconstruction of Georgia, 1865–1870* (Athens: University of Georgia Press, 1997), xix, 222–25; Barry A. Crouch, *The Freedmen's Bureau and Black Texans* (Austin: University of Texas Press, 1992), 3–11, 37–40; Donald G. Nieman, *To Set the Law in Motion: The Freedmen's Bureau and the Legal Rights of Blacks, 1865–1868* (Millwood, N.Y.: KTO Press, 1979), 11, 196–222; LaWanda Cox, "From Emancipation to Segregation: National Policy and Southern Blacks," in *Interpreting Southern History: Historiographical Essays in Honor of Sanford W. Higginbotham*, ed. John B. Boles and Evelyn Thomas Nolan (Baton Rouge: Louisiana State University Press, 1987), 199–253; George R. Bentley, *A History of the Freedmen's Bureau* (Philadelphia: University of Pennsylvania, 1955), 214; W. E. B. Du Bois, "The Freedmen's Bureau," *Atlantic Monthly*, March 1901, 354–65.

Bibliography

Primary Sources

Manuscript Collections

Federal Writers' Project, ed. *Slave Narratives: A Folk History of Slavery in the United States from Interviews with Former Slaves*. Washington, D.C.: Works Progress Administration, 1941. Microfilm of typewritten records assembled by the Library of Congress Project, 1936–38.

National Archives and Records Administration, Washington, D.C.

    Marriage Records of the Office of the Commissioner, Washington Headquarters of the Bureau of Refugees, Freedmen, and Abandoned Lands, 1861–69, RG 105, Microfilm Publication M1875.

    Records of the Assistant Commissioner for the District of Columbia, Bureau of Refugees, Freedmen, and Abandoned Lands, RG 105, Microfilm Publication M1055.

    Records of the Assistant Commissioner for the State of Alabama, Bureau of Refugees, Freedmen, and Abandoned Lands, RG 105, Microfilm Publication M809.

    Records of the Assistant Commissioner for the State of Arkansas, Bureau of Refugees, Freedmen, and Abandoned Lands, RG 105, Microfilm Publication M979.

    Records of the Assistant Commissioner for the State of Georgia, Bureau of Refugees, Freedmen, and Abandoned Lands, RG 105, Microfilm Publication M798.

    Records of the Assistant Commissioner for the State of Louisiana, Bureau of Refugees, Freedmen, and Abandoned Lands, RG 105, Microfilm Publication M1027.

    Records of the Assistant Commissioner for the State of Mississippi, Bureau of Refugees, Freedmen, and Abandoned Lands, RG 105, Microfilm Publication M826.

Records of the Assistant Commissioner for the State of North Carolina, Bureau of Refugees, Freedmen, and Abandoned Lands, RG 105, Microfilm Publication M843.

Records of the Assistant Commissioner for the State of South Carolina, Bureau of Refugees, Freedmen, and Abandoned Lands, RG 105, Microfilm Publication M869.

Records of the Assistant Commissioner for the State of Texas, Bureau of Refugees, Freedmen, and Abandoned Lands, RG 105, Microfilm Publication M821.

Records of the Assistant Commissioner for the State of Virginia, Bureau of Refugees, Freedmen, and Abandoned Lands, RG 105, Microfilm Publication M1048.

Records of the Field Offices of the Bureau of Refugees, Freedmen, and Abandoned Lands, RG 105.

Registers and Letters Received by the Commissioner of the Bureau of Refugees, Freedmen, and Abandoned Lands, RG 105, Microfilm Publication M752.

Selected Series of Records Issued by the Commissioner of the Bureau of Refugees, Freedmen, and Abandoned Lands, RG 105, Microfilm Publication M742.

Virginia Historical Society, Richmond
Eppes Family Papers
Freedmen's School Attendance Book, City Point, Va., February 1868–May 1868

Government Documents and Publications

"Communication from Major General Lew Wallace in Relation to the Freedmen's Bureau to the General Assembly of Maryland." *Journal of the Proceedings of the House of Delegates, January Session, 1865*. Annapolis, 1865. Document J.

Compendium of the General Orders of the U.S. Army. Washington, D.C.: Government Printing Office, 1864.

The General Laws of the Regular Session of the Eleventh Legislature of the State of Texas. Austin, 1866.

Public Laws of North Carolina, 1866–67. Raleigh, N.C.: Wm. E. Pell, State Printer, 1867.

Statutes at Large of the United States of America, 1789–1873. 17 vols. Washington, D.C.: Government Printing Office, 1850–73.

Testimony taken by the Joint Select Committee to Inquire into the Condition of Affairs in the Late Insurrectionary States. 13 vols. Washington, D.C.: Government Printing Office, 1872.

U.S. Congress. *Congressional Globe.* 46 vols. Washington, D.C., 1834–73.
———. *Report of the Joint Committee on Reconstruction.* Washington, D.C.: Government Printing Office, 1866.
———. *Report of the Joint Committee to Inquire into the Condition of Affairs in the Late Insurrectionary States.* 13 vols. Washington, D.C.: Government Printing Office, 1872.
U.S. House of Representatives. "Freedmen's Bureau. Letter from the Secretary of War, in answer to A resolution of the House of March 8, transmitting a report, by the Commissioner of the Freedmen's Bureau, of all orders issued by him or any assistant commissioner." 39th Cong., 1st sess. House Executive Document 70. (Serial 1256)
———. "Report of Bureau Expenditures [20 Oct. 1869]." 41st Cong., 2nd sess. House Executive Document 142. (Serial 1417)
———. "Report of the Commissioner of the Bureau of Refugees, Freedmen, and Abandoned Lands [n.d. Dec. 1865]." 39th Cong., 1st sess. House Executive Document 11. (Serial 1255)
———. "Report of the Commissioner of the Bureau of Refugees, Freedmen, and Abandoned Lands [1 Nov. 1866]." 39th Cong., 2nd sess. House Executive Document 1. (Serial 1285)
———. "Report of the Commissioner of the Bureau of Refugees, Freedmen, and Abandoned Lands [1 Nov. 1867]." 40th Cong., 2nd sess. House Executive Document 1. (Serial 1323)
———. "Report of the Commissioner of the Bureau of Refugees, Freedmen, and Abandoned Lands [24 Oct. 1868]." 40th Cong., 3rd sess. House Executive Document 1. (Serial 1367)
———. "Report of the Commissioner of the Bureau of Refugees, Freedmen, and Abandoned Lands [20 Oct. 1869]." 41st Cong., 2nd sess. House Executive Document 1, pt. 2. (Serial 1412)
———. "Report of the Commissioner of the Bureau of Refugees, Freedmen, and Abandoned Lands [20 Oct. 1870]." 41st Cong., 3rd sess. House Executive Document 1, pt. 2. (Serial 1446)
———. "Report of the Late Freedmen's Bureau for the Year ending June 30, 1875." 44th Cong., 1st sess. House Executive Document 144. (Serial 1689)
U.S. Senate. "Preliminary Report Touching the Condition and Management of Emancipated Refugees, Made to the Secretary of War by the American Freedmen's Inquiry Commission [30 June 1863]." 38th Cong., 1st sess. Senate Executive Document 53. (Serial 1176)
———. "Reports of the Assistant Commissioners of the Bureau of Refugees, Freedmen, and Abandoned Lands [1865–66]." 39th Cong., 1st sess. Senate Executive Document 27. (Serial 1238)

———. "Reports of the Assistant Commissioners of the Bureau of Refugees, Freedmen, and Abandoned Lands and Laws in Relation to the Freedmen [1866]." 39th Cong., 2nd sess. Senate Executive Document 6. (Serial 1276)

The War of the Rebellion: A Compilation of the Official Records of the Union and Confederate Armies. 128 vols. Washington, D.C.: Government Printing Office, 1880–1901.

Other Printed Primary Sources

Alvord, James W. Letters from the South Relating to the Condition of the Freedmen Addressed to Major General O. O. Howard, Commissioner, Bureau R. F. and A. L. Washington, D.C.: Howard University, 1870.

American Annual Cyclopaedia of Important Events. Embracing Political, Civil, Military and Social Affairs; Public Documents; Biography, Statistics, Commerce, Finance, Literature, Science, Agriculture and Mechanical Industry. New York: D. Appleton, 1862–75.

Andrews, Eliza Frances. *The War-time Journal of a Georgia Girl.* New York: D. Appleton, 1908.

Andrews, Sidney. *The South since the War: As Shown by Fourteen Weeks of Travel and Observation in Georgia and the Carolinas.* Boston: Ticknor & Fields, 1866. Reprint, Boston: Houghton Mifflin, 1974.

Atkinson, Edward. "The Future Supply of Cotton." *North American Review* 98, no. 203 (1864): 497.

Avary, Myrta Lockett. *Dixie after the War: An Exposition of Social Conditions Existing in the South, during the Twelve Years Succeeding the Fall of Richmond.* New York: Doubleday, Page, 1906.

Barr, Amelia Edith Huddleston. *All the Days of My Life: An Autobiography.* New York: D. Appleton, 1913.

Berlin, Ira, Francine C. Cary, Steven F. Miller, and Leslie S. Rowland. "Family and Freedom: Black Families in the American Civil War." *History Today* 37 (1987): 8–15.

Berlin, Ira, Barbara J. Fields, Thavolia Glymph, Joseph P. Reidy, and Leslie S. Rowland, eds. *The Destruction of Slavery.* Series 1, vol. 1, of *Freedom: A Documentary History of Emancipation, 1861–1867.* Cambridge: Cambridge University Press, 1985.

Berlin, Ira, Barbara J. Fields, Steven F. Miller, Joseph P. Reidy, and Leslie S. Rowland, eds. *Free at Last: A Documentary History of Slavery, Freedom, and the Civil War.* New York: New Press, 1992.

Berlin, Ira, Thavolia Glymph, Steven F. Miller, Joseph P. Reidy, Leslie S. Rowland, and Julie Saville, eds. *The Wartime Genius of Free Labor: The Lower*

South. Series 1, vol. 3, of *Freedom: A Documentary History of Emancipation, 1861–1867*. Cambridge: Cambridge University Press, 1990.

Berlin, Ira, Steven Hahn, Steven F. Miller, Joseph P. Reidy, and Leslie S. Rowland. "The Terrain of Freedom: The Struggle over the Meaning of Free Labor in the U.S. South." *History Workshop Journal* 22 (1986): 108–30.

Berlin, Ira, Steven F. Miller, Joseph P. Reidy, and Leslie S. Rowland, eds. *The Wartime Genius of Free Labor: The Upper South*. Series 1, vol. 2, of *Freedom: A Documentary History of Emancipation, 1861–1867*. Cambridge: Cambridge University Press, 1990.

Berlin, Ira, Steven F. Miller, and Leslie S. Rowland, eds. "Afro-American Families in the Transition from Slavery to Freedom." *Radical History Review* 42 (1988): 89–121.

Berlin, Ira, Joseph P. Reidy, and Leslie S. Rowland, eds. *The Black Military Experience*. Series 2 of *Freedom: A Documentary History of Emancipation, 1861–1867*. Cambridge: Cambridge University Press, 1982.

Berlin, Ira, and Leslie S. Rowland, eds. *Families and Freedom: A Documentary History of African-American Kinship in the Civil War Era*. New York: New Press, 1997.

Blassingame, John W., ed. *The Slave Community: Plantation Life in the Antebellum South*. Baton Rouge: Louisiana State University Press, 1972.

———, ed. *Slave Testimony: Two Centuries of Letters, Speeches, Interviews, and Autobiographies*. Baton Rouge: Louisiana State University Press, 1977.

Botkin, B. A., ed. *Lay My Burden Down: A Folk History of Slavery*. Chicago: University of Chicago Press, 1945.

Browning, Orville H. *The Diary of Orville Hickman Browning*. 2 vols. Springfield: Trustees of the Illinois State Historical Library, 1933.

Campbell, George. *White and Black: The Outcome of a Visit to the United States*. London: Chatto and Windus, 1879.

Chesnut, Mary. *A Diary from Dixie*. Edited by Ben Ames Williams. Boston: Houghton Mifflin, 1949.

———. *Mary Chesnut's Civil War*. Edited by C. Van Woodward. New Haven, Conn.: Yale University Press, 1981.

Child, L. Maria, ed. *The American Negro: His History and Literature*. New York: Arno Press and the New York Times, 1968.

De Forest, John William. *A Union Officer in the Reconstruction*. Edited by James H. Croushore and David Morris Potter. New Haven, Conn.: Yale University Press, 1948. Reprint, Baton Rouge: Louisiana State University Press, 1976.

Dennett, John Richard. *The South As It Is, 1865–1866*. Edited by Henry M. Christman. New York: Viking Press, 1965. Reprint, Athens: University of Georgia Press, 1986.

Douglass, Frederick. *The Life and Writings of Frederick Douglass*. Ed. Philip S. Foner. 4 vols. New York: International Publishers, 1950–55.

Eppes, Mrs. Nicholas Ware [Susan Bradford Eppes]. *The Negro of the Old South: A Bit of Period History*. Chicago: Joseph G. Branch, 1925.

Eppes, Susan B. *Through Some Eventful Years*. Macon, Ga.: J. W. Burke, 1926.

Fisk, Clinton B. *Plain Counsels for Freedmen: In Sixteen Brief Lectures*. Boston: American Tract Society, 1866.

Fleming, Walter Lynwood. *Documentary History of Reconstruction, Political, Military, Social, Religious, Educational & Industrial, 1865 to the Present Time*. 2 vols. Cleveland: A. H. Clark, 1906–7.

"The Freedmen's Bureau." *Harper's Weekly*, 25 July 1968, 487.

Hahn, Steven, Steven F. Miller, Susan E. O'Donovan, John C. Rodrigue, and Leslie S. Rowland, eds. *Land and Labor, 1865*. Series 3, vol. 1, of *Freedom: A Documentary History of Emancipation, 1861–1867*. Chapel Hill: University of North Carolina Press, 2008.

Higginbotham, Evelyn Brooks. "African-American Women's History and the Metalanguage of Race." *Signs: A Journal of Women in Culture and Society* 17, no. 21 (1992): 251–74.

Holland, Rupert S., ed. *Letters and Diary of Laura M. Towne*. Cambridge, Mass.: Riverside Press, 1912.

Howard, Oliver Otis. *Autobiography of Oliver Otis Howard*. 2 vols. New York: Baker and Taylor, 1907.

Hurmence, Belinda, ed. *My Folks Don't Want Me to Talk about Slavery: Twenty-one Oral Histories of Former North Carolina Slaves*. Winston-Salem, N.C.: John F. Blair, 1984.

Johnson, Suzanne Stone, and Robert Allison Johnson, eds. *Bitter Freedom: William Stone's Record of Service in the Freedmen's Bureau*. Columbia: University of South Carolina Press, 2008.

King, Edward. *The Great South: A Record of Journeys in Louisiana, Texas, the Indian Territory, Missouri, Arkansas, Mississippi, Alabama, Georgia, Florida, South Carolina, North Carolina, Kentucky, Tennessee, Virginia, West Virginia, and Maryland*. Hartford, Conn.: American Publishing, 1875.

Lerner, Gerda, ed. *Black Women in White America: A Documentary History*. New York: Vintage Books, 1973.

Loring, Francis W., and C. F. Atkinson. *Cotton Culture and the South Considered with Reference to Emigration*. Boston: A. Williams, 1869.

McPherson, Edward. *The Political History of the United States of America during the Period of Reconstruction*. Washington, D.C.: Solomons & Chapman, 1875.

McPherson, James M. *The Struggle for Equality: Abolitionists and the Negro in the Civil War and Reconstruction*. Princeton, N.J.: Princeton University Press, 1964.

Myers, Robert Manson, ed. *Children of Pride: A True Story of Georgia and the Civil War.* New Haven, Conn.: Yale University Press, 1972.

Nordhoff, Charles. *Freedmen of South Carolina: Some Account of Their Appearance, Character, Condition and Peculiar Customs.* New York: C. T. Evans, 1863.

Pearson, Elizabeth Ware, ed. *Letters from Port Royal: Written at the Time of the Civil War.* Boston: W. B. Clarke, 1906.

Rawick, George P., ed. *The American Slave: A Composite Autobiography.* 19 vols. Westport, Conn.: Greenwood Press, 1972–79.

Reid, Whitelaw. *After the War: A Tour of the Southern States, 1865–1866.* Cincinnati: Moore, Wilstach & Baldwin, 1866. Reprint, New York: Harper & Row, 1965.

Sterling, Dorothy, ed. *The Trouble They Seen: The Story of Reconstruction in the Words of African Americans.* New York: Da Capo Press, 1976.

———, ed. *We Are Your Sisters: Black Women in the Nineteenth Century.* New York: W. W. Norton, 1984.

Swint, Henry L., ed. *Dear Ones at Home: Letters from Contraband Camps.* Nashville, Tenn.: Vanderbilt University Press, 1966.

Taylor, Susie King. *Reminiscences of My Life in Camp: With the 33d United States Colored Troops Late 1st S.C. Volunteers.* Boston: Author, 1904.

Thomas, Gertrude Clanton. *The Secret Eye: The Journal of Gertrude Clanton Thomas, 1848–1889.* Edited by Virginia Ingraham Burr. Chapel Hill: University of North Carolina Press, 1990.

Trowbridge, John Townsend. *The South: A Tour of Its Battlefields and Ruined Cities, a Journey through the Desolated States, and Talks with the People.* Hartford, Conn.: L. Stebbins, 1866.

Tyler, Ronnie C., and Lawrence R. Murphy, eds. *The Slave Narratives of Texas.* Austin, Tex.: Encino Press, 1974.

Workers of the Writers' Program of the Work Projects Administration in the State of Virginia, comps. *The Negro in Virginia.* Winston-Salem, N.C.: John F. Blair, 1994.

Yetman, Norman R., ed. *Life under the "Peculiar Institution": Selections from the Slave Narrative Collection.* New York: Holt, Rinehart and Winston, 1970.

Secondary Sources

Abbott, Martin. *The Freedmen's Bureau in South Carolina, 1865–1872.* Chapel Hill: University of North Carolina Press, 1967.

Alderson, William T. "The Influence of Military Rule and the Freedmen's Bureau on Reconstruction Virginia, 1865–1870." Ph.D. diss., Vanderbilt University, 1952.

Aptheker, Bettina. *Woman's Legacy: Essays on Race, Sex, and Class in American History*. Amherst: University of Massachusetts Press, 1982.

Araki, Wakako. "Historicising the Ideas of Separate Spheres in the South Carolina Sea Islands, 1862–77." In *Historicising Whiteness: Transnational Perspectives on the Construction of an Identity*, edited by Leigh Boucher, Jane Carey, and Katherine Blinghaus, 190–200. Melbourne: RMIT Publishing in association with the School of Historical Studies, University of Melbourne, 2007.

Axinn, June, and Herman Levin. *Social Welfare: A History of the American Response to Need*. New York: Longman, 1982.

Bardaglio, Peter W. "Challenging Parental Custody Rights: The Legal Reconstruction of Parenthood in the Nineteenth-Century American South." *Continuity and Change* 4 (1989): 259–92.

———. "The Children of Jubilee: African American Childhood in Wartime." In *Divided Houses: Gender and the Civil War*, edited by Catherine Clinton and Nina Silber, 213–29. New York: Oxford University Press, 1992.

———. *Reconstructing the Household: Families, Sex, and the Law in the Nineteenth-Century South*. Chapel Hill: University of North Carolina Press, 1995.

———. Response to "Negotiating the Boundaries of Freedom: White and Black Women in the Reconstruction South." Fifth Southern Conference on Women's History, Richmond, Va., 15–17 June 2000. Unpublished commentary in author's possession.

Basch, Norma. "Marriage and Domestic Relations." In *The Cambridge History of Law in America*. Vol. 2, *The Long Nineteenth Century (1789–1920)*, edited by Michael Grossberg and Christopher Tomlins, 245–79. New York: Cambridge University Press, 2008.

Beale, Francis. "Double Jeopardy: To Be Black and Female." In *Black Woman: An Anthology*, edited by Toni Cade, 109–22. New York: New American Library, 1970.

Belz, Herman. *Emancipation and Equal Rights: Politics and Constitutionalism in the Civil War Era*. New York: W. W. Norton, 1978.

———. "The Freedmen's Bureau Act of 1865 and the Principle of No Discrimination According to Color." *Civil War History* 21 (1975): 197–217.

———. *A New Birth of Freedom: The Republican Party and Freedmen's Rights, 1861–1866*. Westport, Conn.: Greenwood Press, 1976.

———. "The New Orthodoxy in Reconstruction Historiography." *Reviews in American History* 1 (1973): 106–12.

Bentley, George R. *A History of the Freedmen's Bureau*. Philadelphia: University of Pennsylvania, 1955.

Bercaw, Nancy D. *Gendered Freedoms: Race, Rights, and the Politics of the Household in the Delta, 1861–1875*. Gainesville: University Press of Florida, 2003.

Berkeley, Kathleen C. "'Colored Ladies Also Contributed': Black Women's Activities from Benevolence to Social Welfare, 1866–1896." In *The Web of Southern Social Relations: Work, Family, and Education*, edited by Walter J. Fraser Jr., R. Frank Saunders Jr., and Jon L. Wakelyn, 181–203. Athens: University of Georgia Press, 1985.

Berlin, Ira. *Slaves without Masters: The Free Negro in the Antebellum South.* New York: Pantheon Books, 1974.

Berlin, Ira, Barbara J. Fields, Steven F. Miller, Joseph P. Reidy, and Leslie S. Rowland. *Slaves No More: Three Essays on Emancipation and the Civil War.* Cambridge: Cambridge University Press, 1992.

Bethel, Elizabeth. "The Freedmen's Bureau in Alabama." *Journal of Southern History* 14 (1948): 49–92.

Blair, William A. "Justice versus Law and Order: The Battles over the Reconstruction of Virginia's Minor Judiciary, 1865–1870." *Virginia Magazine of History and Biography* 103 (1995): 157–80.

Boles, John B. *Black Southerners, 1619–1869.* Lexington: University Press of Kentucky, 1984.

Boris, Eileen, and Peter Bardaglio. "The Transformation of Patriarchy: The Historic Role of the State." In *Families, Politics, and Public Policy: A Feminist Dialogue on Women and the State*, edited by Irene Diamond, 70–93. New York: Longman, 1983.

Boydston, Jeanne. *Home and Work: Housework, Wages, and the Ideology of Labor in the Early Republic.* New York: Oxford University Press, 1990.

Boyer, Paul S. *Urban Masses and Moral Order in America, 1820–1920.* Cambridge, Mass.: Harvard University Press, 1978.

Bremner, Robert H. *The Public Good: Philanthropy and Welfare in the Civil War Era.* New York: Alfred A. Knopf, 1980.

Brewer, James H. *The Confederate Negro: Virginia's Craftsmen and Military Laborers, 1861–1865.* Durham, N.C.: Duke University Press, 1969.

Brown, Elsa Barkley. "Negotiating and Transforming the Public Sphere: African American Political Life in the Transition from Slavery to Freedom." *Public Culture* 7 (1994): 107–46.

———. "Uncle Ned's Children: Negotiating Community and Freedom in Postemancipation Richmond, Virginia." Ph.D. diss., Kent State University, 1994.

Brown, Thomas J., ed. *Reconstructions: New Perspectives on the Postbellum United States.* New York: Oxford University Press, 2006.

Bryant, Jonathan M. *How Curious a Land: Conflict and Change in Greene County, Georgia, 1850–1885.* Chapel Hill: University of North Carolina Press, 1996.

Burnham, Margaret. "An Impossible Marriage: Slave Law and Family Law." *Law and Inequality* 5 (1987): 187–225.

Burstyn, Varda. "Masculine Dominance and the State." *Socialist Register* 20 (1983): 59–62.

Butchart, Ronald E. *Northern Schools, Southern Blacks, and Reconstruction: Freedmen's Education, 1862–1875.* Westport, Conn.: Greenwood Press, 1980.

Bynum, Victoria E. "On the Lowest Rung: Court Control over Poor White and Free Black Women." *Southern Exposure* 12 (1984): 40–44.

———. *Unruly Women: The Politics of Social and Sexual Control in the Old South.* Chapel Hill: University of North Carolina Press, 1992.

Cardyn, Lisa. "Sexual Terror in the Reconstruction South." In *Battle Scars: Gender and Sexuality in the American Civil War*, edited by Catherine Clinton and Nina Silber, 140–67. New York: Oxford University Press, 2006.

Carlson, Shirley. "Black Ideals of Womanhood in the Late Victorian Era." *Journal of Negro History* 77 (1992): 61–73.

Carpenter, John A. *Sword and Olive Branch: Oliver Otis Howard.* Pittsburgh: University of Pittsburgh Press, 1964.

Censer, Jane Turner. *The Reconstruction of White Southern Womanhood, 1865–1895.* Baton Rouge: Louisiana State University Press, 2003.

Cimbala, Paul A. "A Black Colony in Dougherty County: The Freedmen's Bureau and the Failure of Reconstruction in Southwest Georgia." *Journal of Southwest Georgia History* 4 (1986): 72–89.

———. *The Freedmen's Bureau: Reconstructing the American South after the Civil War.* Malabar, Fla.: Krieger, 2005.

———. "The Freedmen's Bureau, the Freedmen, and Sherman's Grant in Reconstruction Georgia, 1865–1867." *Journal of Southern History* 55 (1989): 597–632.

———. "Making Good Yankees: The Freedmen's Bureau and Education in Reconstruction Georgia, 1865–1870." *Atlanta Historical Journal* 29 (1985): 5–18.

———. "On the Front Line of Freedom: Freedmen's Bureau Officers and Agents in Reconstruction Georgia, 1865–1868." *Georgia Historical Quarterly* 76 (1993): 577–611.

———. "Reconstruction's Allies: The Relationship of the Freedmen's Bureau and the Georgia Freedmen." In *The Freedmen's Bureau and Reconstruction: Reconsiderations*, edited by Paul A. Cimbala and Randall M. Miller, 315–42. New York: Fordham University Press, 1999.

———. "The 'Talisman Power': Davis Tillson, the Freedmen's Bureau, and Free Labor in Reconstruction Georgia, 1865–1866." *Civil War History* 28 (1982): 153–71.

———. *Under the Guardianship of the Nation: The Freedmen's Bureau and the Reconstruction of Georgia, 1865–1870.* Athens: University of Georgia Press, 1997.

Cimbala, Paul A., and Randall M. Miller, eds. *The Freedmen's Bureau and Reconstruction: Reconsiderations.* New York: Fordham University Press, 1999.

Clark, Elizabeth B. "'The Sacred Rights of the Weak': Pain, Sympathy, and the Culture of Individual Rights in Antebellum America." *Journal of American History* 82, no. 2 (1995): 463–93.

Click, Patricia C. *Time Full of Trial: The Roanoke Island Freedmen's Colony, 1862–1867.* Chapel Hill: University of North Carolina Press, 2001.

Clinton, Catherine. "Bloody Terrain: Freedwomen, Sexuality and Violence during Reconstruction." *Georgia Historical Quarterly* 76 (1992): 313–32.

———. *The Other Civil War: American Women in the Nineteenth Century.* New York: Hill and Wang, 1984.

———. "Reconstructing Freedwomen." In *Divided Houses: Gender and the Civil War*, edited by Catherine Clinton and Nina Silber, 306–19. New York: Oxford University Press, 1992.

———. "Southern Dishonor: Flesh, Blood, Race, and Bondage." In *In Joy and Sorrow: Women, Family, and Marriage in the Victorian South*, edited by Carol Bleser, 52–68. New York: Oxford University Press, 1991.

Clinton, Catherine, and Nina Silber, eds. *Battle Scars: Gender and Sexuality in the American Civil War.* New York: Oxford University Press, 2006.

———, eds. *Divided Houses: Gender and the Civil War.* New York: Oxford University Press, 1992.

Coclanis, Peter A. "The Captivity of a Generation." Review of *Generations of Captivity: A History of African-American Slaves,* by Ira Berlin. *William and Mary Quarterly* 61 (2004): 544–55.

———. "Slavery, African-American Agency, and the World We Have Lost." *Georgia Historical Quarterly* 79 (1995): 873–84.

Cohen, William. *At Freedom's Edge: Black Mobility and the Southern White Quest for Racial Control, 1861–1915.* Baton Rouge: Louisiana State University Press, 1991.

———. "Black Immobility and Free Labor: The Freedmen's Bureau and the Relocation of Black Labor, 1865–1868." *Civil War History* 30 (1984): 221–34.

———. "Negro Involuntary Servitude in the South, 1865–1940: A Preliminary Analysis." *Journal of Southern History* 42 (1976): 31–60.

Cohen-Lack, Nancy. "A Struggle for Sovereignty: National Consolidation, Emancipation, and Free Labor in Texas, 1865." *Journal of Southern History* 58 (1992): 57–98.

Colby, Ira C. "The Freedmen's Bureau: From Social Welfare to Segregation." *Phylon* 46, no. 3 (1985): 219–30.

Conway, Alan. *The Reconstruction of Georgia*. Minneapolis: University of Minnesota Press, 1966.

Cott, Nancy F. *The Bonds of Womanhood: "Woman's Sphere" in New England, 1780–1835*. New Haven, Conn.: Yale University Press, 1977.

———. *Public Vows: A History of Marriage and the Nation*. Cambridge, Mass.: Harvard University Press, 2000.

Coulter, E. Merton. *The South during Reconstruction, 1865–1877*. Baton Rouge: Louisiana State University Press, 1947.

Cox, John, and LaWanda Cox. "Andrew Johnson and His Ghost Writers: An Analysis of the Freedmen's Bureau and Civil Rights Veto Messages." *Mississippi Valley Historical Review* 48 (1961): 460–79.

———. "General O. O. Howard and the 'Misrepresented Bureau.'" *Journal of Southern History* 19 (1953): 427–56.

Cox, LaWanda. "From Emancipation to Segregation: National Policy and Southern Blacks." In *Interpreting Southern History: Historiographical Essays in Honor of Sanford W. Higginbotham*, edited by John B. Boles and Evelyn Thomas Nolan, 199–253. Baton Rouge: Louisiana State University Press, 1987.

———. "Reflections on the Limits of the Possible." In *Freedom, Racism, and Reconstruction: Collected Writings of LaWanda Cox*, edited by Donald G. Nieman, 243–78. Athens: University of Georgia Press, 1997.

Crouch, Barry A. "'All the Vile Passions': The Texas Black Code of 1866." *Southwestern Historical Quarterly* 97 (1993): 13–34.

———. "Black Dreams and White Justice." *Prologue* 6, no. 4 (1974): 255–65.

———. "Black Education in Civil War and Reconstruction Louisiana: George T. Ruby, the Army, and the Freedmen's Bureau." *Louisiana History* 38 (1997): 287–308.

———. "The 'Chords of Love': Legalizing Black Marital and Family Rights in Postwar Texas." *Journal of Negro History* 79 (1994): 334–51.

———. *The Freedmen's Bureau and Black Texans*. Austin: University of Texas Press, 1992.

———. "Guardian of the Freedpeople: Texas Freedmen's Bureau Agents and the Black Community." *Southern Studies* 3 (1992): 185–201.

———. "Hidden Sources of Black History: The Texas Freedmen's Bureau Records as a Case Study." *Southwestern Historical Quarterly* 83 (1980): 211–26.

———. "Seeking Equality: Houston Black Women during Reconstruction." In *The Dance of Freedom: Texas African Americans during Reconstruction*, edited by Larry Madaras, 69–89. Austin: University of Texas Press, 2007.

———. "A Spirit of Lawlessness: White Violence, Texas Blacks, 1865–1868." *Journal of Social History* 18 (1984): 217–32.

———. "'To Enslave the Rising Generation': The Freedmen's Bureau and the Texas Black Code." In *The Freedmen's Bureau and Reconstruction: Reconsiderations*, edited by Paul A. Cimbala and Randall M. Miller, 261–87. New York: Fordham University Press, 1999.

———. "'Unmanacling' Texas Reconstruction: A Twenty-Year Perspective." *Southwestern Historical Quarterly* 93 (1990): 275–302.

Crouch, Barry A., and Larry Madaras. "Reconstructing Black Families: Perspectives from the Texas Freedmen's Bureau Records." *Prologue* 18, no. 2 (1986): 109–22.

Cullen, Jim. "'I's a Man Now': Gender and African American Men." In *Divided Houses: Gender and the Civil War*, edited by Catherine Clinton and Nina Silber, 76–91. New York: Oxford University Press, 1992.

Davis, Robert Scott, Jr. "Freedmen's Bureau and Other Reconstruction Sources for Research in African-American Families, 1865–1874." *Journal of the Afro-American Historical and Genealogical Society* 9 (1988): 171–76.

"Documenting the History of Emancipation: The Freedmen and Southern Society Project." *Annotation: The Newsletter of the National Historical Publications and Records Commission* 26, no. 28): 15–16.

Downs, Jim. "The Other Side of Freedom: Destitution, Disease, and Dependency among Freedwomen and Their Children during and after the Civil War." In *Battle Scars: Gender and Sexuality in the American Civil War*, edited by Catherine Clinton and Nina Silber, 78–103. New York: Oxford University Press, 2006.

Drago, Edmund L. *Black Politicians and Reconstruction Georgia: A Splendid Failure*. 2nd ed. Athens: University of Georgia Press, 1992.

———. "Militancy and Black Women in Reconstruction Georgia." *Journal of American Culture* 1 (1978): 838–44.

Du Bois, W. E. B. *Black Reconstruction in America, 1860–1880*. New York: Harcourt, Brace, 1935. Reprint, New York: Atheneum, 1992.

———. "The Freedmen's Bureau." *Atlantic Monthly*, March 1901, 354–65.

———. "Reconstruction and Its Benefits." *American Historical Review* 15 (1910): 781–99.

Dunaway, Wilma A. *The African-American Family in Slavery and Emancipation*. Cambridge: Cambridge University Press, 2003.

Durrill, Wayne K. "The South Carolina Black Code." In *True Stories from the American Past*, edited by William Graebner, 1–15. New York: McGraw-Hill, 1993.

Edwards, Laura F. "Civil War and Reconstruction." In *The Cambridge History of Law in America*. Vol. 2, *The Long Nineteenth Century (1789–1920)*, edited by Michael Grossberg and Christopher Tomlins, 313–44. New York: Cambridge University Press, 2008.

———. "The Disappearance of Susan Daniel and Henderson Cooper: Gender and Narratives of Political Conflict in the Reconstruction-Era South." *Feminist Studies* 96, no. 2 (1996): 363–86.

———. "Enslaved Women and the Law: Paradoxes of Subordination in the Post-revolutionary Carolinas." *Slavery and Abolition* 26 (2005): 305–23.

———. *Gendered Strife and Confusion: The Political Culture of Reconstruction*. Urbana: University of Illinois Press, 1997.

———. "'The Marriage Covenant Is the Foundation of All Our Rights': The Politics of Slave Marriages in North Carolina after Emancipation." *Law and History Review* 14 (1996): 81–124.

———. *The People and Their Peace: Legal Culture and the Transformation of Inequality in the Post-revolutionary South*. Chapel Hill: University of North Carolina Press, 2009.

———. "The Problem of Dependency: African Americans, Labor Relations, and the Law in the Nineteenth-Century South." *Agricultural History* 72, no. 2 (1998): 313–40.

———. *Scarlett Doesn't Live Here Anymore: Southern Women in the Civil War Era*. Urbana: University of Illinois Press, 2000.

———. "Sexual Violence, Gender, Reconstruction, and the Extension of Patriarchy in Granville, North Carolina." *North Carolina Historical Review* 68, no. 3 (1991): 237–60.

———. "Women and the Law: Domestic Discord in North Carolina after the Civil War." In *Local Matters: Race, Crime, and Justice in the Nineteenth-Century South*, edited by Christopher Waldrep and Donald G. Nieman, 125–54. Athens: University of Georgia Press, 2001.

Ely, James W., Jr. "Poor Laws of the Post-revolutionary South, 1776–1800." *Tulsa Law Journal* 21 (1985): 1–22.

Engs, Robert F. *Educating the Disfranchised and Disinherited: Samuel Chapman Armstrong and Hampton Institute, 1839–1893*. Knoxville: University of Tennessee Press, 1999.

———. *Freedom's First Generation: Black Hampton, Virginia, 1861–1890*. Philadelphia: University of Pennsylvania Press, 1979.

Escott, Paul. "'The Cry of the Sufferers': The Problem of Welfare in the Confederacy." *Civil War History* 23 (1977): 228–40.

Everly, Elaine C. "The Freedmen's Bureau in the National Capital." Ph.D. diss., George Washington University, 1972.

———. "Freedmen's Bureau Records: An Overview." *Prologue* 29, no. 2 (1997): 95–99.

———. "Marriage Registers of Freedmen." *Prologue* 5, no. 3 (1973): 150–54.

Farmer, Mary J. "'Because They Are Women': Gender and the Virginia Freedmen's Bureau's 'War on Dependency.'" In *The Freedmen's Bureau and Reconstruction: Reconsiderations*, edited by Paul A. Cimbala and Randall M. Miller, 161–92. New York: Fordham University Press, 1999.

Farmer-Kaiser, Mary. "'Are They Not in Some Sorts Vagrants?' Gender and the Efforts of the Freedmen's Bureau to Combat Vagrancy in the Reconstruction South." *Georgia Historical Quarterly* 89, no. 1 (2004): 25–49.

———. Review of *The Freedmen's Bureau: Reconstructing the American South after the Civil War*, by Paul A. Cimbala. *H-Net Reviews in the Humanities and Social Sciences*, Nov. 2007, http://www.h-net.org/reviews/showrev.php?id=13850.

———. "'With a Weight of Circumstances Like Millstones about Their Necks': Freedwomen, Federal Relief, and the Benevolent Guardianship of the Freedmen's Bureau." *Virginia Magazine of History and Biography* 115, no. 3 (2007): 412–42.

Farnham, Christie. "Sapphire? The Issue of Dominance in the Slave Family, 1830–1865." In *To Toil the Livelong Day: America's Women at Work*, edited by Carol Groneman and Mary Beth Norton, 369–84. Ithaca, N.Y.: Cornell University Press, 1987.

Faulkner, Carol. "A Nation's Sin: White Women and U.S. Policy toward Freedpeople." In *Gender and Slave Emancipation in the Atlantic World*, edited by Pamela Scully and Diana Paton, 121–40. Durham, N.C.: Duke University Press, 2005.

———. *Women's Radical Reconstruction: The Freedmen's Aid Movement*. Philadelphia: University of Pennsylvania Press, 2004.

Faust, Drew Gilpin. "'Trying to Do a Man's Business': Slavery, Violence, and Gender in the American Civil War." *Gender and History* 4, no. 2 (1992): 197–214.

Fields, Barbara Jeanne. "Ideology and Race in American History." In *Region, Race, and Reconstruction: Essays in Honor of C. Vann Woodward*, edited by J. Morgan Kousser and James M. McPherson, 143–77. New York: Oxford University Press, 1982.

———. *Slavery and Freedom on the Middle Ground: Maryland during the Nineteenth Century*. New Haven, Conn.: Yale University Press, 1985.

———. "Whiteness, Racism, and Identity." *International Labor and Working Class History* 60 (2001): 48–56.

Finley, Randy. *From Slavery to Uncertain Freedom: The Freedmen's Bureau in Arkansas, 1865–1869.* Fayetteville: University of Arkansas Press, 1996.

———. "The Personnel of the Freedmen's Bureau in Arkansas." In *The Freedmen's Bureau and Reconstruction: Reconsiderations*, edited by Paul A. Cimbala and Randall M. Miller, 93–118. New York: Fordham University Press, 1999.

Fitzgerald, Michael W. *Splendid Failure: Postwar Reconstruction in the American South.* Chicago: Ivan R. Dee, 2007.

———. "Wager Swayne, the Freedmen's Bureau, and the Politics of Reconstruction in Alabama." *Alabama Review* 48 (1995): 188–232.

Fleming, John E. "Slavery, Civil War and Reconstruction: A Study of Black Women in Microcosm." *Negro History Bulletin* 38 (1975): 430–33.

Flynt, Wayne. *Poor but Proud: Alabama's Poor Whites.* Tuscaloosa: University of Alabama Press, 1989.

Foner, Eric. *Free Soil, Free Labor, Free Men: The Ideology of the Republican Party before the Civil War.* New York: Oxford University Press, 1970. Reprint, with a new introduction, New York: Oxford University Press, 1995.

———. "The Meaning of Freedom in the Age of Emancipation." *Journal of American History* 81, no. 2 (1994): 435–60.

———. *Politics and Ideology in the Age of the Civil War.* New York: Oxford University Press, 1980.

———. *Reconstruction: America's Unfinished Revolution, 1863–1877.* New York: Harper & Row, 1988.

———. *The Story of American Freedom.* New York: W. W. Norton, 1998.

Foner, Eric, and John A. Garraty, eds. *The Reader's Companion to American History.* Boston: Houghton Mifflin, 1991.

Foner, Philip S. *Women and the American Labor Movement: From Colonial Times to the Eve of World War I.* New York: Free Press, 1979.

Forbath, William F. "The Ambiguities of Free Labor: Labor and Law in the Gilded Age." *Wisconsin Law Review* 4 (1985): 767–817.

Fout, John C., and Maura Shaw Tantillo. *American Sexual Politics: Sex, Gender, and Race since the Civil War.* Chicago: University of Chicago Press, 1993.

Fox-Genovese, Elizabeth. "Strategies and Forms of Resistance: Focus on Slave Women in the United States." In *Resistance: Studies in Africa, Caribbean, and Afro-American History*, edited by Gary Y. Okihiro, 143–65. Amherst: University of Massachusetts Press, 1986.

Franke, Katherine M. "Becoming a Citizen: Reconstruction Era Regulation of African American Marriages." *Yale Journal of Law and the Humanities* 11 (1999): 251–309.

Frankel, Noralee. *Freedom's Women: Black Women and Families in Civil War Era Mississippi.* Bloomington: Indiana University Press, 1999.

———. "From Slave Women to Free Women: The National Archives and Black Women's History in the Civil War Era." *Prologue* 29, no. 2 (1997): 100–104.

———. "The Southern Side of 'Glory': Mississippi African-American Women during the Civil War." *Minerva: Quarterly Report on Women and Military* 8 (1990): 28–37.

Franklin, Donna L. *Ensuring Inequality: The Structural Transformation of the African-American Family.* New York: Oxford University Press, 1997.

Franklin, John Hope. "Public Welfare in the South during the Reconstruction Era, 1865–1880." *Social Service Review* 44, no. 4 (1970): 379–92.

———. *Reconstruction after the Civil War.* 2nd ed. Chicago: University of Illinois Press, 1994.

Franklin, John Hope, and Alfred A. Moss Jr. *From Slavery to Freedom: A History of African Americans.* 7th ed. New York: Alfred A. Knopf, 1994.

Fraser, Nancy, and Linda Gordon. "A Genealogy of *Dependency*: Tracing a Keyword of the U.S. Welfare State." *Signs: A Journal of Women in Culture and Society* 19, no. 2 (1994): 309–36.

Frazier, E. Franklin. *The Negro Family in the United States.* New York: Citadel Press, 1948.

Fredrickson, George M. *The Black Image in the White Mind: The Debate of Afro-American Character and Destiny, 1817–1914.* Middletown, Conn.: Wesleyan University Press, 1971. Reprint, New York: Harper & Row, 1987.

Fuke, Richard Paul. *Imperfect Equality: African Americans and the Confines of White Racial Attitudes in Post-emancipation Maryland.* New York: Fordham University Press, 1999.

———. "Planters, Apprenticeship, and Forced Labor: The Black Family under Pressure in Post-emancipation Maryland." *Agricultural History* 62 (1988): 54–74.

Fuller, C. Marchal. "Governmental Action to Aid Freedmen in Maryland, 1864–1869, with Special Emphasis on the Freedmen's Bureau." M.A. thesis, Howard University, 1965.

Ganus, Clifton L., Jr. "The Freedmen's Bureau in Mississippi." Ph.D. diss., Tulane University, 1953.

Gatewood, Willard G., Jr. "'The Remarkable Misses Rollin': Black Women in Reconstruction South Carolina." *South Carolina Historical Magazine* 92 (1991): 172–88.

Gerteis, Louis S. *From Contraband to Freedman: Federal Policy toward Southern Blacks, 1861–1865.* Westport, Conn.: Greenwood Press, 1973.

Giddings, Paula. *When and Where I Enter: The Impact of Black Women on Race and Sex in America.* New York: William Morrow, 1984.

Gilmore, Glenda Elizabeth. *Gender and Jim Crow: Women and the Politics of White Supremacy in North Carolina, 1896–1920.* Chapel Hill: University of North Carolina Press, 1996.

Glymph, Thavolia. "Freedpeople and Ex-masters: Shaping a New Order in the Postbellum South, 1865–1868." In *Essays on the Postbellum Southern Economy,* edited by Thavolia Glymph and John J. Kushma, 48–72. College Station: Texas A&M University Press, 1985.

———. *Out of the House of Bondage: The Transformation of the Plantation Household.* Cambridge: Cambridge University Press, 2008.

Goldberg, Chad Alan. *Citizens and Paupers: Relief, Rights, and Race, from the Freedmen's Bureau to Workfare.* Chicago: University of Chicago Press, 2007.

Goldin, Claudia. "Female Labor Force Participation: The Origin of Black and White Differences, 1870 and 1880." *Journal of Economic History* 37 (1977): 87–108.

———. "'N' Kinds of Freedom: An Introduction to the Issues." *Explorations in Economic History* 16 (1979): 8–30.

Gordon, Linda. "Black and White Visions of Welfare: Women's Welfare Activism, 1890–1945." *Journal of American History* 78 (1991): 559–90.

———. "Social Insurance and Public Assistance: The Influence of Gender in Welfare Thought in the United States, 1890–1935." *American Historical Review* 97 (1992): 19–54.

Gottlieb, Manuel. "The Land Question during Reconstruction." *Science and Society* 3 (1939): 356–88.

Green, Elna C., ed. *Before the New Deal: Social Welfare in the South, 1830–1930.* Athens: University Press of Georgia, 1999.

———. *This Business of Relief: Confronting Poverty in a Southern City, 1740–1940.* Athens: University of Georgia Press, 2003.

Gross, Ariela J. *Double Character: Slavery and Mastery in the Antebellum Southern Courtroom.* Princeton, N.J.: Princeton University Press, 2000.

———. "The Law and the Culture of Slavery: Natchez, Mississippi." In *Local Matters: Race, Crime, and Justice in the Nineteenth-Century South,* edited by Christopher Waldrep and Donald G. Nieman, 92–124. Athens: University of Georgia Press, 2001.

Grossberg, Michael. *Governing the Hearth: Law and the Family in Nineteenth-Century America.* Chapel Hill: University of North Carolina Press, 1985.

Gutman, Herbert G. "The Black Family in Slavery and Freedom: A Revised Perspective." In *Power and Culture: Essays on the American Working Class,* edited by Ira Berlin, 357–79. New York: Pantheon Books, 1987.

———. *The Black Family in Slavery and Freedom, 1750–1925*. New York: Pantheon Books, 1976.

Hahn, Steven. *A Nation under Our Feet: Black Political Struggles in the Rural South from Slavery to the Great Migration*. Cambridge, Mass.: Belknap Press of Harvard University Press, 2003.

Hall, Jacqueline Dowd. "'The Mind That Burns in Each Body': Women, Rape, and Racial Violence." In *Powers of Desire: The Politics of Sexuality*, edited by Ann Snitow, Christine Stansell, and Sharon Thompson, 328–49. New York: Monthly Review Press, 1983.

Harrison, Robert. "New Representations of a 'Misrepresented Bureau': Reflections on Recent Scholarship on the Freedmen's Bureau." *American Nineteenth Century History* 8 (June 2007): 205–29.

———. "Welfare and Employment Policies of the Freedmen's Bureau in the District of Columbia." *Journal of Southern History* 72 (2006): 75–110.

Hartog, Hendrik. *Man and Wife in America: A History*. Cambridge, Mass.: Harvard University Press, 2000.

Hewitt, Nancy A. "Beyond the Search for Sisterhood: American Women's History in the 1980s." *Social History* 10 (1985): 229–31.

———. "Did Women Have a Reconstruction? Gender in the Rewriting of Southern History." *Proceedings and Papers of the Georgia Association of Historians* 14 (1993): 1–11.

Hine, Darlene Clark. "Lifting the Veil, Shattering the Silence: Black Women's History in Slavery and Freedom." In *The State of Afro-American History: Past, Present, and Future*, edited by Darlene Clark Hine, 223–49. Baton Rouge: Louisiana State University Press, 1986.

Hine, Darlene Clark, and Kathleen Thompson. *A Shining Thread of Hope: The History of Black Women in America*. New York: Broadway Books, 1998.

Hoades, Martha. "The Sexualization of Reconstruction Politics: White Women and Black Men in the South after the Civil War." *Journal of the History of Sexuality* 3 (1993): 402–17.

———. *White Women, Black Men: Illicit Sex in the Nineteenth-Century South*. New Haven, Conn.: Yale University Press, 1997.

Holt, Sharon Ann. "Making Freedom Pay: Freedpeople Working for Themselves, North Carolina, 1865–1900." *Journal of Southern History* 60 (1994): 228–62.

Holt, Thomas. "'An Empire over the Mind': Emancipation, Race, and Ideology in the British West Indies and the American South." In *Region, Race and Reconstruction: Essays in Honor of C. Vann Woodward*, edited by J. Morgan Kousser and James McPherson, 283–313. New York: Oxford University Press, 1982.

Hope, W. Martin, and Jason H. Silverman. *Relief and Recovery in Post–Civil War South Carolina.* Lewiston, N.Y.: Edwin Mellen Press, 1997.

Hopkins, Alphonso A. *The Life of Clinton Bowen Fisk with a Brief Sketch of John A. Brooks.* New York: Funk & Wagnalls, 1888.

Horton, James. "Freedom's Yoke: Gender Conventions among Antebellum Free Blacks." *Feminist Studies* 12 (1986): 51–76.

Huebner, Timothy S. "The Roots of Fairness: *State v. Caesar* and Slave Justice in Antebellum North Carolina." In *Local Matters: Race, Crime, and Justice in the Nineteenth-Century South,* edited by Christopher Waldrep and Donald G. Nieman, 29–52. Athens: University of Georgia Press, 2001.

Hunt, Patricia K. "The Struggle to Achieve Individual Expression through Clothing and Adornment: African American Women under and after Slavery." In *Discovering the Women in Slavery: Emancipating Perspectives on the American Past,* edited by Patricia Morton, 227–40. Athens: University of Georgia Press, 1996.

Hunter, Tera W. *To 'Joy My Freedom: Southern Black Women's Lives and Labors after the Civil War.* Cambridge, Mass.: Harvard University Press, 1997.

Hurtado, Ada. "Relating to Privilege: Seduction and Rejection in the Subordination of White Women and Women of Color." *Signs: A Journal of Women in Culture and Society* 14 (1989): 833–55.

Hyman, Harold M. *A More Perfect Union: The Impact of the Civil War and Reconstruction on the Constitution.* New York: Alfred A. Knopf, 1973.

Jackson, LaVonne Roberts. "Freedom and Family: The Freedmen's Bureau and African American Women in Texas in the Reconstruction Era, 1865–1872." Ph.D. diss., Howard University, 1996.

Jaynes, Gerald David. *Branches without Roots: Genesis of the Black Working Class in the American South, 1862–1882.* New York: Oxford University Press, 1986.

Johnson, Walter. "On Agency." *Journal of Southern History* 37 (2003): 113–24.

Jones, Jacqueline. *Labor of Love, Labor of Sorrow: Black Women, Work, and the Family from Slavery to the Present.* New York: Basic Books, 1985.

———. *Soldiers of Light and Love: Northern Teachers and Georgia Blacks, 1865–1873.* Chapel Hill: University of North Carolina Press, 1980.

Jones, Martha S. *All Bound up Together: The Woman Question in African American Public Culture, 1830–1900.* Chapel Hill: University of North Carolina Press, 2007.

Jordan, Ervin L., Jr. *Black Confederates and Afro-Yankees in Civil War Virginia.* Charlottesville: University Press of Virginia, 1995.

Kaczorowski, Robert J. *The Politics of Judicial Interpretation: The Federal Courts, Department of Justice, and Civil Rights, 1866–1876.* New York: Oceana Publications, 1985. Reprint, with a new introduction, New York: Fordham University Press, 2004.

Katz, Michael B. *In the Shadow of the Poorhouse: A Social History of Welfare in America.* New York: Basic Books, 1986.

———. *The Undeserving Poor: From the War on Poverty to the War on Welfare.* New York: Pantheon Books, 1989.

Kerber, Linda K. *No Constitutional Right to Be Ladies: Women and the Obligations of Citizenship.* New York: Hill and Wang, 1998.

———. "Separate Spheres, Female Worlds, and Woman's Place: The Rhetoric of Women's History." *Journal of American History* 75 (1988): 9–39.

Klebaner, Benjamin Joseph. *Public Poor Relief in America, 1790–1860.* New York: Arno Press, 1976.

Kolchin, Peter. *First Freedom: The Response of Alabama's Blacks to Emancipation and Reconstruction.* Westport, Conn.: Greenwood Press, 1972.

Krowl, Michelle Ann. "Dixie's Other Daughters: African American Women in Virginia, 1861–1868." Ph.D. diss., University of California, Berkeley, 1998.

Lebsock, Suzanne. *The Free Women of Petersburg: Status and Culture in a Southern Town, 1784–1860.* New York: Norton, 1984.

———. "Radical Reconstruction and the Property Rights of Southern Women." *Journal of Southern History* 43 (May 1977): 195–216.

Levine, Lawrence W. *Black Culture and Black Conscientiousness: Afro-American Folk Thought from Slavery to Freedom.* New York: Oxford University Press, 1978.

Litwack, Leon F. *Been in the Storm So Long: The Aftermath of Slavery.* New York: Alfred A. Knopf, 1979. Reprint, New York: Vintage Books, 1980.

Low, W. A. "The Freedmen's Bureau and Civil Rights in Maryland." *Journal of Negro History* 37, no. 3 (1952): 221–47.

Lowe, Richard. "The Freedmen's Bureau and Local Black Leadership." *Journal of American History* 80 (1993): 989–98.

———. "The Freedmen's Bureau and Local White Leaders in Virginia." *Journal of Southern History* 64 (1998): 455–72.

Magdol, Edward. *A Right to the Land: Essays on the Freedmen's Community.* Westport, Conn.: Greenwood Press, 1977.

Malone, Ann Patton. *Sweet Chariot: Slave Family and Household Structure in Nineteenth-Century Louisiana.* Chapel Hill: University of North Carolina Press, 1992.

Mann, Susan A. "Slavery, Sharecropping, and Sexual Inequality." *Signs: A Journal of Women in Culture and Society* 14, no. 4 (1989): 774–98.

Marten, James. *The Children's Civil War.* Chapel Hill: University of North Carolina Press, 1998.

Masur, Katherine. "The Price of the Past: Preserving the Freedmen's Bureau Papers." *Perspectives: American Historical Association Newsletter* 38, no. 7 (2000): 9–11.

———. "Reconstructing the Nation's Capital: The Politics of Race and Citizenship in the District of Columbia, 1862–1878." Ph.D. diss., University of Michigan, 2001.
May, J. Thomas. "Continuity and Change in the Labor Program of the Union Army and the Freedmen's Bureau." *Civil War History* 17 (1971): 245–54.
———. "The Freedmen's Bureau at the Local Level: A Study of a Louisiana Agent." *Louisiana History* 9 (1968): 5–19.
McClintock, Megan J. "Binding up the Nation's Wounds: Nationalism, Civil War Pensions, and American Families, 1861–1890." Ph.D. diss., Rutgers University, 1994.
———. "Civil War Pensions and the Reconstruction of Union Families." *Journal of American History* 83 (1996): 456–80.
McCurry, Stephanie. *Masters of Small Worlds: Yeoman Households, Gender Relations, and the Political Culture of the Antebellum South Carolina Low Country.* New York: Oxford University Press, 1995.
McFeely, William S. *Yankee Stepfather: General O. O. Howard and the Freedmen.* New Haven, Conn.: Yale University Press, 1968.
McIntosh, Mary. "The State and the Oppression of Women." In *Feminism and Materialism: Women and the Modes of Production*, edited by Annette Kuhn and Ann Marie Wolpe, 254–89. Boston: Routledge and Kegan Paul, 1978.
McNair, Glenn. "Slave Women, Capital Crime, and Criminal Justice in Georgia." *Georgia Historical Quarterly* 93, no. 2 (2009): 135–58.
Melder, Keith E. "Angel of Mercy in Washington: Josephine Griffing and the Freedmen, 1864–1872." *Records of the Columbia Historical Society* 45 (1965): 243–72.
Messner, William F. *Freedmen and the Ideology of Free Labor: Louisiana, 1862–1865.* Lafayette: Center for Louisiana Studies, University of Southwestern Louisiana, 1978.
Miller, Randall M. "The Freedmen's Bureau and Reconstruction: An Overview." In *The Freedmen's Bureau and Reconstruction: Reconsiderations*, edited by Paul A. Cimbala and Randall M. Miller, xiii–xxxii. New York: Fordham University Press, 1999.
Mitchell, Mary Niall. *Raising Freedom's Child: Black Children and Visions of the Future after Slavery.* New York: New York University Press, 2008.
Mohr, Clarence L. *On the Threshold of Freedom: Masters and Slaves in Civil War Georgia.* Athens: University of Georgia Press, 1986.
Moneyhon, Carl H. *Republicanism in Reconstruction Texas.* Austin: University of Texas Press, 1980.
Montgomery, David. *Beyond Equality: Labor and the Radical Republicans, 1862–1872.* New York: Alfred A. Knopf, 1967.

Moran, Robert E. "The Negro Child in Louisiana, 1800–1935." *Social Service Review* 45 (1971): 53–61.

Morgan, Lynda J. *Emancipation in Virginia's Tobacco Belt, 1850–1870*. Athens: University of Georgia Press, 1992.

Morris, Robert C. *Reading, 'Riting, and Reconstruction: The Education of Freedmen in the South, 1861–1870*. Chicago: University of Chicago Press, 1981.

Morton, Patricia. *Disfigured Images: The Historical Assault on Afro-American Women*. Westport, Conn.: Greenwood Press, 1991.

Mullins, Leith. *On Our Own Terms: Race, Class, Gender in the Lives of African American Women*. New York: Routledge, 1997.

Neal, Diane, and Thomas W. Kremm. "'What Shall We Do with the Negro?' The Freedmen's Bureau in Texas." *East Texas Historical Quarterly* 27 (1989): 23–34.

Nieman, Donald G., ed. *The African American Family in the South, 1861–1900*. Vol. 8 of *African American Life in the Post-emancipation South, 1861–1900*. New York: Garland, 1994.

———, ed. *The Day of Jubilee: The Civil War Experience of Black Southerners*. Vol. 1 of *African American Life in the Post-emancipation South, 1861–1900*. New York: Garland, 1994.

———, ed. *The Freedmen's Bureau and Black Freedom*. Vol. 2 of *African American Life in the Post-emancipation South, 1861–1900*. New York: Garland, 1994.

———. "The Freedmen's Bureau and the Mississippi Black Code." *Journal of Mississippi History* 40 (1978): 91–118.

———, ed. *From Slavery to Sharecropping: White Land and Black Labor in the Rural South, 1865–1900*. Vol. 8 of *African American Life in the Post-emancipation South, 1861–1900*. New York: Garland, 1994.

———. *To Set the Law in Motion: The Freedmen's Bureau and the Legal Rights of Blacks, 1865–1868*. Millwood, N.Y.: KTO Press, 1979.

Oakes, James. "A Failure of Vision: The Collapse of the Freedmen's Bureau Courts." *Civil War History* 25 (1979): 66–76.

O'Donovan, Susan Eva. *Becoming Free in the Cotton South*. Cambridge, Mass.: Harvard University Press, 2007.

Olds, Victoria. "The Freedmen's Bureau: A Nineteenth-Century Federal Welfare Agency." *Social Casework* 44 (1963): 247–54.

Osthaus, Carl R. *Freedmen, Philanthropy, and Fraud: A History of the Freedmen's Savings Bank*. Urbana: University of Illinois Press, 1978.

Oubre, Claude F. *Forty Acres and a Mule: The Freedmen's Bureau and Black Land Ownership*. Baton Rouge: Louisiana State University Press, 1978.

Painter, Nell Irvin. "A Prize-Winning Book Revisited." Review of *Reconstruction: America's Unfinished Revolution*, by Eric Foner. *Journal of Women's History* 2, no. 3 (1991): 126–34.

Pearson, Reggie L. "'There Are Many Sick, Feeble, and Suffering Freedmen': The Freedmen's Bureau's Health-Care Activities during Reconstruction in North Carolina, 1865–1868." *North Carolina Historical Review* 79 (2002): 141–81.

Peirce, Paul Skeels. *The Freedmen's Bureau: A Chapter in the History of Reconstruction.* Iowa City: University of Iowa Press, 1904. Reprint, St. Clair Shores, Mich.: Scholarly Press, 1970.

Phillips, Paul David. "A History of the Freedmen's Bureau in Tennessee." Ph.D. diss., Vanderbilt University, 1964.

Powell, Lawrence N. *New Masters: Northern Planters during the Civil War and Reconstruction.* New Haven, Conn.: Yale University Press, 1980.

Rabinowitz, Howard N. "From Exclusion to Segregation: Health and Welfare Services for Southern Blacks, 1865–1890." *Social Service Review* 48, no. 3 (1974): 327–54.

Rable, George C. *But There Was No Peace: The Role of Violence in the Politics of Reconstruction.* Athens: University of Georgia Pres, 1984.

Rachleff, Peter J. *Black Labor in the South: Richmond, Virginia, 1865–1890.* Philadelphia: Temple University Press, 1984.

Ransom, Roger L., and Richard Sutch. *One Kind of Freedom: The Economic Consequences of Emancipation.* Cambridge: Cambridge University Press, 1977.

Rapport, Sara. "The Freedmen's Bureau as a Legal Agent for Black Men and Women in Georgia, 1865–1868." *Georgia Historical Quarterly* 73 (1989): 26–53.

Regosin, Elizabeth. *Freedom's Promise: Ex-slave Families and Citizenship in the Age of Emancipation.* Charlottesville: University Press of Virginia, 2002.

Reidy, Joseph P. *From Slavery to Agrarian Capitalism in the Cotton Plantation South: Central Georgia, 1800–1880.* Chapel Hill: University of North Carolina Press, 1992.

———. "Slave Emancipation through the Prism of Archives Records." *Prologue* 29, no. 2 (1997): 105–11.

Richardson, Heather Cox. *West from Appomattox: The Reconstruction of America after the Civil War.* New Haven, Conn.: Yale University Press, 2007.

Richardson, Joe M. *Christian Reconstruction: The American Missionary Association and Southern Blacks, 1861–1890.* Athens: University of Georgia Press, 1986.

———. "Florida Black Codes." *Florida Historical Quarterly* 47 (1969): 365–79.

Richter, William L. "'A Dear Little Job': Second Lieutenant Hiram F. Willis, Freedmen's Bureau Agent in Southwest Arkansas, 1866–1868." *Arkansas Historical Quarterly* 50 (1991): 158–200.

---. "'This Blood-thirsty Hole': The Freedmen's Bureau Agency at Clarksville, Texas, 1867–1868." *Civil War History* 38 (1992): 51–77.

---. *Overreached on All Sides: The Freedmen's Bureau Administrators in Texas, 1865–1868*. College Station: Texas A&M University Press, 1991.

---. "'The Revolver Rules the Day!' Colonel Dewitt C. Brown and the Freedmen's Bureau in Paris, Texas, 1867–1868." *Southwestern Historical Quarterly* 93 (1990): 303–32.

Ripley, C. Peter. "The Black Family in Transition: Louisiana, 1860–1865." *Journal of Southern History* 41 (1975): 369–80.

---. *Slaves and Freedmen in Civil War Louisiana*. Baton Rouge: Louisiana State University Press, 1976.

Roberts, Mary Louise. "True Womanhood Revisited." *Journal of Women's History* 14 (2002): 150–55.

Robertson, Armstead. "Beyond the Realm of Social Consensus: New Meanings of Reconstruction for American History." *Journal of American History* 68 (1981): 276–97.

---. "The Difference Freedom Made: The Emancipation of Afro-Americans." In *The State of Afro-American History*, edited by Darlene Clark Hine, 51–74. Baton Rouge: Louisiana State University Press, 1986.

Rodrigue, John C. "Black Agency after Slavery." In *Reconstructions: New Perspectives on the Postbellum United States*, edited by Thomas Brown, 40–65. New York: Oxford University Press, 2006.

---. *Reconstruction in the Cane Fields: From Slavery to Freedom in Louisiana's Sugar Parishes, 1862–1880*. Baton Rouge: Louisiana State University Press, 2001.

Rose, Willie Lee. *Rehearsal for Reconstruction: The Port Royal Experiment*. New York: Bobbs-Merrill, 1964. Reprint, New York: Oxford University Press, 1976.

Rosen, Hannah. "'Not That Sort of Women': Race, Gender, and Sexual Violence during the Memphis Riot of 1866." In *Sex, Love, Race: Crossing Boundaries in North American History*, edited by Martha Elizabeth Hodes, 267–93. New York: New York University Press, 1999.

---. *Terror in the Heart of Freedom: Citizenship, Sexual Violence, and the Meaning of Race in the Postemancipation South*. Chapel Hill: University of North Carolina Press, 2009.

Ryan, Mary P. *Mysteries of Sex: Tracing Women and Men through American History*. Chapel Hill: University of North Carolina Press, 2006.

Saville, Julie. *The Work of Reconstruction: From Slave to Wage Laborer in South Carolina, 1860–1870*. New York: Cambridge University Press, 1994.

Savitt, Todd L. "The Politics of Medicine: The Georgia Freedmen's Bureau and the Organization of Health Care, 1865–1866." *Civil War History* 28 (1982): 45–64.

Schafer, Judith Kelleher. *Slavery, the Civil Law, and the Supreme Court of Louisiana*. Baton Rouge: Louisiana State University Press, 1997.

———. "Slaves and Crime: New Orleans, 1846–1862." In *Local Matters: Race, Crime, and Justice in the Nineteenth-Century South*, edited by Christopher Waldrep and Donald G. Nieman, 53–91. Athens: University of Georgia Press, 2001.

Schmidt, James D. *Free to Work: Labor Law, Emancipation, and Reconstruction, 1815–1880*. Athens: University of Georgia Press, 1999.

Schwalm, Leslie A. *A Hard Fight for We: Women's Transition from Slavery to Freedom in South Carolina*. Urbana: University of Illinois Press, 1997.

———. "'Sweet Dreams of Freedom': Freedwomen's Reconstruction of Life and Labor in Lowcountry South Carolina." *Journal of Women's History* 9 (1997): 9–38.

Scott, Anne Firor. *The Southern Lady: From Pedestal to Politics, 1830–1930*. Chicago: University of Chicago Press, 1972.

Scott, Joan Wallach. "Gender: A Useful Category of Historical Analysis." In *Gender and the Politics of History*, 28–50. New York: Columbia University Press, 1988.

Scott, Rebecca. "The Battle over the Child: Child Apprenticeship and the Freedmen's Bureau in North Carolina." *Prologue* 10, no. 2 (1978): 101–13.

———. "Defining the Boundaries of Freedom in the World of Cane: Cuba, Brazil, and Louisiana after Emancipation." *American Historical Review* 99 (1994): 70–102.

Scully, Pamela, and Diana Paton, eds. *Gender and Slave Emancipation in the Atlantic World*. Durham, N.C.: Duke University Press, 2005.

Sefton, James E. *The United States Army and Reconstruction, 1865–1877*. Baton Rouge: Louisiana State University Press, 1967.

Shifflett, Crandall A. "The Household Composition of Rural Black Families: Louisa Country, Virginia, 1880." *Journal of Interdisciplinary History* 6 (1975): 235–60.

———. *Patronage and Poverty in the Tobacco South: Louisa County, Virginia, 1860–1900*. Knoxville: University of Tennessee Press, 1982.

Silber, Nina. *The Romance of Reunion: Northerners and the South, 1865–1900*. Chapel Hill: University of North Carolina Press, 1993.

Simkins, Francis B., and James W. Patton. *Women of the Confederacy*. Richmond, Va.: Garrett and Massie, 1936.

Simpson, Brooks D. "Ulysses S. Grant and the Freedmen's Bureau." In *The Freedmen's Bureau and Reconstruction: Reconsiderations*, edited by Paul A. Cimbala and Randall M. Miller, 1–28. New York: Fordham University Press, 1999.

Skocpol, Theda. *Protecting Soldiers and Mothers: The Political Origins of Social Policy in the United States*. Cambridge, Mass.: Belknap Press of Harvard University Press, 1992.

Smallwood, James. "Black Freedwomen after Emancipation: The Texas Experience." *Prologue* 27, no. 4 (1995): 302–17.

———. "Charles E. Culver, a Reconstruction Agent in Texas: The Work of Local Freedmen's Bureau Agents and the Black Community." *Civil War History* 27 (1981): 350–61.

———. "Emancipation and the Black Family: A Case Study in Texas." *Social Science Quarterly* 57 (1977): 849–57.

Smith, John David. "'The Work It Did Not Do Because It Could Not': Georgia and the 'New' Freedmen's Bureau Historiography." *Georgia Historical Quarterly* 82 (1998): 331–49.

Smith, Rogers. *Civic Ideals: Conflicting Visions of Citizenship in U.S. History*. New Haven, Conn.: Yale University Press, 1997.

Smith-Rosenberg, Carroll. *Disorderly Conduct: Visions of Gender in Victorian America*. New York: Oxford University Press, 1985.

Sommerville, Diane Miller. *Rape and Race in the Nineteenth-Century South*. Chapel Hill: University of North Carolina Press, 2004.

Stack, Carol B. *All Our Kin: Strategies for Survival in a Black Community*. New York: Harper & Row, 1974.

Stampp, Kenneth M. *The Era of Reconstruction, 1865–1877*. New York: Alfred A. Knopf, 1965.

Stanley, Amy Dru. "Beggars Can't Be Choosers: Compulsion and Contract in Postbellum America." *Journal of American History* 78 (1992): 1265–93.

———. "Conjugal Bonds and Wage Labor: Rights of Contract in the Age of Emancipation." *Journal of American History* 75 (1988): 471–500.

———. *From Bondage to Contract: Wage Labor, Marriage, and the Market in the Age of Slave Emancipation*. Cambridge: Cambridge University Press, 1998.

———. "'We Did Not Separate Man and Wife, but All Had to Work': Freedom and Dependence in the Aftermath of Slave Emancipation." In *Terms of Labor: Slavery, Serfdom, and Free Labor*, edited by Stanley L. Engerman, 188–212. Stanford, Calif.: Stanford University Press, 1999.

Steedman, Marek. "Gender and the Politics of Household in Reconstruction Louisiana, 1865–1878." In *Gender and Slave Emancipation in the Atlantic*

World, edited by Pamela Scully and Diana Paton, 310–27. Durham, N.C.: Duke University Press, 2005.

Steinfield, Robert J. "Changing Legal Conceptions of Free Labor." In *Terms of Labor: Slavery, Serfdom, and Free Labor*, edited by Stanley L. Engerman, 137–67. Stanford, Calif.: Stanford University Press, 1999.

Sutch, Richard, and Robert L. Ransom. "Sharecropping: Market Response or Mechanism of Race Control?" In *What Was Freedom's Price?* edited by David S. Sansing, 51–70. Jackson: University Press of Mississippi, 1978.

Talbot, Edith Armstrong. *Samuel Chapman Armstrong: A Biographical Study*. New York: Doubleday, Page, 1904.

Taylor, Joe Gray. *Louisiana Reconstructed, 1863–1877*. Baton Rouge: Louisiana State University Press, 1974.

Terborg-Penn, Rosalyn. "Black Women in Resistance: A Cross-Cultural Perspective." In *Resistance: Studies in African, Caribbean, and Afro-American History*, edited by Gary Y. Okihior, 188–209. Amherst: University of Massachusetts Press, 1986.

Trattner, Walter I. *From Poor Law to Welfare State: A History of Social Welfare in America*. 2nd ed. New York: Free Press, 1979.

Trefousse, Hans L. "Andrew Johnson and the Freedmen's Bureau." In *The Freedmen's Bureau and Reconstruction: Reconsiderations*, edited by Paul A. Cimbala and Randall M. Miller, 29–92. New York: Fordham University Press, 1999.

Trelease, Allen W. *White Terror: The Ku Klux Klan Conspiracy and Southern Reconstruction*. New York: Harper & Row, 1971.

Tunnell, Ted. *Edge of the Sword: The Ordeal of Carpetbagger Marshall H. Twitchell in the Civil War and Reconstruction*. Baton Rouge: Louisiana State University Press, 2001.

Vandal, Gilles. *Rethinking Southern Violence: Homicides in Post–Civil War Louisiana, 1866–1884*. Columbus: Ohio State University Press, 2000.

van Zelm, Antoinette G. "On the Front Lines of Freedom: Black and White Women Shape Emancipation in Virginia, 1861–1890." Ph.D. diss., College of William and Mary, 1998.

Waldrep, Christopher, and Donald G. Nieman, eds. *Local Matters: Race, Crime, and Justice in the Nineteenth-Century South*. Athens: University of Georgia Press, 2001.

Wallace, Maurice O. *Constructing the Black Masculine: Identity and Ideality in African American Men's Literature and Culture, 1775–1995*. Durham, N.C.: Duke University Press, 2002.

Wallenstein, Peter. *From Slave South to New South: Public Policy in Nineteenth-Century Georgia*. Chapel Hill: University of North Carolina Press, 1987.

Washington, Reginald. "Sealing the Sacred Bonds of Holy Matrimony: Freedmen's Bureau Marriage Records." *Prologue* 37, no. 1 (2005): 58–65.

———. "Spotlight on NARA: The Freedmen's Bureau Preservation Project." *Prologue* 34, no. 2 (2002): 144–48.

Webster, Laura Josephine. "The Operation of the Freedmen's Bureau in South Carolina." *Smith College Studies in History* 1, no. 2 (1916): 121–63.

Weiner, Marli Frances. *Mistresses and Slaves: Plantation Women in South Carolina, 1830–1880*. Urbana: University of Illinois Press, 1997.

Welter, Barbara. "The Cult of True Womanhood, 1820–1860." *American Quarterly* 18 (1966): 151–74.

Wharton, Vernon Lane. *The Negro in Mississippi, 1865–1890*. New York: Harper & Row, 1965.

———. "Reconstruction." In *Writing Southern History: Essays in Historiography in Honor of Fletcher M. Green*, edited by Arthur S. Link and Rembert W. Patrick, 295–315. Baton Rouge: Louisiana State University Press, 1965.

White, Deborah Gray. *Ar'n't I a Woman? Female Slaves in the Plantation South*. 2nd ed. New York: W. W. Norton, 1999.

———. "Female Slaves: Sex Roles and Status in the Antebellum Plantation South." *Journal of Family History* 8 (1983): 248–61.

White, Howard A. *The Freedmen's Bureau in Louisiana*. Baton Rouge: Louisiana State University Press, 1970.

Whites, LeeAnn. *The Civil War as a Crisis in Gender: Augusta, Georgia, 1860–1890*. Athens: University of Georgia Press, 1995.

Wicker, Tivis. "Virginia's Legitimization Act of 1866." *Virginia Magazine of History and Biography* 86 (1978): 339–44.

Wiecek, William M. "The Great Writ and Reconstruction: The Habeas Corpus Act of 1867." *Journal of Southern History* 36 (1970): 530–48.

Wiley, Bell Irvin. *Southern Negroes, 1861–1865*. New Haven, Conn.: Yale University Press, 1938.

Williams, Heather Andrea. *Self-Taught: African American Education in Slavery and Freedom*. Chapel Hill: University of North Carolina Press, 2007.

Williams, Linda Faye. *The Constraint of Race: Legacies of White Skin Privilege*. University Park: Pennsylvania State University Press, 2003.

Williams, Lou Faulkner. *The Great South Carolina Ku Klux Klan Trials, 1871–1872*. Athens: University of Georgia Press, 1996.

Williamson, Joel. *After Slavery: The Negro in South Carolina during Reconstruction, 1861–1877*. Chapel Hill: University of North Carolina Press, 1965.

———. *The Crucible of Race: Black/White Relations in the American South since Emancipation*. New York: Oxford University Press, 1984.

Wilson, Theodore Brantner. *The Black Codes of the South.* University: University of Alabama Press, 1965.
Wisner, Elizabeth. *Social Welfare in the South: From Colonial Times to World War I.* Baton Rouge: Louisiana State University Press, 1970.
Wood, George A. "The Black Code of Alabama." *South Atlantic Quarterly* 13 (1914): 350–60.
Young, R. J. *Antebellum Black Activists: Race, Gender, and Self.* New York: Garland, 1996.
Zipf, Karin L. *Labor of Innocents: Forced Apprenticeship in North Carolina, 1715–1919.* Baton Rouge: Louisiana State University Press, 2005.
———. "Reconstructing 'Free Woman': African-American Women, Apprenticeship, and Custody Rights during Reconstruction." *Journal of Women's History* 12 (2000): 8–31.
———. " 'The WHITES Shall Rule the Land or Die': Gender, Race, and Class in North Carolina Reconstruction Politics." *Journal of Southern History* 65 (1999): 499–534.

Index

abolitionism, 14–15, 16, 18, 19, 20, 26, 28, 30, 56, 79, 144
Adeline (no last name), 70
adultery, 29, 89, 135, 151–56. *See also* marriage
Akins, Malice, 155
Akins, Susan, 155
Alabama, 17, 20, 40, 42, 48, 54–55, 81, 111, 115
Alfred, Barbara, 132
Ambrose, Eliza, 121–25
Ambrose, Harriet, 121–25
Ambrose, John Allen, 122
Ambrose, Wiley, 122–26. See also *In the Matter of Harriet Ambrose and Eliza Ambrose*
American Freedmen's Friend Society, 54
American Freedmen's Inquiry Commission, 26
Anna (no last name), 73
Anthony, Hester, 109
apprenticeship, 10, 11, 34, 55–58, 60–62, 85, 95, 97–118, 120–30, 135, 137–38, 169–71. *See also* children; Freedmen's Bureau; freedwomen; vagrancy
Arkansas, 12, 17, 81, 85, 110
Armstrong, Samuel Chapman, 35–36, 49, 61, 87
Aubriden, Charles, 122

Barber, Phillis, 90
Bardaglio, Peter, 92
Barnett, Judy, 154
Barton, John, 76
Basch, Norma, 157
Bascom, Jack, 112
Battle, Julian, 132
Belcher, Edwin, 101
Bell, Daniel, 94
Bennett, Mary, 150, 157
Bercaw, Nancy, 4, 8, 12, 45, 150, 152
Berry, Virginia, 58, 128

black codes, 99, 146
Bolton, Sarah, 78
Bonesteel, P., 158
Boris, Eileen, 19
Bowdoin College, 17
Brown, Ann Marie, 52–53, 151
Brown, Elsa Barkley, 150
Brown, James, 52
Brown, Julia, 162
Brown, Orlando, 17, 24–25, 53, 82, 146
Brown, Pattis, 75
Bundy, Nancy, 90
Bundy, Sally, 90
Burbridge, John, 132–33
Burch, Mary, 58
Bureau of Refugees, Freedmen, and Abandoned Lands. *See* Freedmen's Bureau

Campbell, Robert, 73
Capus, John, 153
Carbin, Mary, 47
Caroline (no last name), 71, 159
Castle Thunder prison, 91
Cauldfield, Mrs. William, 47
Cecilia (no last name), 88
Cesar (no last name), 154
Chapman, Edna, 117
Charles, Mingo, 77
children, 1, 11, 16, 28–30, 35–37, 39–66, 73, 77, 80, 84–88, 95, 96–140, 149, 150, 151–53, 156–57, 169–70; as orphans, 35, 39, 44, 54–56, 60–61, 100, 102–3, 105, 112–14, 116, 138. *See also* apprenticeship; freedwomen
Childs, Rhoda Ann, 161
Cilley, Clinton, 116
Cimbala, Paul, 16, 20, 107, 134
Circular No. 5, 27, 125–26
Civil Rights Act of 1866, 99, 123, 125–26, 147
Clark, Peter, 152

Clark, Selden, 45
Clinton, Catherine, 5
Clinton, Fanny, 72
Cohen, William, 81
Colburn, Leah, 90
Cole, Ellen, 118
Coleman, Molly, 132
Colored Orphan Asylum, 54
Confederate defeat, 17, 22, 23, 33, 149
Confederate veterans, 2, 69, 120, 162
Connor, Mary, 77
contract ideology, 6, 8–9, 11, 20–23, 25–29, 32, 42, 50–51, 55, 66–68, 71–78, 80, 81, 83–86, 88–89, 91–92, 94, 111–12, 115–18, 119–20, 129, 142, 147, 168–69. *See also* Freedmen's Bureau; marriage
Conway, Thomas, 17, 184*n*12
Cox, Charity, 54, 58
Croudy, Basil, 114

Daniels, Julia Francis, 68
Darden, Sylvia, 57–58, 128
Dartmouth College, 17
David, Dick, 133
David, Hannah, 133
Davis, Jeff C., 184*n*12
Day, Madison, 130
De Forest, John William, 83, 93, 112, 127–28
Debro, Sarah, 38, 136
Delia (no last name), 75
Denby, Caroline, 151
desertion, 36, 45, 47, 49, 51, 60, 84, 87, 100, 101–2, 120, 133, 135, 137, 151–56
Dilsey (no last name), 77
divorce, 8, 51, 156–57. *See also* family; marriage
domesticity, 2, 3, 8–11, 14–15, 22, 26, 28–34, 37, 46, 48–49, 57, 84, 107, 112, 118, 120, 124, 126, 129–30, 132, 142, 144, 150, 152, 155–56, 166, 168–71. *See also* Freedmen's Bureau: and womanhood
Douglass, Frederick, 33
Du Bois, W. E. B., 2–3, 19, 148, 165

Earle, Anna, 55–56
Easton, Mary, 73
Eaton, John, 17, 96–97, 106
education, 2, 12, 21, 30, 35–36, 37–38, 40, 56, 99, 106–7

Edward (no last name), 75
Edwards, Laura, 4, 12, 34, 46, 148, 150
Edwards, Mary, 91
Elder, Eliza, 117
Eliot, Thomas, 22
Eliza (no last name), 77, 89–90
Elliot, Laura, 90
Ellis, Jerry, 152
Ellis, Molly, 152
emancipation, 1–2, 4–8, 10–13, 15–19, 22–30, 32–34, 36–38, 45–46, 48, 50–51, 53, 59, 63, 65–70, 72, 80, 81, 85, 87, 92–102, 104–8, 120–24, 129–32, 136, 140–45, 148–50, 153, 157–60, 162–68, 170–71
Eppes, Richard, 73
Eppes, Susan Bradford, 70
Ester (no last name), 89

family, 2–3, 15, 24, 44–48, 53–54, 57, 59, 60, 70, 73–74, 80, 95, 98–99; and children, 97–99, 101–3, 105–40; and domestic disputes, 150–57; importance to freedwomen, 23, 46–47, 59, 97–98, 149–51; as promoted by bureau, 2, 3, 11, 14, 26–30, 32, 34, 50–51, 52, 61–62, 75–77; in relation to labor, 75–77, 83–90, 93, 97. *See also* children; desertion; Freedmen's Bureau; freedwomen; marriage
Faulkner, Carol, 55
Fields, Barbara Jeanne, 3
Fisk, Clinton B., 14–15, 17, 23–26, 29–32, 50, 82, 107, 134, 141, 152
Florida, 9, 17, 70, 82, 105, 113, 130, 131
Flournoy, Nancy, 46
Foner, Eric, 4, 9, 19, 22, 92
Forrest, Mary Jane, 161
Foster, Louisa, 110
Fourteenth Amendment, 147
Fowler, William, 131
Frankel, Noralee, 4, 12, 150
free labor, 2, 4, 6, 9–15, 22–28, 32–37, 50, 53, 58, 62–68, 70–72, 74–76, 79–82, 84, 86, 92–94, 97–99, 104–5, 107, 111–18, 126–27, 130, 132, 134–35, 137–38, 142–44, 155–56, 166–70. *See also* contract ideology; Freedmen's Bureau
freedmen, 2–4, 8, 10–11, 13–17, 20–21, 24–25, 27–30, 36–38, 41–44, 47–51, 59, 61–62, 66–67, 77, 81–82, 84–87, 91–92, 97, 101, 104, 107–8, 122, 126, 132–

34, 141–46, 148–52, 157, 158–59, 162, 165, 168–70. *See also* gender; manhood
Freedmen and Southern Society Project, 7, 25
Freedmen's Bureau
and abuse complaints, 87–80, 158–65
and Andrew Johnson, 18, 54–55, 69, 106, 147, 190*n*3
and apprenticeship, 55–58, 61, 97–98, 101, 104–9, 111–18, 129, 169
and the Civil Rights Act of 1866, 122–26
and citizenship, 1, 8, 11, 13, 15, 22–23, 25, 27–30, 32, 50, 52, 62, 84, 92, 123, 124, 128–29, 131, 132, 142–46, 148, 165–66
coercion of, 6, 13, 55
and Congress, 1, 16, 18, 21, 22, 28, 35, 36, 39, 40, 60, 104, 126, 143, 146–47, 158, 159, 163, 165, 173*n*2
considerations of inferiority based on race, 44, 50, 96, 127, 137
and contracts, 4, 6, 9, 11, 23, 25–28, 32, 50–51, 55, 66–67, 74–78, 81, 86, 92, 94, 111–17, 147, 169–70. *See also* contract ideology
creation of, 1, 2, 15–16, 22, 23, 173*n*2
and custody disputes, 119–38
and dependency, 10, 11, 15, 28–29, 37, 44–62 passim
and domestic disputes, 155–57
and domesticity, 10, 12, 15, 29, 31–32, 84, 112, 118, 121, 123, 126, 128–32, 142–44, 150, 155, 166, 168–71
and education, 12
extension of, 18, 146–47, 173*n*2
failure of, 1, 2, 3, 7, 148, 165
and freedwomen, 1, 2, 5, 6, 7, 8, 9, 10, 11, 12–13, 29–34, 35–37, 45–51, 56–58, 67–92, 98, 104–40, 155–57, 163–65, 167–71. *See also* freedwomen
and free labor ideology, 4, 22, 24, 33, 64–66, 67–92, 94, 98, 112, 115–18, 142, 152, 153, 155, 167. *See also* contract ideology; free labor
historiography of, 2–3, 6–7, 8, 50, 174*n*5, 175–79*nn*8–15, 181–82*n*26, 202–3*n*2
and judicial tribunals, 141, 145–46
and labor, 36–37, 80–83, 86–92, 94
and land, 20–24, 36, 38, 86, 119, 129, 190*n*3

and manhood, 11, 15, 27, 29–30, 32, 33–34, 43–44, 50–52, 66–67, 75–76, 84–86, 92, 124, 142–43, 150, 153, 166, 169–71
and marriage, 8, 14, 20, 26–32, 75–77, 118, 120, 124, 129, 131, 144, 151–57
paternalism of, 15, 24–25, 29–30, 50, 61, 86, 107, 127, 131, 142, 155, 167
personnel and organization of, 9, 15–21, 33, 106
and poor relief, 37–50, 52, 56
records of, 7, 11–12
and transportation, 53–62
and vagrancy, 11, 29, 57, 65–66, 72, 81–93, 120, 134, 169
and wages, 71–75
and womanhood, 11, 12, 14–15, 29, 30–32, 33–34, 86–87, 142–43, 164–65
Freedmen's Bureau Act, 146–47, 173*n*2, 184*n*10, 226*n*10
freedwomen
agency of, 3–4, 58–61, 67–68, 69–71
and alleged withdrawal from workforce, 51, 64–66, 67–68, 84–86, 202*n*2
assertion of rights, 34, 57, 60, 62, 68, 78, 94, 97–98, 103–4, 109–12, 115–26, 130–40, 142–43, 148–50, 154–55, 157–60, 163–66
and bureau relief, 35–37, 40, 44–49, 58–61, 62
and collective action, 68–69
complaints of abuse, 77–80, 153–55, 158–63
complaints of domestic discord, 151–52, 153–57
complaints against employers, 69–73, 74–80
complaints of racial violence, 158–60
complaints of sexual assault, 160–63
custody disputes with freedmen, 97–99, 130–35, 138–40
and desertion, 36, 45, 47, 49, 51, 60, 84, 87, 100, 101–2, 120, 133, 135, 137, 151–56
as distinct from freedmen, 3, 8, 22
expectations for freedom, 23, 46–47, 59, 67–68, 97–98, 149–51
historiography of, 3–7, 202*n*2
interaction with bureau officials, 1–9, 12–13, 45–47, 51, 54, 58, 67–68, 71–74, 97–99, 104–5, 111–12, 114–17, 155–57, 163–65, 167–70

and marriage, 149–51, 152, 157
and motherhood, 23, 29, 37, 46–49, 55–62, 95, 96–99, 101–40, 149, 157, 177n10. *See also* apprenticeship; children; family
and prostitution, 88, 90–91. *See also* vagrancy
status of, 2, 8, 22, 30, 64–65, 86, 128–29, 142–43, 149–50, 158, 164–66
and transportation, 54–55, 58–60
and wage negotiation, 67–77
and womanhood, 13, 34, 46–47, 62–63, 123, 139, 142–43, 160–65
French, Mr. (no first name), 123
Fuke, Richard Paul, 102
Fullerton, Joseph, 184n12

gender, 28–30, 37, 41, 44–45, 62, 65–66, 77–78, 81–84, 91–92, 98–99, 124, 130–35, 139–42, 150, 154, 157, 160, 162; and bureau policy, 2, 3, 8, 11, 12–13, 166–71; and ideology of true womanhood, 9–10, 14–15, 24, 31, 34, 170; in Reconstruction historiography, 4, 5, 10; relationship to race, 6–8, 11. *See also* manhood; womanhood
Georgia (state), 1, 9, 12, 15, 17, 20, 32, 34, 48, 50, 53, 54, 55, 57–59, 64, 66, 67, 69, 70, 71, 72, 73, 74, 75, 76, 77, 78, 79, 80, 81, 83, 85, 88, 89, 90, 91, 100, 101, 104, 107, 108–9, 113, 114, 116, 117–18, 127–28, 132–33, 134, 135, 137, 142, 149–50, 153–54, 155, 156, 157, 159, 161, 165, 166, 168, 169
Gibbs, Annie, 117
Gillem, Alvan, 152
Glymph, Thavolia, 4, 5, 33, 149
Goole, Frankie, 136
Gordon, Charles, 89
Gray, Emmie, 71
Green, Louisa Bealfree, 75
Gregory, Edgar, 18, 82, 86
Griffing, Josephine, 38, 44, 55–56
Gunter, Agnes Ann, 90
Guntharpe, Violet, 37

habeas corpus, 123, 124, 127
Hagar (no last name), 71
Hall, Charlotte, 102
Hammones, Elvira, 159
Hampton, Harriet, 163–64
Hampton Institute, 36

Hanberry, Harriet, 91
Handy, Julia, 110
Handy, Maria, 90
Hardy, Susan, 134–35
Harper's Weekly, 23
Harrell, Mrs. Thomas, 115
Harriet (no last name), 47, 70
Harris, J. D., 64–65
Harrison, Robert, 3
Hawkins, Margaret, 49
Hayden, Anna, 154
Hayden, Henry, 154
Hill, Jennie, 136
Holt, Thomas, 15
Howard, Oliver Otis, 15–25, 27, 33, 35, 38–40, 49–50, 53–56, 67, 105, 108, 114–15, 118, 123, 125–26, 141, 143–46
Hugan, Harrison, 76
Hunter, William, 134–35

In the Matter of Harriet Ambrose and Eliza Ambrose, 121–26
indenturing. *See* apprenticeship
infidelity. *See* adultery

Jackson, Henry, 154
James, Horace, 48
Jane (no last name), 76, 89
Jenkins, Alford, 156
Jenkins, Grace, 114
Jenkins, Henry, 114
Jenkins, Sarah, 156
Johnson, Andrew (President), 18, 54–55, 69, 106, 147, 190n3
Johnson, Belfield, 152
Johnson, Frank, 153
Johnson, John Calvin, 137
Johnson, Mary, 153
Joins, Kitty, 90
Jolissaint, L., 117
Jordan, J., 85

Kaczorowski, Robert, 148
Kamper, Jane, 110–11
Kate (no last name), 70
Kelson, Bettie, 77
Kemp, Amanda, 78
Kennard, Elizabeth, 118
Kentucky, 14, 17, 50, 107, 158
Kerber, Linda, 6, 88
Kiddoo, Joseph Barr, 106, 184n12
King, Harriet, 89

King, Lucy Ann, 154
King, Wesley, 154
Knox, John, 133–34
Ku Klux Klan, 162–63

Lacy, Moses, 119–20, 126
Lacy, Sarah, 119–20, 126
Laney (no last name), 154
Lay, Phillip, 135
Leach, Feby, 46
Leathy (no last name), 89
Lee, Lucy, 139–40
Lerner, Gerda, 162
Lewis, John Randolph, 184n12
Liggins, Timpy, 91
Lincoln, Abraham, 136, 143
Lindsay, Mary, 71
Lizzie (no last name), 93
Losey, Daniel, 166
Louisiana, 12, 17, 46–47, 57, 70, 73, 77, 80, 85, 88, 104, 110, 117, 126, 128, 135, 153–54, 162
Lucinda (no last name), 59
Lynch, Mrs. Edward, 71
Lyon, Edwin, 84

Magruder, Mary, 74
Maine, 16, 17
manhood, 8, 11, 13, 15, 32, 34, 43–44, 67, 86, 142–43, 150, 153, 169–71. *See also* freedmen; Freedmen's Bureau
Maranda (no last name), 48
marriage, 8, 14, 20, 26–32, 36–37, 45, 59, 60, 62, 75–76, 84, 86, 88, 92, 100, 103, 108, 109, 117–26, 128–29, 131–33, 135, 137–38, 144, 149–57, 170; as a contract, 26–32, 75–77, 92. *See also* divorce; domesticity; family; Freedmen's Bureau; freedwomen
Marshall, George, 133
Martha (no last name), 89, 169
Martin, Catherine, 135
Mary (no last name), 89
Maryland, 52, 97, 100, 101–2, 104, 105, 106, 109, 110, 111, 114, 115, 140, 151, 161
Massachusetts, 17, 56
Matthews, Albert, 157
Matthews, Emma, 154
Mayer, A. H., 106
McFeely, William, 27
McIntosh, Susan, 1, 15
Memphis Riot of 1866, 160

Military Reconstruction Acts, 147
Mississippi, 12, 17, 20, 55, 61, 68, 71, 74, 77, 78, 81, 89, 94, 100, 103, 105, 113, 132, 141, 145, 151–52, 154, 156, 159, 161, 162
Missouri, 17, 136
Molley, Lucinda, 51
Moore, George F., 120
Mosebach, Frederick, 80, 116
Murray, Harriet, 78

Nation, 20
National Archives, 7
National Freedmen's Relief Association, 44
New York, 14, 54
New York Herald, 54
New York Times, 30, 34, 106
Nichols, Maria, 114–15
Nieman, Donald, 144
North Carolina, 12, 17, 18, 29, 48, 53, 57, 72, 82, 100, 103, 105, 113, 114, 116, 121–26, 128, 131, 169
North Carolina Supreme Court, 121, 124

Oakes, James, 144
O'Donovan, Susan, 4, 10, 12, 48, 150
Ohio, 17
orphans. *See* children
Osborn, Thomas, 17

Pace, Jane, 152
Parsons, Rebecca, 104
Patsey (no last name), 133
Pearson, Mr. (no first name), 123
Pease, W. B., 78–79
Peebles, Phillis, 115
Pennsylvania, 28, 30
Phillis (no last name), 110, 128
Phillis (no last name), Aunt, 68
Plain Counsels for Freedmen, 14, 26, 29, 134
Polly, Miss (no last name), 136
Pope, Chuff, 119
Pope, Elkin, 119
Pope, Harry, 119–20
Pope, Leney, 119
Porter, Byron, 75
Porter, Mary, 114
Powell, Betsy, 72
prostitution, 55, 84, 88, 90–91, 135. *See also* vagrancy

Ran, Mary Anne, 118
Randale, Mrs. Martin, 47
rape, 144, 158, 160–63
Rauschenberg, Charles, 155
Reade, Edwin Godwin, 124–25
Reconstruction, 1–13, 15–16, 18, 20, 22, 24–25, 30–31, 33, 36, 44, 50, 65, 92–93, 97, 99, 107, 112, 117, 128, 131, 136, 142–43, 145–48, 150, 154–56, 160, 163, 167, 170–71; as a failure, 2, 148; historiography of, 4, 5, 10, 148; and interconnectedness of public and private, 4–5, 9; as a social process, 4, 13
Reece, Elsie, 68
Reeves, Reuben, 119
Regan, Emma, 75
Republicans, 17, 28, 101, 146, 162
Richardson, Maria, 130
Riley, Ellen, 132
Robbins, Angaline, 73
Robbins, Linday, 111
Roberts, Georgia, 71
Robinson, John C., 105, 121–23
Rosen, Hannah, 4, 12, 158, 160
Ross, Delia, 121–22, 126
Ross, Lucy, 121–22, 126. See also *In the Matter of Harriet Ambrose and Eliza Ambrose*
Ross, Maria, 121–22, 126
Ruger, Thomas, 184n12
Runnels, Sarah, 151
Russell, Daniel Lindsay, 121–24, 126
Ryan, Mary, 5

Sanford, Sarah, 54
Sarah (no last name), 69–70, 154
Saunders, Hepsey, 121–22, 124, 126. See also *In the Matter of Harriet Ambrose and Eliza Ambrose*
Saville, Julie, 12
Saxton, Rufus, 17, 27, 29, 107, 184n12
Scaggs, Maria, 134
Schmidt, James, 117–18
Schwalm, Leslie, 6, 4, 12
Scott, Rebecca, 12
Scott, Robert, 82
Sea Cloud Plantation, 68
Sealy, Angeline, 74–75
Seymour, Rosa, 116
Sharpe, Harriet, 88
Sharpe, Margaret, 88
Sherman, William Tecumseh, 16

Silber, Nina, 38
Silvia (no last name), 154
Simril, Harriet, 162
Smith, Georgiana, 49
Smith, Lucy, 159–61
Smith, Mathilda, 153
Smith, Naomi, 77
South Carolina, 12, 17, 18, 20, 27, 29, 33, 37, 51, 56, 68, 71, 82, 93, 100, 107, 108, 111, 127, 129, 146, 154, 156, 162
Sprague, John, 17
Stanley, Amy Dru, 4, 9, 26
Stanton, Edwin, 17
Sterling, Dorothy, 154
Stevens, Thaddeus, 18
Stickney, W. B., 77
Stiles, William Henry, 100
Strafford, Matilda, 151
Sumner, Samuel S., 78
Swayne, Noah Haynes, 17
Swayne, Wager, 17–18, 115

Taylor, John, 152
Taylor, Martha, 152
Taylor, Rosetta, 74
Taylor, Susie King, 32
Taylor, William, 60, 104
Tennessee, 14, 16, 17, 23, 50, 54, 78, 107, 145, 158
Texas, 12, 18, 40, 47, 50, 51, 54, 56, 68, 70, 74–78, 80–82, 86, 90, 99, 103, 106, 109, 115, 119–20, 126–29, 131, 134, 151, 154, 159, 163
Texas Supreme Court, 120
Thirteenth Amendment, 143
Thomas, Samuel, 17, 141
Thompson, Frances, 160–61
Thorp, Joseph, 85
Tidball, William Sims, 49, 78, 151
Tillson, Davis, 17, 55
Timmins, Mary, 119
Timmins, Robert, 119
Tredway, Thomas, 60, 103–4
Tripp, Ann Maria, 118
true womanhood. *See* womanhood
Tyrell, Mrs. (no first name), 78

Uncle Sam, 159
Union Army, 20, 26, 27, 52, 143
Union veterans, 9, 14, 16–17, 20, 35–37, 44, 45, 47, 62, 102, 106, 110, 149, 159, 161
U.S. Supreme Court, 17

vagrancy, 6, 10–11, 29, 44, 57, 65–66, 72, 81–92, 93, 100, 102, 120, 134, 168–69; relationship to apprenticeship, 37, 56–61 passim, 101–2, 120; relationship to prostitution, 90–91
Victorianism, 8, 10, 12, 15, 29, 79, 163, 168, 179–71
Virginia (state), 12, 17, 18, 21, 24, 25, 28, 35, 36, 39, 40, 41, 43, 46, 47, 49, 51–56, 59–61, 69, 71, 73, 77, 78, 81, 82, 84, 85, 87, 90, 91, 102, 103, 109, 110, 132, 145, 146, 149, 151–53, 157, 159, 165, 167
Virginia (no last name), 88

Walker, Annie, 77, 80
War Department, 1, 2, 39
Warner, Margaret, 161
Washington, Booker T., 36
Washington, James, 76
Washington, D.C., 1, 7, 16, 17, 18, 45, 47, 54, 55, 56, 96, 97, 106, 113, 168
Washington Chronicle, 20
Wesendonck, Jane, 136–37
Wesendonck, Margaret, 136–37
West Point, 17
West Virginia, 47

White, Alma, 91
White, Francis, 91
White, Lavinia, 91
Whittlesey, Eliphalet, 17, 29, 105, 107, 113, 184n12
William, Venus, 71
Williams, Dina, 114
Williams, Dollina, 154
Williams, Lou Faulkner, 162
Williams, May, 91
Williams, Stephan, 76
Wilson, Mary, 91
Winder, Mary, 132–33
womanhood, 8–9, 11–15, 30–34, 46–47, 62–63, 86, 123, 139, 142–43, 160–65; ideology of true womanhood, 9–10, 14–34, 46–47, 168, 170. *See also* Freedmen's Bureau; freedwomen
Wood, Thomas, 184n12
Woodson, Henry, 51, 157
Woodson, Rebecca, 51, 157

Yale Medical School, 17
Young, Caroline, 90

Zipf, Karin, 12, 121, 139

RECONSTRUCTING AMERICA SERIES
Paul A. Cimbala, series editor

1. Hans L. Trefousse, *Impeachment of a President: Andrew Johnson, the Blacks, and Reconstruction.*

2. Richard Paul Fuke, *Imperfect Equality: African Americans and the Confines of White Ideology in Post-Emancipation Maryland.*

3. Ruth Currie-McDaniel, *Carpetbagger of Conscience: A Biography of John Emory Bryant.*

4. Paul A. Cimbala and Randall M. Miller, eds., *The Freedmen's Bureau and Reconstruction: Reconsiderations.*

5. Herman Belz, *A New Birth of Freedom: The Republican Party and Freedmen's Rights, 1861 to 1866.*

6. Robert Michael Goldman, *"A Free Ballot and a Fair Count": The Department of Justice and the Enforcement of Voting Rights in the South, 1877–1893.*

7. Ruth Douglas Currie, ed., *Emma Spaulding Bryant: Civil War Bride, Carpetbagger's Wife, Ardent Feminist—Letters, 1860–1900.*

8. Robert Francis Engs, *Freedom's First Generation: Black Hampton, Virginia, 1861–1890.*

9. Robert F. Kaczorowski, *The Politics of Judicial Interpretation: The Federal Courts, Department of Justice, and Civil Rights, 1866–1876.*

10. John Syrett, *The Civil War Confiscation Acts: Failing to Reconstruct the South.*

11. Michael Les Benedict, *Preserving the Constitution: Essays on Politics and the Constitution in the Reconstruction Era.*

12. Andrew L. Slap, *The Doom of Reconstruction: The Liberal Republicans in the Civil War Era.*

13. Edmund L. Drago, *Confederate Phoenix: Rebel Children and Their Families in South Carolina.*

www.ingramcontent.com/pod-product-compliance
Lightning Source LLC
Chambersburg PA
CBHW022039290426
44109CB00014B/916